Dragon Fighter

Dragon Fighter

One Woman's Epic Struggle
for Peace with China

Rebiya Kadeer

with Alexandra Cavelius

INTRODUCTION BY HIS HOLINESS THE DALAI LAMA

Kales Press

Kenneth Kales, Editor-in-Chief and Publisher
Astrid Cerny, Ph.D., Translator
John Sollami, Senior Editor
Janey Tannenbaum, Senior Editor
Nancy Kotary, Copy Editor and Proofreader
Jamie Wynn, Editorial Assistant

Alim Seytoff, General Secretary of the Uyghur American Association
Henryk Szadziewski, Manager of the Uyghur Human Rights Project
Amy Reger, Principal Researcher of the Uyghur Human Rights Project

Cover design by Laura Klynstra
Map design by Casey Greene for Springer Cartographics

Interior Photograph Section Copyrights © 2009:
Amnesty International
Gabriele Battaglia
Daniel Chanisheff
Choi Chi Chio
Nicolas Monnot
Ricky Ng
Huang Tao
Sharon Tsui
Raffaele Valobra
Feng Xu

Library of Congress Cataloging-in-Publication Data

Cavelius, Alexandra.
  [Himmelsstürmerin. English]
  Dragon Fighter : one woman's epic struggle for peace with China /
Rebiya Kadeer with Alexandra Cavelius; Introduction by His Holiness The
Dalai Lama — 1st ed.
    p. cm.
  ISBN 978-0-9798456-1-1 (hardcover : alk. paper)
  1. Uighur (Turkic people)—History. 2. Xinjiang Uygur Zizhiqu
(China)—History. 3. Kadeer, Rebiya, 1948- I. Title. II. Title: One woman's
epic struggle for peace with China.
  DS793.E2C35 2009
  305.89'43230092—dc22
  [B]
                                                    2008040898

ISBN-13: 978-0-9798456-1-1

Your values become your destiny.

—Mahatma Gandhi

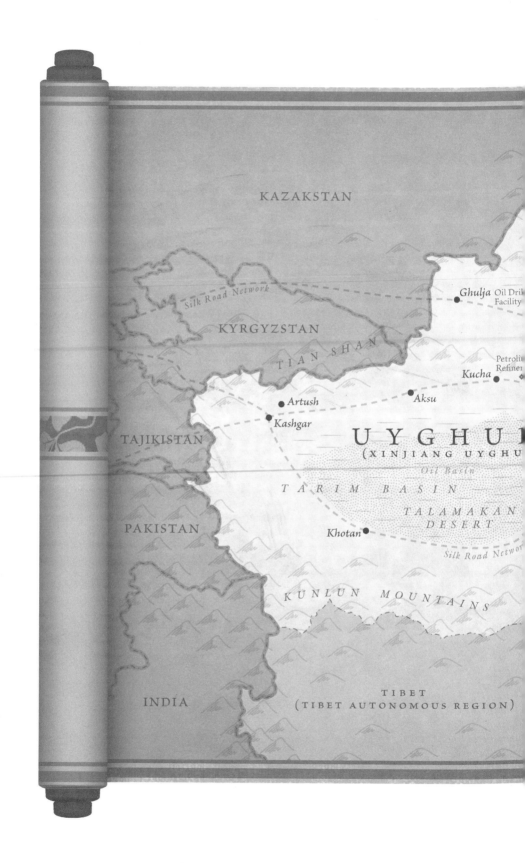

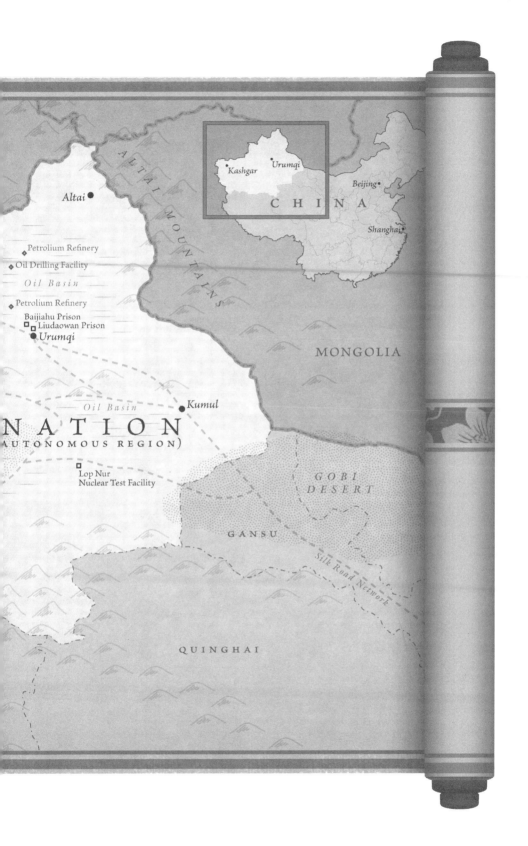

Altai

Petrolium Refinery
Oil Drilling Facility
Oil Basin
Petrolium Refinery
Baijiahu Prison
Liudaowan Prison
Urumqi

Oil Basin — Kumul

NATION
(AUTONOMOUS REGION)

Lop Nur
Nuclear Test Facility

ALTAI MOUNTAINS

Kashgar   Urumqi

Beijing

C H I N A

Shanghai

MONGOLIA

GOBI
DESERT

GANSU

Silk Road Network

QUINGHAI

Contents

His Holiness The Dalai Lama

THE DALAI LAMA

I am glad that Rebiya Kadeer is bringing out an English edition of her life story entitled, *Dragon Fighter: One Woman's Epic Struggle for Peace with China*.

I have been encouraging Tibetans who have undergone experience under Chinese rule to write their stories so that not only the world but the Chinese people, too, understand their situation. Such publication needs to be done truthfully and with a motivation to contribute to the broader friendship of communities.

The Uyghur and the Tibetan people have a history of relationship and in modern times have shared somewhat similar experiences. I therefore hope that this book by Mrs. Kadeer will enable the readers to comprehend the experience of the Uyghur people.

2 April, 2009

Prologue

Within a few hours, the court was going to sentence me to death. The execution was to take place immediately afterward. The whole prison and many of the citizens were already aware of this situation. After months in pretrial detention, my day in court had at last arrived.

I knew the verdict had long ago been decided and that mine, like those of so many others before me, would merely be a sham trial. I wanted to scream out "I will not die!" defiantly and proudly. But my brazen thoughts about a savior angel slowly became melancholy as I turned my mind more deeply inward. I thought *I'm prepared to die in order to become a symbol of hope for our people. I must be fearless— if not for myself, then for my family and the people.*

They asked me which clothes I wanted to wear. For them, it was just a simple errand of sending someone over to the apartment to gather my things. I heard myself speaking my final requests out loud to the guards: "I want to wear my white long skirt and my white leather coat with the fur trimming. I want my '*tomak*,' my beautiful white fur hat. I also want to wash my hair and wear it out long. I want to put on makeup."

"Yes."

"May I see my children one more time?"

"No, that's not allowed."

"May I look at myself in a large mirror?"

This wish was granted. I saw a beautiful woman. When I looked at my reflection, my mind was at peace for the first time in a long time. I took in a deep breath and let the stillness envelop me. But then it all came undone. Everything around me became blurry and jumbled: the guards, the cell, the light, the floor. At first it seemed like I was the only one there who continued to exist. But in a moment the scenario was reversed—*maybe I was the only one there who didn't exist.*

The Chinese guards standing behind me put their heads together and whispered to each other. I could see that they felt sorry for me. I immersed myself in a kind of inner contentment. I was alone with stillness, with death, and with an image in a mirror. Many of the women inmates locked in their cells cried loudly over my fate. Even some of the Uyghur female officers and guards dabbed tears from their eyes as one of the other officers shackled me into hand and ankle cuffs. "All of the wishes that you still have . . . we want to fill them for you."

"As you do not want to let me see my children, I ask only to see myself once more in the mirror with the hand and ankle cuffs on."

A Uyghur officer came into the room and told her Chinese colleague, "You're being asked for by someone. You'd better go." The Chinese woman had hardly left when the Uyghur woman pulled a camera from her pocket. Sobbing, she took a few photographs of me. She asked me what last words I had for her. But I was in a different state of mind— one that no longer had anything to do with her world.

I said aloud, "How beautiful I've become. Someone who belongs to the people doesn't look good in gold chains, but looks beautiful in hand and ankle cuffs. The only human who's truly free is the one who's able to burst through these confines. God will do that for me."

I cannot explain why I spoke like that. Perhaps it was due to my long solitary confinement or that I was facing execution. I do not know. In my mind's eye, I called upon my husband and our eleven children. I asked each of the children, especially Kekenos, because she was the youngest: *How can your father live without me now?*

"Time is up, Mrs. Kadeer . . ."

A group of about thirty officers from the *An Chuan Ting*—the Chinese secret agency for law enforcement, escorted me down a hallway. Another ten prison guards or so marched in front and beside me. They enveloped me in their midst as though it were a dance; I almost enjoyed being surrounded by that many people. Despite the heavy chains, I moved forward with the proper gait and posture of a lady, just as my mother had taught me.

A sudden nervousness took hold of me. I feared that my strength might leave me, so I gave myself courage by saying to myself, *I always thought I would free our land from its occupiers. I didn't achieve this, but like a teacher, I've pointed the way. My death will not be in vain.*

With these thoughts, I found my peace again.

In the courtyard three rows of about fifty *An Chuan Ting* officers each stood facing an equal number of columned Chinese soldiers in combat uniforms. I was escorted to a place between them. Then they shouted unintelligible commands back and forth—presumably in some hand-over ceremony.

I heard my name called, and the soldiers in combat uniforms took over responsibility for me and led me outside through a gate. Someone yelled in Chinese, "The accused Rebiya Kadeer is present!"

There were aisles and aisles of black cars parked one behind the other at the gate. Among the entourage were also two military trucks loaded with soldiers, along with three helicopters circling above.

I slid into the back seat of a black limousine. There were two men next to me and two more up front. Tinted windows prevented anyone from seeing us inside. Five government car sirens started to wail. The two men in front talked about how the original plan had been to transport me in a van in which the prisoners squatted in a cage in the back. But they had dismissed that idea in favor of the current plan, which prevented the population from having much chance of seeing me.

Near the courthouse in Urumqi, the government created a military-only zone and stopped all traffic in an effort to seal off the strategic perimeters. Even state employees who worked nearby were told not to report to work that day, I later learned.

A convoy like this of course made a significantly bigger impression than a van. Soldiers linked hands to form chains along the streets we drove on, sealing them off. People who stood behind the barricades on both sides of the street called out my name loudly. I felt a wish to keep on living stir inside myself.

More than a thousand people had gathered outside of the courtroom, despite the government's prohibition against such a gathering. For a moment, the voices of my children reached me through the crowds: "Mother! Mother!" Those were Kahar and Rushengül! I knew it, but had no time to turn around to them—that is how fast I was pushed through the doors.

In the courtroom the first thing I noticed were many doctors. I concluded from this that they would probably remove my organs after the execution, as was fairly typical of the government. One of them measured my blood pressure. I asked him, "Would you like to sell my organs after you've killed me?"

The courtroom itself was quite large and seated about three-hundred people. But since the trial was "secret," there were only a government prosecutor, a public defender defense attorney, and an *An Chuan Ting* agent present. They led me to the sentencing bench. There the prosecutor and the public defender went through the formalities.

After such a long time in detention, my ability to concentrate was not as strong as I had thought it was when I was back in my cell. Too many things were going on in my head. I had to work hard at putting my words together.

The judge, a Uyghur, came in and read the accusation aloud. Next, the government prosecutor played the evidence—the secret videotape they had made of me while I was unconscious in their *An Chuan Ting* bureau. In the video, my hair was disheveled and my mouth half-open. The documents that the government officials themselves had stuffed into my blouse beforehand were clearly visible.

The judge said, "You may defend yourself now, Mrs. Kadeer."

I responded, "My defense is meaningless to this court. The verdict has already been decided long ago."

"Even if this were true, you should try to defend yourself."

"I think I've led a just life. I've helped safeguard the stability of China. I've financially supported the poor as well as the orphaned, both Uyghurs and Chinese. I've imported urgently needed raw materials, such as iron, for China through my international business arrangements. I've given contracts to several Chinese firms and saved them from bankruptcy. I've exported massive amounts of goods from China and thus earned large profits for all of the people.

"As a representative in the National People's Congress of the People's Republic of China, I've informed the government of the worries and needs of the Uyghur population in order to improve the lives of ordinary people. The government should be grateful that I supported it. The human rights abuses that the Uyghur population suffers, I myself suffer from too. I've been placed before this court today as an important event in the history of our Uyghur homeland.

"If all of you here are innocent and wish to remain innocent, I request of you that you pass a just verdict. So that this can happen, all of the people outside should be allowed to listen in on these court proceedings. I expect a fair verdict from you."

The federal prosecutor and the court-appointed defense attorney pretended to discuss my defense statement. Afterward, the judge announced the verdict: "Mrs. Rebiya Kadeer has revealed state secrets. The way in which she made this error is unforgivable. For this reason, she was originally to be punished even more severely. But because our laws are just, we will punish her only mildly."

The whole trial took about fifteen minutes. For revealing state secrets, the judge sentenced me to eight years in prison. My heart stopped. *Did they not want to execute me?* It seemed as though a barbed hook had been removed from my chest.

Dazed, I followed the policemen back out again through the crowd. I saw my children Kahar and Rushengül through the automobile window. They stood right at the front of the barricades.

People were shouting my name. Others yelled, "Please, Rebiya, take care of yourself."

Suddenly, the driver slammed on the brakes. My daughter Rushengül had thrown herself on the hood of the car. For a second, I saw her wide-open eyes up close. Quickly, uniformed officers pulled her back as she and some others kept coming, breaking through the police barricades to reach me. The driver stepped on the gas and maneuvered into more protection from the convoy.

For a moment, I forgot that I was shackled in hand and ankle cuffs. I looked outside. It seemed to me that I could feel the gentle breeze of freedom.

Like Rain that Falls From the Sky

When I was a little girl, my father told me a fable that has accompanied me throughout my life and moves me deeply every time I remember it. My father said, "This is the fable of a little ant that lived in the wilderness. One day, the ant met a bird.

"'Where are you going?' asked the bird.

"'I'm going to the west,' replied the ant and kept moving.

"'How can you do that? There are high mountains and turbulent rivers along the way.'

"'I can climb over the mountains and swim through the rivers.'

"'But you'll certainly be killed.'

"'Even if a large wave should come along, I can find a piece of wood and cling to it,' replied the ant, and kept walking.

"Many years later"—and here in his storytelling my father's voice would deepen to draw in our attention even more—"the same bird was building a nest in a tree, somewhere far away in a place where he had wandered. Suddenly, an army of ants climbed into the tree and began to aggressively dismantle the nest. The poor bird was about to escape into the sky when one of the ants spoke to him.

"'Hello, my friend. You don't need to fly away. I'll tell my people to leave your nest alone.'

"The bird was more than surprised. 'Who are you? How do you know me?'

"'Don't you remember me from long ago, in a place far away from here, when we spoke to each other?'

"Pausing, then filling with admiration for the ant, the bird replied, 'Well, yes, I do remember. And now you've taught me that we each have the power to unlock the secrets of the world, as long as we have courage and self-confidence.'"

Father was silent for a moment, letting his words sink in. Then he looked at us knowingly and said, "No hurdle is insurmountable. No goal is too lofty."

Why do I mention this fable? I am a woman from a very simple background, who was born in a mountainous area called the Heavenly Mountains in the Tarim River Basin of Central Asia. Our homeland is an ethnically diverse meeting place where Europe, Asia, and Russia come together. It is a place for people to coexist peacefully, but sadly, for others it is also a place to do battle. I am a Uyghur. I am a woman of peace.

For as long as I can remember, Uyghur people have been tortured and subjugated by foreign powers. We have always been menaced by persecution and murder. Truly, I come from a land that has been fighting for its independence and freedom for a long time—today more than ever before. Until now, however, the world has known little about the Uyghur nation. I speak and fight for approximately twenty million Uyghurs worldwide, from whom almost all forms of cultural, economic, and religious autonomy have been stripped away. I want to be the mother of all Uyghurs, the medicine for their ills, the cloth with which they dry their tears, and the cloak to protect them from the rain. My name is Rebiya Kadeer.

Even the name of our Uyghur nation is clouded with politics. The Chinese call it the Xinjiang Uyghur Autonomous Region. It is also known as Uyghurstan or East Turkestan. Its geographic size is immense—approximately three-and-a-half times the size of California. The regents in China have done everything in their power to seal us off hermetically from the outside world as though we are their colony, and they have declared our entire population terrorists. I am not a terrorist—though that is what the Chinese government claims. But they claim the same thing of leaders such as The Dalai Lama, because he advocates for his Tibetan homeland. The Chinese government has also muddled the name of Tibet, calling it the Tibet Autonomous Region. I am doing nothing more than standing up through peaceful means for a humane existence for the Uyghur people.

Today, the Uyghurs, who are among the oldest Turkic peoples in the world, are faced with extermination. Among other fatal afflictions, our homeland is now suffering such extreme air pollution that tuberculosis has become the most common cause of death. Animals and humans have fled due to long-term drought and the encroaching desert. The overall effects of China's environmental pollution have created global alarm.

In 1999, Chinese President Jiang Zemin announced a long-term investment program to definitively tie our sparsely populated Uyghur nation to the rest of China. He explained, "In the middle of the twenty-first century, the western regions will have transformed into a blooming area, where there will be no more unrest, where the ethnic minorities will have become unified, and the beauty of nature can be appreciated." Nobody believed him to be sincere: the subtext was complete domination to exploit the very nature he professed to protect, in particular the oil and coal reserves nature placed in our land for potential export to the West and elsewhere.

There is no doubt that China is a world economic power. It is becoming increasingly influential as one, but this meteoric growth is not the only reason why the West is investing in the Middle Kingdom. What China is deceitfully not revealing to the outside world is that it is so successful financially only because it does not play by the rules of justice. A system without justice is also a system without hope. Thus justice, hope, and prosperity can only be sustained through respect for human rights.

Realizing the truth of this situation is in the long-term interest of the West and other foreign investors in China. Otherwise, they are at risk to lose their money—just like I did. There is no point in averting one's eyes from this reality. Ever since my youth, I have been thinking about the Uyghur people. But every time I said that I wanted to fight for the freedom of the Uyghur nation, those around me rejected the idea. "You're just a little woman," they said, "with a far too vivid imagination."

Later, after I found my second and most beloved husband and told him of this wish, he warned me not to say such grandiose words to his friends, which would cause him to feel shame in front of them. However, words that seemed immodest to him were normal to me. Because I wanted to live as I spoke, I also thought it completely normal to speak as I felt.

When I found myself testifying before the United States Congress a few years ago, in a place where the politics of the world are determined, or when I recently met several times with the president of the United States, then I remembered how as a little girl I was awed by the story of the courage of that little ant.

When I get to a point where I just do not know the right way forward, I purposely call to mind the voices of the people who tried to discourage me over the decades. Despite all the resistance I have encountered, there have been some successes. And every time I experience something great for our people, I also have the fable of the little ant in my mind because today I am the one traveling to faraway places and telling my story with an open heart.

No other Uyghur before me has ever experienced our homeland from as many different perspectives: as a refugee child, as a poor housewife, as a multimillionaire, as a high official in the National People's Congress of the Republic of China, as a political prisoner jailed for many years, and now as a political dissident exiled from my own land. In order to better explain the Uyghurs and myself, I would like to tell my life story starting with my grandparents.

FOR MANY YEARS, OUR HOME was the land of the mostly Turkic Uyghur people and related peoples including the Kirghiz, the Kazaks, the Uzbeks, and other ethnic minorities. It was a land of peace. The Manchus were able to conquer parts of our land for the first time in 1760 and ruled off and on for almost one-hundred years. Their unsteadiness in domination was a result of Uyghur resistance that caused the Manchu Empire to fail in its occupation four separate times during this hundred years. Each time the Manchus were forced to come back more prepared. Uyghur hero Yakub Beg led our people back to independence the last time in 1867. In 1876, however, the Manchu rulers reoccupied the "wild west," which they then violently integrated into the Manchu Empire under the name *Xinjiang*, which means "New Territory."

In 1911, the Chinese Nationalist Party, or *Guomindang*, overpowered the Manchu rulers and founded a republic. The Uyghurs angrily attempted to shake the *Guomindang* occupiers and establish their independence, but in the ensuing decades the territory became more of a haven for Chinese warlords.

Before my paternal grandparents had to flee to the north, they lived along the southern Silk Road in Khotan. This region, as my grandparents had told me, lay alongside the most fearsome desert in the world, the Taklamakan, also known as "The Place of No Return": an area of scorching heat in the summer and bone-chilling cold in the winter. A thousand-and-one cities had been entombed within it, according to the tales of the elders, and the *kara buran*, or black sandstorms that block sunlight for days on end, had buried treasures and gold.

My grandfather was among the fighters who set fire to the palace of the Manchus in Khotan. In order to avoid recrimination from the Manchus, he decided, along with countless numbers of his countrymen, to trek to the city of Gulja with his family over the thirteen-thousand-feet-high Muzart Pass located in the Tianshan Mountains.

For my grandparents' generation, it was possible to ascend through the Tianshan Mountains only on the backs of donkeys and horses. They had to surmount rivulets, walls of ice, and deeply cut ravines. They were a family of thirteen people when they left Khotan, but only seven made it to the final destination of Gulja.

At around the same time, my maternal grandfather was tying up his bundles in Merket, to the east of Kashgar. Like almost all Uyghurs, he too had been active in the resistance. But he was also a playboy. He loved dice games, which were played with dice made from lamb bones, and he loved women. Although a husband's separation from his multiple wives was uncommon and severely frowned upon among our people, he took only his second lawfully wedded wife and his little daughter to make the brutal Tianshan Mountains crossing, leaving behind in the homeland his other lawfully wedded first wife. Yearning desperately for her daughter, our maternal grandmother joined the next caravan. Her companions described how along the way she would call out the name of her daughter: "Tatachahun!"

One night she froze to death. When they found her body, she was clutching to her heart an amulet containing a dark blond strand of her daughter's hair. Our mother often told us this story when we were children. And each time she would grieve, "She was looking for me. I didn't even get to see her put to rest."

In Gulja, there was no jade mining like there had been in Khotan. For this reason, both sets of my grandparents earned their living by raising livestock, especially horses, just as the nomads did. My father was brought up in the north as a refugee child, as was my mother, and it had been previously decided by their respective parents that they would marry when they were old enough. My mother was a perfect, fairy-tale Uyghur girl: discreet, obedient, adept at needlework, and willing to sacrifice everything for her family.

For the wedding, she wore a fire-red dress and a white veil over her forty waist-length braids. It was only after the religious ceremony that my father saw the narrow face of his bride for the first time. She was light-skinned, like our Indo-European ancestors. My father, wiry and small, with a handsome mustache, was about eighteen-years-old, and my mother was at most sixteen when the imam gave them his blessings for marriage.

My father's first name was Kadir. His last name was Kenchi, after the first name of my grandfather. Mother's name thus became Tatachahun Kenchi from that day forward. But peace and good fortune would not be in the future for this newlywed couple.

Father repeatedly told his children, "After the migration from Khotan to Gulja, the Uyghurs never again found peace and tranquility. We were always a toy for the outside world powers to toss around."

OUR PEOPLE HAVE ALWAYS STOOD UP to power plays by Beijing. After the end of the last East Turkestan Republic in 1933, Great Britain, Russia, and China fought for territorial power in Central Asia. Suddenly, our main city, Kashgar, became a center of diplomacy and espionage, as well as the home of explorers and archaeological researchers from all over the world.

Surrounded by mountains up to twenty-three-thousand-feet-high, our homeland borders not only Russia and the states of Kazakhstan, Tajikistan, Kirghizstan, and Afghanistan, but also India and Pakistan. The Uyghur nation is also the part of China that is closest to Europe. Our land is not only of major military strategic importance, but its mineral wealth includes some of the biggest coal reserves in the world, in addition to large deposits of petroleum, gold, uranium, and iron ore.

During the era of World War II, a Kazak named Osman Batur gained prominence as a leader in the Altai region. When Russia was attacked by the German Armed Forces in 1941, it pulled back the Soviets stationed in our land in anticipation of a second attack by Japan.

Along with changes in the constellation of power came changes in alliances such that at times our troops fought with the Russians and at other times against them. Such shifts also occurred in the earlier era of the Chinese *Guomindang*—so that sometimes we fought against them as well. At the cusp of World War II, my mother gave birth to a daughter and a son, but tragically both died as infants. Fortunately, my sister Zohre, who was born in 1940, and my sister Hejer, who arrived three years later, both survived.

In order to help fulfill his dream of an independent Uyghur nation, my father reached for his gun. This period was the beginning of the Three Province Rebellion, so named for the three regions of Ili, Altai, and Tarbagatai. In July 1944, the Uyghurs, Kazaks, and other Turkic peoples once again called for an independent republic. Amidst those unstable geopolitical conditions, our leaders conducted meetings with the Chinese Central Government under Chiang Kai Shek while also secretly receiving weapons and counsel from the Soviet Union.

In the summer of 1946, as a result of these difficult negotiations with the Chinese government—during which our president, Ali Khan Tura, disappeared without a trace—our diplomatic positions for autonomous governance eroded and the Chinese officials asserted their own administrative governance over us soon thereafter upon the passing of our Uyghur Vice Governor Ahmedjan Kassimi. With Chinese oversight, power in our land came to rest in the hands of their trusted allies at the time, the Soviets.

Remaining in Gulja would have been too dangerous for my father in the midst of so much political turbulence. So he decided to go north to organize supplies, weapons, and horses for our compatriots. On one occasion, while he was out hunting, he witnessed a sorry sight that even to this day is difficult for me to recount. Two Chinese soldiers were forcing thirty children of Mongolian, Kazak, and Uyghur descent toward the mountains. They were already poor orphans who had lost their parents during the rebellions. The youngest was four; the oldest eleven. These children were to be executed once they reached the foot of the mountains.

Executions of this kind were a daily occurrence in those days. There was no stable government. Members of the *Guomindang*, in some cases Russian confederates and admittedly some of our own Uyghurs, would scavenge the countryside. For example, a group of rebellious Kazaks stole food and animals from the villages. Then the *Guomindang* soldiers held the village residents accountable for these losses, and as punishment, destroyed entire families. One either became a victim or doomed another to become a victim.

It was quite typical to buy a prisoner's freedom, so my father offered a ransom of two gold pieces to the soldiers guarding the orphans. After some lengthy discussion, he managed to free them. My mother was very pleased, but she also shed many tears when she saw the sorry figures standing before her. She deliberated with the other wives in the neighborhood about what to do. Ultimately, my uncle adopted two Kazak children, and all the other neighbors each took in one or two of the rest. We took in a six-year-old Kazak boy and an eleven-year-old Mongolian girl who soon left for a reunion with her own relatives living nearby, and rarely came to visit after that. Thus, when I refer to my seven siblings I include Jumak, my older brother, as he grew up the same way we did.

I WAS BORN ON NOVEMBER 15, 1946, among the gold miners of the Altai Mountains. My mother must have been about thirty-years-old at the time. Father had put together a group of about twenty miners to explore Altai because it was known to be a place rich with gold. This craggy highland where the men mined was also known as *Altunluk*, or Gold Mountain.

My father promised his workers that he would split any gold they found evenly with them. If they found none, he would pay them a salary out of his own pocket. My mother, who was five months pregnant with me, and one other Kazak woman were the only two females accompanying the gold miners.

For two months, the miners hacked and hammered and sieved and sweated, but they did not find any gold. The atmosphere became more tense as the days wore on. The omen of cold autumn approaching fostered even more unrest. In Altai, autumn signals the arrival of insufferably cold temperatures—as low as minus twenty-two degrees Fahrenheit. Disheartened, my father decided to retreat.

Perhaps it was due to such worries, or the strain of the return journey, but shortly thereafter my mother went into labor. It was too early to give birth to me as my mother was only in her seventh month. It was clear to everyone that under these conditions, a newborn had little chance for survival. Even though it was not far to the next depot where they had previously stored some food rations and fresh water, the miners grumbled as they set up their tents sooner than planned.

But I am told that I was in a hurry to enter the world. My mother had barely laid down to rest when I arrived. Apparently, I was tiny, delicate, and thin as a worm, but with a voice like a full-grown raven. The Kazak woman cut the umbilical cord and wrapped me in a cloth. I survived—which everyone thought was a miracle. My father, a pious man, fell to his knees and thanked God for his third daughter.

In Uyghur tradition, no sunshine is allowed to fall on the bloody linens involved in childbirth. For this reason, my father took the sheets and dug a hole near the rock-face behind our tent. He flung one spade of dirt after another into the air. Suddenly, he stopped.

"Gold!" He shouted until he was hoarse. "I found gold!"

After he paid his workers their share of the find, he still had enough gold left to build a whole new life for our family. The men, who had been complaining about my father for months, now raised three cheers for him and for his new daughter. As a sign of their gratitude, each later threw a small gold nugget into a ritual water basin.

From that moment forward, my parents saw my life as a gift to others: "You don't belong to us, you belong to the people." What that meant for me I would find out only much later.

I WAS ONE-YEAR-OLD WHEN THE COMMUNISTS under Mao Zedong took over our land on October 1, 1949. Then a year later, on October 7, 1950, they conquered our neighbor Tibet. Our immense northwestern region was relatively unknown to most Chinese, as was our language, which is similar to Turkish. Our peaceful culture was foreign to them too. Nevertheless, China had already determined the rules we were to follow.

For nationalistic reasons though, our leaders at the time refused to acknowledge Chairman Mao's rise to power. Our Uyghur vice-governor, Ahmedjan Kassimi, and three others from our government accepted an invitation to attend the People's Congress of the Chinese People's Political Consultative Conference in Beijing. Vice-Governor Kassimi was attending insistent on speaking about our independent and self-determined state.

The Uyghur delegation boarded the plane in Almaty at the end of August 1949. It was not until December that the Chinese government announced that their plane had crashed into a mountain in Manchuria and that none of those on board had survived. Whether it was an accident or sabotage was never clarified. What was clear was that the plane crash was all too convenient for the Chinese government. The death of our leading delegation was too severe a setback for compatriots to overcome, and so our momentum toward independence came to a stop.

After a so-called "peaceful liberation," General Wang Zhen initially took control of our Uyghur nation. Among his first actions was a "cleansing" of the region. Thousands of people were arrested or murdered. Wang Zhen's next objective was to recruit and train local Turkic cadres.

My siblings and I grew up under the watchful gaze of my mother in the small city of Sarsumba, which had a population of about fifty-thousand. Naturally, as children, we did not understand much of what was going on around us. For us, life in the Altai region was like a gift from heaven.

Our house, which had a large courtyard, was located in the middle of the city. Behind it was an orchard with many trees. In the front, my father had opened a beauty salon, a snack stand, and then a bakery, one after the other. There was nothing like it anywhere else in the city. However, he was most proud of his *hamam*, a Turkish bath that could accommodate up to fifty customers. He employed a total of thirty people. I was proud of my father's ingenuity and business skills.

In the following years, my mother gave birth to my sister Arzigul in 1950, my brother Mehmet in 1951, and my sister Heljem in 1957. I spent a lot of time with my maternal grandfather, who lived with us. He was quite lively, just as when he was younger. He sang, danced, and was even a master of many musical instruments, right up to his passing. Every time we visited his grave, we sprinkled grain on the earth. Legend said that if birds ate the grain, it meant that the sins the person had committed on earth would be erased. Maybe God would even forgive him for his womanizing.

Over six-thousand years, our people developed our own religious beliefs, which intermingled with Uyghur traditions that themselves have developed over the centuries under diverse influences. Along the Silk Road, travelers did not just exchange wares, but also different philosophies and religions. Thus, our ancestors prayed to God through versions of Shamanism, Buddhism, Manichaeism, Islamism, and Christianity—as we do today.

The women in Sarsumba did not wear veils. After they were married, most of them wore a headscarf or fixed an embroidered cap called a *doppa* to their hair. If a woman plucked her eyebrows or wore makeup, everybody knew that she was spoken for.

In the Altai region, there were several fabulously rich business people who dealt in exports, owned gold mines, or had large herds of sheep. We did not belong to this elite class, which soon turned out to be life-saving: the Chinese government exterminated all of them in one bloody surprise attack against "capitalistic class enemies."

Every day, my father's workers continued to bring money into the house in three little boxes, and we children would count it. We would trade for bread, eggs, or milk, and sometimes we just gave things away freely. The Altai region was a friendly place where everyone was able to make ends meet.

At the end of the 1940s, the Uyghurs still accounted for three-quarters of the population of our homeland's colorful blend of ethnic groups. The largest in the north of Altai were the Kazaks, and a lot of Russians had also settled amongst us. In one county capital, there was even a Russian elementary school and a Russian consulate.

In 1950, Chairman Mao signed a cooperative agreement with Soviet General Secretary Joseph Stalin in Moscow. In exchange for arms shipments to China, the Uyghur nation was offered as an extension to the Soviet sphere of influence. The Chinese and Russians agreed via contract to share the use of our mineral resources. Uyghurs were not involved in the agreement.

Almost all of the local engineers in the region were Russians. Initially we respected them because we thought that they would support our people. Some of our countrymen even believed that they had a more advanced culture than we did and sent their children to the Russian school. Most of us though believed that ours was an equally respectable culture because literature, music, and painting had always played important roles for us. In addition, educated Uyghurs had been active as scholars throughout Central Asia as early as the Middle Ages.

We had many friends who were Russian nationals. My father even spoke Russian to the wolf-like dogs he had bought from Russians. When I was a child I saw Russians constantly. Many of them were the descendants of refugees who had saved their own lives by fleeing across the border to reach us during Russia's "October Revolution." Up until then, I had not set eyes on even a single Chinese person. I had just heard the term "Chinese" many times by then. If we wanted to tease our parents, we would call out, "Be careful. A Chinese is coming!" "A Chinese" had about the same meaning for us children as "a make-believe ghost."

According to Chinese Communist Party theory, all people should live at the same standard as the majority of the population. In our case, this meant living as peasants. In the years after General Wang Zhen took control of the Uyghur nation, he set about eradicating the rich, the intellectuals, and ideological opposition. Anyone who opposed his reforms was put before a firing squad.

In February 1951, the Chinese executed Kazak freedom fighter Osman Batur in Urumqi as a counter-revolutionary. After that, anytime I heard that someone had been killed, I immediately thought of Wang Zhen. I did not know who his boss was or that his name was Mao Zedong.

WHEN THE TWENTIETH BATTALION of the Chinese First Field Army was stationed in Altai, I was four or five-years-old. I was just playing in the street with a neighbor's child when a man came walking toward us. He was wearing a uniform, looked Asian, had a very flat nose, very narrow eyes, and was shorter than an average Uyghur. The man held a small piece of candy out to us, but we ran home screaming.

That was my first interaction with a Chinese person. My mother came rushing toward me in the courtyard, saying, "Don't be scared, these people are very nice." She took my hand, led me outside, and introduced me to several Chinese soldiers. It was explained to me that these Chinese Pioneers had technical abilities and were here to teach their skills to the local population. For this reason, they were generally welcomed. Henceforth, our parents stopped telling us that naughty children would get eaten by the Chinese dragon.

By March 1950, Chairman Mao had already ordered a program for the mass immigration of Han Chinese—the largest ethnic group of native Chinese—into our homeland, whereby the Uyghur nation would be afforded "mutual help" from their Chinese "brother nation"; in fact, this program was intended to foster socialism. The impetus for this strategic immigration policy was provided by the Soviet Union's General Secretary Joseph Stalin. But this first influx was minor in contrast to that which was still to come. In 1949, there were approximately one-hundred-thousand Chinese living in our homeland. Today, the Chinese population has already grown to an estimated eight million, and at a rate excessively outpacing our own population growth. Unfortunately, there are no reliable measures for this statistic.

The Communist apparatchiks "reformed" the entire populations standing. Landowners, moneylenders, and religious leaders were designated as "sheep" and "goats." Sheep were considered to be elite enemies of the middle class, but in some instances, sheep also belonged to the subcategory "friends," who were viewed as innocent proletarians.

In the top tier of the "goats" were landowners as well as those with rights of inheritance. These people were killed off automatically. After this top tier came other "goats", such as estate owners or small farmers, who also lost their property, but at least kept their lives—that is, as long as their property did not extend beyond a certain size. My father was a member of this category.

Mao Zedong formally declared our homeland as the Xinjiang Uyghur Autonomous Region of the People's Republic of China in 1955 and made statements about the rights of self-determination for the Uyghur nation, including the right to secede from the Chinese alliance. In reality, though, we no longer had any power in our own land.

In the new Communist system, everybody was controlled by everybody else. People were encouraged to incriminate others. The Communists' collectivization of our agriculture took place in July 1955. Their violent socialization of our private trade and industry soon followed.

Because of its size, our region was expected to contribute substantially to the agricultural productivity of China. For this purpose, military farms called *bingtuan* or "production and construction corps" were established. Everything that the Uyghur farmers and shepherds had learned about our fragile oasis ecosystem over the centuries was labeled as reactionary and backward. The invasive transformation of our cultivated landscape through these Chinese military farms would challenge the sustainability of our land to the utmost.

Communist government propaganda claimed that their goal was the equitable distribution of basic foodstuffs so that no one would go hungry and so that no one would hoard.

Not long afterward, twenty soldiers from the Twenty-Eighth Battalion chased us from our home one rainy day. They pulled our whimpering dogs away by their collars. In the chaos, one of the soldiers yelled at my father, "We told you to leave, but you did not! Now we have the right to throw you out!"

I remember how they threw our clothes and furniture out a window and into the street. We watched helplessly, clutching our suitcases.

Because it was raining so heavily, my mother placed a blanket over my head. My sister Arzigul, who was two years younger than I was, clung sobbing to my pants. She looked just like me, only smaller and more delicate. I was eight-years-old at the time.

My mother held two-year-old Heljem in her arms to calm her down. My older siblings Jumak, Zohre, and Hejer cuddled five-year-old Mehmet between them and cried as they asked what kind of people would take our house away. In fact, these were the same Chinese who years before had offered us candy when we played in the streets.

We slept outdoors the first night. In the morning, some kind neighbors took us in. I do not recall that this bothered me particularly as a child. But later, when we were banished for the second time, I felt the pain twice as intensely. If the Chinese government had at that time kept its promises regarding the right to self-determination and peaceful coexistence, I would never have had to tell my story.

MY FATHER ERECTED A SINGLE-STOREY wooden house with five rooms for us in a village about two miles outside of Sarsumba, at the foot of the mountains. The village had approximately one-hundred residents. Its name was Dumbazaar, which means "Trade on the Mountain."

While my father was building our new house—nailing together a bathroom, constructing a stove, installing a water boiler, and clearing a courtyard for us—he would insist: "We will not die. We will be happy again." Meanwhile, my mother planted flowers and hung woven carpets on the walls inside. Back in the city, at our real home, on our property, Chinese troops had torn down all of our shops and built a grocery store for their soldiers.

Father and my older brother Jumak tilled a large field next to our new house, on which we planted potatoes, cabbages, onions, and other vegetables. They sold most of our vegetables to traders.

My father also cut hair in a salon for eight hours a day, then mopped and took out the garbage. Neighboring acquaintances who were dependent on our vegetables helped us work in the fields.

Jumak and Mehmet shared a room. Our parents took my baby sister Heljem into their bedroom. I felt closest to Heljem and younger brother Mehmet at that time. Mehmet was very temperamental, however, and he kept my mother busy.

I shared a bed with Arzigul, who—in contrast to my mother, sisters, and me—did not show any particular interest in housecleaning. Even so, my older sisters Zohre and Hejer defended Arzigul every time I got angry at her for tossing her clothes on the floor. That difference aside, Arzigul and I especially liked to sleep with our oldest sister Zohre.

With our mother, we four girls lovingly embroidered decorative fabric around the bedframes and pillowcases—colorful flowers, grapes, birds, and leaves. Between the rooms was a partial wall and the roaring ceramic-tiled woodstove my father had built. Even in the winter, during bone-chilling below-zero weather, the stove kept the house comfortably warm. I was always careful to make sure the fire did not go out.

In one of the smaller rooms we kept the five dogs that the soldiers had left to us. The smartest among them was named Shark. We kept this pack as guard dogs and as hunting dogs, but also as pets because we loved them.

If we had guests, my father usually took a seat by the door, always ready to lend a hand, while my mother passed around hand-embroidered round pillows for the company to sit on. In the room next door, with my finger to my lips, I would whisper praise to Shark: "You're very polite. You don't disturb the guests."

At the back of the courtyard, goats bleated; cats meowed; and geese, ducks, and chickens chattered. My parents considered animals, plants—all of nature, in all of its manifestations—to be God's work. All of these had souls, just as we humans did—and just like every rock and every animal, we humans were subject to natural laws.

MOTHER ALWAYS CHECKED ON MY FATHER before he left the house, but he did not really care much about his appearance. When he came home at sundown, she had long since prepared supper and smoothed out the blankets on the low *kang* table, so that he could, as always, tell us more stories after supper. My mother favored the more formal usage of our language to address my father because she considered it better cultured, but my father used informal address with her.

Sometimes my father would react angrily toward my mother after a long day at work. But she would always reply with the composed words, "Kadir Khan, our children are present. If you're angry with me, then please tell me in private."

"All right, I'll do that Tatachahun," he would agree.

Peace at home was rule number one. It was even forbidden to shoo a chicken with an energetic "Go away!" when guests were present. A guest was king. My mother taught us girls to sit upright and still—in the presence of men, a Uyghur woman was supposed to put her hands on her lap and lower her eyes.

Father, as a former soldier, was constantly worrying about the future of our land and contemplating large-scale battles. Mother did not. She loved three things: housework, music, and the flowers in her garden. Once a week, she would gather the women from the village and they would play music and dance together.

I inherited my mother's lively spirit, her willing self-sacrifice, and the love she felt for her children. She never complained that she had too much to do. Education, politeness, and respect for everyone were of great importance in our home. We were to do what our parents expected of us. Whoever had more than enough to eat was to give some of it to another in need.

I found moral support in the religious beliefs that my father taught us. I started to memorize the suras in the Koran at the age of six. My faith allowed me to feel as though I were surrounded and led by an extraordinary, strong force. Perhaps others felt it too, and perhaps that was why religion was the first comfort the Chinese government sought to disconnect us from.

As a child, I always felt that my parents preferred my siblings over me. My mother would frequently praise my sisters for their politeness and their elegant ways of dress and movement. Like my father, I was not particularly interested in my appearance. My features were inherited from my father's family: petite stature; light, bronze-tinged skin tone; large brown eyes; and a wide, downward-sloping nose. Besides I did not have time to be interested in how I looked. I was too busy with housework, which my parents considered to be my job.

My father and mother did not always have an easy time with me. In fact, I caused them much worry. There was frequent trouble with my teachers because I said everything just as I thought it. For such reasons, I felt my parents never regarded me as an equal among my siblings. I always felt like I was at the bottom, which made me strive for their love all the more.

❧ ❧

"YOU DON'T BELONG TO US, you belong to the people." I was raised with this belief, which my parents had been saying to me ever since I was born. My mother scolded me, saying, "If you don't help other people, our entire family will suffer for it."

If any one of our relatives fell ill, my siblings would look at me as if there was more I could do. And I would feel guilty. *Had I not been helpful or hard-working enough? Had I not given enough?*

If I took our livestock to pasture to feed, I would also feed our neighbors' livestock too, in order to be helpful. When I returned in the evening, I would pick flowers for bouquets and distribute them among the neighbors. I collected wood for older people. Every time that I completed good deeds such as these, I would stand in our doorway, lift my chin into the wind, and laugh to myself.

But if I fell on the ice while skating in the winter, I would feel an inner twinge. I grew up thinking that way. I was convinced that I was a person whose job was to do work for others.

My father had bought me a donkey, twenty plates, and several extra-large festive tablecloths. I was supposed to learn to use these things not for myself, but for others. If someone were celebrating a wedding, I would lend out my plates and tablecloths. If someone needed a donkey, I would lead it to them.

My father took this all in with satisfaction. When I reflect on this today, in my sixties, it is clear to me that I was under enormous pressure as a child. But overall, it helped me to develop character.

I have kept this habit of letting others partake in what is mine. A large part of what I earned in my life was given to other people. My parents' words remain indelible; they adhere to my skin like a mole.

Even from the moment I was born, my father's workers—the gold miners—were fighting amongst themselves. In that sense, nothing has changed in my life. I am surrounded by struggle and disagreement.

When I was a child, I did not like to hear the story of my birth because it made me feel like an outsider, not like a member of the family. But as I got older, my mother would tell me the story to encourage me. Eventually I was able to understand the story's positive symbolism of working toward peace for our Uyghur people.

AFTER DINNER WAS THE TIME for fairy tales and adventures. We children would get comfortable on the floor around the low *kang* table. Each time, it felt like my father was returning to the places he was describing. My father would begin, in a deep voice:

"A real Uyghur is courageous and honest."

Or "The Uyghurs are fighting an old battle."

He would start with his hand outstretched as if holding a magic wand with which to carry us literally to the scene of his story.

"Every night, there were shots and horrible screams. Many a man had to suffer through standing on nails before he was decapitated."

We would sit spellbound, hardly daring to breathe.

"But did we lose our land every time?" Jumak would ask.

My father nodded to him. "The reason is that the powerful nations in the world have forced us to live under their rules so that they can take from our land what nature has given us. And they'll continue to do this in the future if we don't stop them."

Sometimes he would continue talking as though we were not even in the room. "Victory had been before our eyes twice already. Hundreds-of-thousands of us never returned home. We were happy to fight or to die because we believed the land would soon be ours. And with this belief, it was possible for a small number of men to defeat a much stronger enemy. Every man who was able to carry a weapon joined us. We knew what we had to do. But the one thing we didn't understand were the rules of the game. They kept changing."

After describing this final defeat, my father would seem to succumb to depression. He would ruminate and mumble irrational thoughts to himself, building toward another breaking point, at which point he would be overtaken by a fit of sobbing. Generally, Uyghur men hid their feelings. But my father was a remarkable man: he hugged us and talked to us. To me, he was the essence of love.

Every time my father told us about mass murders, I too would be overcome by a deep sense of trauma. I suffered through many night-mares as a child. In the darkness of night, all of those merciless mur-derers would reoccur in my mind, until I burrowed myself, sweating, under the blankets. In honor of those who gave their lives for our

Uyghur nation, my parents used only the term "East Turkestan" to describe it. That was the name those courageous heroes fought for, and it was the place they had temporarily gained for us, which represented our national self-determination. It was only much later that we would get used to hearing the muddled Chinese description of our nation as the Xinjiang Uyghur Autonomous Region.

My mother never joined us after dinner. She was always busy. In the few minutes of spare time that she had, her favorite thing was to strum on a long-necked two-string dutar and sing. She did not show any particular interest in politics.

THE HAPPY DAYS OF MY CHILDHOOD were short, but indescribably wonderful. "Come along for the hunt, Rebiya!" my older brother Jumek would call out as he pulled me up into the saddle. Shark would bound ahead as we rode through the luscious green valleys enveloped in fog.

Summer was a dreamy time for us as children. We would trek into the countryside with several other families for a few days. We took our musical instruments, the men had their hunting falcons, and we were accompanied by a number of bleating sheep. Like every Uyghur child, I knew how to dance. It also did not matter whether we were celebrating or mourning—we Uyghurs could not live without music.

If we wanted to take a break from the group, we rode horses out to the Kazaks, in the steppes, about twenty miles away. With our faces in the breeze, surrounded by aromas, sounds, and sunshine, visiting them was a journey toward happiness. It did not matter that we did not know any of the Kazaks personally. They would welcome us heartily, as always.

The Kazaks were like relatives to us. They understood our language; we understood theirs. They would prepare their food; we would prepare ours. Then we would exchange our pilaf for their lamb, which was so tender that it would almost melt on the tongue. While our elders drank brandy, we kept to the mare's milk. Sweet and warm, it flowed through our bodies.

When winter arrived, life changed. Buried in warm fur hats, we would come screaming down the mountainsides on skis or on sleighs through the snowy landscape.

Oh, I often wish I could return to the short, happy days of my childhood.

THE CHINESE OCCUPIERS KNEW that they had a bad reputation among our people. So initially, they put a lot of effort into changing our perceptions. It's almost comical now, but on one clear summer day, I saw eight Chinese men hoeing our field and lugging pails of water. They even raked the leaves in our courtyard. At the neighbor's house across the street, two men in white medical lab coats took care of the sick children. They put chairs into the street and called upon the old men to sit down and have their hair cut.

But hospitality was sacred to us. If someone worked for us for free, it was unthinkable for us not to offer something in return. So Uyghurs and Kazaks, who up until that point had avoided all contact with the Chinese, also put chairs, tables, and teacups out in front of our homes. Occasionally, tentative friendships with these Chinese would come into being.

Yet once we realized what their government truly intended for our land, our people immediately retreated to a more formal distance. One result was that Uyghur parents did not allow their children to play with Chinese children, although we really wanted to. And the Chinese parents acted the same way toward us.

"We can tolerate these guests among us for a while, but at some point they'll have to leave," my father would often say.

Because the foreign soldiers showed such model behavior, my sisters and I naively offered our help by bringing water to them when they passed through our area. We thought that they looked rather smart in their uniforms too.

If a unit of troops was passing through, the village leader would demand that we children stand in a row at the entrance to town and clap our hands to greet them. The only one who dared to boldly protest the soldiers was our dog Shark. As soon as he saw the Chinese, he would start to bark. Nobody had taught him to do this. If he growled at one of our people, we told him to be quiet and he obeyed. But with the Chinese, it was no use. The only thing we could do was to chain him up.

The relationships among Chinese and Uyghurs cooled even more dramatically after several thousand of our people were again arrested and killed in the Altai region. During the same period, the loudspeakers that by that time had been installed on every street corner would continuously broadcast the message that local inhabitants and the Chinese were friends and that we should live in harmony and unity forever.

The friendships they spoke of were merely words. In actuality, their words were veiled threats. As we grew wiser, it became apparent to us that those in power in the government generally thought that the only way they could live in peace and quiet was if all of us regional natives were either exiled or murdered.

I remember my father and his friends gathering one night in our dining room and warning, "We have to be careful or they'll murder us too." One of our neighbors whispered, "There are undercover government spies everywhere."

They listened for any noises from outside for a few moments. They said, "We have to be very careful who we speak to. It would be best if we stopped talking about this altogether when we are in the street."

I will never forget how my father first asked us that night to move from the dining room over to another room, then warned us to be quiet. "You're not allowed to leave the room for now or speak in loud voices," he said. It was late, but we tried to be attentive to his directions. Arzigul leaned her head on my shoulder. Mehmet and Heljem were already asleep. Zohre was breathing quietly next to Hejer. There was absolute stillness in the whole house. I thought, *at any moment the door might be ripped open. At any moment, we might be sitting outside in the rain again.*

My father also made it clear to us that whatever we heard at home we were never to repeat to anyone beyond the walls of our house. But he never tried to hide these conversations from us.

Within the family, he never made a secret of his dislike for Mao Zedong: "The man talks this way one day and that way the next." At those times, my mother would reprimand him, "Don't talk like that!" She just wanted to live in peace.

Outside, the loudspeakers continued to blast: "Never forget about class struggle!" and "Serve the people!"

THE FIRST CHINESE SETTLERS had come to our homeland with the military. They had even founded a Chinese school. More and more Chinese were working in the shops, and our people in the village started to buy their goods.

These *bingtuan* who had marched into Altai with the Twenty-Eighth Battalion were different from other armies. In times of peace, they simply worked in the fields. But if a group of Uyghurs gathered outside, in only a moment's time a group of four or five Chinese soldiers would appear near them. Street life slowly began to change.

Every single Uyghur was scrutinized for his or her proper attitude toward the government. In some cases, mere suspicion was enough to get a person executed as a counter-revolutionary. The soldiers plowed through our home like vandals during their routine house searches. On one such search in 1952, they found a few gold nuggets in a gourd where my father had hidden them. At that point, they took not only the gold, but also my father.

Every day they interrogated him as to whether he owned any more gold. Each denial was followed with another beating. After six months under arrest, he staggered home. He collected all of our mother's jewelry and turned it over to the soldiers. From the hallway, I saw my mother applying chunks of raw beef to the welts on his back.

During this period my father slowly started to change and began to raise his voice to us. During the phases between house searches, he was very distant, as if lost in thought. At regular intervals, the house searches continued. But we now just let the searches wash over us like some kind of natural disaster.

My classmate Rahime and my Kazak friend Khinlar told me that in the future, the Chinese would fall from the sky like rain. Khinlar showed with his hands how they would crawl around everywhere like a plague of locusts and take possession of everything. Agitated by this, I exclaimed, "Well, then we'll just have to move into the mountains!"

Chairman Mao and the rest of the Chinese leadership in power would regularly repeat their catchphrase regarding the right to self-determination, first and foremost, for the Uyghurs. Even I, a young girl, was sickened by their lies.

My father began locking the doors behind him at home, particularly when he knelt on his prayer rug. The other Uyghur men did exactly the same. In those days, there were not that many Chinese, yet they were able to keep us all under surveillance. As a counterbalance, though, in the early days of the occupation the Uyghurs were still able to trust each other.

Sometimes my father would cry quietly. Then he would ask questions like, "Why do we have to lead such difficult lives?" In the same breath, he would repeat to himself: "Our people are open-hearted, obedient, simple, modest, and hospitable. We are a people who love art. And trade. A people who were satisfied with our way of life."

IN THE SPRING OF 1957, CHAIRMAN MAO called upon all intellectuals to state their critiques of the Communist Party. They were supposed to offer "complete and thorough opinions of everything." No one was to fear reprisals.

Most people were grateful for this apparent liberalization. In reality though, Chairman Mao had only one thing on his mind. His carefully calculated intent was to "lure the snakes out of their holes." This wretched phrase was actually the official slogan of that propaganda campaign.

All of those lured out by the chairman's call were indeed revealed as enemies of the state. Artists, university students, scientists, and other intellectuals were declared to be "rightists."

Any form of independent thinking was dangerous. Nobody was able to sleep soundly anymore because anyone, through betrayal or contrivance, could be declared an enemy of the state at any time. Everyone was supposed to think the same way and to speak the same way. Everyone was required to be vigilant against "incorrect" thoughts. Otherwise, we were told, the country would be threatened with disintegration. Our school teacher taught us that these words were from Chairman Mao himself.

My teacher at the time, Mrs. Rahima Mamat, was thin and elegant in her every movement. She usually stood at the blackboard in a contemporary two-piece outfit and had sparkling blue eyes. She looked enchanting, and she knew it. But behind her back, a few children would meanly call her "blue eyes." This insult came from the ideology that in the capitalistic West, the class enemy had piercing blue eyes.

At home, my older siblings told me that the things we learned at school were not important, and that we should listen only to our parents. It gave me confidence to have political discussions with my classmates before class in the morning rather than just at home. My father received visits from the teacher twice in rapid succession because I had also wanted to learn more about certain Uyghur heroes. In response to the latter topic, she warned him that our whole family, right alongside me, would be branded and our lives ruined forever if he did not stop telling us such adventurous stories. In class, her actual reply to me was, "Those were not heroes; those were bandits."

My parents could at least be unconditionally proud of my older sister Zohre. To attend the teacher's college, she moved about four-hundred miles away to Urumqi. Though Zohre was not a classic beauty and was the same petite height as me, with her charming character and graceful fashions she looked like a princess. In the family, we always referred to her as "The Lady Consul," because she always dressed like a modern Russian woman.

Conversely, around that time the Communist Party became displeased regarding individualistic styles of dress. That is why Zohre was required to start wearing a Mao-like suit at school. My oldest sister considered the chairman to be a great man. After all, the Party was concerned for each one of its citizens, as if each was its own child. And it provided life with a clear structure. Even the roles for good and evil were defined—when something went bad, the West was always to blame.

Jumak also later went to Urumqi to study agricultural economics, and Hejer passed the exams to attend medical school in Altai.

When Jumak came home for the summer holidays, he helped with work in the fields. He had a lot of respect for me because I had so diligently supported our family. To my greatest delight, he also mimicked my oldest sister Zohre in the way she would prance, lady-like, across the courtyard.

IN THE HISTORY OF THE UYGHUR PEOPLE, there have been many women who became heroines, women who successfully stood up to the limitations of the patriarchal traditions in our culture. My father would often revel in the legends of these famous women. But my favorite story was the one about Iparhan. For Uyghurs, she symbolizes our fight against occupying powers.

Iparhan was the daughter of a respected leader in Kashgar. She was widely known in 1760, legend has it, because her body was naturally perfumed with a God-given captivating fragrance. She had also proven herself to be as brave as any man in the fight against the Manchus. Later, she was captured and taken as a trophy for the imperial harem in Beijing. However, the story goes, the young woman had hidden a dagger underneath her clothes and swore to herself that she would kill anyone who tried to get near her.

Emperor Qianlong was eager to win over this foreign beauty. To ease her resistance, he had fruit trees, musicians, and dancers from the Uyghur nation brought to the palace especially for her.

Despite all of his gifts, Iparhan continued to reject the emperor's advances and decided to refuse to eat, thus jeopardizing her health. Finally, when the smitten emperor realized how determined Iparhan was in her feelings toward him, and that she fully intended to starve herself to death, he asked what last wish he could fulfill for her.

Weak and pale, she answered, "Take my corpse, dressed in my traditional clothing, and bury me in my homeland." The emperor fulfilled that last wish for the love of his life. Today, her grave can be found in the Abakh-Hoja Mausoleum.

"She is a role model for us," my father would say to us children after his telling of the legend. "She kept her dignity and devotion until the very end of her life."

Inspired by the bravery of such heroines, I again confronted our teacher the following morning with the fact that she only ever taught us about Chinese heroes, but never about the Uyghur ones. At that, Mrs. Mamat looked around nervously, then hissed, "Be quiet!"

Time and again, when my father told us a new story about such heroes and heroines, I would allow myself to slip into their personas. I would feel such a powerful strength in me, as if at that moment, I could liberate our people from all of their sorrows.

I believe that in large part, it was those stories about our heroines that made me who I am today.

BY THAT TIME THE HIGHEST POSITIONS in every government office were filled with Chinese. My father met with his friends almost exclusively at our home, where they would talk together in the dining room in hushed tones. They did not attend any of the Communist Party meetings. Besides, those Party meetings were not really meetings. They were indoctrinations at which a person was told how to think, how to feel, and how to love.

Bulletin boards proclaimed in large bold lettering: "LONG LIVE THE GREAT LEAP FORWARD!" and "EVERYBODY MAKE STEEL!" According to

Chairman Mao's directives, China was supposed to develop itself into a modern industrial power. My school friends and I understood only that the whole nation was supposed to gather up every scrap of metal from every corner and turn it in. Furnaces had even been erected on public squares to melt it all down. Pots, pans, and household items of every description landed there.

The search for ores was a top priority. Every family had to participate. But because the farmers had to produce steel, their fields stood idle. And our donkeys could not carry the ore hauls because there was not enough fodder grown by farmers to feed them. Instead, women— including women in late-term pregnancies—lugged the ores for them in large backpacks.

Lunch was eaten at the edge of the fields or in company canteens. Food was strictly rationed and consisted mostly of flour soup. Uyghur women, who until then had been so careful about their appearance, showed faces smeared with dirt.

Before sunrise a soldier would bang an iron rod against a tire rim to tear people from their slumber, forcing the exhausted workers back to the fields. At times the youngest children stood crying at the edges of the fields, yet their mothers had to first ask permission before being allowed to comfort or nurse their babies. Many children died at the edges of those fields.

Even schoolchildren were supposed to contribute half-a-day's labor. With that, we could earn our school meals. We no longer learned reading and writing at school. Instead, we repeatedly jammed our minds full of quotes from Chairman Mao:

> *Unity of the masses, the Party, and the whole country is essential.*
> *Unity of the masses, the Party, and the whole country is essential.*
> *Unity of the masses, the Party, and the whole country is essential.*
> *Unity of the masses, the Party, and the whole country is essential.*

The teacher called us "little soldiers" or the "little army." Many were proud of this.

My father fully dedicated himself to field labor in his spare time. He bribed the overseers with money so that my mother could continue to complete her housework as a customary Uyghur woman. As far as I know, she was the only woman in the village for whom this was possible.

If the neighbors needed potatoes or vegetables, they would turn to Tatachahun. For this reason, they were never jealous of her.

Every time my father came home in his simple blue cotton uniform with the shirt collar buttoned up to his chin, my mother bent over in laughter, saying, "You really look so funny!" He took it in good humor.

My mother decided on her own to protest and not change the way she dressed. In our home and in the courtyard, she continued to wear her long, traditional, colorful garments. She had done this in the beginning as well, when the village held its Party meetings—that is, until the village leader criticized her for being a symbol of the bourgeoisie. After that everyone made fun of my mother, including my teacher.

One day she came back from a gathering and could not stop laughing. My father turned around and looked at her surprised. "What happened?" he asked.

My mother responded, "All the women looked like plucked chickens!" She explained how the women there had cut off their long braids in favor of a chin-length bobbed hairstyle.

In the schoolyard, we felt sorry for each other and for ourselves in our new outfits. "See how terrible I look." Later, we did not have time to worry about how we looked in our clothes. We were busy just trying to find something to eat.

AT SOME POINT, RELATIONSHIPS amongst Uyghurs became unmanageable. Hardened by distrust and further frozen by disillusionment, our old customs of getting together, taking trips to the mountains, and celebrating together did not happen anymore. When we toiled fourteen to sixteen hours a day, there was not much energy left for such pleasures. Our own traditions could only be preserved in the face of this cultural aggression with the resources of time, leisure, and money—and the Chinese had robbed us of all three. We had forgotten how to dance the way we used to because we no longer had the freedom to express our feelings through dance.

I was well known for being a helpful and patient child, but during that time I became more aggressive. I would pick an argument with my classmates over trivial things and would do the same with my siblings at home. I did not understand myself or why I had become so rebellious.

One evening, when my sister Hejer was home for the school holidays, she stood in the vestibule getting ready to go out for the evening. She was wearing the standard Chinese clothing, but she had also put on her favorite scarf to go with it. I accused her of selfishly adorning herself with forbidden articles of clothing. And I said that if she did not stop doing that, our father would be arrested. She went back into her room without saying another word.

We children were supposed to believe everything we heard: all of the lies that were broadcast through the loudspeakers, all of the lies that our teacher told us on a daily basis. The only time I found inner peace was when I listened to my father say his prayers at sunrise. It sounded almost like he was singing sadly in his dreams:

> *God, I beg of you, help us.*
> *Bring joy to us and to our village.*
> *Give us peace and good fortune.*
> *Please return the children of our neighbors,*
> *the ones whose parents are in prison.*
> *Please give our people strength and courage.*

AFTER A MEETING WITH COMMUNIST state leaders at the end of 1957, Chairman Mao began to distance himself from the Soviet Union. In his opinion, his former allies had abandoned the path to socialism. Moreover, it was reported, he felt hurt because the United States and other Western countries had rejected diplomatic relations with China.

Meanwhile, Mrs. Mamat's lessons at school took on ever more bizarre overtones. The chairman had declared sparrows to be enemies of the state because they ate grain from the fields. Schoolchildren were mobilized to fight the "four pests": sparrows, rats, mosquitoes, and flies. Anyone who did not participate was considered to be breaking the law.

We children were supposed to deliver ten pairs of sparrow's feet to school every single day. After we had exterminated almost all of the sparrows in our village, we shot down ravens with our slingshots and delivered their feet to school instead.

In his typically shortsighted way, with this war on the birds Chairman Mao had inadvertently unleashed a terrible plague of insects. Thus, effective immediately, every schoolchild was required to kill fifteen insects per day. We all ran around with flyswatters and collected the insects in a glass. When we turned them in, every single one was painstakingly counted by Mrs. Mamat. It was great fun for us children. But when I think about it today, Chairman Mao killed off not only most of our population, but also a large part of the animal kingdom.

The cadres announced a new campaign almost every week. Once it was "Catch mice!" On another occasion it was announced that women were no longer allowed to wear long skirts, only short ones. Whoever had come up with all of this foolishness must have been either completely crazy or completely terrified.

If Chairman Mao announced, "Today, we will do it this way . . . ," they would nod their heads as usual, no matter how absurd it was. The next day, the command would be "We will do it the other way," and again, everyone would follow without protest—just like a herd of cows being taken from one pasture to another.

CHINESE SOLDIERS CONFISCATED our cattle, chickens, sheep, and goats. Hardly anyone dared to hold discussions about politics. The previously allowed gatherings at a home were at that point prohibited. Nobody mentioned the names of Wang Zhen or his successor, Wang Enmao, any longer. Instead, Uyghurs complained about their general problems in life. "What can we do? Who should we turn to?"

I often heard my father in the next room, noisy and agitated over our fate. He was really a loving person, but he started to yell more and more. When he came home from work, he would toss his jacket carelessly into the corner. If we wanted to ask him something, he would yell at us, "Leave me alone! I'm not in the mood to talk." He also had stopped telling us stories.

We children resented that he ruined everything for us with his bad moods. Hejer, Arzigul, Mehmet, and I got on his nerves the most because we were always pestering him about why he didn't tell us any more exciting adventure stories. I would ask myself *Why was he so unfriendly to us? Why did he treat our mother so badly?*

My mother was an extremely kind woman. Every time her husband's blood started to boil, she appealed to our good consciences: "Please listen to your father. He's a good father." But I had heard with my own ears how he had hurt my mother's feelings with his criticisms.

He was constantly finding fault with her when there was no fault to find. But she always forgave him. We children often saw her bury her face in her hands and cry. We too were upset about her sorrows, but felt helpless, not knowing what to say or to do. Overall, this frustration led to an increasing anger toward our father.

Sometimes, after he had eaten and had a chance to relax, he would become our good father once again. My mother, however, had lost her courage. She was not as carefree as she used to be, she put on weight, and she stopped caring about her appearance. The one thing she continued to be adamant about though was cleanliness.

"Mother," I once asked her, "can we ride together out into the mountains to visit with the Kazaks, like we used to? We haven't left the village this whole summer."

"No. People are too busy staying alive. And I'm not in the mood to go to the mountains."

The Chinese also prohibited many of our festivals, such as the fasting festival called *Bairam*. In the past, neighbors and friends visited each other to eat and sing for this Feast of the Sacrifice. By that point though, we were only permitted three vacation days for it, with no friends, and no singing: just sitting at home.

By then a certain kind of restlessness that had been growing in the village for several months reached unbearableness. One of our neighbors had been forced to flee to the south, into the Tarim Basin at the edge of the deadly Taklamakan Desert. Another was supposed to follow soon thereafter. One of my classmates stopped coming to school. Also, a little Kazak boy and one of our teachers disappeared, never to be heard from again. Soon I was able to count four permanently vacant desks in our otherwise fully occupied classroom.

"Officially" these banishments did not start until later in November 1958, and were termed "being sent down." It was not supposed to be a bad thing. Rather, as it was explained, someone who lived in a city was supposed to move to the rural countryside to bring about a balanced distribution of the population. Even so, in class I asked, "Why are the Communists banishing our friends and their families?"

"That's a law of the Party," answered the teacher. "It's forbidden to discuss it and forbidden to criticize it." It sounded to me like she wanted to apologize.

We would shed bitter tears every time we lost another classmate. I held fast to the belief, though, that this time my family would be spared, that this time we would find mercy. Surely it was not possible to be banished from our home twice, was it?

My perspective that Chinese soldiers were our brotherly helpers had changed. I had to admit that my father and my mother had been right long ago and that the Chinese leadership had been deceiving us from the beginning.

At the dinner table and at school, we children were served the same horrible news day after day, that so and so had been forced to flee, and so and so had been arrested.

THAT JUNE OF 1957 WAS THE LAST TIME my sister Zohre visited us in Altai for the summer holidays. The family accompanied her to the truck that would take her back to Urumqi. From there, she was supposed to move further south to Aksu to start her teaching position. That was the law. Graduates from the north were required to go south after completing their studies and those from the south were required to go north. We were crushed because the long distance probably meant that we would not be able to see Zohre for many years.

The constant complaints from my parents had changed me. I had also lost the last bit of any respect for the Communists. I wanted to stop seeing posters of Chairman Mao's adipose face, with that forever-grinning mouth, plastered over every wall.

Only a handful of Uyghurs were members of the Communist Party. The whole climate was deteriorating, with more and more unrest in our homeland. Too many to count were locked in jails, sent to labor camps, or directly executed.

Finally an eruption came in 1959—the Altai region's entire population rose up in rebellion against the Chinese. The organizers handed out flyers with calls to action, such as, "The Chinese must leave our homeland!"

As I was on my way to school one morning, I heard the clattering of horses' hooves getting steadily closer. About two-hundred Uyghurs and Kazaks on horseback were advancing toward the government offices. I was so curious that I ran after them.

My mother had heard about the rebellion while she was down in the village. Immediately, she dropped everything and came running to look for me. I was small and difficult to find in the crowd, and was startled to suddenly feel her firm grip on my arm, her fingernails digging into my skin.

"The soldiers will be here in only moments! Come on, Rebiya! Great harm will fall on all those still here!" At home, we locked the door securely behind us.

It was an easy task for the Chinese soldiers to quell the rebellion. Many were poor farmers and were simply marshaled off to the infamous prisons in the south. I do not know if my father took part in the rebellion. But I do know that many of his friends came over more often after that. However, my father and his friends no longer let me listen to their conversations. The only thing that I could overhear was some agitated murmuring. In the morning, my mother would say, "Kadir Khan, you're acting very mysteriously." She did not know whether he was involved either.

The word "banishment" circulated through our village like an apparition. By that time, ten families were missing from our community. Those who had resisted being sent away were sentenced to prison terms of up to fifteen years.

For others, a mountain not far away named Chang Kan would bear witness to their fate. That is where they took the Uyghurs and Kazaks to execute them. "Chang" means Chinese and "Kan" means blood. The Chinese had surely bloodied this mountain. "The dead are very useful," Chairman Mao is said to have stated at a meeting of high government officials. "They fertilize the soil."

MAO ZEDONG'S IDEA TO ACCELERATE China's movement into a modern industrial nation from 1959 onward led China into the most catastrophic famine in the history of humanity. Agriculture was dangerously neglected in favor of steel production. The Great Leap Forward turned out to be a devastating step backward into the Middle Ages.

We children would walk the streets with buckets hoping to collect grains of wheat that the *bingtuan* soldiers might have dropped during transport. On occasion, we were able to put a little sack half-full of these grains on the kitchen table. It was also our great fortune that we still had our field with its homegrown potatoes. We even managed to help support the neighbors, as we had done before.

For children under the age of ten, the Communists calculated a ration of eleven pounds of grain per month, assuming that there were crops. Older children had larger rations. Mercifully, the manager at the rationing collective felt sorry for us and added two years in age to my girlfriends and me.

About that time, my teacher, Mrs. Mamat became more sympathetic toward us too. She was constantly asking if we had enough to eat, what the situation was like at home, and how our parents were doing.

Even with all this, I still remember feeling surprised when a neighbor knocked on our door to borrow some sunflower oil and my mother measured out exactly five teaspoons, and not one drop more. Then there was the time that she gave away a bowl of flour, which she had smoothed perfectly flat across the top rim. I was not used to such stinginess from her. But soon I understood her better when I felt in my own body what hunger really meant.

Arzigul and I were there when they shot the neighbors' dogs. In 1960, a group of soldiers also took away Shark and our four other dogs. Our dogs had good personalities. We loved them like family. My father was completely distraught over the loss, to the point of tears. Wherever my father had gone in the past, Shark had always been by his side.

Leaving, Grieving, Believing

In June 1961 it happened. The government gave our parents four weeks to prepare for our forced resettlement under the threat of prison—or even death—for noncompliance. The term "resettlement" would normally imply bringing the community together. A forced resettlement however is hardly that. In fact, it's just the opposite. We felt banished from our community and forced into a life as refugees. Once we received their command, I was even prevented from going to school for that last month.

My father looked gray, his cheekbones protruded more starkly from his increasingly barren face. "We will not lose our sense of calm," he told us as we gathered together in the kitchen. He had succeeded in hiding another one-and-a-half-kilos of gold from the watchful gaze of the Communists. He burrowed about thirty of the gold nuggets into my mother's cloth belt. "Come here, Rebiya, and open your mouth." When I did so, my father explained to me how to test the quality of gold with my teeth.

That night my older sister Hejer gave me a gift of gloves and a hand towel on which she had embroidered a heart with drops of blood. She was not being banished because she was studying medicine in the city of Altai. She was already counted as having been relocated to that population. She made me swear to never in my life become a Communist Party member. "The Communists are responsible for our separation," she whispered, as though afraid of the sound of her own voice. Furthermore, she warned, I was not to tell our parents about this conversation. My father was perpetually worried that the Chinese authorities would catch us discussing politics.

We and all others had to organize our moving arrangements ourselves. So for truck drivers, banishments were good for business. They charged between fifty to sixty yuan. That was expensive, as a typical monthly salary was only forty or fifty yuan.

My mother sewed blankets and heavy clothing for us, even though there was hardly enough room for us to pack them—or much of anything. The garments and other belongings we had to leave behind were distributed around the village by my parents.

We put dried bread into one sack and roasted flour into another. These could be easily mixed with warm water in a bowl for a quick meal on the road. We also packed roasted meat into cast iron pots. Our friends brought us sheep stomachs, lamb fat, and butter to take along too. Our food alone took up ten small sacks and two large ones.

Every day people came by to see us and bid us a safe journey. "We will be back six months from now," my mother would reassure them.

My father was waiting until the very last day of the four-week grace period for us to leave. Then he decided that he alone would stay behind after all, in violation of the command. "Even if these people say they'll kill me, I'm not going to hand over this house to anyone. When you come back, we can live here together again," he said.

He talked to my mother for hours, telling her how to get by in the south and how she could survive with all of us. "You'll go to stay with our eldest daughter in Aksu; that's a nice county." He was convinced that he would be able to get us back, but my mother was more doubtful. However, because he always continued to encourage her, eventually she became just as convinced as he was.

My mother invited her friends over one last time. She strummed her dutar and sang a melancholy song for them. It was a recent melody, written during the days since banishments had become a part of our villages life:

> *Where can I go to?*
> *I cannot go anywhere.*
> *My throat is tied with a rope.*
> *Every step I take*
> *Is watched by a thousand eyes.*
> *Where can I go to?*

ON THE DAY BEFORE OUR DEPARTURE, I got up early and knocked on the doors of all of the neighborhood kids' houses; I ran with them to the places where we had played together, rolled on the ground together, and talked together. We ran to the river where we had always washed our clothes; we walked to the school and passed our fingers over the benches we had sat on.

When Hejer noticed that I kept running off with someone somewhere, she came along with us. Together we visited all of the places we had loved. I would have a thousand times rather stayed in Altai with her. But my mother was against it, saying, "That would only cause problems for your father."

Hejer and I did not sleep a wink that last night at home. We talked incessantly. The only thing I did not want to talk about were my fears, even though talking about them might have helped curb the recurring gruesome images that overwhelmed my mind. I imagined how we would be forced to seek refuge in a desert cave to escape the sandstorms or how the wind outside would stick to us like thick paste, keeping us from reaching any shelter. I was also sure that we would move to a place where there would not be any other human beings. Where we would be all alone.

Hejer and my mother lay clasping each other tightly as the early morning brought an otherwise tranquil day with a sky colored like the blue of steel. The neighbors were already waiting in the courtyard, holding small going-away presents in their hands—a glass jar of yogurt, bread, and dried apricots. "Please take care of my husband," my mother begged of every adult. She gave away her dutar to her best friend.

But there was no loud lamenting to be heard. Perhaps people had gotten used to losing dear friends every day. Or perhaps they were preoccupied with thoughts of when their own day of banishment might come.

Even though it was summer, we children wore the new wool sweaters that our mother had just knitted underneath our short-sleeved jackets, "For when the nights are cold," she had advised. She herself was dressed more attractively than she had been for a long time, wearing her long thin coat over an ocean-blue cotton dress cascading down to her fine leather shoes. A floral-patterned silk scarf crossed loosely under her chin and covered her braided hair.

This was her way of protesting. It has always been customary among Uyghurs to wear our most festive clothes when going out to visit. My mother, in a gesture of defiance to the indignities of banishment, stood tall, dignified, and composed.

It was just before noon when we were finishing with our last bit of packing. Suddenly, I was nudged from behind. It was Shark—somehow he had managed to escape from the soldiers. For the first time in a long time, my father laughed.

Shark whimpered. Sniffing around all of our suitcases, it seemed to me that he had a lot of questions for us.

My friend Rahime stammered as she said something about how I should come back soon. I nodded in agreement. But instead, as fate would have it, she and her family were banished right after us. My friend Khinlar held a small note in his hand, fumbling with it at first, then finally passing it into my own hands. He also kindly gave me a pair of socks.

With the help of a Kazak man, my father had negotiated payoffs to Party cadres who would allow him to return to the village to take care of the house after a few weeks in hiding. My father, having locked the bedroom door, gave the key to my mother and asked her to bury it in a clay pot in the courtyard. He told her that as soon as we were gone, the Kazak man would come by and retrieve it to hold until my father had returned.

The truck was already parked at the gate to our courtyard. My father and a few neighbors heaved an iron-clad wooden trunk onto one side of the flatbed. My father lovingly picked up seven-year-old Heljem, the youngest. He pulled her close and kissed her red cheeks. Next, he hugged eighteen-year-old Hejer. Then came Arzigul, aged eleven, and my brother Mehmet, aged ten.

I was the last one. He kissed me on the forehead. "I've entrusted you first to God, then to your mother. Rebiya, my daughter, now I'm entrusting your mother and also your siblings to you. I beg of you: see to it that your mother never cries; that she doesn't spill even one tear. And I'm sorry that I was never really able to show you my love."

For the first time in my life, I had the feeling that I understood my father—that according to his wishes, I could even take on a role in the family similar to his own.

Standing close together, we looked out upon our village. My father placed his hands on both of my mother's shoulders. Her lips pursed together as if to cry. But because he had praised her courage only moments earlier, she suppressed the feelings.

Again he hugged each of us. Then he went away, at first with hesitation, then ever faster, leftward on the hill toward the village. He turned around often to look at us. Shark trotted beside him. We did not know where our father would go into hiding. It was probably better that way.

Once I had climbed aboard the back of the truck, the neighbors lifted Heljem up to me. She and Mehmet were happy that they were allowed to ride in a truck for the first time.

The motor started.

Hejer ran after the vehicle rumbling down the road, "No! Don't go!" Her jacket flapped in the wind and dirt and stones sprayed out from around her skirt and boots. Although my mother shouted to her several times to stop, she kept running after us. While the truck drove farther and farther away from her, I still saw her running, until she disappeared as a speck in a distant dust-cloud.

MY BROTHER, MY SISTER, AND I sat in the front cabin with our driver— he wore a Mao-like blue suit and was fat, about forty-five-years-old, and a bear of a man. My father had probably tucked some additional money into his pocket because he was always singing his praises: "Kadir Khan is a man of excellent character."

The road went toward the mountains as we passed by meadows, green forests, and horses grazing at blue rivers. "See how beautiful it is where we live," rejoiced the driver. He could not, however, offer us insight into the scenery of our future.

His face reddened as he got angry about the government, saying "We should not be going into hiding! We should be fighting against the Chinese! It was Stalin who sold us off at Yalta in 1945!"

The little ones were quiet as long as there was food and entertainment, which is why whenever they asked for either, we fulfilled their every wish. They would play together a little bit, or eat, and then go back to sleep.

For three days, we traveled through flat land. But then it got more difficult for the driver as the road took long serpentine curves up forested mountains and through the Tarbagatai district. We would need up to twelve hours there to cover a distance of just sixty-five to seventy-five miles.

We spent the nights in state-run lodgings. Every room had three to four beds—there were no bathrooms. We would have no opportunities to wash for days until we arrived in Urumqi.

WE SOON GOT TO KARAMAY. From there we continued along the northern edge of the Tianshan Mountains. Those sky-high peaks divided our homeland into two parts: northern and southern. Between the parts were bountiful valleys and plains. In one of these plains rested the city of Urumqi. "It is the city farthest from an ocean in the whole world," our driver informed us.

Perhaps it was just fatigue from the long drive, but we all felt like we were losing pieces of our inner selves the farther we got from our home. The little ones now constantly had tears streaming down their faces, as did my mother, as did I. I do not know if this was our driver's first trip to the south. In any case, he kept trying to cheer us up: "You don't need to be scared. You'll make many new Uyghur friends. Together you'll be fine."

Although I was only thirteen-years-old, I was already mature enough to understand that we Uyghurs were not responsible for our current life situation. I reasoned that we were experiencing so much sorrow because the leader of the occupiers was such a cruel man, and that the population only listened to him out of fear. In school, our teacher always told us that Chairman Mao came from a simple peasant background. This story, of course, was intended to show that a person who is obedient to the Communist Party could rise to great heights. But I had an alternative interpretation; I told the driver, "Perhaps he doesn't have the skills to lead a country properly, as he is just a simple peasant."

The closer we got to Urumqi, the more sparse the vegetation became. We drove along dusty roads, then through a desert-like steppe. Now and again we would see cows and sheep. The driver was still trying to cheer us up: "Look over there too. It's beautiful. We have everything here, green pastures, white glaciers, and yellow deserts." But in reality, for hour after hour we passed through what looked to me like a rocky moonscape.

My siblings soon began to complain nonstop. First they had to go to the bathroom. Then they were hungry. Then they wanted to know how much longer this would take. It was all so tiring. Sometimes, when the driver spotted a place to stop, we would take a little break. Our fuller sighs of relief only came when we had reached that night's accommodations.

My mother considered rations of tea and dry bread three times a day to be barely palatable, so one day, at a rest area, we sat down to eat our *mantou*, a thin crispy dough stuffed with meat. An old woman with a dirty face and uncombed hair came up to our table. After standing by silently for a moment, she then simply reached into our bowl with her dirty hands and took scoops. Never having said a single word, she hobbled away, *mantou* in her mouth, more still in her hands.

The driver wanted to go after her, but my mother stopped him, "Don't beat her; leave her alone."

We had lost our appetite anyway, and none of us wanted to take any more from that bowl. The driver called after her: "If you wash your hands and make yourself a bit more presentable, you can have the rest."

After only a few minutes, she did come back. She had cleaned up her face a little and now we could see that she was at most thirty-years-old. As she stuffed one piece of *mantou* after another into her mouth, tears ran down her cheeks.

"Why are you crying?" my mother asked.

"My children died of hunger, and my husband left me and threw me out of the house. I don't know where to go or how much longer I will live."

My mother was touched by this, as was I. She also started to cry, saying again and again to us, "Your father would never put us into a situation like that. Your father would never put us into a situation like that. Your father would never!"

As we met more and more destitute people every day, right up until the end of our journey, I was convinced that we would never find happiness again. I was sure that we would end up in the desert. But my mother soothed me, saying, "No, we will go to a place where we have relatives and friends. God is just. Your father will come soon and take us back."

Our father had told us little about life in the south, and our mother knew only a few details such as that summers were long and winters were short; that the north was considered more progressive, in part because it was closer to the Russians; and that people in the south were more deeply attached to their religion.

One night, I woke up long after midnight. At first I had no idea where we were. I looked around and saw my mother hunched over on her bed. I said, "Mother, why aren't you sleeping? You need to sleep— we have to go a long way tomorrow."

"No, first you sleep. After that, then I'll be able to sleep."

But that was easier said than done. Bedbugs and fleas often crawled over the sheets. Once, when none of us could get any rest, my mother went to speak to the woman managing the state-run lodge. She wanted to know what we could do about these pests. The lady was almost amused when she answered that she was sorry, and that she too would love to get rid of them, "But the Chinese cadres are their carriers and have brought them to us from their own homes." Ironically, cleanliness was considered to be a sacred principle among the cadres.

In the early morning, my mother carried little Heljem, still sleeping, back to the truck. We continued down the desolate, bumpy road. The land that we were crossing was uninhabited for miles and miles. Sometimes we would not see another soul for the whole day.

AFTER FIVE DAYS OF TRAVELING we reached the capital city. Surrounded by high mountains, Urumqi was a place of strategic importance to its Chinese occupiers. I was deeply impressed by the paved roads and the number of large stores, to the point that it took my breath away. For the first time ever we also saw two-storey buildings.

Precious carpets lined many carriages, each of which was pulled by one or two beautiful horses. Here the Uyghurs still wore traditional dress, giving me great relief that my mother's own traditional attire no longer stood out by itself. Bearded men in flowing robes also walked the streets.

Still, no one was laughing anywhere. What I did see everywhere were bold-lettered posters heralding the "Xinjiang Uyghur Autonomous Region." I did not see any soldiers. In those days, there were two Chinese for every eight Uyghurs. Today, it is just the opposite: eight Chinese for every two Uyghurs.

I looked curiously around the bus station, where we had arranged to meet my older brother. "Mother, why are there no Kazaks in Urumqi?"

"Because they prefer to live in the mountains."

Mehmet suddenly screamed and started hopping up and down with excitement. "There is Jumak!" Our elder brother was right there—standing before us, hugging our mother first, with tears streaming down his face.

As our father had instructed him by mail, Jumak had found us clean accommodations in which to stay. We spent almost the entire day in the shower, scrubbing ourselves from top to bottom.

After that, to everyone's relief, our mother unpacked meat and bread from the boxes. This feast was in stark contrast to the widespread famine all around us and noticeable even in a large city like Urumqi.

"Where will you work in the future, Jumak?" our mother asked, as she prepared him a plate. He said he wanted to return to Altai. He also said that he was organizing a resistance movement with some other students.

My mother did not reply with words. She let him know instead with one unmistakable look that he should not say such things in front of us.

The two of them then went out together to see his school and his home. We wanted to go along too, but my mother insisted that we stay and get some rest. When she came back, she went straight to her room and cried for a long time.

For most of our visit in Urumqi we sat in our small room, while in the next room my mother had seemingly endless conversations with Jumak. I missed the song of the nightingale back home, and daydreamed about trees swaying in the breezes, about the rushing sound of the river. But I also received something else comforting—a huge compliment from my mother, who said, "You were really a good support for me. I'm grateful for your help."

My mother, Jumak, and our driver, who we had grown to trust, thought carefully about how to sell some of our gold pieces, knowing full well that anyone who was caught selling them would be thrown in jail. After long deliberation, my mother put several gold nuggets into the driver's hands and asked him to buy food ration cards. He refused immediately, out of fear. But my mother was quite stubborn. The poor man: she simply took him, by then deathly pale-looking, with her to the marketplace.

When they came back to the lodging just a few hours later, he roused us all. "Let's go, let's go. We have to get out of Urumqi right now." A short while later, we were huddled together in the back of the truck. I watched as my mother handed a bunch of food ration cards over to my brother. "I may not be able to send you more money, so be careful with these." At that, both of them started crying again; it was contagious, and shortly thereafter, the rest of us started crying with them.

"Stop that, all of you, and let's get on the road!" The driver, still scared to death, was under great stress because they had traded so many gold nuggets for food ration cards.

From that moment forward, we lived in abundance, at least for a while. We were in a good mood as we started south again.

THERE WERE ABOUT FIVE-HUNDRED more miles to go before Aksu. Boulders blocked the way now and again, as the truck climbed steep mountain passes. Our driver honked loudly before every curve.

Where he could not see the way forward at all, he would stop for a moment and stick his head out of the window to listen for oncoming vehicles.

On the descent, we took hairpin turns between tipping boulders, heading toward the second lowest place on earth, the city of Turpan—only the Dead Sea is lower. A network of subterranean water canals fed by glacial runoff from the Tianshan Mountains nourished its luscious vegetation. With temperatures of more than one-hundred-and-twenty degrees Fahrenheit, Turpan is the hottest place in China.

Between the Flaming Mountains, whose snowy peaks glistened in the sun at more than sixteen-thousand-feet, and Lake Aygul, at almost five-hundred-feet below sea level, Turpan was ideal for growing grapes. Lush vineyards stretched out in all directions. "This is paradise!" shouted our driver.

But once outside of the Turpan oasis, we were again surrounded by barren desert.

Arzigul and I stuck our heads out into the wind. In Altai, we fought all of the time, but since we had left, my sister had recognized me, two years older than her, as having parental authority. Yet she still would sometimes get agitated with Mehmet. Mostly out of boredom, I suppose, he would pull on little Heljem's dress until she screamed.

"Leave her be!" Arzigul would shout. But still he would continue. And still the baby would scream, until at last it no longer amused him. Apart from these occasional outbursts, we two older siblings had grown together as if into one person.

We handled the two youngest cautiously so as not to overexcite them, though they needed regular reminding that we must support our mother. Most of the time I sat in front with the driver, Heljem on my lap, and Mehmet next to me. We drove on the old northern route of the Silk Road, through a chain of oases, always along the perimeter of the Taklamakan Desert—one of the largest contiguous deserts in the world—southward toward our next destination: Kucha, the city of a thousand monasteries and Buddhist holy monuments.

At the bazaar in Kucha, the smell of goat soup was in the air. Nearby, a group of bakers hid flatbreads underneath their shirts. They would reveal them for a moment and then, just as quickly, make them disappear back underneath their shirts: "I sell bread. I sell bread." They demanded three yuan apiece, ten times more than normal. The abnormality of course was widespread famine in China. At my request, my mother bought several breads.

I noticed that a gaunt-looking Uyghur woman had been watching us for some time before finally deciding to sidle up to us. Leaning in closer, she quietly asked if we wanted to buy her woolen headscarf in exchange for about one-quarter-of-a-pound's worth of food ration cards. Even I knew that a scarf like hers was far more valuable than what she was asking. I looked to my mother, hoping. "No," she said, "if we keep going like this, we will be standing here one day ourselves, just like this woman."

We started to leave, but in a brief moment that stays with me to this day, my mother turned around once more to this woman. Their eyes did not meet, though they tried to. First one glanced, then the other. But probably the two ladies' spirits couldn't see commonality, or perhaps saw too much commonality. My mother handed the woman one of our breads.

"You're an angel," the lady said repeatedly. "You're an angel." An instant later she was gone, having vanished into the crowd.

Hunger of the Soul

In the early evening of the sixth day, we reached our destination: Aksu, a small prefecture with nine counties. There were perhaps one-thousand families in each of the counties.

My older sister Zohre had planned to pick us up, but she could not find us. We later found out that she was searching for us in the old part of the city. So we made plans to spend the night at a small inn, where the innkeeper kindly assisted us by sending a messenger to Zohre's address.

It seemed as though her arrival the next morning was sudden, though in excitement the passage of time has a way of escaping measurement. Zohre threw herself into our mother's arms. We all talked at once—each of us four children wanted to tell her stories from our journey. For just that moment, I had forgotten all of our problems.

Zohre, an attractive woman, wore a light-colored knee-length dress covered by a hip-length leather jacket. Her shoes did not have even a speck of dust on them. She told us that she had already contacted the office responsible for distribution of refugees and that they had given their permission for us to stay with her in Aksu.

An oxcart was waiting in front of the inn for us. In Altai I had seen only horse-drawn carriages. An ox was a completely new experience. After reloading our baggage onto the oxcart, our driver said goodbye to my mother with tears in his eyes. He advised her that even if the Communists tried to chase us away from there, she must always insist on staying near her eldest daughter, Zohre.

Because our progress was so slow in the oxcart, in the next village Zohre arranged for us to rent a horse-drawn carriage instead. It was already dark when we stopped before a villa. Its wooden entry way was adorned with decorative ironwork that opened into a large courtyard. The roof of the house was supported by stone pillars, and at the foot of each were mud-brick benches that beckoned to us to take a rest. Above the benches were artfully carved wooden panels. The large estate was probably four-hundred-years-old, designed in a southern Uyghur architectural style.

I was proud that my sister lived in such luxury. "I don't own this," she clarified. "I'm just renting it." In fact, the owner, a rich farmer or "goat," had been forcibly stripped of his property by the Communists. Zohre was not sure whether he had been killed or just that his property had been taken.

Two other families had been assigned to live there as well, and they welcomed us warmly. One family consisted of a widow and her son. Her son was twelve years older than me, was unusually tall, and had steel blue eyes and red hair. He took our suitcases and stacked them in the courtyard. Other than the initial welcoming, the second family mostly kept to themselves.

We were happy. My sister had been given two rooms. In one of these, she was preparing noodle soup while talking to us about her new life. All we knew from her earlier letters was that she was a newlywed—we had not even met her husband or his family.

As it was summertime, we ate our soup outside under the velvet blue night sky. Our unfolded blankets fit perfectly across one of the long benches between two pillars. It was one of the same benches that had beckoned to us earlier for resting. As it turned out, we slept outside for several nights under this dark beautiful sky.

The other residents, thrilled by our stories, slept that first night outdoors with us too. We had so much to tell each other—such a lovely evening after such a hard journey.

My mother said, "It seems we've done well for ourselves here. Thank God." The widow, who had a benevolent face agreed with my mother: "Yes, you can see we've found peace here. I hope that you too will be just as well off here." Zohre, however, was more reserved in response to our mother. "Life in Aksu isn't easy. But at least for today, let's be happy."

Despite our sister's protests for modesty, the widow told us that Zohre was quite affluent and was part of one of the few happy families in Aksu. The widow went on to tell us that her son, Abdirim, the one with red hair, was a department head at a bank in Aksu. He had even taken three days off from work to help prepare for our arrival. We graciously thanked him. Families like his and those of others who had civil service jobs were well respected. People believed, rightly or wrongly, that anyone who had secured a position like that would be taken care of for the rest of their lives.

The few Chinese who did live in Aksu either were in the army or were government civil servants. They also filled all of the most influential civic positions such that even in the tiniest Uyghur hamlet, a Chinese native was put in charge. But at dusk they would practically barricade themselves inside their apartments out of fear. As occupiers, they were far outnumbered by the occupied. Sometimes six or seven Uyghur children would chase after a Chinese person on a bicycle, throwing stones and yelling mockeries.

Later that first night, we met Zohre's husband. He was tall and had reddish hair and blue eyes, just like our neighbor's son Abdirim. The other thing the two men had in common was that they were both Party members.

In Zohre's large courtyard, we felt like one big family, and we laughed a lot in those first few days. After a week though, it was not as pleasant to spend the nights under an open sky. My sister took chairs and other belongings out of one of her two rooms to prepare a better sleeping arrangement for us.

Though they did not complain, we began to feel that we were intruding on the newlyweds' privacy. Lovers were not allowed to demonstrate their feelings in the presence of parents—not even by holding hands. That would have been considered immoral. If we wanted to go outside at night or to the bathroom in the courtyard, we had to pass through the young couple's room. That was unpleasant for them and for us. On top of that, my brother-in-law demonstrated some rather unusual behavior. Every time my sister served the soup for dinner, he stood hovering over her shoulder as she ladled it out, making sure none of us got too much. Maybe he came from a poor family. Or maybe he had just not learned proper manners.

During one meal, after we had as usual all placed napkins in our laps while we ate, he reprimanded us for being "bourgeois." "You can't do that!" Immediately he gathered up all of our napkins and threw them into the garbage. On another occasion, as we were walking together in the city one afternoon, he reached for my mother's brand new dutar and smashed it on the ground. This behavior made Zohre extremely uncomfortable. Later, when we were expecting an apology, she instead explained that her husband believed that only "class enemies" played music in private. Thus, there would be no dutar in his home.

On the day of our arrival, Zohre had been able to convince him to wear a suit to greet us. But the very next morning, he went to work at the pedagogical institute in his silly Chinese get-up. Zohre resumed wearing her stylish clothes, which was something the two of them often quarreled about.

If our mother used perfume, my brother-in-law would always complain, "What's that scent of the bourgeoisie that's wafting through the room?" He had no right to speak to my mother—an older person who was due respect—in such a way. He was clever about it though. He would never face her directly, but would instead redirect his comments to me or to Arzigul: "Your mother's ideas originate in the north and are very capitalistic. If she had lived this way in the south, she would have been killed long ago."

My mother did not openly make a fuss about her son-in-law's comments. But sometimes I saw her crying, with her hands covering her face, just like in the old days when my father scolded her. And although she was constantly telling us to listen to what our brother-in-law told us to do, there was one occasion when she could not help but comment, "Send that man to go take someone's hat and he will come back with the whole head."

Fifteen days after our arrival in Aksu, we children were already back in school. I was in the sixth grade with thirty-five other students. To my great surprise, they called me "Little Beauty." As much as I would have liked to believe it, I knew that I was not especially beautiful. I thought that they probably gave me this name because I was always dressed neatly and was polite.

In Altai, my written schoolwork had always been graded quite favorably. After about a week in my new school, I was able to impress my fellow students there as well. In fact, they voted me to be the class representative.

Mrs. Tillahan, our teacher, was an open-minded person. But to be sure, she too taught us about Chairman Mao's theories and harangued us with his "Learn From . . ." campaigns in which we were supposed to act in plays as socialist farmer heroes or self-sacrificing soldiers.

It soon became clear to all of us that a two-room apartment was just too small for seven people, even if we were a close family. Living together had become strenuous. After three months, Zohre and her husband moved to a place closer to her work.

∽ ∼

We helped support the families in our courtyard with our gold pieces. In order to be able to afford the groceries we needed for one month, my mother sold five high-carat gold rings. The situation was such that even those who had money could not always get meat, simply because it was not available. Otherwise, just about everything but food was cheap.

For months we could not find any candy in the markets, at any price. One day, news spread that the government was going to hand out candy. I promised my siblings that I would go and get our ration. About two-hundred people were already lined up in front of the distribution office when I arrived. After waiting several hours, I finally received a number and two entitlement coupons for our family. With those in hand, I was instructed to stand in line at the distribution office's window.

As I approached this second line, I noticed a woman and her children standing on the sidewalk. The line moved rather slowly but at last it was my turn. I placed on the counter my first coupon and greedily awaited the candy. Then I put down my second coupon; this time, the lady responsible for the distribution told me that I would have to go to the back of the line and wait my turn again. Only then would she accept my second coupon for more candy.

When I stepped away to go to the back of the line, the same woman and her two children were standing in the exact place where I had first seen them before. I asked her why she had not gotten in line for candy. She told me that she had come too late and was unable to get a coupon. Without saying a word, I put my second coupon in her hand.

She stood there as if in shock. Then she regained her senses and started fumbling through her handbag. "How much money should I give you?"

"I got it for free and I give it away for free."

In a reverent tone of voice she told her children, "Please show respect for your older sister."

I kissed the children on their cheeks and felt happy about the whole experience as I walked away. I turned around again on my way down the street and saw that the woman was still bowing toward me in gratitude.

On the way home, I thought in general about human behavior. Sharing was a natural response, but of course in times of famine everyone thought only of survival. In teaching by example, I felt that I had become a small role model. I felt that I had just grown up a little bit more.

I could hardly wait to get home and tell my mother what had happened. She offered a wise reply. "The Communists' laws not only demand that we Uyghurs forget our history and our traditions, but they also demand that we forget ourselves. Uyghurs should concentrate on our own traditions, on our moral considerations, so that the Communists can never make us forget ourselves." Aksu was just a small city, so my good deed quickly became well known.

Every time we needed something for the household, my mother took a small piece of gold, sawed it into pieces, and traded the sections in for cash in the city. But that would last at most for just two weeks of supplies. So again she would saw. And again.

In the winter, we burned mud bricks in the oven in our room, both for cooking and for fending off the intense cold. In the summer, we preferred to cook outside.

My mother bought a hand-carved bed frame from a neighboring woodworker. With the mattress and blankets in place, there was hardly any space left to move in our small room. But it was most cozy when Mehmet, Arzigul, Heljem, my mother, and I slept lined up neatly next to each other.

During the day, we used the bed as a place to sit. Then we pushed a low wooden table into the middle of it for a place to prepare meals. Then we moved that aside and used the bed as a place to eat. We cooked, ate, and slept in it.

With every month that passed though, my mother was forced to restrain a little more of her generosity, until one day she announced that from then on, everyone would be allowed to eat only as much food as the food ration cards allotted. We were also no longer allowed to bring our classmates home with us for meals.

Until that time, my mother had been sending us to school with some bread and salad. That was cut to only half a portion of bread and one leaf of lettuce. I would take two or three bites of the bread and during the break give the rest to my girlfriends whose parents no longer had any bread at all. One of the girls dipped the chunk of bread into a bowl with water. First she drank the water "soup" and then she sucked on the little chunk of bread for a long while.

I LEARNED EARLY TO TAKE MATTERS into my own hands. At home, I continued to help my mother with the housework and with raising my younger siblings. But more and more often, people came to me looking for advice. "We have no rice and no flour. What should we do?" Or, "Should we pay the rent or buy more firewood?"

Every month, as a class representative, I addressed students on topics like respect for elders or the best ways to help our parents. The teachers prepared texts for me on morality and honor which I was supposed to then read aloud. As soon as I would get to the lectern though, I put their sheets of paper aside and spoke extemporaneously.

Mrs. Tillihan called me into her office one day and told me that the school wanted to hire me as a teacher once I had completed seventh grade in another year. When I got home, I threw the door open and exclaimed jubilantly, "Mother, I can be a teacher!" To my great surprise, she was not the least bit pleased. Her plans were for me to first finish school and then go on to college.

Within a short time, I had made myself quite popular in Aksu. Every girl wanted to be my best friend, and even the older ladies were eager to talk with me. When I was out and about, I could feel people looking at me admiringly. That was a good feeling, but it was a dangerous one too. With this extra attention, I had also drawn the interest of men.

Never before had I wasted even a single thought on the idea of getting married. And anyway, I could not possibly find a suitable partner for myself in this village.

WE HAD GOTTEN USED TO LIVING with five people in one room and to the fact that our apartment did not have a bathroom or a toilet. The Communists considered private bathrooms for Uyghurs to be "bourgeois" and for that reason had them all demolished. Every week, we got a little coupon that entitled us to a visit to the public bathhouse. Of course, men and women were strictly separated.

My mother would not permit us to visit the public bathhouse though. Instead she had set up a little corner in our room where we could bathe. There was a toilet made of bricks out in the courtyard, which was used by all three families in the house. It was maintained by workers who came by to clean it on a regular basis.

In summer, I actually liked sleeping outside underneath an overhang. There was also a little outdoor table where I did my homework and checked my siblings' homework too.

I grew accustomed to life in Aksu quite quickly. Arzigul, Heljem, and Mehmet each had a much harder time of it. They were terribly home-sick and cried their eyes out because they wanted to go back to Altai. They also complained bitterly about the weather. The south was a lot hotter than what they were used to. There was only one thing they acknowledged as being the same as back home: the tall mountains. Near Aksu are the foothills of the mighty Tianshan range to the north.

In response my siblings of course drew the distinction that at home the mountains were surrounded by luscious greenery. But in Aksu, it was just desert. I tried to explain to Mehmet and Heljem that compared to others, we were still well off; that even back home in Altai, people were suffering from the famine, as our father had written us in his last letter.

We had no idea how our father was surviving. Most recently, he had told us that he was still negotiating with the cadres about our return. In large, cursive Arabic script he had written, "It's good that you left. The amount of crime here has doubled—they enter houses at night and kill the owners in order to take their possessions. The Chinese are flooding our land in waves."

He did not really write much but in one letter—which I remember well—he wrote a poem:

> *The shoes that are flooding into our land,*
> *Have covered it in dirt.*
> *I long for my own past.*
> *Look at the mountain!*
> *The deer and the nightingale in the garden,*
> *have been spooked too.*

Jumak also corresponded with us. Now that his college degree was completed, he tried to obtain permission to visit us in Aksu, but was denied. However, he was permitted to return, as planned, to our home town of Altai. There he first found work in an agricultural cooperative.

Every month, he sent us twenty yuan from his salary. I usually read aloud his letters for my mother, Arzigul, Heljem, and Mehmet. One of his letters in particular stood out among others:

> *Every month I'm allowed only one visit to my father. Every time I go to visit him, I hear a frightening voice coming out from our house. Our beautiful house, which used to be filled with songs, happiness, and friendship, now reminds me of a building deserted in war. I miss you all. I miss the house in which we lived together. I miss the past when we were all so content. I miss our field where we worked together. I miss the warm meals our mother cooked for us. I miss everything and every word you each said to me in those days.*

EVERY DAY, WE HEARD LOUD ARGUMENTS between the neighboring married couple on the other side of the wall of our courtyard. And every time the woman ran outside to get away, still screaming. Another day would bring another screaming argument—until finally I decided to go to their house and check on them.

I stepped inside the house carefully, prompting the husband to release the handful of his wife's hair that he had been pulling on. She collapsed on the floor and lay sobbing, holding her head with both hands. Their apparent poverty was choking them. They lacked the money for even a carpet on the bare ground. They did not even have a bed. The walls were black with soot from the cast iron wood-burning stove. Their cooking area was in shambles—not that they had any food to eat. Their children were cowering in the corner by the stove, looking relieved that the argument was finally over . . . for that moment, anyway.

The wife jumped up and politely offered, "Please, take a seat."

But I did not know where to sit. Excessively nervous, both the husband and wife tried to find something suitable for me to sit on. She was painstakingly apologetic about her difficulty and her embarrassment, but recovered enough composure to show her respect for me, as her guest. Despite the conditions in which she was living, I could tell that she had been brought up well.

Finally, the husband had an idea: "Use the little crate." From under a wobbly wooden shelf in the corner, she pulled out a red-painted wooden trunk and wiped it down with a rag. The red color slowly revealed a shine. The box must have been one of the sort that business-people used as a cash register; a slit on the top looked like a ready-made opening through which money could be inserted. The husband explained to me that the little crate, which had belonged to his wife's father, was their most treasured possession.

I sat down and said, "Thank you."

"He was the richest man in this village," the wife added quietly. "After the Communists distributed his possessions among the poor, they threw away the crate. But we took it home with us and have held onto it ever since." She went on to explain that her husband had been a servant to her family for many years. After her family's household had been dissolved, the only work he could find was hammering metals on an anvil for a blacksmith. Despite how hard that labor was, his weekly wages were not enough to even buy five pounds of flour on the black market.

Then I asked why they fought with each other every single day. They told me that the last time they had anything warm to eat had been several days ago.

"Either I have to go and steal something for my wife and children or we'll just sit here until we starve to death."

I came to understand that he was beating his wife this time because she had not fairly portioned out the last remaining noodles. Instead, she and the children had hungrily devoured them, leaving him out. He felt ashamed. She felt ashamed.

Back in our room, I appealed to my mother's compassionate heart. Could we please help these people out a little bit every month with some of our grain? But my mother, who had always been so generous, reasoned that if she continued to give away our food, we would end up in the same situation as our neighbors. Finally after my continual pleas, she did agree to loan them some food.

After that, I gave the family three bowls of flour. To our astonishment, the wife gave us back the three bowls, filled with flour, just a few days later. Again I pleaded with my mother for more.

"No, I will not give any more."

I knew in my heart this stinginess went against her true nature. Once, I remember, she had cooked a soup out of sheep's head that I had purchased at the market for her. It cost a small fortune. But she still poured some of it off into a smaller pot to share with the hungry neighbors.

This married couple's plight burned inside of me because I knew that before the Chinese had forcibly sprawled across our Uyghur nation, every family in the area had their own orchard in which to grow food. But after the Chinese occupation, the government took over all of the orchards. They stole from us. They robbed us. And there was no compensation.

Instead, Uyghurs were hungry and in poor health from this injustice. In desperation, some first laughed instead of cried. Some just cried. And some trekked straight to the graveyard to pray for their final destiny right there—it was the only relief that they could think of.

THE FAMINE STARTED TO RECEDE IN 1962, but we only minimally felt any improvement in our daily lives then. We were never full, not even from two bowls of noodle soup. For the first time in our lives, we could feel what hunger did to a human being: the way it raged in the stomach like a fire. Then the smoke from that fire clogged the mind with a suffocating lethargy.

I once marched through a vegetable field that had already been harvested and returned home, proudly holding up one cabbage leaf. My mother laughed and cried at the same time: elation and devastation from one cabbage leaf. It was normal for me to share even a find such as my one leaf of cabbage. Every month, I went to the grocery distribution center. I loaded grain, flour, and oil onto my little handcart and raced home with it. I also gained permission from the village head to till a small patch of meadow and plant vegetables near our home. Some weeks later, I cheerfully harvested a few peppers and sweet potatoes for us.

Many people had long ago lost their courage. They were satisfied if they received handouts from the government. But I was not. I bought ten seeds and planted more peppers. I did not understand why others did not follow my lead.

The Chinese government blamed the Soviet Union for the famine. Premier Nikita Khrushchev was said to have unexpectedly demanded repayment from China for a large loan. With that excuse, the Chinese in power had offered to the population an evil creditor upon whom they could project their distress.

That winter, the same neighboring married couple asked to borrow flour one more time. My mother simply agreed. What we did not know was that they had not eaten for several days. Tragically, the next night, only the two children survived. The husband and wife had starved to death.

News of deaths like these were constantly circulating. In the fall, a group of ten farmers diverted—to themselves—some of their harvested wheat. All ten men and three of their helpers were executed. In Bai, to the east of Aksu, hundreds starved to death while waiting endlessly at a grain silo that stored reserves for the city. The Chinese governor, who had once taken part in the Long March as a soldier, droned on about how it was not a serious problem that so many people lost their lives in times like these. An exact mortality figure is not possible, but most sources estimate that the total number of lives lost during those years of famine in China was at least twenty-million people.

The government did not release the real numbers on crop production. Instead, they forced farmers to report bountiful yields, regardless of the truth. Their lies were a part of everyday life, as were the lies the government told about bread rations that were to have been delivered every day.

Mother was more and more discouraged as the days wore on: "My daughter, by the end of the year we will have lost every bit of money we had. I don't know what else we can do."

Part of the problem was that we were registered citizens in Aksu. If we returned to Altai, we would lose citizenship entirely. Without citizenship, we would not be entitled to any grain from the government. But if we stayed in Aksu, what were we to live on? The meager grain entitlement was not enough.

We wrote a letter to our father, and he answered right away: "Tatachahun, how could you have spent that fortune in such a short amount of time when I had spent a lifetime earning it?"

Zohre gave me a gold bracelet and showed me how to disassemble it into individual links. Every month, I could sell one link to a goldsmith to whom she had introduced me. Once a month Zohre would come to visit and would sometimes even leave us ten or twenty yuan. In hindsight, I think she never once asked about our mother's health. But neither did the rest of us have an inkling that there was to be a concern.

I ate my rice soup and put my bread aside for my siblings. Though my stomach growled like an angry dog, hunger was teaching me to make sacrifices.

Starting in 1962, the Communist apparatchiks once again moved to eradicate the so-called "four pests." This time though, they were not referring to sparrows, rats, mosquitoes, and flies, but rather to the Turkic peoples: Kazaks, Uzbeks, Kirghiz, and Uyghurs.

In a massive exodus, between sixty-thousand and one-hundred-and-twenty-thousand people fled our nation for Soviet-ruled Kazakhstan. The Chinese military forces first closed in on these escaping refugees, erected concentration camps to detain and execute them, and then finally sealed the borders completely.

THE SEVERED RELATIONS BETWEEN the Soviet Union and China became obvious at the beginning of 1963 as propaganda from the cadres announced that the truth was that the Russians had sold out to capitalism and were careening toward an abyss. Personally, among other things, this "truth" taught me that such statements can take on various meanings, depending on who is telling them.

Abdirim, our widow neighbor's red-haired son, wanted to marry me and had already sent emissaries to see my mother several times. I was young, more naive about such matters than I cared to admit to, and simply more frightened than anything else. I saw him as some kind of older brother, a nice calm man who visited his mother on Sundays.

My mother would always show Abdirim's relatives the door— politely, of course, but firmly expressing resistance: "I would go begging in the streets if necessary for Rebiya to attend college."

In any case, a true Uyghur union would have been arranged differently right from the beginning. Traditionally, five women sent by the man's side would first introduce themselves as messengers. Each of the women would be carrying a large plate with round flat breads that had been basted in butter and oil, as well as sweets and a variety of fruits. Regardless of whether the young lady received permission from her parents to marry, the gifts would not be returned. If both sides agreed, only then would the young man and young lady be introduced to each other at a big celebration. If the pair liked each other, they themselves would make the plans to meet again. At that second meeting, accompanied by another big celebration, a date for their wedding would be set.

By that time, my future thoughts were only on studying at a university as my mother had planned. So the whole matter of marriage was not yet even a consideration.

When we were down to the last two or three links of the gold chain that Zohre had given us, I told my mother about an idea I had. Whether or not our citizenship made us ineligible to receive grain rations from the government, we could go back to our father in Altai where I would plant our own field with grains, fruits, and vegetables for us to live on.

Though my mother agreed to the idea, the government did not—we were denied permission for the necessary travel documentation that would verify we were registered in Aksu. Unexpectedly, another result from our plan arose.

Apparently our plan had made Abdirim all the more anxious. In a letter to me, he made his feelings known completely, writing: "You have appeared in Aksu just for me, like a star in the sky." I had no interest in reading such nonsense. I tore his letter to pieces and threw it into the stove.

But Abdirim was far from the only candidate who had cast his eye on me. Many other emissaries came as well. To me, all these men looked like wolves circling in on me from all sides, snapping at me with their jaws.

Again, our only option—this time to escape not cavernous hunger but rather ravenous men—seemed to be to flee back north to Altai, with or without government permission. One evening, we decided to do just that.

We packed up all of our possessions into two carriages as all of our acquaintances came over to say goodbye. I bowed politely before the elders. I did not, however, set eyes on Abdirim or the others in his family. I detested these people. I felt that they wanted only to tear me away from my family, from the university, from all of my heartfelt wishes. We steered our carriages away, out of their courtyard, out of their hands. The whole time, I clutched tightly in my hand the money that I had received from selling a half of a link from our gold chain.

WE HAD JUST ARRIVED at our guesthouse near the city of Aksu and disembarked from the carriage when my mother collapsed unconscious onto the street, as pale as though all life had been drained from her. My siblings screamed in shock as four passersby picked her up and put her back into the carriage. Our horse pulled as fast as he could, but in vain, as the main hospital had already closed for the night. For two hours, we searched the city for medical help until finally we found a small clinic.

"Please get me out of here," my mother kept begging me. But for thirteen days she had a high fever and could not leave her bed.

To pass the time for my younger siblings, I told them heroic stories like the ones our father used to tell. I also explained our difficult situation to them. We would have to return to our guesthouse to live, coming back each day to the clinic to be with our mother. I had originally decided to spend as little of our money as possible, but with the guesthouse rent and the clinic expenses on top of that, my plan did not work out. All throughout the day I would count, recount, then count again our remaining coins. I do not know how many times or for how long—it could have been for a minute, it could have been for an hour—I would just stare at the open palm of my hand, my lifelines crisscrossing beneath the one last gold link from our bracelet. Outside in the alleys, noisy children poked through trashcans.

After fifteen days my mother was able to sit up with the aid of two pillows propped behind her back. She did not agree to ask Zohre for additional help, saying "She can only take care of herself, she can't help us."

Zohre had been to see us twice at the clinic and had also given us a bit more money. However, my mother did not like that; she cried heavily each time, which only caused all of us children to chime in. I understood then that we children first needed to keep calm so that our mother could then keep calm. That was the process by which her mind worked.

The doctors had told us that our mother was suffering from a contagious, dangerous disease. To get well, she would need quality medical treatment for one more month.

I had not prayed for a long time. But on that special night I found comfort from seeing God reflected in the sleeping faces of my siblings: each one looked so beautiful, so innocent. I began to pray quietly: "God, please let this difficult time pass quickly."

THE DOCTORS HAD RECOMMENDED that I squeeze a watermelon every day and spoon-feed the juice to my mother. But my mother warned me not to visit her that often or I would get infected too. She also recommended that I eat garlic, rub my fingers and neck with it, and do the same for my siblings to disinfect us. At home, they were nagging me because they missed our mother and wanted to visit her as I was. But I forbid them to leave the room without me.

After three weeks, the doctors allowed my mother to return home as long as I could nurse her properly. After the carriage ride back, once she was settled into her bed, she gave me the following instructions: "Rebiya, drill a hole into a melon. Insert the raw meat of a baby chick. Afterward, place the melon under the coals in the oven. As soon as the meat is cooked, bring me the melon. That'll help me get well." So I made arrangements with one of the neighbors to trade in my mother's long sheepskin coat for three baby chicks. Unfortunately, he was only able to get one chick for it. But he also knew of someone who owned a baking oven and took me there.

After following her instructions, I pulled the hot watermelon out of the glowing embers, put it on a plate, and ran back to her with it. One spoonful at a time, she drank the juice and carefully chewed the meat. After that, she slept for two hours. Every day, I would rush out to get a baby chick and for three days in a row she ate this watermelon potion. On the third day, her fever was gone. We all thanked heaven.

The next morning, we heard a pounding on the door. It was Abdirim: his red hair windblown and messy, his head down. He was accompanied by his mother and his uncle. They had brought bread and a few candies. With what little strength she had, my mother asked me to leave the room.

I listened through the wall from the hallway. The uncle started, "We have heard that you were sick for a long time. If you return to Altai now, you'll not only be denied any food there, but you'll also lose your citizenship here in Aksu. Even if you should somehow manage to make it to Altai to find proof of this for yourself, you must already know now that you'll not get your citizenship back. Not there nor here. So we've come to offer our support."

The widow began her turn: "With two civil servants and a village leader in our family, we lead a good life. If you like, you can even live with us. But we would be happiest if you would give your daughter Rebiya to our son. We would like to also emphasize that our son could marry any girl in Aksu. But he only wants Rebiya. He has been making our lives difficult for a year with this weight on his heart. For the last fifteen days, he has been watching over you. When you were in the clinic, he was close by. When you slept at night, he was close by. When you came back in the carriage, he was close by. But he doesn't dare to stand before Rebiya."

My knees began to cave. I was frightened that my mother would say yes . . . and then she began to speak, pausing frequently, her voice so weak that it was a strain to hear her: "Many thanks that you came to see me . . . under these conditions. But . . . I must tell you . . . my daughter . . . is still too young . . . for marriage."

She must have turned to Abdirim. "I'm honored that you are . . . so attracted to my daughter. She is indeed a particularly lovable girl. But I want to send my daughter to school . . . and after that . . . to return to Altai. Thank you again."

Life had become so complicated. Abdirim's mother cleared her throat. "Even if you don't give us your daughter, we are still your neighbors. We would like to leave our gifts here." Then with more insistence in her voice, she said, "I wish you would think over our offer one more time." The door had hardly closed behind them when my mother fell unconscious once again.

A few days later, when she had recovered a bit more, a letter arrived from our father: *Stay in Aksu! If you come here, they'll throw mother and me into jail. The situation here is very bad.*

My pen flew across the page as I wrote my answering letter. I begged him to come to us immediately. But he wrote back that he could not get the papers, real or forged, to do so.

Seemingly prescient about our hopeless situation, the messengers arrived again—Abdirim, his mother, and his uncle. A lot had been going through my head. I had changed, perhaps out of maturity, or perhaps it was all just a delusion fueled by desperation for our survival.

I went into my mother's room to be alone with her. "Give me to these people, but with conditions. This family must take us all in together and pay the rent for our room. They must also ensure that you're taken care of. If they agree to do this, then they can have me."

She just looked at me, tears streaming down her face. She wiped her eyes with her sleeve, but said nothing as the visitors stepped inside. I kissed her on the forehead. As I reached the door, I turned to her and nodded my head with approval. Then I closed the door behind me.

Listening through the wall, I soon realized that my mother had no intention of following what I had just said. So I stepped into the room myself.

"My mother accepts your offer. You can take us with you." My hands were sweaty.

Abdirim's relatives accepted my conditions, but not with a great sense of trust. His uncle then put forth their conditions. My mother winced as he said, "Rebiya and Abdirim will go to the government office today to turn in their application. Then, they will get married tomorrow morning."

Later that same afternoon, Abdirim came to get me on his bicycle. Without giving him so much as a glance, I sat down behind him on the bike's rack. Less than ten minutes later, our marriage papers were in front of us. I can not recall actually signing my name, but I must have. Just as quickly, my future husband returned me. We did not speak a word to each other during the entire thirty minutes or so that we were together.

The next morning, he arrived again on his bicycle. This time, the ride was to our wedding. My throat felt choked in helpless rage. Through my clinched teeth, I asked if there was a hair salon anywhere nearby.

"Of course." Abdirim seemed elated that I had finally spoken to him.

In the past, many people, and of course my mother, had spoken of their admiration for my long, shiny, black hair. Even just combed through once, it would cascade down my back in little ringlets, all the way to my hips. Abdirim had often given me compliments about how exceptionally beautiful he considered my hair, saying that he would willingly sacrifice himself just to brush his hands through it.

I walked into the hair salon with firm steps. While the hairdresser readied her clippers, I said to her quietly, "These people have come to our aid in a time of great need. But if it had been me in their place, I would've offered my help without demanding anything in return."

As I walked out of the salon toward Abdirim I dangled my cut-off long braids in my hand. I said, "You see, now I've cut off my hair which you'd admired so much." I fervently hoped that with this new hairstyle he would no longer want me. But instead, he bit his lip in silence, then brought me back to my mother's.

It was she who had a dramatic response. Like his though, her response was not in words. She gathered the horse riding gear that she had brought with her from Altai and reached for a leather crop that at one end was sliced into many individual strips. She demanded that Abdirim face her. Then she sent my siblings out, ordered me to take off my jacket and lie face down on the floor. Still sickly, but showing no hesitation or lack of strength, she beat me: one, two, three, four, five. The crop cut into my skin—each long, singular leather strip tore at my back, then whipping wildly in recoil, readied for the next blow.

At first I gladly took each hit as I felt that the pain was worth it if my mother could gain some relief from her own despair.

Having tired herself out, she walked toward Abdirim. She asked him, "What do you want to do now?"

"If you'll agree to it, I'll take her with me."

I laid on the floor, crying softly. The salty taste of my tears reminded me that I was still in the present moment, that it was not just a bad dream.

"Stand up and pack your clothes. You can go now."

At the door, Abdirim turned around once more. "My mother, we'll go now." She turned and walked into the other room.

NOT MORE THAN FIVE MINUTES LATER, my groom accompanied me into the large meeting hall at the bank where he worked. A hundred of his colleagues got out of their chairs—among them seven or eight Chinese—clapping their hands joyously as Abdirim handed out candy to each. It was July 1963. He was twenty-seven at the time. I was fifteen.

Abdirim put a ring on my finger, but I took it off immediately and gave it back to him, saying, "I will not wear a ring of yours, but I'll start a family with you." He still lacked the courage to respond.

At first I was not sure whether this gathering was really meant to be a wedding celebration. Normally, a Uyghur wedding celebration would have been preceded by an engagement celebration. The bride's parents would deliver a crate of expensive gifts, and musicians, singers, dancers, and joke-tellers would all add to the festive atmosphere created in honor of the engaged couple.

At the wedding celebration itself, traditionally the bride would not take part in any of it, but would sit elsewhere with her girlfriends. Later, the older women would provide sexual education for the bride, who was certain to be a virgin. Only in the evening would the couple see each other again to receive holy blessings.

But at this wedding, my wedding, there was no dutar playing, there were no dancers or Uyghurs singing. I did not even have a veil with which to cover my face. Instead, it felt to me like I was an employee arriving for work at this bank. There was a sad poster on the right side of the meeting hall. It said "WEDDING." Underneath it were five chairs, of which the two middle ones were reserved for Abdirim and me.

Usually there would be no Chinese at Uyghur weddings. When I noticed Abdirim's boss, the Chinese head of the bank, I asked my new husband, "What are these people doing here? Why are they disturbing us?"

Abdirim explained to me that his boss had helped to organize this wedding ceremony. He said, "You should thank him."

"You should thank him because if the Chinese hadn't taken over our nation, you would never have been allowed to take me as your wife," I responded.

He avoided my gaze as though it might burn a hole in him. A moment later, his boss pulled Abdirim aside. In those days, I did not speak a word of Chinese, but Abdirim told me later about their conversation. His boss said, "You've taken a lovely Uyghur girl for yourself. She has beautiful eyes, but they're full of hatred. Be careful, or she may murder you this very evening."

"It isn't me she wishes to murder but you."

At that, his boss laughed out loud.

With a few taps on a microphone and hushing sounds spreading throughout the hall, the celebration quieted for a Chinese man who now stood at the front of the room. He gave a toast, which a Uyghur then translated: "Under the leadership of the Communist Party, under the leadership of our worshiped Chairman Mao, and with the support of the Premier Zhou Enlai, our esteemed colleague has managed to gain a beautiful wife. You can see here how happy the couple is."

The speaker suggested that we should eat a piece of candy together, mouth to mouth, but I refused. Finally, he invited Abdirim and me to bow three times to the audience as a greeting. But I did not participate in that either. Abdirim defended me, saying, "I'm very sorry, she is so young. She doesn't have the courage."

The speaker began anew, "If our beloved Communist Party didn't exist, we wouldn't have experienced this great joy." Everyone stood up and shouted in unison, "Long live our venerated Chairman Mao! Long life to our Communist Party! Long live Premier Zhou Enlai!" Then they broke into a chorus of a Communist song.

It was impossible for me to keep listening to this, so I put my fingers in my ears. My husband pulled my hands back down as if I were a naughty child.

Immediately, one of the Chinese men shouted something to my husband. Abdirim told me later what he had said: "Your wife's attitude is incorrect. You must be careful. Perhaps she'll poison you with her ideas."

Two hours later, the guests stuffed the candies into their pockets and left the hall. A number of them accompanied us outside. Directly across the street was an apartment building where the bank employees lived. In Abdirim's room, there were two little beds pushed against opposite walls. On the right wall hung framed pictures of Mao Zedong, Vladimir Lenin, Joseph Stalin, Karl Marx, and Friedrich Engels. In the middle of the room was a small table with two glasses on it. This was supposed to be the scene for our wedding night.

"The celebration is over now. I want to go home to my mother."

At that, he got down on his knees. "No, please. That wouldn't be good for me. What would people say? Dear wife, please you must stay here tonight."

With a sharp voice I rebuffed him: "I don't want to be pestered."

"I accept what you say." Disheartened, he retreated to his bed.

I lay there in the other bed with my face to the wall and listened to my inner voice. Sorrow and pain were blending together to create a black emptiness that ushered me to sleep.

In the early morning, Abdirim brought breakfast to me on a tray: vegetables in a lot of water, and a steamed dumpling. I did not touch the food, but wrapped up the dumpling in paper wanting to bring it to my brother Mehmet. My husband then brought me back so that I could visit with my family.

To my surprise, my mother acted as if she could not believe her eyes seeing me standing there. "What's this? You were married yesterday. Now you have to live with your husband!"

"No mother. I can't live apart from you all."

"My Rebiya, the timidity that every little girl is supposed to have . . . you never had it. You already came into this world as a great mother. You must go back to your husband and prepare for your own family."

"No mother." I won that point and stayed with my family, but my victory came with a much larger cost. At age fifteen, this wedding marked the definitive end of my childhood.

I TRIED TO GET USED TO MY NEW ROLE. Uyghur wives were supposed to be obedient and belong only to their husbands. Twice a month, Abdirim came to visit us; the rest of the time, he spent in his apartment which was only about ten miles away. In order to get in my good graces, he continued to assist my family in any way he could.

When he was visiting, he would sleep at his mother's house. I would continue to sleep at mine. He tried to get close to me, but I ran away every time. Abdirim tolerated this for maybe two or three months, then cleverly rented all of the other rooms in our house and in that way restricted my escape routes. He also transferred his workplace closer to where we were, which was in the old part of the city. It was at that time that my mother absolutely insisted that I move into an apartment with my husband.

In the evening, Abdirim sat down with me. He revealed that every time he looked at me, he did not really know how to behave. "I'm so happy that you became my wife," he told me shyly. "I'm so much in love with you, yet I also know that you don't love me. Still, I will try to be content with this life. Might you as well?"

I did not want a picture of Chairman Mao in our house. The personality cult around this despot was getting ever more excessive. A popular saying was: "Father is close to me, mother is close to me, but no one is as close as the great Chairman Mao." The man was not great, and he was struggling to control his own party. In his opinion, Communism had grown soft. "Only ongoing struggle brings development," he said. He wanted everything in monochromatic colors and everyone in sack-like clothing.

For one year, my husband and I slept in separate beds. Only after that first anniversary did we come together. I knew nothing about sexuality. My mother had tried several times to provide me with some education on the topic, but I interrupted her every time because I did not want to hear such things.

Over time, I grew to see Abdirim differently. Although he marched off to work in his uniform-like jacket, he let me continue wearing our traditional Uyghur clothing. Admittedly, it took me some time to change my attitude toward him, but his behavior helped me. I made a new effort to treat him well and to be nice when I spoke to him.

I was sixteen when suddenly something began to move around in my stomach. Horror-stricken, I rushed to my mother's. She cheered: "You're having a baby!" My mother kept comforting me, explaining to me what to expect, how to nurse a newborn, and reassuring me that I had nothing to worry about.

Later, when I told my husband, he was very excited and wanted to celebrate. When he began to hug me, I pushed him away. Despite my hostile, immature behavior, he became even more enthusiastic. Every morning and every evening, he sang songs and our married life stabilized into a more comfortable relationship. Though I respected Abdirim and held him in some esteem, I was unable to love him like a husband.

IN A LETTER TO US, OUR FATHER WROTE: "If I don't succeed in bringing you from Aksu back to Altai, I'll give up my citizenship here and come to you." That was in January 1964. Not long after, his next letter arrived. "I've finally received permission to depart." He would be with us in just seven more days.

Out of sheer joy, Arzigul, Mehmet, Heljem, and I started to dance. When our father was due to arrive, our mother put on her prettiest dress and powdered her face with makeup. In honor of his arrival, she prepared a fabulous meal. If she heard a voice outside, she ran toward it expecting to see her husband. But shortly after, she would come back inside disappointed. He did not arrive on the appointed day, or the next day either.

It was only on the third day that we received news that Kadir Khan had arrived in the new part of the city of Aksu. Immediately, one of Abdirim's uncles went directly to the city to escort our father home to us.

Remarkably, he had not changed much. He kissed his wife on the forehead, just as he had always done in Altai. She staggered a little from the excitement and held onto the door for balance. Her voice sounded hoarse too as though she had not spoken in a long time. "There are the children," she said. It was as if she was swaying in that spot with only the door keeping her on steady footing. She could not manage to even take one step forward. He wrapped his arms around her tightly and she simply molded herself to his grip. Again she tried to use her faltering voice, and only after some time, managed to say, "The children . . . the children . . . have missed you." He embraced each of us, but was particularly anxious to have a conversation with me. Ignoring the man at my side—my husband—he was seemingly distraught looking at me as I was visibly pregnant.

"But you're still a child," he sobbed aloud. We had decided not to inform him of my marriage because we knew that he would not approve. He scolded my mother, saying, "How could you have let such a little girl get married?"

Abdirim did not show that his feelings were hurt. I respected him for that. Instead, he said, "My father, please take a seat. Can I be of service to you?" Within a short period of time, he had convinced the head of our family that he was a good son-in-law. After dinner, we all listened to my father's travel stories.

"In the city of Altai, there are no more Uyghurs, Kazaks, Uzbeks, or Mongolians. They live only outside the city now, in the villages. There are more Chinese there than you could imagine. They carry baskets on their backs, with children in every one of them."

When I asked about Shark, he looked at the ground sadly. "A few weeks after you left for the south, the soldiers came back again and told me they would return in a few days to pick him up. The following night I had bad dreams, about you all, about our animals, about Shark. In the morning I had an odd feeling, so I went outside, through the snow, to the courtyard gate. When I opened it, I saw Shark. He had frozen to death right there during the night.

"I dug a hole at the edge of the field to bury him. A few days later, the soldiers came back to pick up our dog. I explained to them that Shark had passed on. I was beside myself with disbelief when they kept demanding that I turn over the corpse.

"'No,' I said to them, 'At least Shark's body must be at peace in this place.' For three days they harassed me until finally they ordered that I would either have to pay a fine of one-hundred-and-fifty yuan or turn over the dog's dead body. That was three months' salary. But I decided to pay them their fine."

On his way to Aksu, my father had spent two days looking around Kucha. He had calculated that he had a good chance of finding work there. So his plan was to move to Kucha with our mother and us children. I admit that it was a lot for me to think about. At the same time, I was calmed by my father's unstoppable spirit.

AFTER A TWO-WEEK STAY WITH US, our father loaded the family's furniture onto a carriage for their two-hundred mile trip to Kucha. For the first time ever in my life, I was to be separated from my mother and siblings. They felt as badly as I did. Our father helped calm us down:

"Tatachahun, if you miss your daughter, you can come visit her here. And Rebiya can visit us in Kucha any time." Within weeks, both Zohre and my second oldest sister, Hejer, with their husbands, followed the family to Kucha.

I constantly felt a dull pain in my spine that traveled down to my legs. It made me want to just sit down with my big belly and not think about anything. I had between twenty and thirty days left until the birth. My mother had hoped that I would give birth to my first child at her home in Kucha, but even I rejected that idea. My father was new to the city and had not yet found work. I did not want to add a newborn to their burdens.

I cried for two days after they left. I had mixed feelings, but I knew that I had to get used to this new life. If I caught my husband singing and dancing with his anticipated joy of fatherhood, it gave me goose bumps all over my body. However, I also hid from him, as well as I could, my feelings of alienation. The only thing I could not take, and could not fake, was if he tried to touch me—definitely not in front of others, and not in the daytime.

In the evenings, I cooked for Abdirim and served him dinner. At the dinner table, Abdirim talked with me about problems of the day at work. Whatever we happened to be talking about, he would add that he was the happiest man in the world because of me. The apartment, the laundry, and our clothing were all sparkling clean. I emulated my mother in all of the housework.

The doctor at the hospital was worried about me because of my young age and my slight body frame. This would be a difficult birth he thought. But the opposite came to be. After I gave birth to my son Kahar, on February 10, 1964, the doctor told me that I had gone through childbirth like a woman who had already given birth to several children.

I was back home after three days. With Kahar in my arms, I no longer felt as lonely as I had before. For forty days, I was surrounded by relatives, friends, and neighbors. My mother-in-law was quite helpful, standing at my side. She had become a close friend to me, and soon we grew to know each other well. A child does not belong only to its parents; it belongs to the whole community. Everyone held themselves responsible for our new little citizen.

If I was not busy in the house, I read. Abdirim had a lot of books, and he always got upset if I bent or stained a page. The funny thing was that he had not read a single one of these books. With concerted effort, I worked my way through almost his whole library. Among the books were translations from Russian, Japanese, and Turkish.

At home, Abdirim and I spoke openly about the political situation in which we lived. From the outside, things appeared to be stabilizing in the country. Under leading Chinese politicians of the time, such as Deng Xiaoping, a more sensible economic policy than before had been put into practice. Farmers were at least allowed to sow the fields partially for their own use.

On October 16, 1964, two days after the downfall of Soviet Premier Nikita Khrushchev, China set off its first atomic bomb in Lop Nur, an area in the Uyghur nation on the eastern edge of the Taklamakan Desert. The government commemorated the event as China's biggest success of the century. My husband explained to me how dangerous these tests were for us. The ground nearest the test area would be contaminated for decades to come, and the surrounding areas far around it would also become radioactive from the fallout. He surmised that was why the Chinese had not detonated the bomb on their own land, but on ours.

Tragically, the authorities had not sealed off the test area or surrounding region. The nearest settlements were only about thirty miles away. Turpan was the nearest city. Victimized unknowing residents who went to collect firewood in the area became exposed to radiation. Years later, with my own eyes, I would see the true extent of the catastrophe.

I was finding Abdirim more attractive the more I grew to know him. He was attentive and taught me many things. It was around this same time that his jealousy appeared, along with an unexpected rage. Uyghur men are raised to believe that they are the supreme rulers in the family, and the women are taught to accept their subordinate role to them. Ironically, it was Abdirim who seemed to suffer from inferiority. As soon as another man came near me, perhaps at a festival, he would growl jealously that I was to look away.

In the village, word was that Abdirim, of all the husbands, had done the best for himself. In my opinion, I was not prettier than the others— but I was different from all of the rest.

Red Revolution, Blue Dissolution

The bureaucracy gave us along with my mother-in-law, a new two-room apartment in the center of the city. I spent a lot of time with Kahar and devoted myself even more to being a good housewife for my husband. But strangely, Abdirim began to change as soon as I began to improve my behavior toward him. He became ever more stubborn with me. I was sure this change had something to do with his monthly salary because on seventy yuan he was expected to support Kahar, his mother, and me. Well, at that time there were just the three of us.

But I was pregnant again, and we simply could not afford a second child.

So we started to borrow money from the bank. But even that was not enough, so we took out more loans. I calculated that we would not be able to survive in this way much longer.

In the previous few months, I had also gotten in touch with a lot of people who had been banished from their homes. They were, in essence, refugees struggling with the government's inhumane relocation policy—just as my family had done and was continuing to do. I visited these people on a regular basis. I was always ready to step in where I could to provide solace or protection for others.

I believed that Chairman Mao was afraid of losing his power. For that reason, he wanted a population more vigorously Communist. His campaign called together young people to meet at Tiananmen Square on several occasions between August and November 1966—I particularly remember August 16, 1966, when more than one million people gathered. The Red Guards cheered in unison for the "most favorite chairman" and promised to "destroy everything old—exploitative thinking, old culture, traditions, and habits." It was no longer the construction of a country, but a witch-hunt for real and imagined political enemies who stood in the forefront of governmental politics, and for those who hid in the shadows of an underground rebellion.

The goal of the great proletarian revolution was to establish new bureaucratic elites, meaning the rebels decided that any form of traditional authority must be destroyed. Adrenalized Communist youth, whose membership emblem was a red armband, sought to destroy everything that evoked even the most distant memory of what had been traditional China. Nobody was safe, as it would turn out—not even the chairman's leading supporters. Schools and universities stopped teaching, and students, in a bizarre reversal of authority, tortured and beat their teachers with no repercussions.

Outside, every wall and every fence was plastered over with huge posters on which individual citizens were portrayed as Chairman Mao imagined them to be—his imagination came complete with individual and national happiness, prosperity, and devotion to him. His battle cries—such as "First destroy everything, then construction will take care of itself"—ensured that everyone was fighting with someone, with anyone, all of the time.

Shortly around the start of this Cultural Revolution, Abdirim brought home a rolled-up poster of Chairman Mao which we were supposed to unfurl and obediently display in our home. Instead, I kept it in its roll and placed it behind our bed. Not long after, the Red Guards began a search of all houses. I could not imagine what would be of importance to them in our home.

Then they found that poster still rolled up. Condemning me for disloyalty, the Red Guards immediately paraded me through the streets to bring me to the Party training center in order to subject me to a *pi dou hui*. In English a *pi dou hui* was referred to as a struggle-session, relating their re-education program to Chairman Mao's concepts of gaining salvation through human struggle. My pregnancy was still in its early term, so I must have appeared to them to be physically fit. Had I been showing, I do not know if they would have pushed and pulled me by my arms, spat on me, and swore at me as they did.

I was told that I was considered one of the "black elements." That was their term for referring to counter-revolutionaries. But I was lucky. The people in the community held a protective hand over me, saying that I was just a simple mother and that they would undertake my re-education themselves.

The Red Guards did not consent to this idea entirely. I was escorted to a stage, with several other accused people, where I was ordered to stand on a chair and bend over so that the audience could better see me and so that some others could better humiliate me.

As I accepted my punishment, the impassioned leader of the Red Guards carried on with the other defendants assembled. I remember him approaching one man whom I knew quite well. I always bought my fruit in his shop.

"Capitalist!" The Red Guard kicked the man in the knees from behind, forcing him to stumble forward before hitting the ground. The shopkeeper was around fifty-years-old and someone had recently pinned to his shirt many, many small pictures of Chairman Mao. In order to deflect the Red Guard's violence elsewhere, the shopkeeper shouted, "Some of you are disrespectful toward our honored leader! You don't carry his picture with you, or display his picture on your clothing like I do!" With his fists raised to the sky, he continued: "Do you know what I would like to do most? I would love to open my chest and carry the pictures of our beloved leader in my heart."

Standing up then, he pointed to me: "Do you know who gave you your clothing? And your bread? Was it not Chairman Mao? You should be beaten until you're unconscious. And then killed!"

Some of my neighbors applauded him and loudly condemned me. I thought to myself *Surely they nor anyone else seriously wanted to lift a hand against me, much less kill me . . . did they?*

A woman stepped toward me, yelling, "You have to carry it, this picture, it's important!" Then she came even closer, in a whisper, "Pin this picture to yourself." Not wanting to cause me to lose my balance atop the chair, she went ahead and pinned a picture of Mao Zedong to my blouse. My heart was beating wildly as I stood before this seething crowd. Amongst them I also saw sitting quietly several of my friends, elders whom I highly respected, scientists, and teachers. They made me feel not so alone.

The principal crime of most of the defendants that day was that we possessed knowledge, wealth, or influence. At later assemblies, I would be regularly shamed by being cordoned off with loyalist government supporters. I secretly wanted to be grouped with those who had more common sense, who could still differentiate between good and evil. Still, I was better off than those the government categorized as having lost control over themselves. When I returned home that day, I sat down on the bed, exhausted, and removed the picture from my blouse.

As further punishment for the rolled-up poster hidden behind the bed, I was put on view fifty days in a row, standing on a chair, bending over before the struggle-session assembly. At first, the Red Guards did not notice that I had removed the picture of Chairman Mao from my blouse. After four or five days, however, one of the loyalist government supporters from the audience screamed with outrage, "She's not wearing a picture!"

As I was still bending over, a soldier pushed my head down further, then jerked my arms upward into an airplane-like position. Suddenly, ten loyalists were pushing toward me. Soon, there were about fifty. Beyond them, approximately one-hundred more jeered. Soldiers prompted them to chant, "Long live Mao! Long live the Communist Party!" After that, they prompted a chant of "Rebiya should be annihilated! Rebiya should disappear!" The rest of the audience was required to greet this with equal cheer.

A young loyalist muscled through the crowd and rushed toward me. "I'm the son of Chalidem," he whispered to me.

His mother was a good friend of ours, and fortunately, the boy was smart. He shouted, "Rebiya didn't wear a picture of our beloved chairman because she didn't consider herself worthy of it! She was a counter-revolutionary and now only wants to wear his picture when she's developed into a true loyalist!"

His words were well received. Chalidem's son then called out to me, "You come down and sit. As long as you haven't changed your mind, you've no right to wear a picture of our chairman!" The Red Guards nodded their approval.

We were automatically found guilty if we behaved like our true selves, as Uyghurs. People talked differently from how they felt. Only those who acted aggressively were considered to be real revolutionaries. At the struggle-sessions, it was more of a contest between villages than a denunciation. The reputation of a village leader rose with the number of loyalists he gained in his village. Mao Zedong bibles or stickpins bearing his likeness were common rewards for loyalists. In homes across China, many had drawers stuffed full with these mementos.

The tide had turned against my husband. Admittedly, some of it was my fault, as the Red Guards held against him two things—the first, his rebellious wife; the second, his authoritarian position as department head at a bank. The previously highly respected work of civil servants was downgraded due to the absurdly irrational anti-authority programs of the Cultural Revolution. Literally, those with authority lost it, those without authority gained it: doctors mopped floors, and janitors treated patients.

Abdirim eventually lost faith in the Party, but not as a result of my influence. Rather, he simply saw through the Communist lies. It did not take long for the Red Guards to lead my husband away. They confined all of the bank's department heads and bosses inside a meeting hall in Aksu's old city. Abdirim's monthly salary was only twenty-five yuan during parts of his confinement. If I had not started earlier that year to sew together children's shoes from corduroy and plastic soles and make undershirts for women, my son and the unborn child growing inside me would not have survived.

I gave my fabrications to Bouhatcher, a neighbor who made her livelihood as a black market dealer. She was not my best friend, but she was a patriotic Uyghur and respected me for my love of our homeland. Bouhatcher was as short as I was, but approximately three times as wide. She floated along like a steamboat. With my earnings, I was able to bring an additional thirty to forty yuan a month to our home. That was a lot of money.

Meanwhile, Abdirim was forced to memorize Mao Zedong's philosophy, along with twenty others who had held management positions at the bank. He was allowed to go home only when he could recite a book-length of material, page for page.

THE RED GUARDS LEARNED from one of the victims at a struggle-session assembly that we had an entire library at home, and even worse, that we would occasionally lend our books to acquaintances. Less than one hour later, the Red Guards stormed into our house.

They started a bonfire in the middle of the street. While some of the Red Guards dragged our books outside for burning, others held my scarves and my coat up in the air: "A member of our society isn't allowed to wear these." After that, they rummaged through the entire house, grabbed all of our nice clothes, and threw them onto the firepile as well.

Four soldiers took Abdirim and me to a big square, in the middle of which lay hundreds of books among them many religious texts. Like madmen, several of the loyalists stomped on top of the prayer books. One of them cursed, "God be damned! People say it's a great sin to say such things. But I'm saying it anyway, and I haven't had any problems because of it!"

They lit the books on fire. Uyghurs lost a great percentage of our written heritage during the Cultural Revolution's book burnings. Once everything had gone up in smoke and flames, they smashed doors and windows in some nearby buildings and herded pigs inside. Zohre and her husband were counted among the best loyalists. In one hand, she held the flag of the People's Republic of China; its red star went well with the crowds clamoring and starry-eyed enthusiasm. My oldest sister was of the opinion that her path was right and that the path I had chosen was wrong.

My sister Hejer and I were more alike. She even joked about those "uninhibited Red Guards." Zohre's husband thought that we had crossed the line. He condemned us both and declared us to be enemies of the people.

The Cultural Revolution's sadism and bloodlust knew no bounds. Uyghurs, Chinese, Mongolians, other ethnicities—just people, just ordinary people—were boiled in oil, had their faces cut in patterns, and had clumps of hair pulled from their scalps by soldiers' bare hands.

Those in Kucha, of course, had not overlooked my father either. They accused him of praying in secret. But he never complained out loud. Instead, he seemed deeply lost in thought. Probably he was just immersed in his prayers to God.

A FEW WEEKS BEFORE MY DUE DATE, I explained to Abdirim that I wanted to go to Kucha to give birth to our second child at my parents' home. Hejer, who had studied medicine in Altai, would be able to assist. My parents knew about our financial situation and considered this a good idea.

Zohre's husband opened the door for me. He was wearing a blue Mao-like suit, and while we drank tea he prattled on about his plans to eliminate all of the counter-revolutionaries. When I had listened to him talking at me, not with me, for long enough, I cut him off, "I'm sorry that I have to say this to you, but you're thinking very simplistically. I'm ashamed for you. But, I'm also convinced that Chairman Mao is a smart man because he has succeeded at making you all crazy."

My brother-in-law just glared at me. Then he adjusted his posture and looked down on me with a punishing expression. "You're clueless, but then again, you didn't have a chance for an education."

"And you just attended the university and became a teacher. Learning once isn't enough. You have to keep educating yourself and read different books for a change."

My brother-in-law replied, "You've been poisoned by the books of the bourgeoisie."

Despite this exchange, Zohre still loaned me the money to cover the hospital costs for the birth of my daughter Rushengül, on July 18, 1967.

Two days after giving birth, my mother came in a carriage to the hospital to bring Rushengül and me back to my parents' home. Life was moving along normally. Mehmet and Arzigul were in school, with whichever of their teachers had not been imprisoned. My father worked at a barbershop when he did not happen to be on stage at a struggle-session assembly. Ever since my parents had reunited, my mother seemed to have blossomed. But this outward appearance hid what was really going on inside of her.

When mother and I were sitting together in the kitchen at night, she seemed very melancholy. She brought out her dutar and strummed a song for me:

> *Black, black, black*
> *Nothing in me is black,*
> *Not like the ergot among grain,*
> *There is no sin in me.*
> *My falcon flew from my hand,*
> *Where are the guests today?*
> *Don't get involved,*
> *My heart is wearing mourning today.*

She continued, "My daughter, do you miss our homeland in Altai? Do you think I'll ever be able to lead my old life again?"

I tried my best to lighten these dark thoughts that had nested firmly in her mind. During that first night, we slept together in one room. Rushengül was sleeping beside me. All of a sudden mother began to twitch and make a gurgling sound. I jumped up and pulled her head into my lap, and in the same moment, she vomited a surge of blood.

At once, with my father's help, we brought her to the nearest hospital. It was an agonizing wait for the diagnosis; however, I would have rather waited an eternity than to experience the agony of what the doctors concluded: stomach cancer. I was overcome with despondency. But then I pulled myself together and swore that I would bring my mother back to Altai. This was the day that I decided that it was my duty to liberate the Uyghur nation from its occupiers.

The family decided that we would withhold the diagnosis from our mother. The next morning, she was sitting up in her hospital bed, with a smile playing about her lips.

"My daughter, all of my pain flowed out of me through that blood. From my truest heart, I can talk to no one else but to you. Maybe the blood was just waiting for you to come. I'm very sorry that I showed you my pain in this way." A week later, we transported her back home in a carriage.

A short time later, she was scheduled for an operation in the large hospital in Aksu. As we were getting ready to leave, my mother chose a mauve-colored traditional dress, one that she liked to wear as a young woman. In the year 1967, this type of attire was met with severe punishment. But the doctors in the hospital said nothing. Everyone knew that she did not have long to live anyway—as it came to be, she had just another forty-eight days. My mother lay on the stretcher, ready to be taken into the operating room. My father stood next to her, telling her, "You've become very beautiful my wife."

Awake after the anesthesia, she whispered, "Have the doctors removed from my stomach what was giving me such great pain?"

I caressed her hand, which seemed now to merely be skin and thick protruding veins: "Yes, mother, they've removed it."

Within the next few days, the doctors informed us that the cancer would devour our mother. After the operation, she could no longer manage to sit up. Every morning, I selected one of her favorite dresses for her. Over and over she repeated, "When I'm well again, we'll return to Altai." She turned to me. "You'll bring me there, won't you Rebiya?"

Her stomach became more swollen and ever larger. We knew that she felt the wings of approaching death passing over her.

One morning, when it was still very early, she asked for me. She told me, "My daughter, I'm so sorry that I haven't managed to make you happy. You've made great sacrifices for our family. And I took happiness away from you. But you're capable of surmounting all difficulties. You'll find your freedom. You don't belong to me, you belong to the people.

"You've no place to work, you've no money, but you have a big heart. If you want me to die in peace, then please let me shift the responsibility for your younger siblings over to you."

"Yes, mother."

"Your eldest sister went to university; she has a clean heart, but she isn't as smart as you. She doesn't know how to live. Your second oldest sister is sickly and often argues with her husband, and your brother in Altai is far away. Now bring me your three younger siblings."

When Arzigul, Mehmet, and Heljem were standing before her, she slowly opened her eyes, as though it were a tremendous effort for her. She told them, "From today onward, Rebiya is your mother and your father."

She looked tired and strained. After a pause to breathe, she asked one more thing of me, something completely unexpected: "Rebiya, turn Rushengül over to your older sister. She isn't able to have children. Your sister is a good person. But how can she spend her whole life without a child? Please, give her Rushengül."

"Yes, mother, I will do that."

Then she asked me to get my father.

He sat down on the bed with her and took her hand. "My dear husband, I will not allow our three children to stay with you. You can't feed them. Promise me that you'll give the children to Rebiya."

"Yes, yes, yes, of course. But don't speak of dying."

"After I've died, please wait one year. Then you can marry someone else." She coughed. "You also need to consider finding the right one. If the woman can't cook and take care of you, you'll experience great problems. And, my dear husband, for the times I've angered you, please forgive me."

Finally, she asked for her two oldest daughters.

"Rebiya is responsible for the younger children, effective immediately."

"No," Zohre protested. "Each of us will take a child home with us. We can't expect Rebiya to bear the burden alone."

"No. Nobody is allowed to separate the three children from each other."

In a voice barely more than a whisper, my mother pulled me closer to her. "It isn't that easy to breathe my last breaths. I will have a lot more pain until then too; maybe I will even . . . urinate. If something like that happens, please change the sheets quickly and clean me up so no one sees."

She also asked me to dress her in one of her prettiest dresses. "And please comb my hair beautifully one more time."

In her trunk, she had a white Tatar dress with a red top and ruffles along the bottom. She had been keeping it for a very long time. It would be perfect for her. She looked like a queen wearing it.

I wheeled my mother directly next to the window, a bright place with much sunshine. While I was smoothing the blanket, she spoke as if to herself, "This land is our land. Now bring me Heljem."

When I arose to bring in my little sister, I watched a single tear detach itself from her eyelashes and roll slowly down her cheek. It was then I understood that she had released herself for her final journey.

Traditional funerals were considered outdated during the times of the Cultural Revolution. But we found beauty in tradition and did as we wished to honor our mother. After my father had dug her grave at the large cemetery in Kucha, he decided at that very moment that the plot next to her site should be set aside for him when the time came. Approximately fifty friends and relatives took part in the funeral ceremony with us on September 28, 1967. Sadly, many people from the village who had wanted to take part did not, out of fear of retribution. But there were some loyalists who took part; such was the respect my mother had acquired from so many.

I stayed with my father for forty days. When I was preparing to return to Aksu and had already packed my bags, Zohre came to me and demanded to take Rushengül with her. I had promised our mother. "Remember," she insisted.

I turned around. "If my third child should happen to be a girl too, then you can take Rushengül home with you."

Somehow I placed hope in the idea that I would continue in a pattern—first a boy, then a girl—and then, God willing, a boy again. With this hope, I rode the bus back to Aksu, together with Rushengül, Kahar, and my three young siblings.

I HAD LEFT FOR KUCHA with one child and returned to Aksu with five. Abdirim smiled. He said he had been expecting something like that.

Right after I got back, I unpacked my sewing kit and began producing shoes and undershirts. I never felt overwhelmed with children and housework, even though at nineteen I was still rather young. I loved the little ones more than anything and was happy being together with them.

Throughout the entire country, Red Guards were being sent to remote Uyghur villages in order to "learn from the peasants." The destructive energies of youth, especially of those who were educated, according to Chairman Mao, would be tamed through hard physical labor and the diligent study of his teachings. It seemed that the high tide of senseless butchery had receded.

Abdirim fulfilled his basic duties as a father, but he was not very loving and generally kept his distance from the children. Perhaps he did not know any better. A year-and-a-half after my mother's death, my beloved mother-in-law was also taken from us. After I had lost these two important people in my life, I gave birth to my third child. To my great sorrow, the earlier birth pattern did not hold, and it was a girl.

The day after Reyila's birth, on April 10, 1969, Zohre was already kneeling before me, saying, "You should keep to your promise." Everything around me seemed to be spinning. I looked my oldest sister in the face. Her eyes had dark circles underneath them from not having rested in a long time. I reasoned with myself and considered my mother's wishes. Zohre would never find happiness if hers was a life without children. In our Uyghur culture, a woman's life had essentially no meaning if she had no children.

I took a deep breath before I talked with Abdirim that evening. I lowered my voice before I said the words, as though I could remove some of the weight from them. But my deep breath and lower tone were of no use.

"We can't just give away our children! Rushengül is already a year-and-a-half-old. What are you thinking?"

Insistently, I explained my mother's last dying wishes. We discussed it with each other all night long. In the end, we agreed to entrust our second-born child to my oldest sister out of respect for both Uyghur tradition and my mother's deathbed plea.

When we handed Rushengül to Zohre, we negotiated that she would bring our daughter every two months for a visit. I cried for several days, unable to accept my own decision, unable to forgive myself.

However, Zohre did not keep to our agreement. Instead, I would travel to Kucha once a month to visit my little girl. Each visit I got onto the bus with the intention of bringing my daughter back home with me. But every time I had to acknowledge that my sister adored the child as if she were a princess. She cared about nothing else all day long except my little girl—it was always, "Rushengül said this, Rushengül did that."

Zohre had taken my child so firmly into her own heart that Rushengül did not even want to come back to me. How then could I separate the two from each other? As if to console me, my fourth child was soon growing inside of me.

Zohre and her husband, as staunch Communists, were against the bourgeoisie, against traditional clothing, against everything that was not strictly Mao-sanctioned. These beliefs of course worried me with regard to my daughter's upbringing. However, over time I got used to the idea that my daughter would grow up in another family. Once, when I had sewn for Rushengül a matching set of jacket and pants out of black silk fabric adorned with decorative roses, Zohre and her husband proudly let her wear it. That made me feel good.

Soon I could afford to visit Rushengül only every three or four months, which seemed to prompt my sister to become more spiteful toward me. In fact, she told me she did not want me to visit as often anymore. Because I realized that Zohre and her husband really loved the child and that Rushengül had gotten used to her new parents, my pangs of loneliness eventually healed. Today, Rushengül calls both Zohre and me "mother."

WITH A BIT OF LUCK, we were able to find work for my twenty-year-old brother Mehmet at the vehicle licensing bureau once he had finished middle school. My sister Arzigul became a packer at a company that produced food, and soon thereafter she started her own family.

While everyone in our village was going about their lives in their Mao-like suits, Mehmet dressed himself up like a film star. Every day we had new worries about him. He was passionate, almost reckless, and often expressed out loud his displeasure with the government. Every time he demanded that we Uyghurs should finally throw the Chinese out of our homeland, the *An Chuan Ting* secret police beat him up and threw him in jail. Then I would have to go to them again and beg a thousand times to get him back out alive.

Because of his clothing, the locals nicknamed him "The Albanian." Every time the soldiers cut up his tie, he put on a new one afterward.

Mehmet also liked to drink which meant getting into fights, and to gamble. I think that the traits of his maternal grandfather probably coursed through his veins.

But most of all, Mehmet was prone to embellishment and exaggeration. In one of his favorite stories, the first time it was two girls, the next time four girls who had been flirting with him. But one day, he surprised us all by expressing his intention to marry. His chosen bride was a girl he had met not long ago, the daughter of the governor of Aksu.

I tried by all means possible to dissuade Mehmet. But he would not be put off and asked me to help him. He tried to prod me into helping him, claiming that only I could succeed in convincing the parents of his goddess to accept him as their son-in-law. That made me laugh. He had really exaggerated even his high opinion of me.

For two more days he continued to try to persuade me while I tried not to be distracted by the growing child kicking inside my stomach. Finally, I reasoned that he was my brother and I would not forget that our parents had raised us as true Uyghurs: honorable and fearless.

But when I entered the government grounds on his behalf, it went as expected. The guards would not even let me through the gates.

I looked for another solution. I asked Mehmet to bring the girl to me. "Do you love my brother?" I asked her.

"Yes," she answered shyly.

"In that case, I would like to help the two of you. But in order to do that, I will need to know if your father has good friends or relatives here in the city."

She mentioned the names of some high officials at the courthouse. I packed something to eat and a few small presents into a basket for them, bringing her as my escort. The governor's friends—mostly judges—welcomed us warmly. But once I had let them know that I had come as an emissary for the girl, they gave me confused looks.

"It is true that my father is a hairdresser and the girl's father is a high official. But one shouldn't forget that my father also was once a very affluent man. Maybe even your family was poor at some time. Our world is constantly changing.

"Among many other reasons, I also honor my father because he fought for the freedom of our nation. He was a soldier in the Three Districts Revolution."

After that announcement, the atmosphere in the room got much better, largely because one of the governor's friends had also taken part in the rebellion at that time. He rummaged through a drawer for a large black-and-white photo. Finally finding it, he brought it to me without a word. I recognized my father in the fourth row, in the back corner. I pointed him out.

"Your father is Kadir Khan!" All of the sudden I found myself in the arms of the judge, who then kissed me on the forehead. I hardly knew what was happening. He had completely lost himself in the moment, this powerful civil servant—and I was just a little mother.

As an emissary for our family, the judge went to see his friend the governor. But he met with no success. So he went to see the governor several more times. At some point though, the governor's curiosity got the better of him and he asked to see me. He said, "Why do you ask for our daughter? We are of a much higher social standing than you."

"It has never been a desire of mine for my brother to seek a bride from a family that works for the Chinese."

I expected that he would show me the door, but instead he smiled. He was a Uyghur and he loved his people. "Give me your hand." He held it for a moment, thinking. Then he said, "I will give our daughter to your brother."

I had really hoped that Mehmet would give me a visible sign of his appreciation. But he did not seem the least bit surprised. He even dared to say that he knew all along I would succeed.

After the wedding, our standing improved dramatically. My husband's Chinese colleagues kowtowed, and Abdirim was promoted to the directorship of the bank even though he had previously been demoted.

But my brother's union was not a blessed one. His mother-in-law constantly reminded him of their class differences, and after two years, he and his wife separated. He married three more times in rapid succession. To our family's further disappointment, my brother never wanted to study or develop himself professionally. Later though, he would write his own chapter in Uyghur history.

THE CULTURAL REVOLUTION CONTINUED, its rage threatened Uyghurs more than other obstacles had done through many generations. Again and again, the Communists accused me of having worn a jacket other than one that was allowed or having visited the wrong friend. The reasons did not matter, really: the aim was public humiliation. It was in this political environment that I gave birth to my fourth child, my son Adil, on March 10, 1971.

Unfortunately, the public humiliations did not subside. Sometimes I was forced to bring my children with me because during the Cultural Revolution, the misdeeds of deviants had come to be considered hereditary. In essence, descendants were to suffer with their parents, their parents' parents, and on. With his head bowed, my seven-year-old Kahar stood on the stage holding newborn Adil in his arms, with his two-year-old sister Reyila tucked between his ankles. Occasionally, my children were permitted to stay with an uncle when I was yet again placed on the pillory. But often they had to stay home alone all day long.

One evening, we were invited to our neighbors' home for dinner, and just as we were about to take our first bites a huge picture of Chairman Mao hanging on the wall came crashing down onto the tablecloth.

I half-joked, "Not even while eating steamed dumplings can we find peace."

To my regret, the next day our dinner host told this story around the neighborhood. Thus there was another reason to haul me back up on the stage. This time, they wanted to keep me there all day long. However, another neighbor spoke out against that: "Let her go—she doesn't have a lot of schooling. She doesn't know what she's saying."

This woman knew me very well and knew exactly what I thought of the Chinese government. Intellectuals were punished many times harder than simple housewives like me. Zunun Kadeer, the creator of realist Uyghur prose and president of the Writer's Guild in our nation, was one of these intellectuals. They had given him nothing more than a small, drafty room to live in. One day, on my way home from the market, I witnessed the Communists tormenting our famous writer. They had stripped him down to his underwear and had slathered white paint on him from head to toe. A large wooden sign held with iron wire dangled from his neck, reading in bold letters: "Counterrevolutionary, follower of Soviet-bourgeoisie, and nationalist. Zunun Kadeer must be annihilated."

I could see that the weight of the wooden sign was digging the wire ever deeper into his skin. It would have been naive for me to plead with that crowd for a milder treatment. I would have been arrested as well. Without thinking much, I reached in my jacket pocket for the bills that I had earned from selling my home-made shoes. Then I discreetly approached the young leader of the crowd, took his hand, and dropped fifty yuan into it. Leaning in closer, I whispered, "If you continue on like this, the man will die. Please release him."

That was a high-risk undertaking. If this Communist were to announce that I had just given him money, it could have cost me my head. But thankfully, he commanded, "Stop! The man has lost blood! We shouldn't kill him because we still have much more to punish him for, and for a long time. Maybe, maybe we should let him think for awhile, then maybe he will speak freely from his heart about all of the evil he hides inside of himself."

Afterward, he turned away from the crowd and released the writer. I surely could not have accomplished more than that with my fifty yuan. But to my astonishment, the young leader stood squarely before the others, announcing: "We will stop for today."

A cold shudder passed through my body. *I actually held the power to make a difference with my money.* That revelation gave me the courage to continue. So a few hours later, I visited that young Communist leader at his apartment. Just for him, I put my hair up and powdered my face with some subtle makeup.

"If it is within the realm of possibility for you, please take on more mildly the other counter-revolutionaries. If you have relatives or friends in the city who need anything, just let me know. I'll do my best to get it for them."

In such situations, Abdirim stood behind me. After all, Zunun Kadeer was a highly respected figure. Any Uyghur would have been proud to help such a distinguished man. We had seen him ridiculed many other times—lying in the street, sometimes painted red, sometimes black. A lot of the intellectuals could not endure these constant abuses and committed suicide.

As MY CHILDREN GREW, my husband started to beat me. Kahar, Reyila, and Adil were terrified—they were constantly frightened of everyone and everything. Each night when Abdirim came home from work, they would hide. Kahar, who earlier had attracted attention for being a hard worker, then no longer fared as well in school.

I knew how much my husband loved me, but the surrounding conditions distressed him to the point of violence. Often he was barely through the door at home when he came after me: "Who are you? Why are you acting so aristocratic? I'm sorry that I married you."

If I was silent in response to this attack, he would put his face so close to mine that I could see in his eyes my own reflection and shout, "Why don't you answer me? Didn't you hear what I said?"

If I still remained silent, he would slap me in the face with his hand. "You must consider yourself so superior that you don't need to answer me!" he accused.

One day Abdirim came home drunk, his eyes in a hollow stare. "You're uneducated. You don't work for the government. You can't even speak a word of Chinese. Even when you go anywhere or do anything, you don't take responsibility for yourself. That's how I know you aren't well-suited for me."

"You're right," I said as I continued chopping the vegetables.

Within a moment he started beating me, fists flying and legs kicking, until I was knocked to the ground as I tried to shield my face with my hands. "If you conceive one more child from me, I will leave you."

I did not understand. He wanted our children. He loved our children. He conceived our children.

"You're a woman who can never be quiet, not even for one second!"

With one swipe, he smashed the glasses and plates off of the table. "Your wishes to liberate the population have very little to do with reality! You have to understand that you're only a woman. Despite children and a household, you think you can take on such a massive task. Those are just fantasies in your head! You'll never accomplish this!"

For a while, the air settled between us. But it turned out to be only a short time before Abdirim beat me again. I told him, "If you continue to constantly beat me up like this, I will leave you. I will raise our children on my own."

From that point on, he was a changed man, very nice to me and to the children. He said, "I'm so sorry that I treated you like this. I don't even recognize myself."

There was a long period of peace between us. And then it started all over again.

SHOEMAKER ABBAS HAN LIVED in the old part of Aksu with his family. He and his wife were like parents to me. Once a week, I visited them and discussed everything that was on my mind. I even told them the whole story about what I had accomplished for the esteemed Zunun Kadeer. Unfortunately—though I was sure it was not Abbas Han or his wife—someone in his family leaked this information to the Communists.

An elevated sense of paranoia had developed during the Cultural Revolution. If three people shared a secret, each of them would eventually convince himself that it would be revealed somehow, some way. In an act of self-preservation, each of the three individually would do what was best for himself—proclaim to the authorities that he or she had come upon a secret held by the other two. Thus, the first to betray an alliance to the government had maneuvered into the best possible position.

I had experienced betrayal before. But this was the first time that I had been betrayed by friends, so I was especially sensitive about it. I cursed myself for being so trusting. At least I had not mentioned any names in front of Abbas Han and his family. Still, not only had I jeopardized my own well-being, but potentially also that of my young Communist accomplice. It was not just a mistake that I had made—it was an error of life-and-death proportions.

The next day, the Communists forcefully brought me to a struggle-session assembly, demanding for hours and hours to know the name of the Communist accomplice I had bribed. "Traitor!" "Tell us the name!" "Step on her head!"

At some point, I lost my nerve and started to scream. I no longer had my senses about me and had neither time nor space as reference points. I did not know what I was saying, how fast or slow my words were passing over my lips, how loud or quiet my voice was.

I reached with both arms to the sky. "Why, God, is everything so difficult." At first, my hallucinating felt like relief. A multitude of white stars, so beautiful, so peaceful, floated before my opened eyes. Then just as quickly, all faded to black as I sank to the floor in a heap. A moment later, I was conscious again, but crying uncontrollably. By the grace of God, they let me leave for the day. Tomorrow, though, the questioning would resume.

That whole day, a thunderstorm had been brewing. As I left the assembly, suddenly it began to thunder and lightning. Heavy rain poured, washing down over me just as it was washing down through the gutters. As I was running home, I saw the shoemaker standing there before me. He also had attended the assembly. When our eyes met, he sank to the ground. His whole body was trembling. His eyes rolled upward as he reached his arms toward me. He said, "Forgive me." I had no idea those were to be his last words.

His relatives came running up from behind. The next moment, his sister grabbed me by the throat. She scratched my face in a fury. Within minutes, not even deterred by the pouring rain, a mob of two-hundred people had come to watch. Many of them had witnessed the shoemaker falling down on his own, but Abbas Han's sister yelled out that I was a witch and had killed him.

He died? My friend had died? I was bewildered.

A few men helped me free myself from his sister. At that time, I did not yet know that it was his sister who had betrayed me to the authorities. But from that day onward, she would throw rocks at me any time she saw me walking in the street. It was odd too, how the Uyghur people in the village began to spin fantastic tales about me, about my curse, my thunderstorm, and my sentence of death for a poor sinner. They said that I had the power, the anger, to unleash destructive heavenly spirits.

After these occult rumors about me had spread, the Red Guards were afraid to put me back on the stage to humiliate me. Instead, I was asked to sit in the front row with the Communist loyalists. Only Abbas Han's sister continued to rant about me until she was noticeably absent from the assemblies and the village.

To my surprise, the shoemaker's widow, whom I still considered to be a kind person, invited me to her home. Truthfully, I was not eager to accept her invitation and stir up again the traumatic experience for us all. I had already forgiven the family and decided for myself that the real culprit was not the shoemaker or his sister, but the Chinese government.

I felt depressed when I entered the widow's home. On one side of the room was a bed in which Abbas Han's sister lay, with her hands and feet tied spread-eagle to the posts. My heart ached as I waited for some words, any words from anyone, to help explain life's complications.

"She has rabies." This flat, monotone diagnosis was all the widow could muster. She and her two children looked at me, their eyes red from crying. Together we picked up the sister, put her on a cart, and took her to a hospital. A month later she was dead.

As usual, I was sewing shoes and undershirts almost every night. With the money I earned, I could attend to Zunun Kadeer and others who suffered. I even helped support Abbas Han's family. His wife was appreciative, but his two children did not love me for it.

Abdirim, for his part, mostly kept silent about my activities. Once, however, he did say half in mockery, half in flattery: "That story about the thunderstorm, the dead shoemaker, and the rabies—that was just coincidence. But you really are an amazing person. Things are always coming together for you in some miraculous way."

IN 1972, PRESIDENT RICHARD NIXON visited China, which until that time had been politically isolated from the West. One of the results of this momentous détente was a sudden appreciation of knowledge and education. But the improvement lasted only a short while, as the "Gang of Four"—a political group under the leadership of Chairman Mao's wife—continued to strike terror in people's hearts.

On November 13, 1973, I gave birth to my fifth child, Ablikim. My husband constantly spoke poorly of me. If we were invited out, he would seek to humiliate me in front of the other guests. Despite everything, I was more respected than he was, and I think this made him jealous.

By mid 1974, I was pregnant again. Abdirim looked at me derisively. "Okay, so you'll give birth to your sixth child. But no one will want you after I leave. You think you're something special. You're beautiful, that's true. But you're also aged." I was twenty-seven-years-old when I gave birth to my son, Alim, on February 29, 1975.

As goes the cycle of life and death, on September 9, 1976, the loudspeakers bellowed all day long: "Our great leader Mao is dead."

Turmoil immediately began to spread among us Uyghurs, as it did for beggars, civil servants, the unemployed—really for everyone, as we came together in the streets. Uyghurs seemed to have been awakened from a nightmare. Of course, nobody dared put themselves in danger by openly showing their joy. The cadres ordered our entire village to meet in the big town square for mourning.

Zohre's husband cried to the point that his whole body twitched. Zohre herself seemed to also be taken aback, but her pain was expressed more discreetly. Even though one of the most despicable mass murderers of the twentieth century had died, a person who was responsible for the death of some seventy million people, it was impossible to know who was mourning with genuine feeling because everyone had learned long ago to choose their best public face to suit each occasion.

Though Mao Zedong's wife and the other members of the "Gang of Four" were tried and convicted, not much essentially changed after the passing of the dictator. Even today, his portrait hangs, larger than life, at the entrance to the imperial palace in Beijing.

Soon, a new Communist leader emerged. His name was Hua Guofeng. But his style was not new: it was derived from his predecessor. The only extraordinary event during this phase was that many prisoners were released.

After some time, many began quietly to denounce the government loyalists. My brother-in-law, the duly devoted Communist, was transferred from teaching at a large middle school to a small elementary school. The only ones who remained in their positions during this post-Mao transition were Chinese citizens. Among them were a few who had even murdered and tortured with their own hands. Yet they too were retained or promoted.

Zohre's husband had sacrificed himself for Communism; in turn, Communism only demanded more sacrifice, never offering reward in kind. He and others had willfully carried out the Cultural Revolution in support of the Chinese government. In an incomprehensible twist of logic, the Chinese government then blamed him and others for carrying out its commands.

IN THE EVENINGS, I SEWED until late into the night, then in the daytime, I delivered goods to the black market via Bouhatcher. My youngest sister, Heljem, married a chauffeur in 1976 at the age of twenty-six. Thankfully, again a financial burden was taken from us. In the house at that time, only seven people were left, including my husband.

One afternoon, Abdirim came home for lunch accompanied by a well-known Uyghur singer who was quite beautiful. We knew this singer from our secretive meetings with friends, where she would occasionally sing Uyghur songs for us. She could mesmerize us with her lovely melodies from the old homeland.

After lunch, I was astonished to see my husband put his hand on her shoulder. I told him, "Stop that. Those are bad manners."

At that, he jumped up and slapped me in the face. When my husband was reaching out to do it again, the singer moved between us and held his arm back. Breathing heavily, Abdirim left the room. She expressed her sympathies and then left as well.

Meanwhile, the black market dealer Bouhatcher had been arrested at the bazaar. It came as no surprise because everybody knew the black market was risky. A person could not conduct business in private though there was in place somewhat of a black market code of silence to help reduce the risk for the benefit of all involved in it, which was virtually everybody. In truth really each person was on their own. That same afternoon two *An Chuan Ting* officers came to arrest me as a result of information from harshly interrogating Bouhatcher. They had strung together on a line some corduroy shoes that I had sewn. They hung it around my neck. One of the men shoved against me a pile of embroidered undershirts that I had sewn. As they forced me outside, they pressed a metal rod into one palm and a stone into the other. I was told to bang them together each time they announced on the street: "Rebiya Kadeer is a capitalist! She is a black marketer! She should be annihilated!"

I had to pass through the old city several times like this. Men, women, and children ran beside me, teasing me. But I knew that I had made the right decision with the black market. As a mother, I was responsible for supporting and loving my children, and I also helped five other families with the money I earned. Despite appearances, I actually began to feel like a heroine in front of this crowd. With my head held high, I walked like a woman whose dignity had never been tainted.

It was only later that night that they let me go. At home, Abdirim hung his head, deeply ashamed. His superiors had been pressuring him heavily for a long time. I soon found out that the pressure was not about work. What I did not know was that his superiors had been pressuring him to divorce me. If he did not divorce me, they said, he would lose his position as head of the bank. Abdirim had worked at this bank since his youth. He did not know any other place of work. Truthfully, he did not have any other strong skills with which to obtain different work.

His shoulders tensed up. "You'll have your marriage application returned to you. From the very beginning, you thought I wasn't good enough for you, but I didn't say anything. Over the years, though, I've balanced out your hatred for me with my own hatred for you. With this many children, you'll never find another husband. You'll live alone for the rest of your life without ever experiencing the love of another."

The grief that was lodged deep in my throat permitted me only to whisper, "Do you really not love me?"

"No. I do not love you." His words hit like punches. "Nobody loves you. If one would throw you, like slop, to a dog, even he wouldn't want you."

"I beg of you. I kneel before you. Please don't separate our children from their mother."

But he was no longer listening to me. Still, my mind raced with the unthinkable of a Uyghur woman with six children separating from her husband.

"Please, Abdirim, allow me to work like a maid for this family and live together with our children."

No response. I knew then that I had to immediately begin to reflect on my direction, or my life would pass hopelessly by. The more desperately I fought for this man, the more I felt my opposite wish to finally leave him. I got up off my knees, bolstered by the strong courage I felt in my heart. Defiance and anger arose inside of me. I was a proud woman. Why should I not be able to raise my children by myself?

"I will not allow you to drive the children away from their mother. Outside on the street, I see hundreds of children who have to live there without their mothers. I will give up everything for my children."

He had already opened the door. "Let's go to the courthouse."

I heard myself agree, and I followed him.

EVERYTHING WAS FINISHED IN TEN MINUTES. It was the thirteenth year of our marriage when I signed the documents stating that I would not receive any remuneration from my ex-husband. The judge handed us the confirmation of our divorce.

As our eyes glanced at each other, I felt some things inside of me welling up, demanding to be spoken. "Look at me carefully once more. Maybe you've never really seen me before. Right after this, I will remove the headscarf under which I've been hiding from the world. I want you to know that I'm not the Rebiya who has been living beside you all of these years. I carry my secrets in my heart. I'm not a person like you, so humiliated as you.

"You've accused me of being uneducated. I will show you what I'm capable of. You'll miss me, but I will never again belong to you. You'll feel what you've lost as soon as you go home. Starting today, I will take care of my children myself. Right now I don't have my own apartment and I don't know anyone with whom I can live. For this reason, and this reason alone, the children should stay with you for now, but I will pay for them myself."

He responded, "You don't have a place of work. How can you make such a promise? Do you intend to sell yourself?"

I lifted my chin a notch higher. "With that you insult not only me, but yourself too. I'm the mother and you are the father of our children. For the rest of my life, I'll not let anyone who is unclean or unjust so much as touch my hands. First of all, I'll keep my courage for the sake of my children. Second, I'll keep my heart pure for my country and for my people. And third, I'll keep my pride for my own sake."

The next words passed across my lips as though they had been waiting forever for their moment to be heard. "As the mother of our children, I was forced to stay with you. I'm aware that you aren't the only one at fault for this situation. From this moment forward though, I'll introduce myself as the true Rebiya Kadeer and live accordingly. I'll look for the answer to my mother's tears. Our children will also cry. But even for their tears, I'll find answers."

Typically, a mother would take the children with her after a separation and the father would provide for them financially every month. I rejected this dependency. I had no idea how I could earn money. I only knew that I was smart enough to prove to others that I could manage to keep living, even without a man. I had faith in my abilities.

Abdirim looked sullen as he contemplated what I had said. They were words that he had never heard me speak before. Uncomfortable, he shifted his body away from me. "It hasn't even been a minute yet, and already you've lost your mind. You're talking nonsense."

I took off my earrings and other jewelry. "Give these to our daughter Reyila."

After I had left the courthouse I just kept walking. I did not go home to my children to say good-bye to them. I did not want their sparkling eyes to turn sad again, or to cause them to cry again, or to burden them with my pain. I just went away.

Usually, tragedy awaited Uyghur women who were divorced. At home with their parents, they would wait to see if another man came to marry them. Most of these women, however, stayed single with their children and were condemned as outsiders. They were vilified as being immoral.

I stopped just before an intersection, not knowing where to go. I did not have a single yuan in my pocket. Of course, I had friends in town, but they were my ex-husband's and mine together, not just mine alone.

My first wandering led me to Bouhatcher. I described my situation to her. With her thick fingers, she rummaged around and pulled out ten yuan as a loan. Next, I went to my brother Mehmet.

Matter of factly, I reported to him my divorce, yet he reacted as if I was helpless. "How inhumane Abdirim has been toward you. How can he do such a thing? The best idea right now is to go back to him. If he doesn't take you, I'll go to him and ask for you." I completely rejected this proposition.

Mehmet lived in a single room with his new wife. I could not and did not want to burden them in any way. From his monthly salary of forty yuan, he gave me thirty. With a total of forty yuan in my pocket, I left for Kucha to see my father. For twelve yuan, I bought a bus ticket, and for one yuan, I got something to eat on the way. That left me with twenty-seven yuan.

When I got to my father's house, I found, just as my mother had advised in her blessing to him, that he had remarried after one year. I discovered that in addition to his new wife, her two children were also living in their apartment.

That night I overheard a heated conversation between my father and his wife. She said, "What a shameless woman your daughter is. How can we raise our children if someone like her wants to stay here?"

My father tried to quiet her down, "Please speak softly; please speak softly." But she would not. "I'll leave you."

The next morning, I went to Zohre. My nine-year-old daughter Rushengül smiled at me innocently. But between Zohre and her husband, my presence caused great tension. My brother-in-law had never really possessed a decent sense of justice. It quickly became obvious to me that I would not be able to stay there either.

So I asked Zohre to allow me to bathe there and said that I would be on my way afterward. I also asked her if she could loan me twenty yuan. My sister had saved one-hundred yuan and gave me all of it. I told her I planned to open some kind of business in Aksu.

My sister Hejer came to Zohre's house just as I had finished bathing. Skipping pleasantries, Hejer reasoned out loud, "My sister, it's best if you don't stay in Kucha. It'll be unpleasant for the rest of us if people speak poorly about you."

Zohre defended me, "First, I ask that you not speak badly of our unhappy sister. Besides, Rebiya isn't as you see her. I'm absolutely sure it's entirely her husband's fault. I also don't care what people say about her divorce."

"Zohre, does Rebiya seriously look like an unhappy woman to you? No, she is acting as though she has no problems. Look at how pretty she has made herself. As though she were on her way to a wedding—"

Zohre cut her off. "You can't look inside Rebiya's heart. You're heartless. She isn't like you."

The next morning, I returned to Aksu on the first bus. Not far from the courtyard where my brother Mehmet lived, I rented a room on a small cross street. When I discovered that a little spring flowed behind the property, I knew what I needed to do. That is when I decided to open a laundry service.

With thirty yuan, I paid rent for three months. With another thirty yuan, I purchased five bars of soap in the market, a large washtub, three washing boards, and additional equipment. Then, in a used furniture store, I bought a bed for two yuan.

I told Mehmet only that I had moved into an apartment in Aksu and that I was going to open a new business. He immediately wanted to see my room, but I did not allow it. With his lips tightly pressed together, he lovingly handed me a simple sheepskin carpet, a pillow, and a blanket.

For thirteen years of marriage, I had followed and respected the Uyghur traditions. I had been obedient and submissive. But no longer. The image of being constantly tied to a man like Abdirim was far more terrifying than being penniless. Instead, I wanted to see myself as a woman who could throw off that suffocating blanket of helplessness.

I would prove to everyone that there was a different Rebiya inside of me, one who was self-confident and sure, one who would claim victory, and one who would achieve not only her own freedom, but also that of her people.

Everything Besides Death is a Pleasure

J was a modestly attractive woman who was only twenty-eight-years-old, and I did not want to gain the attention of other men. In addition, men and women in the laundry business were considered to be at the lowest rung of society. I did not want someone to recognize me and tell my children what lowly work their mother was doing for employment. Had he known, it is possible that my brother Mehmet would have even forbidden my business venture.

So on the second day of my new life, I went to the bazaar, selected a brown mesh cloth, and covered my face with it. I also wore an ankle-length dress of the sort usually worn by older women. Then I arranged my glittering *doppa* on top of my head, draped another longer veil over the *doppa*, and covered the rest of my head in a cocoon-like wrap. Though it was rare to see women who hid their faces under veils in Aksu, my concealment remained in place even as the curious gazed at me. Only my landlord knew who was underneath this protective layer.

First, I scrubbed the floor in my room, then I whitewashed the four walls and wrote on a large piece of cardboard: "Laundry service: one pair of pants—one-half yuan, one jacket—one-half yuan, one blanket—one-half yuan, one shirt—one-half yuan." Underneath this I wrote, "Give me your old clothes and you'll receive them back as if they were brand new." I hung the sign outside on the wall to the house.

My landlord also owned a restaurant next door. He kindly allowed me to advertise for business among his customers. Almost immediately, the young, unmarried men wanted to know how old I was, but I ignored them.

The next day, one of the customers from the restaurant brought me his pants, a shirt, and a jacket to wash. I thought to myself that he must be exposed to petroleum or grease at work because his clothes were stiff with filth. I had never before held things so dirty in my hands. I dunked them into soapy water with the tips of my fingers. They stank to high heaven. While I was working, I had to run outside twice to vomit. Finally, I dragged the washtub over to the spring. I changed the water that first time and so many other times afterward that I lost count of the water changes. All I knew was to keep on changing the water until the stench no longer took my breath away. Then I pulled the tub and his clothing back into my room and continued working on them.

At the market, I had bought a special soft stone that we were accustomed to using to wash clothes. It dissolved when you placed it in water. Once I had treated the clothes with it, I noticed that it had removed not only the dirt, but also some skin from my hands. My fingers burned like fire.

After the clothes dried, the only things left to do were to replace a few buttons on the shirt and pants and fix a few tears. It was already dark outside when I heated coals to do the ironing. The next day, the clothes really did look like new. Proudly, I handed them over to my customer.

The good man was speechless with amazement. He wanted to take me to lunch immediately to thank me. But that was out of the question. So, offering what would be more valuable to me anyway, he instead highly praised my services to his friends. From my first payment for services, which was one-and-a-half yuan, I laid aside one-half a yuan for my children. I was absolutely convinced I would be successful.

The next day, I took in four men's suits and two women's skirt suits. Fortunately, they were not nearly as dirty as my first customer's clothing had been. The third day, I had no customers. In a way, I welcomed the break after the ordeal of settling in anew. On the fourth day, I had eight suits, then the next day ten, then twelve, and then fifteen. All of Aksu had heard about my laundry service—even my brother. But he had no idea that it was his own sister who ran the business.

My knees, hands, and back were in great pain. To protect my skin, I designed leather gloves for myself. By then I had also acquired several washtubs, all of which were lined up in a certain order so that I could work faster. With my new method, I managed to wash eighty to one-hundred-and-twenty items of clothing every single day.

If I took even just a moment's rest, I saw my children before my eyes. With such motivation I could tolerate little rest, as my yearning for my children kept my stomach in a constant knot. To try to ease my anxiety, I would wring, hit, and whip the laundry. But even with the increasing workload, I was unable to protect myself from those feelings. I would force myself to try to sleep for four to six hours a night. Sleep was a compromise of sorts in my mind because either those feelings or physical exhaustion would eventually break me down anyway.

The landlord had given me permission to string six laundry lines in the backyard. In return, I had to clean his backyard every day. If the weather changed, I quickly took the laundry down. As soon as the sun was shining again, I hung the laundry back out.

My customers were very kind to me. They thanked me with gifts of fruit and bread. After three-and-a-half months, I had taken in nearly five-thousand yuan in revenue. I knew it was unlikely that anyone else in Aksu had the amount of cash that I had earned. With that realization, I lifted my veil, took my sign down from the wall, pushed the washtubs back underneath the bed, and closed down the business.

For fifteen days I wandered around the bazaar picking out for my children clothing made of fabrics that were particularly soft to the touch. I bought socks, pants, and undershirts—a complete, high-quality set for each of them. I also put candy into little packages I had made. I felt good at the thought of my children opening the packages, imagining how they would giggle and laugh. I swore to myself that starting from that day forward, they would never lack for comfort. I still had four-thousand yuan left after my shopping for the children. From this, I paid off all my debts.

I went to my brother Mehmet to ask him to deliver to Abdirim my children's presents and also to give a letter I had written to them:

> *My dear children,*
> *These presents are from your mother, who has made herself hard like a stone for you. As your mother, I will earn more money and come to get you from your father.*

Through Mehmet, I also expressed that I would not be able to visit them in the next six months, but that I would be sending money for school supplies soon.

Suspicious, my brother asked where I had gotten so much money.

I looked him in the eyes and said, "Do you trust me?"

"Of course. I know you aren't a bad woman who would sell herself," he responded.

"Then you'll have to wait until I've achieved a certain stature with my business. After that, I'll tell you what I'm doing."

But the uncertainty made him nervous. "I want to see your room."

"No. I live in a different city now and do my business there."

Mehmet later told me that Abdirim had gasped for air like a fish out of water when he saw all of the beautiful presents. He was unable to imagine how anyone could earn so much money in such a short amount of time. He demanded that my brother tell him where I worked. Mehmet answered nonchalantly that I was running a business, to which Abdirim muttered something about me probably being arrested soon anyway.

AT THE BAZAAR IN AKSU, a new idea came to me. I collected cheap wares from across the city: combs, jewelry, soaps, and headscarves—all for a total of one-thousand yuan. The rest of my earnings I hid in my belt. In a *hotshu*—which is a pole with a sack attached to either end and balanced on the shoulder—I carried my purchases down the street, blending in with so many others doing business as usual with their wares. My thinking was that I would not bring any attention to myself by going about my plans in this way. I walked toward the bus station. My destination was Kucha.

As fate would have it, my seat companion on the bus passed some favorable information to me: "I've heard that it is possible to get lambskins for quite cheap in Shaja. If you were to bring those to the bazaar in Kashgar or even to Kargilik, you're sure to make a one-hundred percent profit."

That sounded promising to me. So instead of Kucha, I exited the bus in Shaja. I went from mud-brick house to mud-brick house and inquired whether anyone was interested in trading goods for sheepskins. I had intended a generous offer of four pieces of soap for a single sheepskin. But, to my astonishment, the merchants eagerly accepted a deal of up to five of their sheepskins for only one piece of my soap.

I asked the people what else they were missing in their households and made notes on my writing pad. Listing under each of their names their desired items, such as "sweaters" or "a pair of socks," I promised them, "If you collect sheepskins for me, then I will bring back everything you need the next time I come."

By the end of my visit to a second nearby village, I had acquired so many sheepskins that I needed to rent a handcart. I had not yet had time to even count how many there were. The people would simply deposit them with me, then take some of my soap or jewelry and go away.

In the end, I had two-hundred-and-twenty sheepskins. This included fifty somewhat more valuable larger ones from full-grown sheep. Many of the skins appeared slightly deteriorated. In fact, some of them had most certainly been lying in the garbage. How could I ever get them clean again? So I asked a *tomatchi*, a sheepskin hat-maker, for advice.

But the conversation went nowhere because the man kept urging me to go home to my husband—or rather my ex-husband—which in his opinion is where I belonged.

So I sought out a second *tomatchi* and offered to purchase two of his hats if he would help me learn his craft. He agreed, but asked me with a grin in how many months was he supposed to teach me all of his knowledge.

I said, "No, not months, in the next five minutes. I will write everything down and learn it fast."

He shook his head and said that would be impossible.

I tried a different approach but remained cautious not to reveal too much. "Maybe I can be helpful to you as well. I've bought sixty sheepskins but some of the skins are hard and dry. I don't know how to treat them."

He laughed so hard he had to wipe his eyes. "You may look like a simple woman, but you're certainly not one. You came up with this business idea and I think it's very clever of you. So I will help you."

His remedy was as follows:

First, bury the skin in the ground. Then, rub the skin side with salt and lay it in the sun. After that, beat the skin with two sticks. Finally, knead it by hand.

The *tomatchi's* recipe for treatment of the skins performed miracles, bringing about beautiful furs with lush curls. Originally, I had planned to travel to Khotan with a truck driver. Something about this idea left me feeling overcome with doubt though. So I changed my plans, deciding it would be safer to travel with a lot of people by bus. The bus driver roped my skins to the roof. I had a journey of about six-hundred miles ahead of me, first toward Kashgar, then around the Taklamakan to the west, and finally along the southern Silk Road to Khotan.

I was happy to arrive in Khotan. Once it had been the most important center of Buddhism on the southern Silk Road. Here, in the hometown of my grandparents, I learned about the way the Uyghurs used to be. It was impossible to argue with these people—they were so courteous. With a smile on their lips, if a family had two sheep, they would give away one of them to a guest. Although these people were far poorer than we were, they had managed to uphold an elegance that was no longer practiced by us, their brothers and sisters. It felt to me like I had made a trip deep into a foreign country.

First, I rented a room at the nearest inn. Then, with three sheepskins under my arm, I went out into one of the street markets. Doctors and traditional healers were selling their herbs and homemade medicines there. Down the next street, the hat-makers were sewing. "Do you happen to need sheepskins?" I asked the first one.

When the other *tomatchi* saw me standing there with my sheepskins, they came over and looked at me for a while. Then they wanted to know how many skins I might be able to sell them.

"Ten."

"What are you charging for one?"

"You tell me." I knew enough to not say a number without having first checked the prices in the bazaar.

"I will give you twenty-five yuan for each one," said one of the *tomatchi.*

"No. Give me thirty yuan."

He whined that he did not have that much, but in the end he paid it.

"Do you need any more? Because actually I have thirty in total."

"That isn't right to be deceitful! Just now you were talking about ten skins."

"I'm sorry, I was afraid."

It became clear quite fast that this kind of business had to be done in absolute secrecy. Back-stabbing betrayal ran as thick as blood through this market. The man whispered that he would introduce me to a wholesaler who could use that many skins.

The wholesaler, with a sun-tanned face, received us politely. He said, "You know, I'm responsible for the complete distribution of all the sheepskin hats in the regions of Khargilik, Khotan, and Yarkand."

In Khargilik, I knew the men wore tall hats made of sheepskin, similar to those of the English palace guards. The wholesaler's wife poured green tea for us.

As we drank tea, I came out with a larger portion of the truth, "Actually, I have one-hundred sheepskins."

"A great businesswoman has arrived in our midst." My intermediary gasped with excitement. The wholesaler, who was calmer, said that he was ready to take all of them.

I felt caught in my own web. In a voice that was meant to sound more confident than it did, I explained that actually—really, seriously this time—I did not have one-hundred but rather two-hundred sheep-skins in stock.

This time, I made even the biggest dealer in Khotan gasp. He called for two other men to enter the room. Meanwhile, my excited intermediary must have already starting thinking about what he was going to spend his yet-to-be-earned commission on as he boldly asserted that I should demand fifty yuan per piece. The wholesaler gave him a dismissive look.

"We don't have enough cash for all of your sheepskins. But if you'll agree to it, we can offer you carpets in exchange."

I knew that almost every family in Khotan wove carpets. Finally we came to an agreement that they would give me cash for one-hundred skins and for the other one-hundred-and-twenty—at some point, I had admitted to the last twenty—they would give me carpets. In total, I received thirteen carpets in different sizes. Not since our banishment from Altai had I seen such exquisite woven art.

"You can believe us." The wholesaler coughed. "We've really given you a good deal for our carpets. You're a courageous woman coming here. We've made an agreement and now you're responsible, effective immediately, for delivering the sheepskins to us here in Khotan."

With my inexpensive wares that I had acquired for one-thousand yuan at the bazaar in Aksu, I had made a profit of eight-thousand yuan in Khotan within ten days.

Of course, I also knew what would happen to me if I were caught: I would be locked up for a minimum of five years. With that in mind, I decided to do business only in places where no one knew me.

My next plan was to haul the carpets by bus to Hami, a town deep in the eastern part of our Uyghur nation. The journey before me would be about ten days.

The sheepskin dealers had given me the name of a man to contact during the stopover in Urumqi. When the older man with a white beard saw that I had managed to get thirteen carpets all the way there, he put his hand to his heart and stepped back respectfully, saying, "A rich woman has come, a very rich woman."

It was the first time in my life that I had heard the word "rich" mentioned in conjunction with my name.

With the help of my new business partner, I sold the largest carpet for five-hundred and the smallest for three-hundred-and-fifty yuan. I left the older man a generous commission. After selling the remaining carpets in Hami, at a great profit, I returned to Urumqi.

There I put together a suitcase full of presents and money for my children. Of course, I did the same for my father, my stepmother, and all of my siblings. Once back in Kucha, I rejoiced with Zohre, Hejer, and my father. At that point, something had definitely changed for my father's new wife. Suddenly, she was insisting that I not leave. I recalled the opposite sentiment from her when I was poor.

Back in Aksu, Mehmet forwarded the children their presents through my ex-husband, as before. Into each of the school notebooks I had bought for my children, I had written on the first line, "You need to study hard if you want to be happy." In my name Mehmet also gave the children's nanny, who Abdirim had hired, a pretty outfit and thirty yuan.

A short time later, when I returned for a second time to Shaja, I carried myself more professionally. I divided my newly collected sheepskins among several trucks. The drivers covered each load with long cloths and delivered them to my business partners in Khotan. Thus free from the fear of being stopped by the police, I followed after my skins in a bus.

Many people considered me crazy in those days. But for me, stepping into life as a businesswoman was liberating. In the stories my father used to tell us as children, he always presented businesspeople as wise, prosperous, and the freest members of our earth-bound world. I wanted to be like them too.

It was my goal to earn fifty-thousand yuan. For thirty-thousand, I could buy a house in Urumqi, bring my children there, and send them to school. With the rest, I wanted to open a restaurant or a bakery. Then I would be able to live a normal life surrounded by my loved ones. The marketer to whom I delivered my sheepskins was by now one of the richest men in the area, but he reached a point where he was unable to distribute all of my sheepskins on his own. So he generously offered me contact information for other dealers.

On the way to visit one of them, my escort showed me the mulberry and cotton plantations that the *bingtuan* had planted and for which they had diverted water from the rivers. The Chinese soldiers by then were settling wherever our soil was fertile. The previous inhabitants, Uyghur nationals, had been chased away by these *bingtuan*.

Entire lakes and rivers had dried up due to the reckless land reclamation of the Chinese government. What was particularly hurtful to those of us who loved our land was that the *bingtuan* gave not a moment's concern to the spreading salinization damaging our soil, the receding vegetation, or the encroaching life-threatening desert, all of which were of grave concern to Uyghurs.

After that drive, I asked my escort to take me to the slums. He was somewhat surprised, but agreed. There I made the acquaintance of families who slept ten people to a room, with not even one blanket to warm them. In particular, many of them had no clean drinking water. I asked them if they had been short of water in the past too. They had not. Before, their traditional agriculture protected the soil from the sun so not much water was used or evaporated. In fact, they had never been short on water or anything else in the past.

What had changed then? "They are drinking up our rivers," one farmer asserted. For the first time, I began to feel involved with this problem. I no longer wanted just to be a rich businesswoman. I wanted to know the exact condition of our Uyghur nation.

I realized too that it was not only my children I needed to support, but that there were so many other people who also needed help. I revised my goal of fifty-thousand yuan to one much larger. I would have to move my business forward in grand style because in the end, financial development would be the deciding factor for progress in our land.

Twice more I repeated the sheepskin transactions. My money had multiplied to about forty-thousand yuan. But by that time, the sheepskin dealers of Khotan were copying me, and they went to Shaja themselves to directly acquire sheepskins. Thus, my idea had been profitable up to the point when the price of sheepskins in Shaja had increased so much that it was no longer worthwhile for me to continue as a skin supplier to wholesalers.

My carpet trading was no longer as successful either. So I decided to do something new. Together with a few colleagues, I planned to bring inexpensive goods from China's interior back to our homeland.

I HAD BEEN PLAGUED BY HOMESICKNESS for years. By this time in my life, I had the financial stability and the freedom to undertake a journey back home to the Altai region. When I placed my feet on the soil of my childhood, the heavens seemed to cry along with me as a fine rain misted in the air.

I went from house to house, but Chinese people were watching me from every doorway. In the past, there had always been colorful flowers blooming in the gardens and fresh bouquets in lovely vases on the tables outside. But I saw no flowers anywhere as I turned my head, and then my whole body three-hundred-and-sixty degrees in search of a flower. The streets stank of trash.

In my family's old courtyard were grunting pigs, but inside the house, it all looked very much like it had sixteen years ago. A Mongolian family and a Dungan family—Muslims of Chinese origin—now shared the house. The brook along the village road looked as if it had dried up long ago. And the weeping willows looked like they were indeed weeping in their withered state.

The Communists had no relationship with nature, and because the people owned nothing, they felt no sense of responsibility for the environment or property around them. While I was standing there at my family's old house, feeling lost, a Mongolian man approached me. I asked him who was responsible for our old house. In response, he took me to the director of the hospital, who vaguely understood why I was there. I explained to him that I would like to buy back our old house. But he explained that to do so would be impossible because it was now a government building.

Back in the village I finally saw a face I recognized—the daughter of an old neighbor. She cooked pumpkin for me and put me up for the night. The next morning, I started my search for my adopted brother Jumak. I asked everyone I met but nobody had any idea what had become of him.

So I rented a carriage and scouted the outskirts far beyond the village—stopping, asking, hoping. Near a hut at the foot of the mountains, my coachman brought the horses to a stop. I went to the hut and asked the man in the yard about my brother. He answered, "Who are you?"

"I'm the daughter of Kadir Khan."

At that, tears began to roll down his face. A Kazak woman came out of the house with two children. She called to her little daughter, "Rebiya!"—And I knew then that I was standing before my brother.

The last few years had been difficult for him. He and his family had been chased from village to village until they washed up on the shore where he stood. Through boulders that had been dynamited to pieces, he sifted for gemstones for a Chinese company. From that income, like the other residents in the area, his family was barely able to survive. Jumak apologized for not having been able to take part in our mother's funeral. He explained that he had been under arrest. We cried and hugged each other a lot that night.

The next morning, we saddled two horses. We wanted to go up into the mountains to the places where we had been so happy as children. Along the Irtysh River, we saw Chinese panning for gold with a sieve. The forest we had loved, which had been full of evergreen and deciduous trees, had been cut down to the ground.

I spurred my horse forward. On top of the mountain we had once found only nature, alone with herself. But even here there were Chinese gathering things from these mountains and placing them into their baskets. When I saw so many Chinese even in this place where I had hoped to find peace, I remembered a friend's prediction that I had heard in childhood: "One day it would rain Chinese from the sky."

All those years I had wished for nothing more than to revisit the places of my childhood. I had been there a week already, but nothing was the way I had remembered it. I cried when I arrived, and also when I left. When I think back to this visit, I still feel pain in my chest, even to this day.

Years later I would return again as a millionaire. I wanted to secure at least one memory for myself by buying back our old house. I planned to furnish the rooms as they'd been in the past and settle a poor Uyghur family into it. I was prepared to pay any price demanded. But the government still would not sell the house to me.

I PLANNED TO TAKE MY NEXT BUSINESS TRIP to Shanghai along the third longest river in the world, the Yangtze. Previously I had met several times with four other Uyghur businesspeople. Together we had sought out advice from other well-traveled traders on buying and selling wares via Shanghai. With that background information, we traveled by train for four days, crouched in overflowing corridors and squeezed together amongst soldiers, farmers, and chickens, until we finally arrived.

My first impression of the Shanghai trade and industry center was not positive. It smelled horribly from automobile fumes and the industrial and chemical smokestacks spewing out factory residues—it smelled a lot like burning sulfur. I suffered from a constant urge to vomit and was barely able to stomach the food from the little street-side kitchens.

The hot and steamy climate was also difficult to get used to. If a typhoon passed over the city, water rose knee-deep in the streets and the rickshaw drivers tripled their prices. But I got used to it over time, just as I did the noise of the street cars, the honking automobiles, and the shouts of the coolies. Other than that, Shanghai was everything I had hoped it would be—a source for inexpensive, beautiful goods.

First we looked for a Uyghur to be our translator. Once we had accomplished this, I bought silk headscarves, men's cotton undershirts, and rose-shaped brooches.

Uyghur businesspeople had always given each other nicknames. My companion Abdirim, for example, earned the name "America" because of his large eyes and prominent nose, which gave him a more western appearance. We called my other companion Hussein, who looked more like a Russian with his blue eyes, red hair, and white skin, "Urs." As for me, I must confess I cajoled my way out of being nicknamed.

I felt like I was living two lives in two different worlds. Still, it was easy for me to cross the border between rich and poor since I knew both worlds well. I was aided in both worlds by the clean hearts and helpful manners of Uyghur people. They quickly transformed me from being relentless and suspicious into a warm-hearted, open person.

My colleagues had a great fear of getting too personal with me as a woman. If they did, they understood clearly that I would no longer do business with them. They were expected to and did behave respectfully and treated me as an equal.

On my business trips I was also eager to get to know the land and the people. I wanted to understand what kind of people the Chinese were and how they lived. Even without being able to speak much Chinese, I was able to communicate quite well. I met friendly and helpful people, and it became clear to me that in regards to the injustices against Uyghurs, it was not the average Chinese population but solely their government that was responsible. The Chinese traders informed me just how greatly Shanghai profited financially from the Uyghur land and our natural resources.

In the earlier days when the Chinese occupation of the Uyghur nation was just taking hold, people in Shanghai and other Chinese provinces did not want to relocate or help to establish settlements in our homeland. In fact, though many were vehemently opposed to this practice, they complied because to do otherwise would have led them directly to jail. Those who voluntarily pushed forward into our homeland were mostly from impoverished and overpopulated provinces such as Sichuan and Anhui. Many settlers were also ex-convicts who had just been released from their labor camps in exchange for commitments to settling in our land.

The Chinese traders also provided us with wonderful business transactions on our trip. Each of us purchased five or six sacks full of goods. As my colleagues and I had learned from earlier experience, transporting our wares back with us was perhaps the most dangerous part of our venture. We made our way to the train station with our sacks carried over our shoulders. We then placed them directly in the pile of baggage, amongst all the other passenger luggage. As the expression goes, we were "hiding in plain sight." If an officer accused us of wrongdoing, we could simply deny that the sacks were ours. Each of us managed to get five or six sacks into Urumqi. We made a one-hundred percent profit on our sales. At that point in time, I had taken in over two-hundred-thousand yuan. Of that, I had hidden fifty yuan with my brother Mehmet.

After I had bought goods in Shanghai twice and successfully sold them to the traders at home, my name began to be known both there and at home. It had reached a point where it was impossible to keep working in secret. To continue would at some point lead to my arrest. In addition, now that my family knew of my ventures as well, my father and brother tried to persuade me to stop my black-market trading.

In the meantime, I had brought gold and silver jewelry from home and sold it in Shanghai. After news of that transaction spread, the authorities did indeed put a warrant out for my arrest.

It felt like I was facing an icy headwind once the *An Chuan Ting* was looking everywhere for me. But to achieve the larger goal I had promised myself to accomplish, I would have to overcome that obstacle in addition to all of the others before me. To me, my transactions were moral. I was then and I continue to be a person who contemplates my own ethics and morality. It is the Uyghur way.

I had concluded in my mind and heart that it was the government officials denying responsibility for their economic policies who were immoral and without conscience. Their ineffectual economic program of forbidding trade, stifling ingenuity, and turning a blind eye to rampant poverty and starvation was not only policy, it was cruelty directed at innocent, suffering human beings. The tragic effects of their economic policies were clearly visible by the hollow stomachs and sickened bodies of Uyghurs and others suffering every day.

Apparently I was not the only one anguished about the impoverished because at that decisive crossroad in my life, the laws changed. All of the sudden, it was broadcast from every corner that anyone and everyone was allowed to do business.

"To get rich is glorious" was the new motto for China's future, as announced by Deng Xiaoping at the Thirteenth Communist Party Congress in 1978, thus closing the book on "noble poverty" under Chairman Mao's socialism. Markets opened everywhere, and people's standards of living improved dramatically.

With my newfound freedom to do business, I went back to Shanghai for more transactions. While I was there, Zohre had received a letter in Kucha for me from my children. She was worried that the letter would bring me much sorrow though, so she gave it to my father and asked for his advice. After he read it, I am sure he thought he was acting in my best interest when he made the decision to take the letter, go see Abdirim, and ask my ex-husband to take me back.

However, Abdirim was already in the midst of wedding preparations. His new bride was both a civil servant and an educated woman "with a future." So he suggested to my father, and that my father express the same to me, to wait and see if he could find happiness with his new wife. After all, he thought, I could lose nothing by waiting for him, as it would be impossible for me—as the mother of six children—to find another husband anyway.

My father could not believe his ears. First, he explained to Abdirim that he had come without my knowledge. Second, he had come only out of concern for his grandchildren. And third, he was not at all sure that I had any interest in coming back to him.

Right after I returned from Shanghai, my father told me what he had done and then handed me the letter from my children:

> Dear Mother,
>
> The things you sent us in the little suitcase are very beautiful. We've never seen such beautiful clothes, such pretty notebooks, and pencils. Every time we put on our clothes, we seem to see the picture of our mother before our eyes.
>
> Actually, we had hoped to find a photo of you in the suitcase. All together, we searched through the suitcase, but there was no picture of you in it. We wished for a letter from you, but didn't find that either. Nobody is affectionate with us; nobody tells us stories anymore.
>
> These clothes, these pretty things, we don't need—it's only you we need, our mother. With the money that you sent us we sewed a new blanket. This blanket is very beautiful. When you come, we'll give it to you.

Each of my children had put his or her fingerprint on the letter and signed it.

When my father saw me sitting there, a picture of misery, he shook his head and demanded that I go to Abdirim and ask him to let me live with him and the children again.

"No. I will take the children home with me, but first I need to earn more money."

I HAD SENT MANY PRESENTS and much money to my children but it had been a full year since I had last seen my darlings. I could not stand another second without them, so I asked my brother to bring the children to me.

My God, how they had grown. The children screamed with joy. We talked about everything that had happened to us and everything we wished to have happen.

My oldest son Kahar dreamed of spoiling me in the future with sweets and delicious dishes because he himself enjoyed eating. His round, good-natured face beamed.

Rushengül, my second born, who lived with Zohre, spun in a circle, showing off her new clothes. "I'm the most beautiful!" She was always looking for things she could improve upon and was lightning-fast at finding faults in others.

My third child, eight-year-old Reyila, was the cutest of all—very open, very straightforward, a true free spirit. She also knew how to get what she wanted.

Adil, the fourth in line, did not talk much. My six-year-old read a lot and was already reciting his first poems.

Ablikim, my fifth child, was at four-years-of-age the diplomat in this tribe. He would counsel his siblings when they pulled each other's hair that they should not fight, that they were not enemies, and that our enemies were those who had occupied our land and we should fight against them instead.

My youngest had been just six months old when I left the marriage. But even then, I could see an intelligence gleaming from his eyes, just as it did at this time too when he was nearly two-years-old. Alim had the ability to mesmerize people with his adorable looks and inviting personality. One day he would take over responsibility for my holding company.

All of my children had such individual character. We sat together closely, each child wanting to touch a part of my skin. Although it was not easy for me to tell them about my plans, they deserved an explanation. "It wouldn't be enough if I earned money only to support you and myself. I already have that amount. What I need is to earn more money for our people too. I hope you can understand this. You may be too young; I don't know for sure. As your mother—as much as you need me and I need you—I'm asking you to make sacrifices along with me for our people."

"If my father brings this new woman into the apartment," Kahar said, "I'll not stay with him. I would rather move to Aunt Zohre's house." I gave Kahar my permission to do so. I said, "When I come the next time, I will bring you to Aunt Zohre's house. Later, I will come to get all of you."

In the early light of morning, we went to sleep, nestled closely together.

The reunion with my children gave me new energy. In Urumqi, I also reunited with my old colleagues "America" and "Urs". "America" had learned that there were many opportunities for economic gain on the southeastern edge of China. At the port in Canton located on the coast of the South China Sea, now known as Guangzhou, a constant stream of new, inexpensive goods was arriving from all over the world. From there, it was just a short train ride to Hong Kong.

I thought about "America's" idea. I liked it. I liked the idea of a change of venue.

I WAS ALMOST FEVERISH WITH EXCITEMENT over our new challenges as we arrived in Canton. We were particularly interested in jewelry and women's clothing. We had survived the Cultural Revolution, and clothing had once again become important. Our usual plans for business trips to bring our goods to market for riches were sanctioned under the government's new program, which proclaimed, "To get rich is glorious." Having nothing to hide felt good.

On our journey home with a fully loaded truck, we made a stop in Shantou, an important export center. Within a short amount of time, rumor had spread throughout the town that some foreigners wanted to take goods from Canton back home with them. We found little of interest in Shantou and so moved on, not realizing that we had inadvertently invited some neighbors to join us.

A few miles later, as we crossed a bridge, about fifty policemen approached. A few of them held up their hands like stop signs, but none had weapons.

I leaned back calmly saying to my companions, "We have all of the required documents. So we've nothing to fear."

One of the men asked brusquely, "Who's in charge here?"

My colleagues, who I had considered to be equal in stature, pointed to me. That was the first day of my career when I became head of a group. For the next twenty years, I was automatically the boss.

The policemen were from the neighboring small village and had grown accustomed to seizing all goods that were being transported through their region on the way to Canton—so they seized our truck and all of our goods as well. They were nothing more than robbers. If anyone tried to sue them, no court in China would take the case. They took almost everything. They actually considered themselves generous and fair because they let us keep just enough money to buy return train tickets.

In the ten minutes of that robbery, my four colleagues looked as if they had aged several years. I felt that we had been lucky up to that point. It had to catch up with us eventually. I saw this stroke of fate as a temporary setback: the blame was not to be found in our behavior—we had done everything possible but had fallen prey to uncontrollable external circumstances.

On the way home, I tried to get the men to laugh with a variety of stories, including the Uyghur saying, "Everything besides death is a pleasure."

Once back in Urumqi, my colleagues wanted to know how we should proceed. I explained to them that I would first go out to look for a suitable husband and then I would continue with business.

They stared at me in surprise. Until then I had always insisted that I never wanted to marry again. I had wanted to keep men at bay so much that I had even gotten carried away saying that I would try to reconcile with the father of my children. True, I needed time to heal after the failure of my first marriage, but I had also noticed glances from two of my colleagues that revealed how they saw me: not only as a business partner, but also as a desirable woman. It may be true in other cultures too, but without a shadow of a doubt, it is no simple matter for an unmarried Uyghur woman to do business with Uyghur men.

As word traveled, other businessmen started sending emissaries to me too. Out of necessity, I sought refuge at my brother Mehmet's house. From there I made my way to Shanghai—thankfully alone. I then transported my wares directly back to my relatives in Kucha.

A Feather Fell Down From One Angel

When I got back from Shanghai in 1979, the minute I set foot in my father's apartment my family was already waiting for me. They let me know that they intended to turn me over to a new husband; they were unanimous in their belief that a woman could not just go anywhere she wanted to without an escort. Otherwise I would be considered immoral and my family would lose face.

Especially adamant about this plan were my second oldest sister Hejer, my new stepmother, and Zohre's husband. Zohre was a bit more reticent but generally agreed that it would be best if I were to remarry.

After I had gotten over the initial shock of their unified opinion, I explained to them that I had already reached that conclusion on my own. I advised them that they needed to allow me to at least sell my goods from the last business trip. My relatives agreed, but only with the condition that I not leave the house, not even to accomplish my business dealings. Instead, businesspeople would have to come to see me at home.

I agreed. But I was not prepared for my family's pressure. On one occasion, a businessman had hardly finished his purchase of some shirts and blouses when he was quickly ushered out while Hejer shoved me back into another room and locked the door behind me.

Every day my father, my siblings, and my other relatives gathered around me and lectured me on how I should either go back to Abdirim or decide on another man. I suppose, of course, that fleeing was another option for me. But that did not suit my character. On the third day, Hejer informed me that someone would be coming to see me.

The door opened. For a moment, he took my breath away. But not in a good way. I was more aghast than anything else. They had picked out a butcher for me. He had a thick handlebar mustache combed upward along his rotund face. He held his hands crossed over his large belly.

I must confess that I have always been afraid of men who looked like this, so he was not off to a good start. I examined him speechlessly and then turned to Hejer. In a calm voice, I said, "You can leave your husband and choose this man instead. His face is a lot like yours."

The butcher took offense, as I suppose anyone would. "I'll not take this person for a wife. She's crazy!" He looked at Zohre. "You also told me that she has six little children. How should I take care of six children?" Without waiting for an answer, he was gone.

When I had sold all of my goods, I distributed a portion of the proceeds among the family. After that, I requested to see everyone together once again. In retrospect, it seemed like that day was a rehearsal for my first public speech before a crowd of Uyghur people.

"My father, I'm not your daughter. My dear siblings, I'm not your sister. I'm not the mother of my children.

"I'm the daughter of our people. I'm the daughter of our land. This feeling has gradually developed inside of me, without me having consciously chosen it. These words have collected in my heart for a long time.

"Zohre and Hejer, you two have gone to universities. But you didn't experience the banishment from our homes and the misery as the rest of us did. I felt that pain, which continued until my decision to put it to rest beside our dear mother in her grave. But I made a promise at her burial. I will never, never accept the conditions under which our mother passed away. We have personally viewed how many parents and children lost their lives through those forced relocations that turned each of us into desperate refugees.

"If all Uyghurs live only for themselves and forget their roots, then how can we continue to exist as a people? I'll work for our nation; I'm already on my way and in doing so, I'll never forget that I also lost my own children because of the Communist Party. You all who sit here with me, you're lying to yourselves when you say that you live in peace. You've yet to recognize the truth of my words. Instead you compare me to the worst women in the world, ones who sell their bodies to other men. But you should know that I will never forget my honor. Even if others slander me in the streets, you should at least lead by example and not speak badly about me. Then I can work in peace for our people."

I looked at each one of them in turn. "I promise you that just as our traditions demand, I will marry a new husband. But I tell you, from my heart, that I've never known true love for another man. Still, I carry a deep certainty inside—I see a young, good-looking man with a good heart before me. At this moment, I don't know who he is or where I will find him. But I will ask this unknown man just as soon as I do meet him whether he will take me as his wife."

Hejer was unrelenting. "Who would want to have you with six children? We found someone for you, but you didn't want him. Think about this—we believe that you're decent and good, but the men don't."

"Get a pencil and paper Hejer, and I'll tell you the criteria that my future husband must meet."

"How can you even think to make demands in your situation?"

At that, Zohre picked up a pencil, saying, "Okay then, I'll write them down."

"He should be good-looking, at most three to five years older than me, and be a university graduate. It should be love at first sight for both of us. This man should've already been in prison for his principles—okay, that one isn't a requirement, but he must never have betrayed anyone and he must have made sacrifices for our people. He must be ready to fight for the freedom of our nation."

Hejer said, "You've really lost your mind. Do you expect to take to the streets with this man and fight the Communists? You seem to have forgotten that even if you should happen to find such a man, you both would soon end up with bullets in your skulls."

"It's of no consequence to me whether I take a bullet. But first, you'll need to find someone like that for me."

To his credit, my brother Mehmet got right on the job, looking around and getting his friends to look for a suitable partner for me. I also went to visit Bouhatcher at her home, where I told her all about the meeting within my family circle.

"My God, I know someone like that! This man is exactly as you describe," she said.

Breathing excitedly, she told me of this nameless man in complete detail. He was living in Artush, his family's homeland, and while he was in prison, his wife left him and took their one child. Bouhatcher kept talking, hardly pausing to take a breath. He had studied literature; he did not have any money, not even enough to get the hair shaved properly from his temples. With eyes shining, she said, "Maybe he's the one you're looking for."

I was fascinated! Bouhatcher's husband, who in contrast to his wife showed no enthusiasm or inflection, added another morsel of information: "This counter-revolutionary lost a leg while he was in prison. Other than that though, he's a good-looking man."

I banged my outstretched hand on the table. "I'll marry him! He lost a leg for our country! From now on we'll fight together!"

IN 1968, WHILE I WAS STILL MARRIED to Abdirim and living in Aksu, news had spread like wildfire that a great resistance movement against the Chinese government had formed. On May 16, 1968, two years after the start of the Cultural Revolution, the organizer of this resistance movement had, along with eight of his friends, rallied fifteen-thousand people into the streets to protest for their freedom and independence. His name was Sidik Rouzi.

In those years, many Uyghurs were grateful to receive a matchstick as a present—that is how needy they were. They had nothing left to lose—not even their will to live. To those fifteen-thousand protesters, Chinese soldiers pointing their weapons at them were barely a deterrent. Even though no shots were fired, soon thereafter the Chinese government announced that any other demonstrators would be put in prison. The result though was not as the Chinese had expected. Instead, protests increased—and so did the ensuing wave of arrests all across our land.

About a year later, some acquaintances introduced me to a woman who had just started as a new hire at the pedagogical institute in the old city of Aksu. She was a small person with a large face. Her little girl slept in her arms. This woman's husband was in jail; perhaps he had already died there some people whispered. But most believed him to still be alive. His name was Sidik Rouzi. He had been incarcerated on January 17, 1969.

From that day forward, the wife of this resistance fighter was among my closest friends. At first, she confided in me that she had become pregnant for a second time by her husband who had only recently been imprisoned. But then just a few months later, she told me that she had decided to marry another man. That seemed rather dishonorable to me, and I told her so. Still I listened to her reasoning that she was not sure whether her imprisoned husband was even alive.

"If I had a husband like that, I'd be glad to wait a lifetime for him. Even if I grew white hair into my old age." Regrettably, I had not chosen my words carefully. Abdirim, who had been listening, gave me a resounding slap on the face and said, "Sidik Rouzi would never take someone like you as his wife."

Later, my friend's little daughter was weakened by a cough and died from a lack of medicine. My friend, at that time with her new husband, gave birth to her second child, a son.

WHILE BOUHATCHER WAS EXTOLLING the virtues of this intriguing man, she finally mentioned his name: Sidik Rouzi. I could not believe that this was the same person I had heard about way back in 1968. *It must be a mistake* I thought, or someone with the same name. I was sure of one thing however, I had to meet this man!

The next day, I got off the bus in Kashgar. I took a room in an inn for one night. I asked one of the guests if there was a man named Sidik Rouzi living in Artush. I added that he had been one of those put in jail during the Cultural Revolution. The man thought for a moment, stepped away, and returned a few minutes later with another man at his side.

The second man said, "Unbelievable—all of the beautiful women want to see Sidik Rouzi." Without responding to his joke, I asked for Sidik Rouzi's address and directions to get there.

I took the bus to Artush, which was about sixty miles to the north, and got off at a pass in the foothills of the Tianshan Mountains. The directions specified that from there I was to walk another two or three miles. It was a hot summer day as I walked along the stone-scattered road. Sweat was sticking to my brow as I entered a dusty village. Every building looked dilapidated. I asked a boy at the side of the road if there was someone living in the village named Sidik.

"Yes, we have two Sidiks," he chattered. "One is the good Sidik; the other the bad Sidik." I asked him to explain. "The good Sidik is our Communist Party secretary in the village."

"And the 'bad' one?"

"The bad Sidik was released from prison about five months ago. He'd been there for eight years. He came from a wealthy family, so everyone thinks he's still supposed to pay penance for his guilt until the end of his days."

"I'll take the 'bad' Sidik."

But the boy did not want to take me to him, saying, "Nobody dares to set foot in that man's home."

Then I placed two yuan in his hand, which abruptly changed his mind, and he just about flew down that road in front of me. At a field of grain, where several former prisoners were taking in the harvest, he stopped and waved to the leader of the work group. They spoke.

The work group leader called Sidik Rouzi to come over: "Someone's looking for you." He pointed toward me.

So this was Sidik Rouzi. I was deeply impressed. He was unbelievably handsome: tall, muscular, thick black hair, and clear dark eyes like dewdrops. He was wearing simple black pants made of a synthetic material and a white shirt with pale vertical stripes. It only took one look for me to see that he was different from the others. It would have been clear to anyone, not just to me.

And as a pleasant surprise for me, he also had two legs! It was not true what Bouhatcher's husband had said. I was smitten. It was love at first sight. I decided at that moment that I would become this man's wife.

He walked over to me quickly and bowed politely with his hand on his chest, saying, "Who are you? Which wind has brought you here?" As he was quite shy, he flashed only a quick look at my face while we walked toward his house.

In the front of his house was a rain barrel, and further toward the side was a stone oven. There was a small vegetable garden surrounded by a mud-brick wall. Overhanging branches from a few fruit trees protected the garden from excessive sunshine. I followed him inside through the open front door. To be kind, I will just say that the house was in need of maintenance.

Sidik's mother did not know how to honor her unknown and unexpected guest. After some deliberation, she placed a blanket that had been patched in several places onto the stamped dirt floor for me, saying, "Please, have a seat."

"Thank you. And thank you for allowing me into your home. I apologize that this visit comes as a complete surprise to you without any earlier communication. I've come to show my respect to your son as a resistance fighter."

She looked at me as though I was a guardian angel that had arrived in her sitting room. Without replying verbally, she went back to the stove and began to serve a pot of noodle soup that she had been cooking. I waited in silence, as did they.

We began to eat, and Sidik gave me a passing glance. To me it was meaningful, and apparently it was to him too as he blushed at being caught. After that one glance though, he did not dare look at me a second time. With his eyes lowered, he finished his soup.

A storm was raging inside of me. Maybe this was the love that I had been pining for for so long. Maybe this was the love that I had always seen in my mind's eye, in my dreams, in my thoughts, in my prayers.

After lunch, we went outside and sat on a log at the edge of a field. Without much further thought, I told him about my past and my future goals. I told him, "I'll liberate this land!" I could see from his facial expressions that he was annoyed by my words. Still I continued. "You've done so much for our country, but your vision isn't finished yet. I think that if we work together, we can achieve our goals together."

He started laughing and said, "That's a funny wish, a very romantic wish. But it shows me that you're an emotional person." Then he lowered his head again and his voice became stern. "The work isn't as easy as you imagine it to be. Back then we also believed, just as now you believe. Many of my friends fled to foreign countries; others were beaten to death by the Chinese." His gaze wandered into the distance and his voice became melancholy and lonely: "Your unusual wish honors the position of Uyghur women."

"What I really want to say is that I'm twenty-nine-years-old. Of the ten qualities that my future husband should hold, you meet nine of them. There is only one that's still unknown. Do you think you can love me?"

I did not know where I found the courage to say those words. His face again blushed, even more so than before—this time it was almost beet red. He also began breathing heavily, like someone who had just run too far and too fast.

I continued, "I don't have less to offer than other women. I need someone who loves me and who also needs my love. It's true that I've already given birth to six children and already been married once. However, my love is like that of an untouched maiden. I've been in love with you from the first moment I saw you."

He turned aside and chuckled quietly, "I can't believe what I'm hearing, I don't know what to say."

I added, "I could tell from the way you looked at me for the first time that you were attracted to me. You have to admit that."

He stared at me, fidgeted, stood up, sat back down again, then cleared his throat and said, "No, I can't marry you. It all seems like this is happening too quickly."

He then settled into his own anger. "Despite your current situation, you dare to speak such pompous words. You live on the earth, but you speak as though you're from the heavens. First, you said you've no house. Second, you said that you've six children. In the same breath though, you admit that your family is putting great pressure on you to go back to your ex-husband. I think it would be good for you if you go and seek out the father of your six children. If you succeed at raising your children well, then you'll have accomplished as much as if you had liberated our nation."

Yet his deep eyes revealed even more of his inner feelings I knew he had for me. I said, "You've fallen in love with me. But I can't love a man who has no self-confidence. I thought that you'd certainly have a magnificent personality. But now I recognize instead that you've lost all hope. Why were you in prison? Do you want to tell me that in those days you dreamed of hiding in this village afterward?"

"If you've been keeping yourself busy with simple tasks since your release, it's time now to use your intelligence and finally get back to work with a purpose. Your highest wish will be fulfilled only with me as your companion. If you can find a woman who will cook *laghman* noodles for you, you might be able to lead a reasonable life with her. But it'll also be the end of you."

"Leave me alone! I want to live out my life in peace with my people and then die. So now please tell me the truth that you work for the *An Chuan Ting*!"

That was really too much. The blood shot to my head as I stood up and slapped him. "I think I made a mistake. You aren't the man I imagined you to be." What impertinence! He called me a spy, me—of all people.

After a moment, my head cleared. When I saw him sitting before me with his eyes aflame, I fell even more in love with him. "What kind of a person are you? Instead of being elated about my love, you speak so badly of me. I don't understand."

I was so angry on the inside yet at the same time I was flooded with feelings of utmost joy—it was making me feel almost physically ill. Initially I had an inkling that this was the man I had been looking for in my heart, but in that moment I was filled with certainty. I placed my hands on his head and gently turned his face to me. "I'm absolutely sure that you'll come looking for me, but I'll not be that easy to find."

From that day forward, whether he would admit to it or not, I knew that Sidik was hopelessly in love with me. I told him, "I'm leaving now."

It was already evening and there were no more buses. So I had no choice but to stay overnight in Artush. I stayed up late talking with Sidik's mother. Tearfully, we talked about the past. She said, "He made us so proud then as he still does now. Oh God, there are Uyghurs who still respect my son."

I could feel Sidik sometimes sneaking a look at us from the next room. But I pretended that he did not exist for me. After contemplating my options, I decided that I would let him start courting me.

Thick blankets were spread across the carpet for his mother and me to sleep on. However, I could not sleep and tossed and turned all night. I am not sure why though. After all, I knew with absolute certainty that in the end Sidik was going to marry me.

Once I returned to Aksu, I immediately continued with my business, but I could not get this man out of my mind. I had never known that feeling before of being madly in love. Wherever I went, I was haunted by a desire that he would pop up around the next corner as a surprise for me.

Every day, I stared into the street like a madwoman. Every night in my dreams, I fought passionately with this man and swore at him. Finally he would come toward me and take me into his arms—and then I would wake up.

At some point, I started to regret rejecting in the way that I had my ex-husband Abdirim. I began to understand what pain he had endured because of me—his first true love.

APPROXIMATELY HALF-A-YEAR had gone by since Sidik and I had met. Because I still did not have a permanent address, I rented a room in Aksu which allowed me to see my children as often as possible. I met them at friends' houses and also in the courtyard at their home. I did not want to go inside the house. Besides, Abdirim always wanted to keep some distance between us.

My business activities at least forced my wildly beating heart to calm down a bit, but again and again my thoughts would come back to Sidik. Inside my mind, I was carrying out a duel with him that had no end in sight. In the winter of 1977, still absolutely miserable, I surrendered to the pangs and decided to go back to Artush for a second time. Remarkably, immediately upon surrendering to my unrelenting heartache, I received a message from Bouhatcher that Sidik had arrived in Aksu.

I nervously adjusted my white fur hat in front of the mirror before stepping outside, trotting down the alleyway in my little white boots. From the first moment I entered Bouhatcher's house, I was already asking, "Have any other guests arrived?"

Bouhatcher grinned widely at me from her moon-shaped face, saying, "Yes, oh yes, we have a guest. It's good that you've come over."

I could see from the hallway that Sidik was sitting together with other men in a room. Bouhatcher left me there alone, but a moment later Sidik approached with a little notebook in his hands. He gently offered it to me. He said, "These two-hundred-and-sixty poems express my love for you. I've written all of my feelings for you in these lines. I've found an answer to every one of the words we exchanged in Artush."

He told me that since I had left his home village, he had not been well. He no longer knew what to think—what was right or what was wrong. All he knew was that he longed for me and that this feeling got stronger and more painful every day.

I rushed back to my room with his written pages in my handbag. I read the poems half-way through the night:

"I can no longer bear the fire of light, I toss and turn. I want to burn in your fire."

Silently I mumbled along with every word, and when I was done, I started over again from the beginning.

The bullets of the Chinese had not injured him, but love had. I knew I was lost in Sidik and he in me. His words shined down upon me like stars. Reciting one of his poems as I lay down for the night, the beautiful tranquility accompanied me into my own peaceful dreams:

> *When in the skies,*
> *Many angels had flown up,*
> *A feather fell down from one angel.*
> *And that was she . . .*
> *Piles of stars, just like diamonds,*
> *Circle constantly around the moon,*
> *The star that is longing, that is I,*
> *My beloved, she is far from me . . .*

"UNFORTUNATELY, THERE ARE SOME among us who once enjoyed the respect and tradition of the Uyghur people. But they've now developed into followers of the Chinese government. We need a leader, one who should arise from the ordinary people, because no one understands their problems like someone from their midst." This is how I told Sidik that he was the right person for the leadership of our movement. I pictured two other intellectuals with leadership characteristics who could stand by his side: the poet Osmanjan Sawut and the writer Abdurayim Ötkür. Both men had spent many years in jail and were highly respected among the people.

In addition to the collective experience of these three thinkers, money would also have to play a significant role in our fight for freedom. Without the necessary financial foundation, a revolution would be impossible. I saw my job as generating money for our movement. I did not want to take on a different leadership role for myself at that point.

"After our wedding, our first task will be to liberate the land." Sidik laughed at me but I was not listening.

"You should also accept that I can't be a housewife. I don't fit into the sky, or the earth. I need freedom. I will not stay under your control. But you can be absolutely sure there's nothing to doubt about my morality.

"I have to tear down the barricades that are limiting the possibilities for our people because the government will never willingly give back what they've stolen from us. That's why it's important for us to first amass a fortune in order to gain influence. First and foremost I have to serve our people but you can't be sad because of me."

My dearest looked at me with great concern.

I continued, "Sidik, perhaps you'll never live in security or peace after you've married me. Perhaps too you'll have problems, because despite the traditions among Uyghurs, you'll have to allow your wife the right to move about freely. I've said several times this evening that by marrying me, you'll have to make sacrifices. But it should be our goal to serve the people together."

He was forceful in his response: "You don't know how this revolution will continue to develop, or what will come toward us next. I've been to prison myself and have heard with my own ears how badly people spoke of me. It was only after my release from prison that I found out more about the operations the government had put into action to have me arrested. You haven't experienced any of this, so there is no way you could know. Although you can sacrifice yourself for your goal, the hardest part is to win over the people. Who are you? Who am I? Who knows us anyway? Even if we risked making our wishes public, no one would follow us.

"Uyghurs are honest and forthright people. We trust easily, but to our disadvantage, we are also easily won over. The Chinese government knows this and they cast webs of lies and deceptions to take advantage of us.

"Maybe you too have a very lively imagination. You've read many books—among them is surely the one about Don Quixote. You don't own your own home, yet you have a goal of becoming rich. Maybe I can support you so that you can learn to think in a more practical way. Plus, we Uyghurs aren't a small community. There are several million of us."

I said, "If you aren't prepared for this Sidik then we can't marry."

He grabbed my hand and calmed me down, saying, "You're very emotional Rebiya Kadeer. You shouldn't rush things. Of course I'll do my best. I'll accept all of your conditions. But I ask you not to tell anyone what you told me today, because people would find such talk ridiculous."

He put his hands on my shoulders. "Turn what you just told me into reality. When you've achieved your goal, you'll no longer need me and those other two men. You'll be able to take over the leadership position yourself. I'm pleased to hear these words that will radiate with great strength into the future. Many millions of people among us have this hope for our freedom. Rebiya, keep fighting."

I wished he could have said that we would be successful in making our dream come true.

"I HAVE A REQUEST," Sidik said one day.

"Yes, my love." Cheerful, I was bustling with activity in planning our wedding.

"Go to your ex-husband once more and ask him if he's willing to take you in. If he agrees, I'll celebrate your wedding with you and then go back to Artush." At that point Abdirim still had not married the teacher he was engaged to.

Sidik had every reason to ask me to return to Abdirim. He was being criticized by all of his family and friends for wanting to marry a woman with six children. Meanwhile, my relatives and friends were equally critical, never missing an opportunity to remind me that Sidik had been in prison, had no job, and had no money.

While I was away on business and without my knowledge, some friends of mine took my six children to meet Sidik for the first time. This act was intended to finally stop our impending marriage. Their thinking was that the children's anticipated displeasure with him would certainly end the deal. In addition, they made their own case to him, arguing that he had no right to marry me.

But because he was a man with a big heart, he spoke to my children for a long time. Only my daughter Reyila rejected him. She believed that he stood in the way of reconciliation between Abdirim and me. My other five children however, had a lot of respect for him.

Still, Sidik could think of no remedy for the enormous pressure we were under from our families except to send me away. "I'll isolate myself as a poet and live alone for the rest of my life. I'll be happy just with the sound of your name. That's enough—your name. I'm asking you for the last time to go back to your husband and fulfill your responsibility as a mother. When you go back and live with him, I'm prepared to continue fighting with you for the sake of our nation."

I could have screamed with anger. With this rage in my gut I went to see Abdirim, along with two of my girlfriends. Beside myself with overwhelming emotions, I cried uncontrollably on the way there. Then I had to laugh with joy because I had finally found someone in my life who I missed.

I was afraid that because of our six children, Abdirim might actually agree to take me back. But then he would have had the unhappiest wife ever at his side. I would be a woman giving up everything, a woman shackling her life next to his.

At least I had the notebook with Sidik's poems to comfort me. I could have kept reading those for a lifetime. With him, I could be a happy woman—a woman allowed to experience loving a man and receiving love in return.

I had intended to stand coldly before my ex-husband. But upon arriving at Abdirim's home, I chose instead a more conciliatory tone.

I said, "I can no longer live alone. It isn't good for a mother and such a young woman as I am to do otherwise. I'll marry Sidik. I've fallen in love with this man and he feels the same as I do. That's why he sent me to talk with you now. I'm doing as I was told."

Abdirim seemed to want to put me down—this woman in love standing before him: "Sidik will never marry you. And I'll not take you back either."

"You mean you wouldn't marry me again?"

"I will not marry you again."

I took each of our children into my arms. "You'll never be without a loving family. As long as I live, you're loved."

That shamed and angered Abdirim. "Don't talk such nonsense. And get out of my house, now!"

When Sidik saw me coming across the courtyard, he practically threw himself at me, saying, "I'm so sorry. Please forgive me." His eyes were swollen thick from crying.

"Nothing happened."

"Nothing happened?

"No."

"Thank God. If you had been taken from me that would've been the greatest loss of my life."

THERE WAS NO LONGER anything standing in the way of our marriage. At the Aksu civil registry office though, we had to haggle with the officer-in-charge who ultimately refused to give us the needed paperwork because he was a good friend of Abdirim.

Soon thereafter, the governor of Aksu also called me into his office and gave me a lecture on morality: "What exactly are you planning? Don't forget that the father of your mother-in-law was a leading official in Aksu. How can you give your hand in marriage to someone who doesn't have a home, let alone citizenship?" Sidik had lost many rights, including citizenship, after his arrest.

My father and my siblings also remained opposed to our intentions. Many people in the village, including the intellectuals, were of the same opinion—that I should not enter into marriage with this outcast. All of Aksu was busy gossiping about us as though their own personal happiness depended on it.

During this time, Sidik wrote poetry that was largely based on his life story. In contrast to himself, he wrote about how many of his university classmates had become rich and well-respected. But he had chosen for himself a different path because he wanted to work for his people. He wrote of his hurt when those previously erstwhile companions had snubbed him and treated him as small and inconsequential.

Those in our social group considered Sidik a beggar, someone who possessed neither shoes nor a homeland. Through his poetry however, he found a way to respond to these rejections. As no one wanted to help us in Aksu, we decided to get the paperwork for our wedding in Artush.

At around this time, Abdirim tragically suffered a stroke. For six months, he lay in the hospital recuperating. Until the very end, he doggedly tried to foil our marriage ceremony. He never believed that he could lose me forever.

After his release from the hospital, he finally married the teacher. My eldest son told me later that their father had said he was proud to have been married to Rebiya Kadeer.

ON JULY 31, 1978, SIDIK AND I WED. He wore a black suit and white shirt—my garments were simple, but pretty. Sidik had no money with which to buy me a ring. I kept only ten yuan in my handbag because I did not want to shame anyone by having more money than the others.

Sidik's family was shunned because of his history, so nobody dared to congratulate us. There were only six of us at the wedding, including Sidik's brother, his two sisters, and his mother. The imam was not even allowed to conduct the wedding in public, so instead he came to the house. In his own personal way, Sidik was a believer. In contrast to myself though, he prayed only once a day.

The mood in the little cottage was lovely. We ate rice pilaf and carrots in a pot and Sidik's family accepted me and grew giddy with happiness. They laughed and were unanimous in the belief that an angel had descended from heaven to visit their home.

Wistfully, I sank into my own thoughts for a moment. I prayed for my children. They really should have been there. But despite that sorrow, I felt overjoyed on this day for the first time in my life. I had filled an important piece of my life that had always been missing.

Each time I looked at Sidik, he became more handsome. His eyes were shining and seemed even larger than before. As if I were still a schoolgirl, he made me crazed with happiness. I could feel for the first time how beautiful love could be when carried on a noble road. I was experiencing in reality what before I had only read about in books.

Sidik's mother clapped her hands energetically. "Regardless of whether guests are coming today, we are going to celebrate. Sidik will play the dutar and I will dance. Since the occupation, this is the first time that we are all laughing here. Today is also the first time since then that I lift my arms to dance. God gave us back joy and honesty."

My husband sang with a deep, strong voice. His eyes were full of tears. I moved close to him, asking, "Why are you crying? Today is our wedding day. We should be joyful."

"You know you're my greatest love. But I'm not in a position to buy you even a simple ring. I wish that I could've given you the stateliest wedding gown too so we could have paraded hand-in-hand through the village."

I felt tears welling in my eyes. "If you really think that, then give me your hand." He put his hand in mine, his skin calloused from hard labor.

"The two of us will liberate our land. I've bought a ring for you, but I'll not give it to you yet. I'm waiting instead for the day when our land will be free. That's when you'll give me my wedding gown too. But until then, let's be patient."

Sidik pulled me tightly toward him. "My wife who speaks such great words, I accept your wish. May God grant us this day."

Because my love for Sidik had swelled my heart, because I loved our land, and because I had followed my innermost urges to take action, I was the happiest woman in the world at that moment. I was glowing with the joy of life.

Sidik is such a noble man. In our two hearts, a strong love was to be our shared destiny. To this very day, it is inconceivable for me to be separated from him. I am sure that I would not have survived this struggle without him.

Further Into the Yellow Desert

ventually my family calmed down once I was back under the protection of a man. Only Hejer continued to have fears about how Sidik would worsen my situation because he had no money and had been in prison.

For a year, I used Artush as a base. My children remained with their father. I visited them as often as I was able and sent them presents and messages to cheer them up. Because he was a former prisoner, the village officials stubbornly refused to give Sidik permission to travel with me on business trips. As I caught the next bus to Kashgar, he stayed home and wrote poems.

Kashgar, the oldest Uyghur settlement in our nation, was famous throughout Central Asia for its impressive bazaar. For centuries, dealers gathered there from all directions, traveling from as far away as Pakistan in their donkey carts. I loved this city, with its interlocking mud-brick buildings, its houses decorated with Arabic ornaments, and its crooked alleys reminiscent of the Middle Ages. Ninety percent of the population was Uyghur. Kashgar is two time zones away from Beijing. No city in the Chinese kingdom is further away from the capital. Yet, the government mandated that clocks there run on Beijing time. Only a handful of loyal Chinese who lived in Kashgar disregarded the earth's rotation and did as Beijing commanded. The rest of the population, for practical reasons, set their clocks according to the usual regional time.

I considered getting into the livestock trading business. However, when I went to the bazaar to do research on it, I became fascinated instead with the timber business. I asked one of the sellers where he got his wood and how profitable the business was.

The man readily told me that near Kashgar, there was little wood to be had. But there was plenty in Karlac, which was about three-hundred miles away. Taking note of my interest, he kindly added that the wood business was not easy work. I thought about his answers carefully. Transporting a load of timber would cost one-hundred-and-fifty yuan.

The livestock business would be more expensive. So I went to Karlac immediately to inquire about tree trunks.

I had one-thousand-five-hundred yuan with me. With that amount, I was able to purchase one-hundred-and-fifty tree trunks. I talked with suppliers to reserve for me another five-thousand. I was aware that this business opportunity could be gone quite quickly because of competition, as had happened with the sheepskin trade. With that in mind, I decided to acquire a huge quantity in one transaction, thus limiting the available supplies for others. I was glad because the dealers trusted me, and they were glad because they had reached an agreement valued at fifty-thousand yuan.

I worked hard at this business. I had logs transported from Karlac to Kashgar by truck to be sold in the market. Three or four times each week I traveled the dusty route to Karlac. I gave twigs and branches to the poor for their firewood and in return, they sawed entire trunks into smaller portions for me.

I was on the road for three months and was so occupied with work that there was little opportunity for Sidik and me to spend time together. That was a difficult challenge for both of us. I had heard from acquaintances how miserable Sidik felt when I was away; that he did not shave for days; that he had lost weight. Once he sent me a poem that he had written, with the lines, "Why did I not die in jail? Why on earth did I meet Rebiya?"

When I finally came home, my sensitive poet was hurt; he could not look me in the face as he spoke quietly, saying, "I know that you're a special woman, but after all, you're a woman. You know that there's no Uyghur man who would allow his wife to do what I'm granting you."

His facial expression was tortured and full of sorrow. "I feel like I'm being made to feel melancholy. It leaves me unable to look into the eyes of our friends and relatives. Unfortunately, you've become very special to me. Had I fully realized this, had I known you would be the only woman for me, that there could never be another and one who was also as beautiful as an angel, who could drink a glass of water for me so that I could watch as that water coursed slowly down her throat—then perhaps I would have been better prepared for the torment that comes when you go away for so long."

His sorrow made me feel sad as well, and I vowed to make every effort to get my husband to come with me on my travels.

⤳ ⤲

AGAIN AND AGAIN I TRIED to gain a travel permit for Sidik from the village bureaucrats until finally they consented. After that, my husband was a great inspiration for me in the business world and took care of me as sensitively as if I were made of crystal.

However, Sidik did not care one way or the other how much money we made. Instead of thinking about making money, he thought about buying books. Every time he found a new literary work on a trip, he would begin to read it and would then be in harmony with himself and the world. I had married Sidik with the hope that one day he would take over the leadership of our people. But I soon realized that he was an inward soul—he was a thinker more than anything else.

One time we stopped in the middle of a gravel desert in order to better tie down the timber load. While I pulled on the ropes, the wind loosened my headscarf. It first fluttered to the ground and then floated away, dancing from stone to stone as if pulled by a ghostly hand.

Sidik watched it briefly. "I will not allow the wind to take your headscarf," he said and ran after it, further and further into the yellow desert.

The driver and I waited for more than half-an-hour until finally a dark speck appeared in the yellow void. A figure approached; its face and clothing were covered in dust and sand. Wordlessly, Sidik handed me my scarf.

"Why'd you do that?"

"I'll never allow anyone to take anything from you."

The driver had overheard us and could hardly contain his laughter. "I already knew this man loved you," he said, "but I didn't realize how madly in love he is with you."

Sidik shrugged his shoulders and said to the driver, "For you, I'm abnormal. But you know nothing of the deeper meaning of life, so you can't fathom what I think, what I feel."

The meaning of life, Sidik once said to me, could be found even in a tiny pebble.

Days later, we were traveling along the same route when our load of fifty logs slipped loose. Sidik climbed on top of the load and pulled the logs while I pushed from behind to get them back into position. When I switched directions and tried to pull a log toward me, other logs shifted and rolled dangerously so that one wedged against Sidik's foot, clamping him down, while others pinned me down tightly at the neck. Neither one of us could move. We called to the driver for help, but the man had fallen asleep in the distance. We were in the middle of the desert. Other than our deep-sleeping driver, we could see no one in any direction—the desert stretched as far as the horizon with only solitary tamarisk shrubs dotting the landscape here and there. The heat shimmered in the glaring midday sun; dusty sand scratched across my face. After what must have been hours, everything became a blur and I lost consciousness. Sidik stared at me helplessly while still trying to rouse the driver.

From out of nowhere, a farmer appeared, pedaling his bicycle up the road.

As soon as he saw us, he threw his bicycle aside and immediately came to our aid. He first freed me from the logs as I regained consciousness, then turned his attention to Sidik. My husband had hardly a chance to thank the farmer before the man was on his bicycle again, pedaling away just as quickly as he had come. I still think about that today—*how did this man happen to come along?* It was like a little miracle.

We needed to take a break after that ordeal. A former classmate of Sidik's lived in a village that we had passed on the way to Kashgar. It was one o'clock in the morning when we arrived. At first we thought about knocking on his door, but then we realized it would be best to let the family keep sleeping undisturbed.

Sidik's friend had a beautiful garden. Pumpkins and melons were stored underneath a wooden table. My husband tore down some large leaves and arranged them into a mat for us. We covered ourselves with a few more leaves. But because it was so cold in the desert, Sidik and I embraced tightly. I fell asleep to the beating of his heart in my ear. He would often tell me later, and even today, "That was my nicest night of sleep with you."

My brother Mehmet said, "Officers are constantly inspecting us right here on the street. The other day they even took a young man named Yolwas, only seventeen-years-old, into custody. Just because he happened to be walking by their station. For hours, three government security officials beat him up in the courtyard. Then they shoved a broom handle down his throat."

Their son had not died violently *An Chuan Ting* officials assured the parents as they handed them ten-thousand yuan. The payment came with two conditions: that the peasant family would not speak about the circumstances of Yolwas' death, and that they would bury their child promptly. These poor farmers, who barely had enough to eat, agreed; yet news about the boy's agonizing death spread anyway.

My brother Mehmet finished with this news in his summary of happenings over the last few months in Aksu. It was 1978, during a period when Sidik and I were spending some time there. I was angry and asked my brother to take me to this family.

Three security officials were standing guard at the family's door. They wanted to know what business I had there. I said that I was the sister of the farmer's wife, so they let me in. Yolwas' body was respectfully placed behind a curtain, true to Uyghur tradition. Typically, Uyghur women are not shown the corpse of a man, but I glanced at the body anyway. One side of his face was a deeply bruised blue-green. His bludgeoned eye looked like a plump fig.

His mother sat nearby. Her body was shaking and heaving with grief. I told her, "I've brought twenty-thousand yuan for you."

She looked up at me and said, "We are scared of the *An Chuan Ting*."

I caressed her back with my hand. "I heard how your son lost his life. I can imagine his pain. It was wrong of the police—especially wrong for them to tell you that your son died without violence. I would like to have Yolwas examined in a hospital, please."

The boy's mother agreed. I told the officials in front of the house that I was taking the boy to the hospital for an autopsy. The men made telephone calls until they finally received permission from their superiors to entrust me with the corpse. Quite possibly, they did so because they feared that there might otherwise be an uprising. By that time, three of my brother's friends had arrived.

Though they let us leave with the body, the government immediately took countermeasures. They contacted the coroner in charge to make certain he would prepare an "appropriate" autopsy report. My counter-countermeasure was to give the physician some money along with a request that he do his work accurately.

We waited in the hallway at the hospital. Later, we were told that a surgeon had also been brought in to remove a piece of the splintered broom handle from Yolwas' lungs.

During the procedure, the chief of the local *An Chuan Ting* bureau also arrived. When he was informed that the young man had died from puncture wounds to his lungs and blunt trauma to his head, he expressed complete surprise at the findings and solemnly declared that those responsible would be severely punished. But, he added, we should let the boy rest in peace now. I nodded, though pursued a different course.

Once we were back at Mehmet's apartment I gave him instructions. "Sidik and I have to go to Shanghai on business, so I'm giving you a major responsibility. You'll show homage to this murdered young man and to all of the other innocent victims who've lost their lives through such brutality.

"Take Yolwas' corpse to his memorial service tomorrow. As soon as you get there, hang signs on both sides of his casket with the following inscription: "STOP THE ETHNIC KILLING." Explain to the mourners the circumstances under which Yolwas died. Then pass through the whole city, respectfully carrying the casket that holds his remains."

My brother made his doubts about this plan known quickly: "But there are only a few of us."

"That's right, but when you take to the streets, many more will join you. But nobody should lay a hand on another. Nothing should be destroyed. Nonviolence only."

Sidik repeated to Mehmet a warning he'd shared with me earlier: "Nobody can know that Rebiya is involved in this. Otherwise, we'll not be able to realize our larger goals."

Before we left for Shanghai, I impressed upon my brother one more time: "Nonviolence only."

The next day, just as the imam was about to start reciting prayers, my brother stepped forward and with one tug pulled the cloth back that was covering the tortured boy's corpse. The crowd immediately became so enraged that they stormed through the doors and into the streets. The news spread through Aksu as fast as lightning. Within an hour or so, more than ten-thousand people had taken to the streets. The demonstration was peaceful as a whole as evidenced by the security officers showing restraint to almost all. But admittedly, my brother no longer had organization over the crowd and a few pockets of those outraged destroyed a security station and temporarily took hold of an outpost. There were no reports of injury thank God. Again, the episode taught me another lesson on nonviolent resistance—this one more tactical regarding behaviors of large crowds in consideration of the risk that some may become too excited. So I took to heart lessons about keeping large groups calm and organized and have not repeated the mistake of creating unnecessary risks for peaceful gatherings.

The next day, my brother and his friends held a memorial service and buried Yolwas in peace. The authorities had arrested many demonstrators but in the end they released everybody. Eventually though, my brother and his friends were identified as chief suspects in the demonstration and were kept behind bars.

From Shanghai I went directly to Beijing and submitted a formal protest to the government officials responsible for ethnic affairs. I reported that many people in our homeland, like Yolwas, had been tortured and killed without reason. Even Ismail Amat, chairman of the Xinjiang Uyghur Autonomous Region at the time, could not accept the cruel treatment of Uyghurs. As a Uyghur himself, unfortunately he was not a particularly influential member in the central Chinese government.

Interrogators tried to force my brother to confess that I was the one who had instigated the uprising. But Mehmet would not give in. He said that he had only been expressing his indignation over the murder of an innocent person. After six months, he and his friends were set free. I had paid a ten-thousand yuan fine for the release of each of them.

Many Chinese civil servants, soldiers, and farmers fled back to China after the uprising. The Chinese head of the local Aksu government was transferred back to Beijing. Of the group of government officers who had murdered Yolwas, several were transferred into the *bingtuan*. None that I am aware of were punished. The government then released several more prisoners to try to appease the population.

Overall however, there was no significant, notable change in Aksu—not even in my brother. For him, there was still a fire burning in his eyes, as though he was not afraid of the Chinese or of death.

IN THE SPRING OF 1979, Sidik and I were on a business trip in Bai, an ancient city along the northern Silk Road. I noticed that my husband had begun to look very pale. He got out of the truck and vomited behind the bushes. I thought that he might have caught a virus.

We drove to Kucha where my sister Hejer was working as a doctor. She prepared a bed and prescribed medications for him. But his fever continued to rise. On the third day, it had reached an alarming one-hundred-and-six degrees Fahrenheit and continued to climb. Two women helped me dunk towels into ice-cold water and wrap them around him. After about two minutes, we repeated this procedure with more ice-cold towels. Then we tried filling the bedsheets with ice. But his fever remained high without any hint of breaking. For forty days, my beloved was only barely holding on to life. None of the medications had any effect.

Day after day I spoon-fed him a few mouthfuls of watermelon juice, which was the only thing he could manage to keep down. What was hardest for me was when the doctors gave their dire last prognosis, shaking their heads in resignation. In their minds, he had at most only a few days left. The whole time he was in the hospital, I sat next to his bed and looked at him, full of hope.

While I was placing cool cloths on his forehead, I continuously thought about what could have caused his illness. Shortly before his release from prison, the Chinese doctors had taken a great deal of blood from him and predicted that he would not be able to enjoy his freedom much because he would not have long to live. It seemed implausible that this occurrence was related, many years later, but my mind was spinning in search of answers. I began to imagine that they had injected some kind of bacteria into him when he was in prison, then dismissed this as ridiculous thinking.

Sidik had told me often and in great detail about his time in prison—mostly about the vicious dogs they would let loose to attack the prisoners and about the interrogations to force him to reveal names, places, and plans.

He also talked about the black handcuff—a torture device in which both hands would be bound together behind the back in a single shackle. An iron bar would then be staked between the hands. One horrifying consequence of this treatment, likely due to a traumatic drop in blood circulation, was that after about five minutes the tortured prisoner's tongue would begin to swell. It would get bigger and bigger until it could not fit inside the victim's mouth. His whole body would quiver, he would lose control over his bodily functions and urinate and defecate on himself. After a while, the victim's eyeballs would also protrude.

My husband told me, "While I was laying on the ground, so weakened, I could hear the guards talking to each other, saying, 'If we leave the handcuff on just a minute more, he'll die.'" I cried whenever Sidik told me about those times in prison.

When Hejer told my father about Sidik's serious illness, he came to the hospital immediately. Without saying much, he sat down at my husband's bedside and felt his pulse. I sat next to my father, saying, "But he loves me."

"If he really loves you Rebiya, then he'll not leave you alone. You have to hope with your full heart that he'll survive."

My father rushed from the hospital and came back about an hour-and-a-half later with a Uyghur traditional medicine of a black, paste-like substance. My father said, "Rebiya, help me—you need to push his tongue down." Then he squeezed the paste down Sidik's throat. "Now we have to wait. I didn't have enough time to prepare more, so I'm going out again quickly to get some."

It was the forty-third day of Sidik's high fever. He was getting visibly paler and weaker. Ninety minutes after the treatment, with my father by my side again, Sidik's temperature miraculously dropped to one-hundred-and-two degrees Fahrenheit. We shouted with joy, but my husband was barely conscious.

In the evening, my father fed him the paste once again. Around midnight, his fever climbed back up to one-hundred-and-seven degrees Fahrenheit. He could hardly breathe—it was more of a wheeze.

After a few hours, his temperature dropped again. For the rest of the day he maintained only a slightly elevated temperature. My father fed him spoonfuls of chicken soup with the paste mixed in it. On the third day, Sidik opened his eyes. My father measured his pulse and pronounced: "The man who loves you so much has come back."

My other half had found his way back to life, and I felt like a whole person again. We have never discovered even to this day what had brought him to the brink of death.

AT THE END OF 1979, SIDIK and I moved from Artush to Urumqi. Over time, the government was allowing more and more freedom to merchants. With a few of my old business partners and my husband, I went to Shanghai once more. At first, the number of Uyghur business people was still small, but after a few months, there were more and more of us. Our profits thus diminished day by day.

On our journeys through central China, I discovered that the population was not as well off as the government had proclaimed. Most people survived on the edge of existence and under the control of the boss at their workplace. A Chinese boss could determine almost every aspect of his workers' lives. In short, what he wanted, he got. I watched Chinese workers toil away like animals—oxen, mules, or water buffalos—they seemed resigned to the fact that they had come into this world with no rights at all.

But at the end of the Cultural Revolution, many Uyghurs began rediscovering their national identity. Monuments were erected all over the Uyghur nation; figures were sculpted from stone to represent the Buddhist aspects of Uyghur heritage; and other works of art were created depicting animals that were important to us, such as sheep and wolves. Even the open-air bazaar blossomed again.

There was talk of reform in our land. We listened very cautiously, since all of the Chinese reforms so far had been directed against our countrymen. This time, though, there were some positive signs, such as some nomads having their livestock returned to them. It also became permissible to distribute religious literature, and writings in various scripts were reintroduced. There was discussion of freedom of religion as well. Some Muslims, Buddhists, and Taoists were even permitted to go on religious pilgrimages again.

When I heard of these new developments, I thought to myself that the government had finally realized they could no longer hold onto our population through constant suppression—the only way to live in harmony was for them to let us be free.

There were even rumors that the government planned to recognize the independence of our Uyghur nation. For the first time since the Manchu conquests more than two-hundred years ago, the government also publicly confirmed that our people were of Turkic descent, not Chinese.

With China's openness toward capitalism, the face of Urumqi and other territories began to see a real estate and construction boom. Though the uniformity of the Communist architectural style had nothing in common with our Uyghur architecture, undeniably progress was being made in our homeland.

For a long time, government officials had refused to assign suitable work to my husband. Just like many intellectuals and religious figures who had recently been released from prison, his every step was under surveillance. But at my request, several Uyghur civil servants spoke up on Sidik's behalf.

For a researcher like Sidik, it was a great accomplishment when he finally received a teaching position at the university. Sidik was not a businessman; that was not what he was born to do. My husband was employed from 1980 onward at the university to train elementary and middle school teachers on the subject of "New Chinese Literature."

Under the control of the Chinese government, the university was limited as to what teaching materials were allowed in the classroom. Professors, unlike in the West, were not given permission to choose freely. My husband circumvented those restrictions as best as he could by subtlety selecting texts on subjects like the Cultural Revolution and democracy in the West. After all, students were supposed to acquire tools for critical analysis. Sidik had to find ways for introducing new thinking to the students that the government would not object to. For example, he cleverly compared Communist East Germany with democratic West Germany, and thus, through implication, alluded to the situation in our country. Although the conditions were difficult and the restrictions frustrating, Sidik found that his work made him happy.

In the same year, I began to bring my children from Aksu to Urumqi, one by one. Only Adil stayed in Aksu. He accepted the government's offer to take over his father's job at the bank. The three-room apartment in the middle of Urumqi that the university had temporarily provided for us was unfortunately quite small: its total area was just over five-hundred-square-feet. The five of us, including my children Kahar, Ablikim, and Alim, lived on the second floor of a six-storey building. It had no private bathroom, so we went to the public showers once or twice a week to wash.

The public toilet was literally next door to our apartment. We actually shared a common wall. Every day, a thousand people went in and out. The smell left behind was beyond description. The toilets did not have running water so a constant stench hung in the air.

A new apartment building near the university had already been constructed; this is where the Chinese employees lived. To our great relief, rumor had it that another new building was also being constructed for the remaining university employees. We heard that Sidik's name was one of those near the top of the list.

CHINA'S INCREASING OPENNESS toward business at the beginning of the 1980s was an epochal turning point. It brought not only open markets, but the Communist government also tentatively allowed intellectual life to flourish again. Encouraged by the improved political climate, Uyghurs sought more work and more autonomy.

However, they received the opposite of their desired goals of work and autonomy, as the government again tightened controls on our people. Every expression of our desire to improve our quality of life, to them, was equivalent to a treasonous expression of separatism. According to Chinese law, talk of separatism was a crime against state security and could be punishable by death.

At that time, I was tempted to go back to Canton. Under Deng Xiaoping, that coastal province was developing into the richest and biggest market in China. To facilitate growth, the government established special economic zones in the Pearl River Delta between Canton, Shenzhen, and Zhuhai.

This region, with its rich diversity of available goods, was especially attractive to business people; that is, it was attractive in theory. But in reality, every person was subject to the arbitrary decisions of the region's security officers. Sometimes you could enter the province; sometimes you could not. Sometimes you could leave the province with the necessary papers deemed to be in order; sometimes you could try to leave the province but would be detained because the necessary papers were deemed to not be in order.

Unfortunate "arbitrary" occurrences seemed to happen more often to Uyghurs than to others. Sometimes the Chinese officials would allow our people to deliver inexpensive wares into Canton from Shantou, across from the coast of Taiwan. From personal experience I can relate though that when these same officials arbitrarily changed their minds, they would simply close off our route and confiscate all of our commodities.

For a person to arrive in Shantou by himself was extremely risky because the locals would assault and rob trade dealers. Once when I was in Shantou, a few hundred of my Uyghur business colleagues were in residence. We found strength in numbers and would spontaneously get together somewhere, even though it was forbidden to organize into such groups. Sometimes we would live together in the same hotel, eat in the same restaurant, and then decide at some point, "Let's do business together."

On one occasion I was meeting with about twenty men. In order to avoid confiscation of our goods, as we had experienced the last time in Canton, I took the extra precaution of paying off two Chinese officials. Every time we were inspected, they were supposed to confirm that our wares had been acquired by legal means.

Near Canton, my colleagues and I bought electronics and rayon fabric. Chinese garments did not fit Uyghur women very well, primarily because Chinese women were built differently. We therefore bought beautiful fabrics so that our women could sew their own clothes. The fabrics were better in terms of colors, patterns, and quality than what we could buy at home. Finally, I reconfirmed my agreement with the two government officials who said that they would accompany our convoy of trucks through Canton and secure our safe passage.

I had invested approximately two-hundred-thousand yuan in this enterprise. With my usual sense of certainty, I assumed that nothing would happen to us because we had paid the appropriate taxes, had official state receipts in our pockets, and had followed all of the other laws for this transaction.

On the return trip, we stopped at a restaurant in a small town. The two government officials escorting us enjoyed their meal right along with the rest of us. While I was settling the bill the two disappeared without me realizing it.

Only a few minutes later, roughly two-hundred policemen stood outside the restaurant, facing us like a wall. Other officers were already swarming over our five fully loaded trucks. Seven of our colleagues stood up to them, trying to convince them with words, but they were just pushed aside. It was impossible to tell who first lifted a hand against whom, but I saw how they pushed our colleagues back, started roughing them up, beat them more and more with their batons, and then once they'd been knocked down, kicked them mercilessly.

"Stop that! Stop that!" I shouted. Other Chinese residents who were nearby joined my pleas: *"Ting yi xia! Ting yi xia!"*

But our pleas fell on deaf ears. Groups of six or eight officers kept kicking my fellow businessmen who had been knocked to the ground. It was a long time before they let up. Of our seven colleagues, four were taken to a security station. Of the other three, one was clutching his abdomen, another had a broken shoulder, and a third could not manage to get up off of the ground at all.

At the station, we showed each and every document proving the legality of our trade. But the chief confiscated our papers, just as he had done with our trucks and their contents: "If you continue to blabber on about how all of this is legal, we'll throw each of you in jail for a year."

We begged him to at least leave us some money for our families. This request infuriated him to such a degree that he threatened to have his officers beat our colleagues again. I tried to calm him down, saying, "Keep our goods, but please give us back our documents." But the chief refused that too. He concocted an argument that our Uyghur homeland, which he referred to in Chinese as *Xinjiang*, was not a Chinese district and did not belong to China. Ironically, he did not know that my life's work was precisely to turn this distinction into a reality.

After we left the station with all of our colleagues together again, we found a guesthouse in which to recover. We were too short of funds to pay even the medical expenses for our battered colleagues. Some of the other colleagues asked me to please help them find some money. Most of what they had invested, as is our Uyghur custom, had been borrowed from friends and relatives. They would not be able to show their faces back home if they returned with empty pockets. Right then, I made a firm decision that I would help them regain their losses.

It had been six months since I had last seen my husband. I had to see him. With a heavy heart, I went back to Urumqi. My knees like rubber, my hands raised as if in prayer, I went before him, crying, "Ah, Sidik, my husband. This time I experienced the same thing again. I've lost my money and my goods."

"Are you healthy? That's the most important thing."

"Yes."

"Then to keep your health, you have to stop with this business now that you've had losses like this for a second time." He took my hands, "I need you, Rebiya. I can support you and the family. Please, stay here."

But I could not stay. Aside from my dream to free the Uyghur people from oppression, I had the practical and immediate responsibility of paying off my debts, including interest. Friends had loaned me fourteen-thousand yuan for my trip.

So back to Canton I went. Our group discussed matters in a Dungan restaurant, as I encouraged them to agree that we could not accept defeat, but rather, that we should start over again. Each of us gave our last amounts of cash, totaling one-thousand-seven-hundred yuan. I sought out several more Uyghur partners as well as some Dungans whom we had befriended. Some of them joined in our venture too, with each contributing five-thousand yuan.

I sent two of our men to Shantou to once again buy goods, cassette recorders, and other electronics. Another group built a Uyghur oven in which to bake our traditional wheat bread in both flattened and ringed form. Then we rented a small room and opened a restaurant, serving hand-pulled noodles and other Uyghur delicacies.

In the meantime, our colleagues in Shantou acquired and sold electronics at a profit. The money we made from the restaurant was reinvested in the purchase of additional electronic goods and other merchandise in Shantou. With a greater sense of urgency, we also wholesaled our wares to businesspeople in Canton.

For three months, we pursued these different businesses intensively until we had finally pooled together three-hundred-and-fifty-thousand yuan. I divided the money equitably among the twenty people involved. But my colleagues offered me an additional one-thousand yuan bonus for acting as the organizer. At my suggestion, we donated this bonus one-thousand yuan to a poor boy who had recently arrived in Canton. When we parted ways, a few from our group tried to elicit a promise from me to continue working with them.

"You know that I only wanted to help you get back the money you lost in the last venture. We've taken in enough money. That's as far as I go."

I WAS SIX MONTHS PREGNANT. Sidik placed my hand on his chest, saying, "I ask you once again, from my heart, please stay home. Even if we have to live in a cave and use a rock for a pillow, for me that would be the most beautiful life. Please stay here, at least until our child is born."

I agreed. First, I paid back my debts and took care of my children. Over the next two months, I searched for a location in Urumqi suitable for me to do business. With approval from the authorities, I picked a patch of asphalt between two trees and on a side street where no vehicles were allowed. I placed a board between these two trees and every day I spread out fabric and clothing that I had left over from previous dealings. In the evenings, I placed everything back into a large box and stored it with a nearby family. My single board between two trees quickly grew into more boards, with more merchandise.

One day, another woman came. She had a board wedged underneath her arm. The next day, she brought two more boards and lined up all three on the asphalt not far from me. She put out her old clothes just like I did and sold them at low prices. Eventually, her small shopping space was comprised of twenty display boards.

I inquired with the authorities whether we could set up an open-air market in the location I had found. The idea was well-received. They agreed to my plan and named me director of this bazaar. After that, I rented out spaces to merchants who wanted to participate. I had a roof built to cover the area intended to be the bazaar. Each person was allocated a small stand or kiosk. Within a short amount of time, several hundred merchants had rented individual kiosks.

My store number was fifty-eight, and my kiosk was painted a sky blue. The bazaar soon had its own main entrance and grew from my single stand to many stands, shooting up from the ground like mushrooms. A quiet part of town had been turned into a lively market square in only three months. Because this had been my idea, the cadres nominated me to be vice president of the Urumqi chamber of commerce.

After three months of this work came the birth of our daughter Akida, on July 13, 1981. When Sidik and I were walking along the streets with our baby carriage, people turned to look at our newborn because she was so beautiful.

After giving birth, I worked at my store during the day and went back home in the evening to be with my husband and baby. But just after our daughter turned one, I began to feel dissatisfied with my earnings. My monthly average from store fifty-eight was between ten-thousand and thirty-thousand yuan.

I said, "I have no time to lose. I think I should go back to China again." My plan, as before, was to bring inexpensive goods from Canton back to Urumqi.

"No! If you leave us alone again, then stay away forever! Akida is still young. Plus, you told me that you might be pregnant again. Why don't you treat yourself to a rest and be satisfied with what you've accomplished already."

"Please—" I started.

"We will buy a courtyard house and live there. We don't need that much."

"Before we married, I told you that I'd always have to be free. We're working toward a larger goal."

"No, you'll not go!"

"But you agreed."

"Look into Akida's eyes. Then you'll see that I've already met your conditions for freedom long ago."

When Sidik left for the university the next day, I did the unthinkable, and left him a letter:

> *Dear Sidik,*
>
> *I love you and I also love our daughter. But in order to fulfill this plan that we made, I have to leave for a short period of time. Please never forget how much I miss you. As painful as this separation is for all of us, you will later hear good news from me.*
>
> *Love,*
> *Rebiya*

I put the letter into Akida's shirt pocket and brought her to an uncle in Sidik's family. She was crying when I left. I told her, "I'm so sorry; please forgive your mother for going away. I love you, but I have no other choice."

When Sidik found the letter, he went into a terrible rage. He was considering whether we could even continue living together. My sisters, my brother, and my father all judged my behavior harshly as well.

From Urumqi to Canton, my heart burned. But I ignored the pain as much as I could. I was enwrapped in a cause that I could not shake myself loose from and perhaps never would be able to. *But at what price* I thought, while trying to convince myself that Sidik would stay with me.

MY UNTHINKABLE ACTION BECAME WORSE when I soon confirmed that I was indeed in the early stages of pregnancy with our second child. With a new life accompanying me wherever I went, the next six months in Canton were quite profitable ones. I worked together with seven of my old colleagues, and we were successful in trading fabrics.

I had paid over two-hundred-thousand yuan in taxes and planned to fly back home with my profits of nine-hundred-thousand yuan. My pregnancy had gone well and I was thinking how proud I would be to show Sidik my six-month "bump."

From Canton I telephoned Sidik at the university, but my call was routed instead to a secretary who told me, "Sidik said that he wants to get separated from you. He can no longer live with an immoral woman who is even capable of leaving behind her small child." I did not know what I thought would happen when I called Sidik, but I was stunned.

I planned to fly home on the next flight out of Chengdu. The bundles totaling nine-hundred-thousand yuan were packed in my small rolling suitcase, the currency stuffed between my clothes and the presents for our children. As cash had never before been confiscated from business-people, I was certain that I would be able to take my money home without any problems.

But *An Chuan Ting* officials had been watching me for a long time. I had hardly opened the door to the departure gates at the airport, pulling my small suitcase behind me, when I was surrounded by twenty uniformed officers. One of them stepped forward and showed me his badge, saying, "Are you Rebiya Kadeer?"

In a small office, two of the uniformed men lifted my suitcase onto a table. I stood only a few steps away as a Chinese officer opened it. He slowly took out the clothes I had bought for my little children. An instant later, when he discovered the banknotes underneath them, he and the others standing around looked at me in disbelief. "How much is that? How much money is that?"

I had adjusted after the first two major confiscations. But this time, I was beside myself. I had risked my child, my unborn child, and my relationship with my husband. I was dizzy—everything seemed to be spinning. I became nauseous from my own thoughts—thoughts of lunging at them, one after the other. I asked them, "Why are you doing this? I have documents proving that I paid taxes."

"We've been watching and waiting for you to become rich. You and all Uyghurs should never forget that it's an impossibility for you."

When I got home, I found the door locked. Immediately, the neighbor stuck her head out of her apartment window and shouted, "You can't set foot in there anymore; Sidik won't allow it."

Although it was a boiling hot July day, I shivered.

I FIRST WENT TO THE UNCLE in Sidik's family with whom I had left Akida, to find my little girl. With her hands on her hips, his wife reprimanded me firmly.

"What kind of times are these? When you feel like it, you just abandon your family and drive off to wherever you want? And when you're in the mood, you come back again with a swollen belly? Don't forget that we belong to a respected family and can't accept that someone like you would affront us like this. Sidik has already prepared his divorce from you, and you're also not allowed to see Akida."

I responded, "Please tell me where my daughter is." She slammed the door in my face.

I only had fifty yuan left and did not know where to turn. Finally, I went to a friend, the writer Zunun Kadeer. He was a man whom I greatly respected and who was held in the highest regard throughout the entire Uyghur community—a true Uyghur of strong character. I was already ashamed of myself; he too was of the opinion that I had been wrong to abandon my family and children.

I then went to look for my husband, but nobody at the university would even speak to me. They all knew what I had done, and so I was shunned.

I tried to corner an acquaintance who was also a teacher at the university. "Where's Sidik?"

But he turned me away just as the others had. I said, "Tell me where he is."

The teacher said, "He's in Khotan selecting new students. But when he comes back, we'll look for a moral, beautiful wife for him."

My heart was racing as I rushed to the post office and dialed the number for the education center in Khotan. I asked if there was someone there named Sidik. The secretary said, "He's busy right now but will be back here tomorrow morning."

I explained that I was Sidik's wife and that I was in the late stages of pregnancy and did not know where to give birth to our child. I said that I would wait for my husband to call me back at this post office at twelve noon tomorrow.

The next day, I was at the post office by ten in the morning. For two hours, I waited in front of the telephone. Every time it rang, I would flinch.

I thought *maybe destiny will decide my future today. If he calls by twelve o'clock, regardless of whether he has good news or bad, that means he doesn't want to leave me. But if he doesn't call, I would agree to whatever he demanded of me.*

I knew that I had been wrong. I understood that I had hurt my husband badly. It could not have been easy for him, with an important job, to be alone and left to take care of Akida. I prayed to the depths of my soul: *please don't separate me from my beloved. But even if the whole world turns its face away from me, I believe that you God will stay with me.*

At twelve noon sharp, the telephone rang. I had trouble bringing the receiver to my ear. I heard Sidik's voice but was afraid. "Hello . . . hello . . . hello . . ."

"It's me," I said.

"What's wrong with your voice? What's wrong with you? You don't need me anymore? You don't need the children anymore?"

My insides were swelling with tenderness, but my voice would only half-way obey. I started to cry loudly.

"You stay right there. Don't move from that spot. I'll send someone to pick you up."

All of my guilty feelings would have kept me there anyway, unable to move, immobilized.

About an hour later, a car stopped in front of the post office. The driver said, "I'm Sidik's friend. Come on. I have a key. You can freshen up in his apartment and change your clothes."

Before Sidik had left for Khotan, he had entrusted Akida to his sister who lived in the Ili prefecture. The baby had already been there for one month. Sidik had left word with his sister that someone should bring my baby girl to me as quickly as possible. But all of his relatives had decided firmly against that.

Together they conspired to separate Sidik from me. But he threatened that his relatives would encounter major problems if they did not bring my daughter to me. He explained that whether we became separated or not, every mother had the right to see her child.

On the third day, his sister came to the house with Akida. Sidik's brother then brought Akida and me to Artush to stay with my mother-in-law while Sidik was away.

THE SUFFOCATING HEAT had even stopped the birds from singing. Everyone in Sidik's home village spoke softly and pointed accusing fingers at me. Only his mother, her eyes wet with tears, could not let go of me in the courtyard. She consoled me and caressed my hair.

"Regardless of what the others say about you, you're my daughter-in-law who swept into this house like the sun. That will not change. You aren't only a daughter-in-law—you're everything I always wished for. You are the woman my son needs. And that will not change. If the people here don't show regard for you and don't look at you anymore, that doesn't matter. Just don't forget: I will continue to look at you and respect you. And when my son stands here and looks at you, that will suffice for all of the others."

Life on the edge of society had shaped this woman's heart.

"We are having a small gathering today," she said. "I want to take you there with me. I'm afraid that if I leave you here alone, perhaps my children will speak badly to you. But I'll not allow it. So for now, please come along."

Since the birth of Akida, Sidik's mother had only one wish—to see her grandchild before her own passing. Cheerfully she took her grandchild in her arms and carried our little girl outside. In the courtyard my sister-in-law scoffed, "Look there, the great businesswoman has come."

My mother-in-law sat down with Akida in her arms. But in the next moment, she collapsed to the ground, though Akida remained safely cradled close to her. "I've seen the child of my son Sidik," she gasped. "I'm so happy."

Those were her last words. Sidik was called to come back home. When he arrived in Artush, we hardly spoke a word to each other. That night, when I knelt down on the hard ground next to him, he laid down some soft blankets. He called his sister to him and scolded her. "How could you treat a guest like this without proper blankets? Regardless of what she did or who she is, she is our guest!" My sister-in-law did not answer him. Sidik also grew silent. That is how we spent the night.

Sidik's mother was buried early the next morning. After her burial, the family held a mourning feast in her honor. The courtyard was filled with tables as the neighbors and others prepared for the more than three-hundred guests. In this region the Uyghur mourning ceremony involved simultaneous singing in celebration of life and loud wails and crying for the loss of life, each person's words stumbling over the others', somehow still combining into a freely expressed harmonic, rhythmic chant.

Joining in with the others, my personal grieving began. "The people who are here have no right to take the name Tachihan between their lips because they're the ones who didn't accept her when her son was in prison. They didn't leave this woman in peace."

Slightly louder, I continued: "The mother of Sidik is also my mother. She had waited such a long time to see her grandchild. Where are you, my mother-in-law? Did you not say that you wouldn't accept any harm coming to Sidik and me? But the people do it anyway. Where are you now? The birds have flown here and have injured us with their sharp beaks."

After all of the guests had left late that night, I spoke with Sidik. "You've had enough trouble because of me, and you've also seen how the people are appalled by me. If you so wish, you can go your own way in the future and live your life. You can find an educated woman for yourself and live happily at home with her. I'm prepared to put our child into this world and provide care by myself."

The corners of his mouth lifted into a smile. "I have to agree that I really have had much larger problems with you than I could have ever imagined. But that's the way of your character. I can't change that. The only way to live with it is to accept your nature and understand it as such. So first, you should give birth to our child."

I said, "I have about ten to fifteen days left."

"After that, rest for six or seven months. Then we can decide how we want to proceed. We've lost all of our money, but don't discount our love. I'm your husband. I'm your Sidik. And my children are your children. My arms are always open for you. Only death can separate you from me. I know with certainty that you also love me."

"I'm sorry Sidik. In Canton I worked while others stopped. I kept on because what they always said about me was, 'Rebiya feels a deep love for money to support her Uyghurs. That's why she can never stop.'"

In that moment, Sidik started to again believe in me, believe in us, and believe in our dream to liberate our homeland.

Because You Are a Woman

To fight back against the most recent confiscation of our money in Canton, my colleagues and I hired lawyers to file a complaint in Beijing. For eight years after that, we received the same answer to our demands for justice: an investigation was in progress. Then we gave up.

In Urumqi, I reopened my sky-blue store in the bazaar. In thirteen days, I had again taken in about two-thousand yuan. After the birth of our son Mustafa on August 1, 1983, I stayed home with our newborn infant. From home, I worked on expanding my business beyond Urumqi throughout our Uyghur nation. In our land, it was common to be given two nicknames: a good one and a bad one. My bad nickname referred to flight: a woman always on the run from her home, her husband, and her children. My good nickname came from the Persian language—*djahangir*, a person who continues onward regardless of the end result.

My intention to gain recognition from a people of several million was not easy to put into practice. But soon, the Uyghur people began to hear the name "Rebiya Kadeer" and to accept me. Until then, all Uyghur women had been convinced of their destiny to stay at home, cook at the stove, and nurture their children. Young women who left the home after marriage to do business were considered to be vulgar and without morals. After I had managed to make a name for myself though, other women began to believe that they too could also achieve meaningful work.

THE COMPETITION AT THE BAZAAR had gotten so fierce that I began looking for new possibilities. I decided on a variation of my existing concept: retail and wholesale combined. I also had to offer more goods to more customers at lower prices.

When I first started, I was happy if I sold a pair of shoes or a shirt in one day. Now I had a hundred pieces of fabric and a hundred pairs of shoes on display. Merchants from near and far sought me out in order to purchase twenty or fifty units wholesale. I had fostered their trust in me.

The other resources, they had decided, did not have enough experience in trading or instincts for what retail customers wanted to buy. I was also well known for being able to acquire quality wares at inexpensive prices and bring them to market through a distribution network I had formed.

At one point, a colleague of mine went to Shanghai to acquire new merchandise. Among the items he found was a particular jacket. It caught my attention at first sight. It was made of an inexpensive synthetic material with a delicate black and white dotted pattern. I thought that this garment could be worn by farm wives just as easily as by businesswomen. Immediately, I advised my colleague to sign a contract with the manufacturer for forty of these jackets.

By the time the first delivery of jackets arrived, I had designed a suitable matching black skirt and had it manufactured by a local seamstress. When the outfit was complete, I distributed it at no cost to respected ladies in society, including college instructors, civil servants, and politicians' wives in Urumqi, Artush, Khotan, and Kashgar. I did this because the women in our homeland had a peculiarity about them. If ten or fifteen ladies in the same place had taken a liking to a particular item of clothing, the rest of the women in that place would also buy the same article. They strived to dress in uniformity. It took only a few of my female role models to like the skirt suit to make it highly fashionable for practically all Uyghur women.

Of course I wore this same outfit myself. My acquaintances in the bazaar complimented me on how good the clothing looked on me. For the next delivery, I increased my order to two-thousand jackets.

My colleague in Shanghai was sworn to secrecy about our transaction details, suppliers, and transporters. Upon the delivery of the two-thousand jackets, I supplied inventory to a few other women's clothing dealers as well. They had the option to pay me up front or after the sale of the jackets. In a short amount of time, I had sold one-thousand garments.

Soon dealers from other cities came streaming into Urumqi to purchase the jackets wholesale in large quantities. By then I had lowered my wholesale price to half of what it had been; in essence, I was passing my volume savings from the manufacturer on to my wholesalers. In a short amount of time, I had sold one-hundred-thousand jackets.

But one day, to my great distress, a shopkeeper on the other side of the street began selling a jacket remarkably like my own. Also, she told me that she had two-thousand pieces in stock. I immediately confronted my colleague in Shanghai but he vehemently defended his honor and the vow of secrecy we had made. We already knew that many Uyghurs had been urgently searching for the manufacturer of our jacket. Together we surmised the inevitable that our one factory amongst thousands was finally discovered by the others.

I quickly sold the rest of my inventory, about one-thousand pieces, for less than the wholesale price but still made a profit. Then I informed my Shanghai colleague that we were ending the jacket trade and instead moving into discontinued remnants of silk and synthetic fabrics. I had found these gems at manufacturers I had visited in my previous travels. Most of the remnants were printed with flowers in different colors. For this enterprise, I invested all of my earnings. I wanted to do this business only once, and as profitably as possible. Besides, I already knew in advance that other merchants would copy me as soon as they were able to.

Among the fabrics that my colleague had acquired were some high-quality weaves. Most of them however, were slightly damaged. Women who liked such clean, sharp colors however were quite happy with these fabrics, flawed or not. And besides, a good seamstress could largely work around or conceal many fabric flaws. Almost immediately, wholesalers from other cities again besieged me and purchased large quantities of these fabrics. Sidik, recognizing that I was concentrating deeply, let me work in peace. I suspect that he also did not want an argument about my persistence or what sometimes truthfully could have been called my stubbornness.

News of the bazaar's success traveled fast, and soon many Chinese merchants established competing bazaars in Urumqi. They offered huge quantities of clothing and other merchandise that were far superior in variety and assortment to ours, and at lower prices. In truth, it was not a fair fight. The Chinese easily acquired and transported imports from Shanghai and Canton whereas the Uyghurs were stopped, robbed, and beaten for those same operations.

Not only had it become difficult for my countrymen to earn a living, but it also had become increasingly clear that the Chinese government had in place a *de facto* policy prohibiting Uyghurs from ever gaining positions of economic influence.

For me, it was unappealing to copy other people's work and I had no interest in repeating what I had already done. I was attracted to what was new. So it became a period of transition for me. During this time,

Sidik and I took every opportunity to be with our children. We had hired a nursemaid for the little ones. I was always in contact with the older ones and sent them money regularly. Kahar had also moved to Urumqi so that we could be closer, and he even started his own business. I had brought Reyila to Urumqi as well while my second-born daughter Rushengül was studying to be a teacher at a nearby university.

During this sabbatical, I contemplated my next venture and discovered my interest in building construction. So naturally I decided my next business would be in real estate development.

ONE DAY, MY SIX-YEAR-OLD DAUGHTER Akida came home with a tear-stained face. She wrapped her arms tightly around me and put her head on my shoulder. I asked her, "What happened my love?"

Sobbing loudly, she told me that her classmate's mother had been burned to death baking bread at home. It was said she had accidentally fallen into her oven—a traditional kind for us, one similar to a Spanish beehive design; five feet tall and five feet in diameter. I was immediately suspicious of the circumstances of her death. In addition, her three children had become orphans, as they had already lost their father in an earlier uprising against the Chinese authorities. Teachers as well as students came to me to ask if I could help the orphans in any way.

Akida's classmate, Honzohre, was a seven-year-old girl; the middle brother, Tayir, was ten; and the oldest brother, Turjan, was twelve. Through a Chinese forced relocation, or, as Uyghurs experienced it, banishment from our home towns, the widow and her three children had become refugees from Kucha and ended up housed in barracks in an immigrant neighborhood of Urumqi. That particular part of town had little Uyghur community support and was mostly a settlement for Dungans and other Chinese. I also learned that ten-year-old Tayir had suffered a bad head injury during a much earlier street fight and had sustained permanent brain damage.

I offered to take the children in. However, it became clear that Turjan, the twelve-year-old, did not want to stay with us and by the next morning had disappeared from our apartment. After searching everywhere, I found him in a sadly impoverished Dungan settlement. His shirt hung down nearly to his knees and his ragged pants dragged in the dirt. He was so thin that practically every limb looked more like a bamboo shoot. But I could see that he was a handsome boy with a straight nose, well-formed features, black hair, and white skin. Yet he was still just a boy—a boy filled with fear.

It was well-known that the neighborhood gangs preyed on orphans like Turjan and resorted to kidnapping young boys from unsuspecting families. The gangs would then train these boys to be thieves or drug dealers. I had to forcefully pull Turjan out of this slum.

But he insisted on returning there again. I wanted to pull him away from danger once more, but this time I asked him to come with me. Turjan looked at me with wide eyes. One tear spilled, but he wiped a second one away before it revealed itself. He looked at the ground. "Mrs. Kadeer, nobody's ever kissed me on the forehead before—only you.

"If I stay here, Tayir will be safe. And then when I'm a grown-up, I can take care of him. They said that if I go with you, they'll murder my little brother. They want to make him a drug dealer too. And they also want Honzohre. Though I get something to eat every day for doing their business, I also get beaten like this—"

He lifted his shirt and showed me his back: it was covered in wounds, bruises, and slashes from beatings. He begged me to talk to no one about this and I agreed completely.

He also showed me burn marks on his legs where the gang members had extinguished their cigarettes.

"When did the burns happen?" I asked.

"When my mother was still alive."

"Did your mother know about this?"

"No."

"Were you at home every day then?"

"No, every five days I would go back to my mother. I never told her that they kept me. She might have found out about these people though because she said she wanted us to move away. We were out when she fell into the oven."

According to reports, she had been found with her feet protruding from the oven.

I said, "Come on, let's go to the authorities."

But that made Turjan scream hysterically. "No, please not that. Otherwise, I'll kill myself. Don't you know the police are in on it? I see how the gangs drink with them every night."

"I'm not afraid of these people. I'll destroy not just one of them, but all of them."

But Turjan dropped down before me and clapped his hands open and shut in prayer to beg me, saying, "Please, no." For three more days, I tried to convince him to come with me and also to find out what kinds of activities he was being used for. But he did not reveal anything more.

Three months later, Turjan disappeared. I sent people after him several times but finally went out on my own to find him. The Dungans I spoke with told me all kinds of lies about how he had gone away. I filed a report with the authorities and insisted that they start a search for him. Seeming bored with such a task, they told me they would work on it.

Tayir, meanwhile, spent his days in our apartment. Sometimes he would act normally and other times completely irrationally. Every day when I came home from work I would discover that he had driven my husband half-crazy. He smashed out windows and relieved himself next to the toilet or in the hallway.

Sidik had reached his breaking point. He was so upset that he could no longer even grade student exams at home without being disturbed. "This child needs special medical care. Care that we can't provide. We should admit him to a home where they can better look after him."

"I love you Sidik." I leaned my head against his shoulder while caressing his hair.

"I love you too Rebiya. Sometimes he's just fine, but sometimes he needs so much medical attention that I don't know what to do to help him."

I had become fond of Tayir, and it would be difficult to give him up. But I too had come to realize that despite our strong efforts to integrate the child into his new environment he needed acute medical attention that we could not provide him by ourselves. Finally, we decided it best to support his stay at an orphanage. I visited him there once a week with Honzohre. The relationship between Honzohre and Tayir was strong and intimate—more so than I had experienced even among my own children. When I would amble sleepily down the hallway on Sunday mornings, Honzohre would already be sitting there, freshly combed, with a little package in her lap waiting for us to go see her brother.

No Uyghur had yet dared to take a major step into the real estate market, but I considered life to be a challenge and saw good prospects in the field. In the middle of a project to expand a mosque with an adjoining apartment building, some Uyghur developers came into financial difficulties. Seeking relief, they were in negotiations with the *bingtuan* to lease the ground floor to them.

I asked the developers, "Why do you want to give the ground floor to the army? You could do much better by selling it to me."

The developer looked at me. "Really? But we owe the *bingtuan* three-hundred-thousand yuan. If you can take over the debt, we'll do business with you."

I immediately paid off the debt with the *bingtuan*. For this act alone, the sixty holy men and businesspeople involved in the project praised me to the heavens. Then, for one-million yuan, I rented the first two floors for a period of ten years. Over that time period, I proposed to pay installments at a certain rate every year. Within the retail space of about seven-thousand-square-feet, I installed one-hundred-and-fifty small shops. My plan was to lease out each of these stores to merchants. I also invested three-hundred-thousand yuan into remodeling the floor plan.

When the last nail had been driven into the new renovation, the developers responsible for the building asked to meet with me. They explained that they would not be able to lease me the two floors after all. The reason for their sudden change of mind was that I was not religious enough, that I did not wear a headscarf, and that I danced. They could not allow a woman like me to enter a building that also housed a mosque. As a suitcase filled with money was moved toward me, they explained that they had leased out the floors to someone else who was reimbursing me entirely for my payoff to the *bingtuan*, as well as my remodeling expenses.

It was impossible for me to hide my disappointment. "A short while ago you were praising me and now you're showing me the door. This part of the house of God, which you wanted to turn over to the occupiers, I brought back to the Uyghur people. But you would rather give these floors to the Chinese who caused your fathers and mothers great pain. You didn't take me seriously because I'm a woman. But don't forget that your wives and daughters are women like me. You don't comprehend that in this same moment you are also insulting your wives and your daughters.

"To tell an untruth is a sin. You're lying to me in this holy place—a place where you're meant to liberate yourselves from your sins. I'm thankful to God because He did not allow me to work in this holy place with you. You've simply calculated for yourselves how much money you'll make with this bazaar that I've built for you. That's why you've taken it away from me."

I grabbed the suitcase with the money and quickly walked away.

STILL AGGRAVATED BY THE TURN OF EVENTS, I finished up at the bank after having deposited all of the refunded cash. As I went out, I noticed an entrance gate to a two-storey shopping center where Chinese people sold vegetables and flour. I was pulled as if by a magnet through the passageway that led into a large square. It looked more like a garbage dump than a shopping center. There was plastic, glass, scrap wood, and burned garbage everywhere. A strong smell of decay hovered in the air. No one had lived there for quite a while since it was labeled as "bourgeois" and targeted for devastation during Chairman Mao's austere Cultural Revolution.

The area encompassed about ten-thousand-square-feet total. Single-storey houses on two sides of the square sat vacant; some of their front doors, barely hanging on hinges, swayed occasionally in the light breeze. It seemed to me that God had led me directly to this pile of rubble. I imagined for myself just how beautiful this could be if it were cleaned up. The square was centrally located between important parts of town through which many Uyghurs passed. Back out on the street, I asked the first public security officer I found who was responsible for that location. He directed me to the land registry office.

Then I spoke to the head of this office about whether I could be permitted to rent the location and set up an open-air market. He asked, "How can a private person do such a thing?"

I ignored his sense of disbelief and instead explained, "Of course, the first thing I would do is clean up all of the trash."

"Are you going to pay in cash?"

"Yes."

A few minutes later, the office head, three of his Chinese colleagues, and I were walking together toward the square. When they passed through the gate, it took their breath away. They took only a quick look around and then fled outside. They whispered to each other quietly, laughing at the same time.

"How much money do you have?"

"I have forty-thousand yuan." I thought *why on earth did I not say ten-thousand?*

"If you give us forty-thousand yuan, you can have this location for three years. But let me remind you that you'll have to clean up this garbage at your own expense."

Back at their office, the Chinese officials immediately began writing a rental contract. Though I read and spoke some Chinese at that point, when it involved a contract such as this one, I requested and was granted the assistance of a Uyghur to translate for me. I signed the contract and wanted to get the money from the bank but the officials insisted on accompanying me for security reasons. When I handed the money to them, they thanked me. I could see from their faces how excited they were.

I had negotiated into the contract that if the government voided our agreement—that is, if another agency overruled that office's authority to lease the square to me—I would be entitled to a full refund of my forty-thousand yuan plus any other damages. I had also negotiated that city residents be notified effective immediately that they would no longer be permitted to dump their refuse in the square.

I told Sidik about my new plans, and he was worried. Still, he let me keep going, and I considered him to be a great source of support. My children—especially the older ones—completely backed my plans. Twenty-three-year-old Kahar had no doubts: "Mother you can achieve anything."

The next day, I led six business colleagues to "my garbage dump" and explained how I wanted to build a bazaar there. They just shook their heads. I had actually expected that they would want to participate in the enterprise. But they were not at all interested.

One of them joked with me, "When a woman earns money she immediately loses control of herself. It's good for you to experience a situation like this one. So Rebiya, I'm not upset that you led me here and wasted my time. You're, after all, only a woman."

I learned something from that first guided tour. For the second one, before I invited any other potential investors, I hired people to help me clean up the entire square. I was so busy doing this for three weeks that I had no time to come home. Instead, I set up a small office nearby and slept there overnight on a couch.

There were about fifty Chinese and one Uyghur couple working at the large vegetable shop at the entrance to the passageway. The government had assigned nearby apartments behind the shop to these people. I heard their constant whispering as I passed by: "She is a Uyghur . . . a crazy woman. A nutcase."

Every so often men from the land registry office would stop by and take note, seemingly with a look of satisfaction that no apparent progress was being made.

But I was comfortable with how things were going. There is something about me that I have seen in others as well. I am a person who once convinced of something will commit myself to believe in its success. For example, before I start something, I live with it in my mind. I make plans and prepare myself internally for success. When I get started with the work, I am so focused on it that nothing else exists around me. That is why the Chinese later gave me the nickname "The Adventuress."

Finally the clean-up operation was completed. We had installed new roofing. We also hammered together fifty crates so that merchants would be able to lock up their wares at night. Sidik had only come to visit the "garbage dump" once, right at the beginning. He had shaken his head in dismay and had not come again until the end of the clean-up work.

My planned bazaar was a topic of conversation all over Urumqi. People were sure that this time I had gone completely out of my mind. Until the end of the clean-up work, I gave no one else permission to set foot in the square. In total, thirty-six full dump trucks had hauled away all of the garbage and I had invested into the restoration one-hundred-and-seventy-thousand yuan. At that point, everything was shiny and new.

I had the entire square, the shops, and even the entranceways decorated with colorful synthetic flowers. It was quite possibly the first time since the Cultural Revolution that we Uyghurs had seen such decorations in our homeland.

My first official invitations for a tour went to the men from the registry office.

"Really great! Really great! *Zhen bang*!" they said, repeating their praise constantly and timing their words rhythmically to bowing with their hands before their faces.

Another expressed himself quite sincerely: "We regret that we didn't believe in you as you believed in yourself."

"*Zhen bang! Zhen bang!*" echoed through the passageway as they left.

After that inaugural tour, I invited sixty business colleagues to take a look, but only two came. And the opinions of both were frustrating. They said things like, "No customer is going to come down this long passageway. You've really cleaned this square up nicely. Maybe you can even move into one of these apartments here. Now go home and cook for your husband."

I did not want to waste any more time with such fools. I sought out the local women's association. I knew that the association had kept colorful fabrics in its storage halls since the beginning of the Cultural Revolution. So I requested politely that they sell these fabrics to me. But they did not take me seriously.

At this point I felt I had no other choice but to negotiate directly with the fabric factory outside of the city. I asked the managers if they would sell to me at inexpensive prices remainder fabrics that they had not been able to sell at all. In total, I acquired fabrics with a retail value of 1.6 million yuan at a discounted rate of six-hundred-thousand yuan. We arranged monthly deliveries of ten-thousand yards at a time. Their last condition that I had to fulfill was giving a one-hundred-thousand yuan security deposit. Once we had concluded our agreement, I closed my eyes and said quietly, "God, I've undertaken this business in your name."

The first collection of fabric was transported to me in a small truck. When I unfurled the rolls, I could not believe my eyes. They were of the highest quality, purest cotton, in a variety of colors and styles.

Rather than abiding by the monthly delivery schedule, I immediately had the next ten-thousand yards of fabric delivered. I thought to myself: *you never know, this deal might be over tomorrow.* When I put the third shipment of fabric in storage, the Chinese factory manager praised me. "You've really done well." I think he was especially happy that I paid him every time with cash in hand. "Can you take another twenty-thousand yards?" he asked half-serious.

I hired thirty poor girls from the neighborhood as workers and sent them to all corners of the city in search of inexpensive fabrics. If they found some, I would negotiate the price. The biggest profit gains were to be made from the large government stores. In one of these stores, the manager told me that their synthetic pearl necklaces were slow sellers and that he would like to negotiate a close-out agreement with me. We reached an understanding and I purchased his entire inventory of necklaces.

I CHOSE MARCH 8, 1987 as the bazaar's opening because it was International Women's Day, and I had named my business the Women's Bazaar.

In order to publicize the event I recorded five advertisements, which I arranged to have played at several markets around town: "Welcome, women of all nationalities. Please visit the Women's Bazaar opening on March 8th."

I wanted to sell some of the items for less than their value, and others for only one or two yuan more. My thirty employees were spread throughout the bazaar. One boutique had shoes, another fabrics, a third clothes, and so on. There was no special ceremony planned for the opening day. I knew that the most important businesspeople would not attend anyway.

At nine o'clock in the morning, the first visitor of the day stumbled in—a beggar. I gave the poor man ten yuan. He looked around thoughtfully and said, "Looks like you don't have any other customers." Then he bought three white pearl necklaces with the ten yuan.

After ten o'clock, a few women wandered in as a group. I hoped that they would buy something immediately. I unfurled before them with great care some rolls of fabric. When they saw the floral patterns and shimmering colors, they were thrilled. Each of them bought about twenty yards from me. They also put several strands of pearls into their shopping baskets. When they had spent all of their money, they said they would go home to get more.

Many businesswomen who had heard my advertisements came to see the bazaar just out of curiosity. Once they noticed how inexpensive my offerings were though, they began to buy merchandise on a grand scale. Immediately I had to set a store policy that no more than ten yards of fabric at a time could be sold to any one person. In a short time, masses of people were pushing around each other, all of them wanting to load as much as possible into their bags.

One of the ladies whispered to me in an embarrassed tone, "I'm from the women's association. Please, please give me more than ten yards." I expressed my apologies that she could not purchase more than any of the others.

Journalists from television stations and newspapers arrived. They interviewed me, asking why I had opened the Women's Bazaar and what my goals were.

That very same afternoon, the stations broadcast their footage. When Sidik turned on the television immediately upon getting home from work, as was his habit, he was so startled that he dropped his glass of water. I had not let him know about the opening because I wanted to see how everything would turn out first.

There I was, flickering on the screen amidst the tussle of shoppers, with my hair disheveled and my *doppa* askew. No matter which station he switched to, he saw my face on nearly every channel. They announced, "As one of the first successful businesswomen in China, Rebiya Kadeer has dropped the prices on her merchandise just for International Women's Day, and in so doing has offered a wonderful present to the women who are celebrating this occasion."

They even showed before and after pictures of the bazaar: a stinking garbage dump before, and a flood of people shopping in the bazaar afterward. Once Sidik saw me on television, he came to the bazaar immediately. When he arrived, we embraced joyously. He told me, "You're a wonder my wife."

My colleagues meanwhile were less surprised by my business success, but rather more surprised that I had become the first businesswoman in our Uyghur nation to appear on television. Furthermore the business colleagues who had previously declined my offer, now all wanted to lease several shops from me.

There were also a lot of poorer women who had contacted me and expressed wishes to open a store of their own at the Women's Bazaar. To thirteen of them I offered free retail space and promised to provide my support and advice on an ongoing basis. I reserved the last two stores in the inner courtyard for myself as locations from which I could conduct my wholesale trade.

Spurred on by my success, I immediately made new plans—or rather, revisited unfinished ones: to gain a strong footing in the construction and real estate business. I was already a millionaire. But in 1987, I really began to increase my profits.

IN THE BEGINNING, our neighbors in the Chinese vegetable store cursed us bitterly, but after I succeeded in opening the Women's Bazaar, they really got angry. One evening, some of my female workers came running to my house, saying, "The Chinese neighbors have left excrements on the cupboards and have filled the square with trash again."

We all rushed back to the bazaar together. On the street side, on a wall that we had painted white, they had drawn a donkey. There was a man sitting on him facing the wrong way. The writing underneath said, "The Uyghurs should leave and go look after their donkeys. Otherwise, we will not let them live in peace for the rest of their lives."

I instructed my employees to get rid of the mess and to mop the floors clean. However, they were to let the picture of the donkey remain on the wall as possible criminal evidence. Then I went to find the manager at the vegetable store.

"Is it possible that we could become good neighbors? After all, if my business runs well and we have a lot of customers, it'll only benefit you in helping you sell more vegetables."

"No. We can not be friends."

"I think you may have answered too quickly. Please think it over once more and I'll come again in two hours."

A few minutes later, he—along with others—came to me. They totaled about a few hundred. The one Uyghur couple who worked there was in the front of the pack with their Chinese co-workers and other angry militants standing behind them. All of them were wielding sticks. I approached them, then stopped with my legs firmly planted wide. At that, the Uyghur couple threw down their weapons and started to turn away. But one of the Chinese grabbed the woman by her hair; three other Chinese grabbed her husband and demanded that he fight with them against us.

There were a few hundred of us as well, including from the Women's Bazaar three saleswomen and another nine men who worked as our security guards. In addition, word had spread fast and more of our own supporters quickly rallied with us. When I saw how the Chinese had treated their own colleagues, the Uyghur couple, I could no longer control myself. It was not really my style to resolve conflicts with physical force. I was aware that we lived among the Chinese and that by now they were more numerous than we were. But we Uyghurs are fearless, even when we are up against a larger power. That had already been proven time and time again throughout history.

"The boards over there are our defenses," I said to our group. "Take them!" I was the first to reach for what was normally just a board on which we would hang our merchandise. Our employees and our street brigade grabbed their own defenses and engaged with fierceness, all of us screaming primal battle cries that came up from the depths of our guts.

I had intended to allow only a little scuffle. But this fight got more intense, much more so than I had anticipated. We Uyghurs quickly overpowered our adversaries. I was honestly afraid that someone would be critically wounded among the Chinese, so in order to prevent anything worse from happening, with my arms spread wide I placed myself protectively between the fallen Chinese and us victors. I told my employees to hurriedly lock the front and back gates to the bazaar to prevent any more of the Chinese neighbors from running away. Most of the rest of them simply surrendered, with their arms raised. A few of the Chinese men were still rolling around in pain on the ground, and, regrettably, two of my security guards continued kicking them. I stepped in between, telling them, "Stop it! They aren't fighting back anymore!"

The next day I spoke again to the vegetable store manager. I demanded first that he apologize to the Uyghur couple whom he forced into the brawl. The manager was decidedly repentant and even promoted the Uyghur man to a higher position of responsibility.

In the end, we came to an agreement. We would not get in each other's way any longer. Over time, our neighbors actually became nice. If our customers came into their stores, they would get priority service and receive only the best quality. As far as my own personal development in embracing non-violent resistance, I was disappointed in myself and took to heart the lesson learned. I have never repeated that poor judgment again even to this day.

AS SOON AS A UYGHUR GAINED INFLUENCE within the population, the government promptly assigned the person an appropriate title. It was actually a ploy intended to gain favor with the Uyghur through propaganda that would eventually benefit the government. Of course their ploys were well disguised through appointments to influential positions which also carried privileges. If the Uyghur complied well with the government, he was baited with even higher and higher positions.

Through my successful establishment of the Women's Bazaar, I had demonstrated to many people that I was capable of significant achievement. One result was that the members of the government elected me to a five-year term as a representative in what is officially known as the "National People's Congress from Xinjiang Uyghur Autonomous Region." Among all of the citizens of all of China, I was offered an honorable distinction, along with three others, as a "Flag Bearer of the Eighth of March"—International Women's Day.

My duty as a delegate consisted of expressing the wishes of our population to the government. But because the rulers negated the wishes of our people, in actuality delegates were simply there to pacify their fellow citizens.

My overall reputation rose with the achievement of these positions, yet some of my countrymen accused me of aligning myself with the Chinese government. Trying to outsmart the Chinese ploy of elevating my status was indeed a perilous path to walk—some watched expectantly for signs of my capitulation.

After I was awarded the "Flag Bearer of the Eighth of March" title, several high officials governing our Uyghur homeland invited me to their houses. They were quite accommodating and let me know that naturally they would recommend me for even higher positions. But they would be keeping a close watch on me as well. And, amidst the sparkling wine and fancy hors d'oeuvres, they indicated that I should also keep my distance from my nationalistically inclined fellow Uyghurs.

In those days I held a false belief that the officials governing our homeland were well intentioned but simply did not understand the true problems of our people. I thought that in my new position as a delegate it would be a straightforward task for me to better inform them. That is why I tried sincerely each time to describe the problems in detail. For example, I told the officials that the Uyghur students in the southern region sat under an open sky and wrote on slates with a piece of coal, while the Chinese students' learning institutions in the southern region had modern equipment. At the end of this discussion, the politicians applauded and I thanked them for listening. Looking back now, I am embarrassed by my own naiveté.

On another occasion I asked a group of politicians where all of our natural resources were going and why the Uyghur population became poorer day by day.

In reply, one Chinese politician slapped his thigh, snorted loudly with laughter, and said, "I can see that you're very impatient. But you're a noble woman—that's why we have hope that we'll be able to work with you. Of course we'll try to solve these problems you speak of. And if we can't solve them ourselves, then we'll pass them up the chain of command. Everything you've brought to our attention is correct. But you can't let that be known outside. We know that you feel sympathy for your people. However, as long as there remains instability among you, we can't even begin to speak of normal development. That's why you have to work especially hard for Chinese–Uyghur friendship: to bring the Uyghur people in line."

"Great. I'm compliant. But we have to make efforts to solve the problems I've mentioned."

"Of course," he replied, as a look of satisfaction spread across his face.

As night fell, Sidik and I sat in our living room and discussed with our friends the state of affairs in our land. The writer Abdureyim Ötkür and the poet Osmanjan Sawut were among those present. These two were the same men I had envisioned as true leaders for our people, together with Sidik, before our wedding.

Abdureyim Ötkür seemed particularly insightful: "In our nation, it's impossible to stand up against the government. As soon as we rise up, we'll all be killed. We also have no way of organizing a massive demonstration. That would bring genocide upon our population. Whoever wants to take the leadership role on behalf of our people has to go abroad and work from there. Between 1949 and 1972 alone, I was a witness to sixty major Uyghur rebellions. Three-hundred-and-sixty Uyghurs lost their lives and another half-a-million were locked up in labor camps. I haven't the strength to lead; my eyes have already seen too much."

Osmanjan Sawut breathed a heavy sigh and said, "There is really no point in us reaching for public leadership now. That would be no different from leaping to our deaths. We must work secretively. I can't be a leader. Neither can Sidik. He can give advice and he can support you every step of the way. I think it rests in your hands alone, Rebiya, because you're a woman who has the character for it, the stamina, the will, and the ability to be alone in the world."

Maybe my friends were right in their thinking. The idea of going abroad however was not something I had even remotely considered.

MY BUSINESS COLLEAGUES were awakened by my recent success and began building new shopping bazaars for themselves. So naturally I wanted to move forward and achieve something even better. I planned to build a department store with an apartment complex behind it for the employees to live in. This arrangement—employment with adjoining employee housing—was a fairly common practice for larger businesses and factories throughout China.

Up to that point, in all of China, a private individual had not yet been permitted to build even a two-storey structure. Only single-storey houses were allowed. The government was the only one authorized to construct anything beyond one-storey. The idea of a private individual undertaking such a project was in itself revolutionary. I did not tell Sidik anything about my intentions. I knew that he would be worried about me.

On short notice, I invited roughly two-hundred businesspeople to a meeting at the Women's Bazaar. We had prepared a traditional cup of tea and provided a comfortable chair for each of them for my brief presentation.

I told them, "If you would like to, you, that is, we, can earn a lot of money together by building a large department store that would accommodate up to one-thousand shops offering merchandise of all kinds."

One attendee responded, "I'm simply one man from Kashgar. For my part, I certainly will not participate in your offering. Your talent is indisputable. But the government doesn't allow private individuals to construct such buildings. Yes, you've been successful with the Women's Bazaar; however, surely you don't believe that you can discard all reasoning and be so bold as to convince yourself you'll have success at everything."

Others' opinions echoed his. No one among the invited colleagues wanted to build a seven-storey building with me. Such being the case, I went ahead on my own. First, I prepared all of the necessary paperwork. With this in hand, I needed to find a way to meet with the Chinese Vice Governor of the city of Urumqi, Zhang Guowen. His office was located amid other governmental buildings situated in a large area similar to the more well-known Tiananmen Square in Beijing.

A simple Uyghur woman like me could not conceivably gain a meeting with the governor. The only way then for me to have an appointment was with a little creativity.

A girlfriend of mine was employed as a government secretary. I explained to the guards at the gate that I was going to visit her. She was surprised to see me, but even more surprised when I told her the true purpose of my visit. Hesitantly, she led me one floor up, pointed toward the governor's office, and then hurried downstairs back to her work.

A kindly attendant in the anteroom greeted me. I briefly described the matter of constructing a seven-storey building by myself, causing him to shrink back in fear and seemingly seek escape from me by going into his boss's office. Of course, the governor wanted to see this crazy woman immediately and had me brought in. When I approached his desk, he grinned at me, showing off two rows of strong, yellow teeth.

He said, "Do you even know what a skyscraper is?"

"I—"

"How can you possibly do that by yourself? Do you actually, seriously, believe it is even possible?"

"Gov—"

"It seems that you've lost your mind after all of the praise you received for something . . . a bazaar or something. I believe you're a Uyghur. Is that true?"

"Yes."

"Then you should work in a field and sip your soup out there."

"You're right Governor. Because it's only the people who have sipped their soup in the fields who have the strength and ability to construct the building that I propose."

He angrily told his attendant to escort me outside.

But I did not go home. Instead, I went directly to the central government building to pay my respects to Chinese Vice Governor of the Xinjiang Uyghur Autonomous Region Huang Bo Zhang who was responsible for—among other things—city planning. But the guards denied me access to his building. For an entire week, I was unable to pass by these guards. So I decided to corner Vice Governor Huang Bo Zhang when he was outside of his office, perhaps walking on the street or possibly when he drove by in his car.

Finally, a black limousine approached. Out stepped a stocky man I immediately recognized as the famous Huang Bo Zhang. Apparently he saw me coming toward him too and jumped backward as if in horror, lifting both of his hands in the air with his palms out, telling me to stop moving. So I stopped.

I called out to him: "You're the Vice Governor of our land, why don't you want to speak to a Uyghur woman?"

He studied me for a moment. "Oh yes, I've seen you on television."

I handed him the documents with plans for my proposed building.

I said, "You seem to be a nice man. I request that you please sign here."

"What? What is it you want?"

"I want to buy a piece of land to build a house."

"You? A woman? You want to build a house?"

"Yes."

He signed the documents without even reading them: "It is permitted that Rebiya Kadeer constructs a building." Then brushed by me probably having assumed that I wanted to build a small, one-family house.

Then I went in search of the Governor of Urumqi, a Uyghur named Yusuf Eysa. I told him of my conversation with the higher-ranking Huang Bo Zhang. "It's been confirmed that I'm allowed to construct this building. And so now Governor I request that you too please sign the necessary documents."

Governor Eysa seemed petrified. "Can you really build a sky-scraper?"

"Yes."

He scratched his head, looked away for an instant, then signed his name to the paper.

My next step was to go back and visit again Chinese Vice Governor of the city of Urumqi, Zhang Guowen. He leafed through the documents. When he realized that two other higher ranking men had already given their signatures permitting construction of my proposed building, he just clutched his head in disbelief. Then he telephoned Governor Yusuf Eysa for confirmation that he himself had in fact signed the documents. Again he clutched his head. "This is crazy." Muttering obscenities quietly to himself, he scribbled his signature underneath the other two.

The next day, I visited Governor of the Xinjiang Uyghur Autonomous

Region Tumur Damavat. He was a Uyghur and officially the highest ranking authority in the land. Unofficially, he was a puppet of Chinese Communist Party Secretary Wang Lequan.

Tumur laughed with amusement when he saw all of the signatures. He said, "It's clear that you are not able to construct such a large building yourself, but since the others have already signed, I will too."

At first the land registry office and various other departments, one after the other, each gave me their blessings when I presented my documents. Every time I walked through the halls of the ministry for construction, the employees would run from their offices to have a look at who was behind this proposed building.

Next, I sought out future investors starting with the businesspeople who had rented shops from me at the Women's Bazaar. I offered them commercial space in my new department store—all of them eagerly wanted to participate. Now, with the necessary documents in hand, the mood among my colleagues had decisively tipped in my favor.

My earlier pleasantries with the bureaucracies turned out to be short-lived. I soon discovered an additional, longer, more difficult bureaucratic path before me. In order to construct a high-rise building, many smaller bureaus also needed to give their stamps of approval. Although at that time I was pregnant with my third child with Sidik, these critical governmental procedures required me to work with the bureaucracy myself, though it is something I would have much rather delegated. For many of these additional stamps, I was required to revisit the same bureaus at least fifty times, waiting and waiting for my turn. Each stamp of approval peeled away only a fraction of the bureaucratic layer. I thought that anyone else would have given up on this project just because of the bureaucracy alone.

Perhaps sensing my frustration, a Uyghur man in the city planning office pulled me aside quietly and said, "The department manager doesn't like it if you show up here every day without even some presents."

The next time I brought five-thousand yuan with me. It was possible that he might report me for attempted bribery, but I had to try something to hasten the process. I wanted to build this building more than anything else in the world. I waited in the office until all of his colleagues had left. Then I tentatively approached his desk.

I said, "I've brought five-thousand yuan with me. Please help me get this matter taken care of as soon as possible."

He quickly opened his desk drawer. He said, "Put the money in here," and after I had done so, he closed it just as quickly.

"Give me your documents."

I laid the papers on his desk, and a moment later he had signed every one.

The city planning office was next on my list. The process at that stage was for their office to mark on the construction renderings green lines that would indicate the perimeter of my lot. I had already been there at least twenty times, and each day, the department head told me to come back tomorrow.

Following the last eye-opening experience, I asked him straight out, "How much do you want?"

Grinning at me, he said, "One-hundred-thousand yuan."

I refused to pay him that amount. I had actually considered the amount to be at most five-thousand to ten-thousand yuan. Finally we settled on thirty—thousand yuan. He wanted his money immediately, but I only had five-thousand yuan in my purse so I rushed home and came back with the rest. When I arrived back at the office though I was told that he had already left for a meeting.

The next day, I arrived early in the morning and handed the department head the thirty-thousand yuan wrapped in a newspaper. He assembled three people to draw the all-important green lines for me. He asked me to wait and then left.

Right up until lunchtime, his three colleagues sat around a table and played cards together. They did not even glance at my papers. When I had finally reached the end of my patience, I called upon the one sitting closest to me to please look at my documents.

He responded, "How can we work on your case with nothing in our stomachs? You have to invite us for lunch first."

Grinding my teeth, I accompanied the men to a restaurant, then afterward bought them cigarettes and brandy as they demanded. Back at the office, they drew one of the six lines and said, "We will do the rest tomorrow. But let's meet first again for lunch at that nice restaurant."

The next day they again drew only one line.

Effective immediately, I was required to feed them throughout the day. Despite my schedule, they also required that I stay in the office all day and sometimes into the night. They rarely let me go home to my children after the workday, but instead usually demanded that I be present during their drinking binges.

If their wives were present, I had to sit at their table. Otherwise, the men would direct me to a separate table, somewhat aside from theirs. While they gorged themselves on expensive wine, brandy, meat, and all kinds of delicacies, I made do with soup. I made every effort to hide my feelings by presenting the most bored expression I could muster. I was in a mental battle with myself to repress my constant, overwhelming rage.

But I also thought to myself *If I can't take the pressure, then I haven't earned the right to aspire to such a lofty goal.* I reflected on the experience I had gained when my merchandise was confiscated in Canton. That experience had made me tougher. Later when the government had confiscated all of my money, that experience also made me tougher.

On the tenth day, the three men finally completed marking the green-lined perimeter.

Now it was time for the red lines.

I had to go to three important addresses to get placement of the building marked in red within the now green-lined lot perimeter. With the increasing importance of the departments, the amount of the bribes automatically increased. The big money was not paid for the construction of the building itself, but for the bribes involved.

These officials instructed me to give certain leather jackets as presents to their friends and relatives. Each one of these jackets cost four-thousand yuan. In addition, some of their wives also wanted clothes and jewelry. Then there were their children whose wishes I was also supposed to satisfy.

One day all of this became too much for me. Until then I had taken this abuse without a single outburst. But when I got home that day, I started to cry loudly and uncontrollably.

My husband encouraged me: "You've already accomplished so much. You just have to be a little more patient until the construction starts. The bigger the hurdles you confront, the bigger the problems associated with them. You just have to keep believing in your goal."

I leaned my head on his shoulder.

He added, "*Kam namus.* No honor. The Communists are people with no honor."

Those years before construction began taught me to either ignore dead ends or to find my way back out of them. A number of the merchants who were tenants in the Women's Bazaar had grown quite rich by that time. Some of these protégés had also become my best backers. But there were also many Uyghur investors who lost their patience and wanted their money back. As soon as one had left us though, another one would ask to join in.

WE WERE STILL LIVING in our small university apartment. In order to work with fewer disturbances, I had set up a small office with a telephone for myself in the Women's Bazaar which I also occasionally used as a living space. I had an assistant and a secretary working for me. Next door was the salesroom, which contained mass-produced goods for my wholesale clients. I managed to get by with this arrangement until the hot summer arrived. Maybe all of the pressure with my building plans had gotten to me.

Or, maybe the air in our apartment was weighing us down from the heated stench coming from the public toilet directly next door. We were able to survive the location only because of the hope that we had been placed on the list to receive a new apartment. When the multi-storey university employee building was finally finished that summer, our hopes rose even higher until we were told that there was no apartment available for us after all.

The rector of the university was an Uzbek; his deputy was a Tatar named Rawup Ewsi. After all of our hopes were dashed, I lost my temper. Angrily, I went to see the university rector and complained that apparently we had not been taken into serious consideration during the distribution of the new apartments. "The only reason my husband agreed to our awful living conditions is because his work means so much to him. It is completely irrelevant which new apartment you give us. The only thing that matters is that we don't live next door to the toilet anymore!"

He responded, "But you're just a housewife and I've heard that you're buying and selling things." The standing of businesspeople among these intellectuals was even lower than that of thieves. "You must also not forget that you're the wife of a man who sat in jail for a long time."

"You've no right to speak to me like that! Why do you and the Chinese want to keep us Uyghurs down? If you were a Uyghur, you wouldn't be sitting in that chair today. You didn't get to your position through your talent or intellect. You got there because the Chinese handed it to you! Who are you to speak to me in this way?"

"Please, please, be quiet. I can't listen to you any longer," as he waved me out with his hand.

When my husband heard about this he got very upset with me. "That's my workplace! You've only made things worse. That wasn't necessary!"

A short while later however, the deputy rector did make a small apartment available for us on the second floor of the new apartment building. He told my husband, "Sidik, regardless of what wishes you have, please come to me yourself next time." He also warned: "Your wife needs to watch what she says, especially about the Chinese government. Otherwise, she'll find herself in jail for a long time."

Do You Hear the Rooster Crowing

There was a big demonstration in Urumqi on May 19, 1989. The impetus for this march, besides calls for democracy and freedom, was a book that was shocking to many Uyghurs. The book was about the sexual practices of Muslims, and had been published in Shanghai. The Dungans and the Uyghurs demonstrated in front of government buildings together. The relationship between our two ethnic groups had been full of animosity for ages, but on this issue regarding our commonly held religion, we demonstrated together.

The entire population of the provincial capital city was on edge. Pupils, college students, and even officials joined in the demonstrations. My husband was teaching a class at the university when his students got up to join the demonstrations. There was only one young man left in the lecture hall. Though this young man also wanted to join the others, Sidik requested that he stay behind as a witness to prove that my husband had not taken part in the demonstrations.

They waited about two hours before going downstairs together. Just as Sidik was leaving the university, I rode up in a taxi and called to him to get in. My husband got in the back seat with me. There were perhaps as many as thirty-thousand people demonstrating in the streets. Chanting loudly, they demanded the end of the Communist dictatorship. I wanted to join them, but Sidik was against it and directed the driver to my office. Once we got there, I got out of the taxi, very frustrated. I was angry at Sidik and at the same time disappointed that he was so fearful.

After the Chinese officials ignored the demonstrators, the crowds next moved to the Communist Party's headquarters. Finally, the government responded. But their response was with brutal violence against the demonstrators. Many were arrested. The government's response also continued beyond that one episode. They initiated a new period of strict political measures that included more arrests—some people were sent to prison, others to labor camps.

The first inquiry from the *An Chuan Ting* to the university chancellor was whether Sidik Rouzi had also taken part. They had already interrogated and tortured the demonstrators and also locked up those named in the interrogations. When I heard about this, I understood how right Sidik had been to not take part in the demonstration.

Less than one month later, on our television screens we followed the events of the Beijing Tiananmen Square massacre. We excitedly supported the protesting Chinese college students in their demands for human rights and freedom of opinion. These values were the same as ours. Still, it was completely beyond our belief that the Chinese in power would have their own children gunned down.

I predicted that Communism had come to its end and that we had won. But Sidik was much more reserved about the toppling of the regime: "Don't rush things. You weren't in the streets yourself. You don't know exactly what's going on in Beijing."

We did not see on our television much about the tanks that were sent in. For example, we were never shown the now-iconic image of one young man standing directly in front of a tank, halting an entire column of tanks lined up behind in single file. An announcer simply reported that students had lynched and set fire to a Chinese soldier. That horrific image was shown, but with no explanation of the surrounding activities leading up to the soldier's death.

In our media, the official death toll was one-hundred-and-eighty-six demonstrators. The true number of victims is still unclear today. It was years later, when I was living in exile in the United States, that I first learned the details of the brutal crackdown at Tiananmen Square.

The massacre was Deng Xiaoping's response to the students' demands for democracy. The government's pathological strategy was that it first needed to bludgeon all opponents before it could hold civil discussions with them. Even though the way the Chinese government violently ended the demonstrations was disheartening, we could feel that something was changing in the world. There was an atmosphere of transition. Deng Xiaoping stepped down from his position as Chairman of the Military Commission five months after the bloodbath. Jiang Zemin replaced him.

IF ONE WANTS TO ACHIEVE GREAT THINGS, one has to overcome resistance and take a leap of faith into the unknown. The old apartment buildings behind the Women's Bazaar were scheduled to be torn down and replaced with new ones. The government had allocated new apartments elsewhere for the Chinese residents, including the employees at the vegetable store. But the vegetable store owner refused to move after the government's notification and directed his employees to blockade all demolition and construction efforts.

I asked for help from the city Office for Public Order as well as from other authorities, but nobody was willing to confront the noncompliance of these people. So there was nothing left to do but for me to go myself and speak with the vegetable merchant in his office. To support my arguments that it was in everyone's best interest to demolish the old apartment buildings, I put together a large basket of groceries for him and included two-thousand yuan in an envelope. Admittedly, I was a little fearful about this attempted bribery. After all, the vegetable merchant also held a position in the Communist Party. But I could have spared myself the worry. He not only took the money without hesitation, but demanded an additional three-thousand yuan. Surprised that the whole thing was so simple, I counted out the three-thousand and he telephoned his people.

After the apartments had been leveled and the vacant lot cleared for forthcoming reconstruction, I called upon the same two-hundred business people I had invited once before as potential investors in my Women's Bazaar. This invitation was not for the bazaar however, but for a much larger undertaking. This meeting was for an inspection tour of the vacant lot where I had decided to construct my seven-storey building. It was also to show them a miniature model of the high-rise department store concept. The model sat elegantly on a long table where I directed everyone's gaze. Then I began my brief presentation, once again suggesting their participation in the enterprise.

The next morning, one by one, these colleagues began to come by and leave their financial deposits that committed them as partners. They just laid the bills right down on the table without even asking for a receipt. In total, I received four-million yuan, about twenty-five percent of the planned expenditures. Up to that point, the bank had not considered me for a loan. My holdings were founded largely on the capital and trust of my Uyghur friends. There were even some who had generously entrusted loans to me without any interest.

I negotiated with the construction companies to pay eight-million yuan up front and the rest over the next five years. I calculated the total costs to be sixteen-million yuan. In the end, with a more truthful accounting that included the bribes, total costs were nineteen-million yuan.

CHASING AFTER BUREAUCRATIC rubber stamps and the daily grind of dealing with deceitful people really used up a lot of my strength. But real estate development was certainly not the end of my bureaucratic entanglements with the government.

This other matter was much more personal. The government had remained steadfast in carrying out its abortion policies, although not as severely as they were in carrying out other laws. In my seventh month of pregnancy, the birth control bureau took notice of me. Until then, I had been able to hide my pregnancy relatively easily, as had also been the case with my previous pregnancies. With my ninth pregnancy though, I directly experienced this area of policy as it applied to my own body.

Officially, non-Chinese ethnic groups living in a city were allowed to have two children; in the countryside, three were allowed. In every village and neighborhood, there were groups of five or six women, mostly Chinese, but admittedly also some Uyghurs, who worked as public servants on behalf of the government's birth control policy. In essence, they reported on expectant mothers in their area. In Urumqi alone, there were approximately ten to fifteen birth control bureaus, with adjoining medical rooms in which forced abortions were often carried out.

Without an authorization to give birth, a woman was not allowed to have a baby delivered in a hospital. Therefore, only a handful of pregnant women who had already given authorized birth once or twice would risk going to a clinic for what would likely be their last authorized birth. If they became sick during their pregnancy, they would not go to the doctor at all out of fear their authorization would be revoked.

To manage this situation, many pregnant women went to different cities to give birth, staying one step ahead of the bureaucracy. The strategy was to have an authorized baby in one city and another authorized baby in a different city, with the hope that the bureaucracies remained uncommunicative with one another. Regardless of where women went though, there were birth control bureaus in every location.

In a sense, it was essential for the parents to involve these bureaus in the birth of their children because if a couple kept a birth secret from the bureaus, the babies were denied recognition as citizens by the government. From their very first breath—and for their entire lives—these children did not exist according to the state. Often the parents would also lose their jobs as punishment.

"The ladies from the birth control bureau came by again," my husband announced as I closed the door behind me after a long day at work.

"Oh, Sidik, it doesn't matter whether I'm at home for them or whether I'm at the land registry office or the municipal building—or anywhere. They follow along at my heels."

There were times when I hid in the shadows of a house entrance, turned suddenly into an alleyway, or left a shop through the back door. They would dress normally to blend in with regular pedestrians, so I never really knew how far I could get before they'd be onto me again. But as soon as they caught me, their attempts to "educate me ideologically" would lead to heated verbal battles.

My response was always, "Uyghurs never needed birth control. Our land was always able to accommodate many children. It's only because of the government's planned influx of Chinese here that there are these population pressures. You yourselves made these mistakes. Your birth planning policies are just you loading your problems onto our shoulders."

Once, on the way to my office, I could see from a distance that female officials were waiting for me at the door. I waited in hiding nearby for two hours until they finally left. The next day, four ladies surprised me at my desk at noon. They were accompanied by armed police and demanded that I go with them to the hospital.

I slammed my hand on the table: "I'm nine months pregnant! My child has almost come into this world! How can you still want to kill it?"

The birth control officials treated me somewhat gentler than other Uyghur women, but with well-known individuals like myself, they could not make any exceptions. In their minds, they reasoned that if they managed to abort even Rebiya Kadeer's child, then they would be able to argue more easily with other pregnant women to do the same. That day they allowed me one more reprieve.

The next day, I was busy with construction details. I was at the city planning office in the afternoon dealing with more paperwork, when officials from the birth control bureau suddenly came up behind me and forced me to go with them to their offices. There, another official told me that the next day they would open my stomach and remove my child.

At that very moment, I felt a pulling in my lower abdomen. "Oh

God, the contractions are starting," I said. My fourth daughter came into the world on December 25, 1989.

The next morning, a young Uyghur nurse came to my bedside. She comforted me for several moments but stopped suddenly and said, "Mother Rebiya, you're in bed number eighteen."

"What's eighteen?"

"You have to leave quickly with your baby if you want to save her."

The nurse held a tray in her hand. On the tray, five syringes were laid neatly in a row, their stems pulled back ready to plunge the liquids they held into bodies. But whose bodies? The nurse mumbled to me to sit up. It was then I could see that one of the syringes had the number eighteen labeled on it. This syringe number eighteen was meant for my daughter—and they planned to kill four other children too!

With a jolt I tore the tray out of the nurse's hands. She cried, "No, you can't do that! They'll fire me."

I told her, "God will provide you with a more suitable place of work."

Without thinking further, I ran outside into the corridor. There were other female patients lying there and a visitor standing next to one bed. I quickly took money out of my handbag, pressed it into the visitor's hand, and begged him to go to my home and get my husband.

Then I rushed into the next room which was the nursery where the newborns were, and began to make a lot of noise. I called out loud the numbers inscribed on each syringe, yelling that these infants were meant to be killed. Mothers raced into the room with horrified faces, pulling their babies from the cribs.

A minute later, the director of the hospital arrived. He grabbed my arm and pinned it to my back. Sidik arrived at the same moment, accompanied by many men. My child and I were saved as we hurriedly left the hospital.

The punishment for this unscheduled birth and my reaction in the hospital was the demotion of my husband. His salary was downgraded by two levels, and he had to pay a two-thousand yuan fine. My fine was fifty-thousand yuan.

We named our daughter Kekenos in honor of a magical bird in Persian mythology. It was said of this bird that it could live five-hundred years.

At the time Kekenos was born, a forced abortion usually required the husband's permission. But within a few years, the government expanded the powers of the birth control officials so that husbands did not need to give their permission. After that, there were incidents of women being forced onto the operating table against their will. Doctors also performed forced sterilizations on men and women alike. When babies were born in spite of the planned birth regulations, doctors received orders from the office for birth control to murder the newborns.

THE ACCOMPANYING APARTMENT BUILDING for the department store employees and associated business people had been completed in 1990. There were fifty or sixty apartments, of which we sold some and kept the rest for our staff. I had planned to reserve the entire second floor for my family. It would be the most modern apartment in all of Urumqi, complete with five bedrooms, a living room, a kitchen, a bathroom, and a toilet.

Visitors were taken aback by the large size of the apartments. Even Rawup Ewsi, the vice chancellor of the university, came by to tour the apartments. After he had walked through room after room, he honored my service at the next university meeting:

"We should all learn from this woman. I'm sixty-six-years-old, and I've lived to see both the Russian and the Chinese Communists. After our wonderful Communist Party came to us, I've experienced for the first time a woman who has been able to have a vision and carry it out: to construct a beautiful, spacious apartment building and take her husband with her. In the past, this same woman scared me. But now we are good friends. I'm proud of her. And I'm also proud that this woman's husband works with us."

Sidik still could not believe that he would finally have his own office and a huge library at his disposal. He said, "You've given me everything I wanted. You've given me the children, provided an office space for me, and built this apartment.

"But in my eyes, you've still not yet arrived at peace with yourself. I feel like I can't reach you. If you would just live here together with me, we could be the happiest family in the city. Rebiya, I'm worried about you building all of these businesses. Maybe the time has come when you can finally stop. Don't you want that?"

My silence and his after this question told us both what we each knew of the other's answers. So neither of us pressed any further. Despite our mutually agreed upon non-responses, I could tell how happy he was and how happy our children and relatives were. Kahar, Rushengül, and Reyila moved in with us. The other children visited us whenever they could.

Soon thereafter, I planned the construction of my department store that would reach for the skies. Until then it had existed only as a miniature model and architectural renderings. When the backhoes finally arrived, more than five-thousand people came to the ribbon-cutting ceremony at the construction site. They carried clothing or money in their hands as offerings. Some of them led sheep on ropes.

Yusuf Eysa, the Uyghur vice governor of the city, cut the ribbon with a pair of scissors and then made a speech: "I see how many people have come here today. My heart hardly fits inside my chest at the sight of so many Uyghurs. An indescribable strength is almost helping me to fly. Yes, I feel like I'm flying. I understand our people. Finally, its heroine daughter has stepped onto the world stage. I can see that all of the dreams, all of the expectations—yes, even the future of our people rests in the hands of people like her. I too will learn from the strength, the courage, and the spirit of Rebiya Kadeer. This is a huge building that's taking shape here—the first and the biggest in our history. In it we can see how well the Communist Party, the central government, the people, and also our autonomous region have developed together."

His speech increasingly deteriorated into an advertisement for the Communist Party. I believe he felt he had no choice in making it.

"Rebiya Kadeer has supported the reform policies of the government. I request of you, please, now support Rebiya Kadeer. Today's politics are excellent; they allow one to gain wealth. Please take advantage of this opportunity. Thank you."

The crowd applauded. It was an uplifting feeling to look into all of those happy faces as it became my turn to step forward to the microphone. I said, "Thank you. We shouldn't praise ourselves too much. But we should believe that all people can achieve great things. You've seen it today. This dream has become a reality. At first everyone assumed that this was only an idea—and a crazy one—that could never be successful. So starting today, we want to make stronger efforts to break open doors that have been previously closed to us."

A cheer of joyful agreement roared out from the crowd. "I believe that your joy and my joy have the same roots. Let's enjoy this common feeling. But I also want to tell you two more important things today.

"First, every human being should choose to go into battle because that's the most valuable life and death there is. Please don't misunderstand me. I haven't said that one should die in battle with weapons.

Uyghurs were once a people with a remarkably developed culture. Now we've lost almost everything and the main responsibility for correcting our course remains with us. If we want to change something, we must take the initiative and do it together.

"Second, regardless of whether you're begging because you're poor or you've fallen to the ground because you're weak, in all cases you must send your children to school. Our children are the future of our people! Thank you."

The crowd chanted: "Rebiya! Rebiya! Rebiya! Rebiya! Rebiya! Rebiya! Rebiya!"

I had actually intended to host a dinner at a fancy restaurant, just for the honorary guests such as the vice governor. In fact, the tables were already reserved. But it seemed inappropriate at that point. What about the other five-thousand people who were shouting my name?

So instead of leaving for the fancy restaurant, Yusuf Eysa and his entourage suggested that we all stay and dine together with the people. Lambs were slaughtered and soon thereafter meat was steaming on the table. The aroma of pilaf, our national dish, wafted through the air.

People sat everywhere and had fun. My relatives, my children, my husband, and my father all sat at a long banquet table. Everyone had come, even people who had demanded bribes. They would have rather gone to the fancy restaurant, but when they noticed that Yusuf Eysa and his friends were also staying, they could hardly insist upon it. They smiled—as always—making it impossible to see their true feelings or their true faces.

Musicians played drums, fiddles, *tambur*, and flutes. Others danced and sang. When I looked around, men, women, and children were waving to me from the rooftops and balconies. It was so crowded that they had not been able to find a spot below.

My husband edged close to me and whispered, "Did you see the people? You've won them over."

I replied, "You said they'd be difficult to win." At that I couldn't control my laughter. Then he laughed too. On that day, I had the feeling that the pain within our people was being released through song, dance, and joy.

Yusuf Eysa shook my father's hand and told him, "You can be proud of your daughter."

"Yes, my daughter is quite unusual. Sometimes she makes us cry; sometimes she makes us laugh. She never leaves us Uyghurs in peace."

Poet Osmanjan Sawut, who had taken a seat with us at the table, recited one of his works which included the lines: "Do you hear the rooster, who crows in the early morning? Wake up! The dawn has come. Do you hear the rooster crowing?"

DESPITE OCCASIONAL MOMENTS OF JOY such as at that opening ceremony, our people were leading a desperate fight for survival. There was much unrest, and it did not take much to incite us. In Baren, which is located south of Kashgar, a rebellion broke out on April 5, 1990. There had been many rebellions since the end of the Cultural Revolution, but this one was the biggest. I sincerely hoped that it would lead to victory. The government called for an emergency meeting.

Especially in the southern part of our homeland, which unlike the rest was not yet dominated by the programmed influx of a Han Chinese majority, the Uyghur population was fighting for independence from China.

In the meeting hall of the People's Congress, the Chinese leader of the military commission made his position clear, saying, "We will put down the rebellion with weapons. We have to act immediately. Otherwise, it could be that we lose Xinjiang. We may even bomb the area with planes to prevent foreigners from backing the rebels in Baren."

My heart ached when I heard this. First of all, his point about foreign support was an absolute fabrication. There was no support from either the Soviet Union or the West. These rebels were just simple people, mostly farmers, protesting in the streets. Still, the government reacted with a heavy hand by declaring the entire Baren region be closed to foreigners.

In Urumqi too, Uyghurs were calling for independence. The television news shows reported on the "sinful plan of a handful of nationalistic extremists" who wanted to achieve "the partition of our great motherland." These "separatists" were purported to have conspired with foreigners for decades and to have published reactionary literature.

After work, I called a secret meeting with friends in Sidik's office. We considered how to best handle this situation. Initially, we unanimously agreed that it should not only be one village but all villages that would rise up in unison. But in the end, we concluded that this plan would be impossible to organize. We valued the courage of the people in Baren. Yet we worried that there would be many casualties there and elsewhere.

Fortunately, Baren was not bombed. Still brutal but less so than incoming air raids, the Communists sent in two-hundred-thousand infantrymen to crush the rebellion. There were about one-thousand Uyghur deaths for us to mourn. The government now seemed more fearful though as a result of the rebellion. They were afraid that Uyghurs would see as role models neighboring countries on the verge of independence resulting from the imminent collapse of the Soviet Union—role models such as Kazakhstan, Uzbekistan, Tajikistan, and Kirghizistan.

Immediately, brutal measures for the "encirclement of the criminals" were implemented. Our people were branded as "nationalists" trying to destroy unity between the Chinese and other ethnic groups. The number of arrests increased dramatically throughout the entire Uyghur nation. Hundreds of schools were closed. Thousands were forbidden to work. Tens-of-thousands of people were subjected to searches and scrutiny. Officials and youth under eighteen were no longer allowed to pray. Birth control mandates were more strictly enforced. Uyghurs permitted to work had an even harder time finding employment. For example, among sixty employees at a company in our own nation, at most ten would be Uyghurs. The rest of the employees would be Chinese planted in our land to grow free and to take all of the sunlight, while we were to wither away underneath them.

AFTER THE FIRST TENTATIVE ATTEMPTS at reform in the vanguard of *perestroika* and *glasnost* under the general secretary of the Communist Party of the Soviet Union, Mikhail Gorbachev, the Union of Soviet Socialist Republics was dissolved in Almaty, Kazakhstan on December 21, 1991. It was replaced by the Commonwealth of Independent States in which all of the Central Asian Republics were decreed to be sovereign nations.

The Uyghurs were happy that our relations—the Kazaks, Uzbeks, Tajiks, and Kirghiz—had their own nations again. Our people had great hopes. Maybe we Uyghurs would get our own recognition back again too. But the Chinese officials in power thought otherwise.

To quell any hope of independence, the government's propaganda program began in earnest almost immediately. We were told over and over that the Chinese and Uyghurs were inseparably bound together by a mutual interdependence and that our Central Asian neighboring peoples were no longer our friends. The official media also reinforced the idea that the declarations of independence in the neighboring countries had been flawed decisions.

Those who did not agree with this viewpoint lost their jobs. Even elementary school children were forced to parrot the official Communist Party lines to their teachers.

The level of Chinese government intimidation was daunting. For me however, the regained freedom of our neighboring friends indicated that we too had a chance. Our neighbors and Uyghurs formed one cultural community as evidenced by thousands of years of heritage together. Our history, our language, and our architecture were examples of this common culture.

With the collapse of the Soviet Union, new business opportunities opened up for me as well. If a businessman came from the Central Asian republics, he first looked for me. It had become fashionable among Uyghurs to wear Central Asian and Western-looking clothing. Our neighbors in Central Asia, however, were interested in Chinese dishware and inexpensive fabrics.

So I started to revitalize my business contacts in China. My initial plans were to have suitable fabrics manufactured specifically for Central Asia. I was eager to travel to the neighboring countries myself. For a Chinese merchant to take this kind of business trip would have been easy. But as a Uyghur, I had to factor in a waiting period of up to two years. Some of my colleagues, in order to speed the process for their own travels, had paid fifty-thousand to one-hundred-thousand yuan in bribes.

In my position at that time, it would have been unwise for me to try bribery, largely because the government under Chinese Communist Party Secretary Wang Lequan had decided to deny me a passport. One approach I thought about was how the only Uyghurs who easily obtained passports were those who worked as translators for the Chinese. But for me to pose as one of these translators would mean that the real translators would be put at greater risk.

Several times I asked some of the highest government officials why they did not want to provide me with travel documents, although they themselves were constantly touting the opening up of commerce to the West. Patience, I was told. I should have patience.

IN 1992, MY DEPARTMENT STORE OPENED. On the seven floors I had created selling space for about one-thousand merchants and their employees. Despite being very eager to participate, many of the merchants had yet to learn anything about business. My first priorities for mentoring were women and poor people.

I had spent much of my wealth on bribes. But I had erected my department store with the financial backing and trust of fellow Uyghurs. There was no building like it in Urumqi. It was the first, most modern, and most beautiful department store in our entire Uyghur nation, and it became an important business nexus in the region. The same Uyghur businesspeople who at first had not wanted to invest even ten-thousand yuan in a shop now patronized me, inquiring whether I could find a place for them in my department store at this late date. Some of their wildly inflated offers were as much as fifty-thousand yuan.

If I had accepted these many offers from the top bidders, I would have been able to pay off my debts quite quickly. But I did not want to engage in those sorts of deals. They were unethical and unsettling. As word spread about these wealthy bidders, the businesspeople who had leased their shops from me in mutual good faith became frightened. Many had arranged their leases at a time when the building was still more of a dream than a reality. Rumors were swirling that I would now demand a higher rent, which caused them great worry.

I appreciated that once they had invested with me, their money had been unavailable to them for nearly three years with no return whatsoever. Expressing my gratitude to them was more important to me. In order to clarify this matter, on opening day I gathered them all in the main restaurant and told them, "Your help means much more to me than you could imagine. Today your retail shops become yours. How much rent do you want to pay for them? Please decide for yourselves."

The merchants started to loudly negotiate prices. The lowest offer was five-hundred yuan. I raised my hands slowly to calm them down. "Okay then," I said, "you can have each of the shops for three-hundred yuan."

The people shouted in joy and threw their hats into the air. I yelled above the uproar: "And next year and the year after I will not ask for any rent at all from you!"

At that, the merchants clapped their hands and cheered. Then they opened their shops. Moments later, my department store opened to thousands of visitors who flocked into the building. They were like a huge wave that came rushing toward us. What an amazing first day!

MY DEPARTMENT STORE was not simply as it appeared. It would change the course of my life. The building introduced me to Uyghur people in the way that I had always hoped it would. It embodied my strength and my spirit of resistance against opponents. At some level, it encapsulated my existence.

It was a symbol of a Uyghur woman achieving what even some men were not able to accomplish. Regardless of what those in power think about the building today, and even if the government destroys it soon, it remains eternally in my spirit.

Nothing I built afterward came close in significance to this department store. Other Uyghurs built many such buildings after me—ones even taller than mine. But the people in the street told stories about my building. They spoke about the difficulties I overcame during its construction. Those stories, as is the Uyghur tradition, were told and continue to be told as metaphors for teaching lessons in life about will and self-determination.

The government itself later constructed its own modern bazaar built in the Turkish style. It cost them many millions of yuan. They even imported businesspeople from Kashgar and from other Uyghur provinces across our nation. They filled their shops with Uyghur wares, Uyghur traditional clothing, Uyghur delicacies, and Uyghur everything. Yet the local people were unshakably faithful to our store.

My building today, looked at from the outside, appears somewhat dilapidated. The government will not allow it to be renovated, but many people still stream into it. Uyghurs have grown to believe that it will bring them good luck. They recognize each other by their faces, by their language, and by their love of their land. In that building, they feel at home because outside of it they have become a minority in their own country.

In this regional capital of Urumqi, my department store became the center of commerce. Many outside merchants attempted to gain a foothold there. But after a short while, they gave up because nobody would buy from them. The Chinese government had also experienced great distress because of this building. For me, despite how many blessings it brought, the building may have also hastened my arrest and subsequent eight-year prison sentence.

REBIYA KADEER DAYS BEFORE 1999 IMPRISONMENT   *Urumqi*
Photograph courtesy of Amnesty International

UYGHUR WINTER PANORAMA   *Kanas*
Photograph by Ricky Ng

SEA OF CLOUDS   *Tian Shan*
Photograph by Sharon Tsui

SAILIMU LAKE GRASSLANDS   *Bortala*
Photograph by Huang Tao

VAST SANDS   *The Great Gobi Desert*
Photograph by Nicolas Monnot

SUNSET *Ili River Basin*
Photograph by Feng Xu

UYGHUR MELODY *Kashgar*
Photograph by Choi Chi Chio

UYGHUR BOY   *Kashgar*
Photograph by Choi Chi Chio

TWO UYGHUR BOYS   *Kashgar*
Photograph by Gabriele Battaglia

IN MEMORIUM TO THOSE LOST UNDER MAO ZEDONG

MAO ZEDONG STATUE   *Kashgar*
Photograph by Anonymous

UYGHUR WOMAN ROTATING THE WHEEL OF LIFE   *Hetian*
Photograph by Choi Chi Chio

UYGHUR CONTEMPLATIONS   *Kashgar*
Photograph by Choi Chi Chio

UYGHUR IN A STORM   *Taklamakan Desert*
Photograph by Nicolas Monnot

UYGHUR WISDOM *Kashgar*
Photograph by Raffaele Valobra

OIL FIELD   *Jungar Basin*
Photograph by Nicolas Monnot

STREET SWEEPER *Urumqi*
Photograph by Daniel Chanisheff

The Wealthiest Woman in China

$\mathcal{F}$or two years I had been waiting for my passport which would allow me to travel to Central Asia. It made no sense that the government would bar a successful businesswoman from engaging in commerce with neighboring foreign countries, especially while they permitted others to go without delay. Because my stature within the community was valued, the government's unequal treatment in denying me travel created discord among Uyghur high officials. The government finally relented in the face of serious complaints from these officials, and a passport was at last granted to me.

My first trip consisted of a long drive through Kazakhstan. My driver, Rehmutulla, and I brought several athletic-wear outfits with us that were already popular among Kazaks. Many Uyghurs, Chinese, and others became millionaires within a short time in Central Asia in part because demand had been severely suppressed under Soviet rule. When open market imports such as athletic wear became available, they were like manna from heaven.

Even in this atmosphere, however, once again Uyghurs lost their riches to the Chinese government. When the Communist Party saw how quickly we had become wealthy, they became uneasy. Soon thereafter, we were forbidden from receiving import or export permits. Only Chinese merchants were allowed to continue conducting business through their own firms. One concession they did allow us was that we could continue to do business with Central Asian government-related firms, but only if we shared ten percent of our profits with the Chinese government itself.

The government continued to harass us with various laws that applied only to us. We not only had to register with the authorities before we left for Central Asia, but we also had to notify them if we were going to stay longer than they had originally authorized. The lack of a reliable distribution network in Central Asia at that time required us to drive with a quantity of wholesale goods in tow from which a merchant could then purchase on the spot. Larger special orders would be delivered separately. In essence, we were traveling warehouses, selling goods out of the backs of our trucks.

To exploit this deficient distribution system, the government levied special taxes on certain goods we brought with us, regardless of what we actually sold on the trip. To give a clearer example of the economic catastrophe this essentially created for us, a Uyghur businessman told me that he was once bringing goods to Central Asia with a total wholesale value of four-hundred-and-eighty yuan. Yet the special levy demanded that he pay one-thousand yuan in taxes. He had to stop doing business.

I strove to be the most diligent of all the merchants. I watched closely over the bazaars in the neighboring countries. I was not concerned with what the government was up to. Around every new roadblock, I found a new road. I circumvented most of the government's special taxes by building my own distribution network that substantially reduced government exploitation of my business. For merchandise that was popular, I immediately ordered huge quantities from Chinese factories and arranged for direct transport to Central Asia. I arranged for a local driver and a truck to be at my disposal in each country. Thus I largely eliminated the Chinese government's role and still continued a little business through the "old-fashioned" traveling warehouse plan.

In those days, I was the most active businesswoman in all of Central Asia. I did not break existing laws and paid the required taxes. Although most Uyghurs specialized in one category, I remained generalized. The fabric and clothing trades were only a few of the many possibilities open to me.

When I found out that there was a huge demand for scrap iron in China, I secured multiple contracts in Kazakhstan and collected iron in all forms, including old cars, retired army tanks, and junked bicycles. The Chinese government purchased one ton of iron from me for just under four-thousand yuan. Through this first scrap iron transaction, I established positive relations with the Kazak government. Thereafter, the Kazaks and I sold many more thousands of tons of iron to China.

I was delighted to hear on one occasion that there were fifty Chinese government trucks stopped at the border. Behind them, one-hundred of my trucks loaded with iron approached in a cloud of dust. While other vehicles had to wait ten to fifteen days to get through the border, the officials waved my trucks through. As the Chinese government was trucking

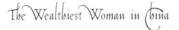
back one-thousand tons of my iron, I would have already procured five-thousand more tons before their trucks had even come to a stop.

In the first year after the borders opened, trade went relatively smoothly. With the start of the second year though, there were unfortunate changes. Locally organized gangs patrolled the main roads into Central Asia. If they dared rob the Chinese, the embassy immediately became involved. They also knew better than to interfere with merchants from other countries. But the gangs quickly realized that we Uyghurs did not have our own country, our own embassy, or our own Chinese protectorate. So they came after us. They robbed us, murdered us, and then fled—with no consequences.

Even through the borders and into Kazakhstan itself, only business-people from the Uyghur nation were targeted. To intimidate citizens, these organized gangs murdered two of the wealthiest Uyghurs. One of them was Tursun Sakal. He was an acquaintance of mine and a nice man. First they took his money. Then they slit his throat, decapitated him, and mounted his head on a plate by the road with a note reading, "We'll kill anyone who doesn't voluntarily give us their money." The second Uyghur was also decapitated.

In Kazakhstan, criminals soon attained key positions in government and society. There was a similar situation in Kirghizstan. The gangs liked to call themselves *rekit*, which is the Arabic word for "mafia." If they saw someone on the street wearing a watch, they would tear it from his wrist. If a victim went to the government to file a report, it was he—not the perpetrator—who would be locked up.

In order to work in Central Asia with the least disturbance possible, it was vital to know at least one strong mafia boss. If he let his underlings know not to bother someone, then there would be no problems. If not, the consequences would be horrific. Thus, in Kazakhstan, I found it necessary to open communications with many of these bosses. Once I asked one of them why he had become a member of the mafia. The man laughed and explained to me that he was not a member of the mafia. It was just that if he presented himself as being so, customers were more apt to buy his goods.

To MANAGE MY INCREASINGLY busy working life, I employed a large staff to help me with my itinerary of meetings, speeches, and dinner engagements. Government meetings rarely took place without me, and at home we entertained famous actors, scientists, and poets.

Every other day my image was flickering on television screens across China with such headlines as "Only because of the support of the Communist Party has this woman accomplished all that she has." Hearing such nonsense, my husband would mimic, "Most women were obedient but Rebiya Kadeer was not one of them. Only because of this has she managed to become who she is today." I was not only wealthy but I had become influential, and the Chinese government wanted to reap rewards from my position.

The decadence of the rich sometimes shocked me though. For example, a Chinese company near Shanghai invited me to dinner. The person seated next to me explained with great mystery that I would be served a delicacy that was reserved for only a select few. A moment later, the waiter rolled out a cart with a silver chafing dish. With white velvet gloves on, he lifted the lid and a monkey was looking at me. I gasped in disgust.

They had cut open his head. His brain was exposed to spoon it out. The poor animal looked as if he was still alive with his eyes gaping at me. Two men had to accompany me outside because I was so revolted and had to vomit. Full of repulsion, I returned to the hall afterward and explained to my hosts that I would not do business with them in the future. At the very next People's Congress session, I proposed to the delegates that the inhumane treatment of animals should be against the law. The other Chinese representatives just laughed at me.

When I was poor, I was sick of poverty. When I was rich, I was quickly sated by wealth. More money brought more responsibilities—but also many opportunities for investment for the benefit of other people. I felt money was the easiest means through which to teach people what democracy offered. It was only with a full stomach that one could ponder freedom.

Normally a person would be expected to feel good in such a position of privilege as mine. And sometimes I did. Sometimes I indulged, and in retrospect, sometimes I feel embarrassed by my excesses. But more often, a nervous restlessness would consume me. Every night before I went to sleep, I saw children in the streets with no shoes, even in the winter. When I saw poor people in the streets, I was ashamed of myself. When I was driven to my department store in a limousine, I felt as

though I was being insensitive to my countrymen. I thought they should share in my wealth. It all led me to feeling an increasing sense of loneliness. It became a burning pit inside of me. I began to think about what more I could do for our people. I had to help liberate the Uyghurs from poverty. I had to help Uyghur parents send their children to school. I had to help Uyghurs succeed in their vocations.

IN MANY RESPECTS, the exact same law would be applied in two distinctly different ways: one way for the Uyghurs and another way for the Chinese. Looking out of my office window one day, I watched as one of my merchants bought goods from a Chinese vendor. He had already heaved twenty full sacks from the man's truck onto the ground. Almost immediately, two officers from the taxation bureau raced up to the Uyghur like bloodhounds to levy a tax on each sack. I later found out that the amount was five-hundred yuan per sack.

The man explained to the tax collectors that his goods were inexpensive and that he could not sell even an entire sack for the amount of their tax. At that, they took him to the taxation bureau. Later the merchant reported to me that even though he had already paid for the goods and was their rightful owner, the tax officers returned them to the Chinese vendor, who also kept his payment. Uyghurs were particularly targeted for this kind of tax corruption.

The people in government also demonstrated far more consideration for Chinese businesspeople. Uyghur officers who were on patrol for the taxation bureau were reported and suffered consequences if they tried to bribe Chinese merchants. In addition, Chinese tax collectors were advised to be more moderate with Chinese, whereas both Chinese and Uyghur tax officers were unbridled in their corruption against Uyghur merchants. In its simplest terms, whoever paid more in bribes paid less in taxes.

I had gone through a considerable number of unfortunate experiences with that bureau. But the simple business owners would literally begin to quiver as soon as they saw them approaching. The tax officers were immediately recognizable: aside from their uniforms, they were the ones overly adorned with gold chains and jewel-studded rings. If they set foot in a bazaar, all of the Uyghurs would stand at attention.

Finally, after numerous complaints, the government established a bureau against corruption and bribery. The people who worked there almost immediately began to receive bribe money themselves from the tax officers. If merchants complained about the means used by the tax collectors, their shops would be shut down the next day. This happened constantly. We would see the tax officers and men from the bureau against bribery and corruption playing cards and dining together at the big restaurants. Among them were also Uyghurs who had discarded their heritage and their honor like an old coat.

Not only did the two bureaus not disturb each other, but they actually collaborated in determining in advance who would cash in from which business at which market. In effect, this was organized crime within the government.

There were also times when the head of the taxation bureau came to my department store and tried to trick merchants into reporting any of his officers who wanted to collect bribes. That ploy was an easy trap to avoid.

More difficult though was avoiding problems during his next visit to the department store when he pointed to an article that would have a visible price tag of three-thousand yuan, for example. He would ask innocently how much he would have to pay for it. If the businessman was smart, he would answer that the tax man should pay as much as he wished. Then the head of the taxation bureau would ask if he could pay five-hundred yuan. Again, if the businessman was smart, he would agree to this amount. The taxation official would praise him, "We'll apply the discount to your next tax bill."

As a People's Congress representative for our homeland, I was assigned to work with a committee named "Business and Communication with the Common People." In the grand meeting hall of Congress, I would stand and describe conditions for average Uyghur businesspeople. Each time, the Chinese chairman would thank me for my service and promise to provide immediate relief. About forty-five or fifty people would meet for discussions on the matter. Among them were the bribed officers from within the bureau against corruption and bribery. The five or six Uyghur colleagues present would always remain silent at the meetings.

They were perpetually surprised that I had not been relieved of my position long ago. They believed that anyone who had ever spoken out in the way that I did ended up in prison and died there. They advised me that it would be better to remain silent in the future, particularly since not one single suggestion I had made led to any improvements. In private however, they would pat me on the shoulder afterward for having dared to raise these issues.

Ignoring their advice, at the next Congressional session I again stood up for the interests of the Uyghur merchants. This time several of the representatives insisted that I provide proof of my allegations. So, in what I soon learned would be a catastrophic mistake on my part, I named several victimized merchants and described in detail what they had experienced. The consequence of this was that the merchants whose names I had mentioned were driven into financial ruin. When word of their fates reached me, I understood at that very moment that all of the government offices from top to bottom were not only corrupt but also working together. The businesspeople I had tried to protect would not even look at me anymore. Soon, none of the Congressional representatives wanted to hear from me anymore either. However, I decided to wake up this lazy organization and took the floor again at our next Congressional session.

I said to them, "Millions of people have great confidence in us and expect us to help them. That's the basis for us telling them that we're here to lead the population into prosperity. They're told that all they have to do is follow the slogans of the Party. But we're lying to them. I'm a Uyghur woman. I don't speak Chinese well. I only know the conditions under which our people live. Perhaps the Chinese experience a similar situation as we do. I don't know though because every time I try again and again to describe the living conditions of our population, instead of helping, you deny that these truths even exist.

"Why? That answer I already know. It's because you yourselves are among the people who accept the bribes. The common people know by now that you're lying to them. That's why in the streets Uyghurs don't speak of this body as Congress, but instead as *kikesh*. The people call us 'Political Puppets.'

"I understand now that this is a place where our people aren't taken seriously. But even if you don't want to hear it anymore—I will never stop talking about them."

A commotion slowly started to rumble, with a few shouts counterattacking me. But then things settled back down. After the meeting, many of us went together to a restaurant. On the way, several of the other representatives were conciliatory: "You really spoke well." Another said, "Wonderful."

As they all jostled for a seat near me at the dining table, one asked me, "Rebiya, why is it that we like you so much?"

By way of answer, I said, "Please don't be angry with me for telling you the truth. You and everyone else here attract those unseemly people to you and then you and everyone else here also get to pass judgment on them. Basically, you're all very similar to the criminals, with one major difference. You hold the power. You make the laws. If lawmaking were in the hands of justice, then you too would receive your punishment just like ordinary criminals."

One of them laughed aloud as though I had just told a hilarious joke: "Do you really believe that we are like thieves, whores, and murderers? That we belong to the lowest rung in society?"

I said, "You're the masters of that rung."

Then they really broke out in laughter, like a bunch of drunkards.

AT THAT POINT, THE SCOPE of my political responsibilities had been limited to our Uyghur nation. In 1992, the leadership appointed me to the National People's Congress for the entire People's Republic of China. The government had also made me a member of many organizations, and all of a sudden I was sitting at the same table with China's President Jiang Zemin and other members of the government debating current affairs.

At a grand meeting once a year about three-thousand representatives from provinces throughout all of China, certain well-deserving party cadres and financial leaders like myself who had been serving themselves as well as society as a whole through their business enterprises, gathered together in the Great Hall of the People in Tiananmen Square.

For two weeks, the responsibility of the National People's Congress was to officially release the new laws of China. There was no legislating in our sham legislative body. In reality, the Party elite dictated their agenda to us through various plenary and committee decisions.

At one of these gatherings the regime had chosen a translator for me who also served as my escort. When I arrived at the meeting hall, a Chinese official relayed a message that the President of the Beijing United Front wanted to see me for an individual meeting. The other representatives upon overhearing this shook my hand.

My heart beat fast with excitement. Even if on the inside I felt like

cheering about this opportunity, my feelings about this powerful man were quite mixed. After the first assembly, the president had not made a good impression upon me. To me, he seemed to have an unfriendly look in his eyes, and his laugh sounded dishonest. A person like that, in my mind, was not suited to be one of the central leading figures of a country.

Within the building housing the National People's Congress was a separate section for what they called *Xinjiang*. As I have mentioned previously, that was the Chinese name for our Uyghur nation, and it was in this section where my powerful host awaited me. The room was decorated with traditional Uyghur wood carvings. Carpets hung on the walls, as did a large picture of blooming fruit trees. The president stood up immediately and greeted me warmly: "Welcome, Rebiya. Come in, Rebiya."

I said, "I'm sincerely grateful that I'm being received by the President of the Beijing United Front. I feel very honored."

In that moment, I felt a little ashamed of the negative things that I had long thought about this man. Even though I did not feel comfortable, I tried my best to look cheerful for him.

There were eight of us in the room. At my side sat the translator and the three men who had brought me to the president. Then there were also three other men from the president's staff sitting next to him. The president crossed his legs. We all turned toward him. Presumably, I had been invited into this gathering because they had plans to elevate me into an even higher position. But first they wanted to test me.

After we had exchanged a series of niceties and established a polite atmosphere, the president began to ask me questions:

"Which laws in your region do you think are bad? What are the largest problems in your region? What injustices exist among the high officials in your region?"

My first thought was that at last the Chinese leadership was seriously interested in finding appropriate solutions for the problems that Uyghurs faced. I was permitted twenty minutes to answer the president's questions.

One after another, I sketched out the main problem areas, including the behavior of high officials such as Wang Lequan, Chinese Communist Party Secretary of the Xinjiang Uyghur Autonomous Region. Without hesitation, I cited corruption, the tax burden, and the large unemployment rate. I spoke of how, in contrast to our own people, Chinese inhabitants had no problem finding jobs. I also said that even Uyghurs with higher education degrees had limited chances to find work.

I continued, "You said yourself that there should be elementary education for all. Then please don't demand such an expensive school fee from the families. They can't afford it.

"The Chinese settlers are ruining our land. They chop down our trees and deplete our forests. They dam and divert our rivers so that our own fields are drying out. Please revisit your population settlement policies. Please put a stop to the massive Chinese migration into our region.

"Furthermore, our impoverished farmers should have free hospital treatment. Thank you."

The president gave me an encouraging look and said, "Please keep going."

I continued, "Thank you. You take so much petroleum and natural gas from our land and speak of our immeasurable reserves as second only to Saudi Arabia. Yet in our villages and cities, we don't even have water pipes. It is well known that you have the wealth transferred to the interior.

"I ask that you please educate and send abroad at least one-thousand Uyghurs using the income derived from our natural resources. Unfortunately, I can't expand on everything in detail in the time that has been given to me today. There is simply too much to say. Maybe you aren't aware of these conditions. I just wanted to inform you of them. Thank you."

He told me, "You've given me a great amount of interesting information. An improvement in the Uyghurs' standard of living is among our most important tasks. You can believe that we'll concern ourselves with the problems that you've spoken of. Our reform policies have just started. You must have already noticed that in comparison to earlier times, things are already much improved."

One of the president's staff underscored, "Yes, you've become very wealthy in the meantime. You would never have been able to sit here together with us if you had stayed poor."

The president added, "If anything is weighing you down, please report it directly to the central government. Please don't take this outside to the common people. We trust you."

"Thank you," I replied. One of the most powerful men in China had

made a good impression on me. Back in Urumqi, I told Sidik about the conversation.

"It's wonderful that you described so many problems to him. But look here, you forgot this problem, and that problem, and this one here. And why didn't you speak more forcefully to him? Don't be so trusting, they don't always have our best interests at heart."

"Please. I had only twenty minutes. But I hope that he'll take what I said to heart and help our people."

At that, Sidik put his hands to his head. "Oh, that's what it is. After you saw this man you lost your mind. Don't take yourself so seriously. They only want to calm you down. This is only a game."

"Sidik! One day when you've succeeded in meeting the President of the Beijing United Front then you can tell me everything you said!"

He laughed, saying, "They will never receive me."

Soon after my husband would prove correct in his assessment.

CHINESE COMMUNIST PARTY SECRETARY Wang Lequan of the Xinjiang Uyghur Autonomous Region ordered me to his office. He criticized me bitterly while wearing a permanent grin on his face that I would have loved to wipe off. When he talked, his face wobbled. Every word he spoke contained undertones of his brutality.

Although he was Chairman of the Communist Party in our land, he did not bother to learn the Uyghur language—and neither did the other Chinese living in our nation. It was only one more example of the oppressive, dismissive policies of the Chinese occupying our homeland. Two translators assisted us.

He told me, "You always talk about 'my people.' Remember one thing. They're not 'your people' and it was we who introduced you to the central government. I think we made a big mistake in doing so. If you continue to say bad things about us, then you'll experience more problems than you can imagine.

"Don't forget that you're just a simple businesswoman. We have tried to support you. But when the opinion of a person is not in accordance with the central government, then we are prepared to introduce all manners of educational measures. If you don't control yourself, you too will experience such treatment. And one other thing—we believe your husband is an unsavory person."

Until then he had never before mentioned Sidik in any conversation. Although by that time I could speak Chinese well enough to have been able to respond to him directly myself, I instead spoke Uyghur and incorporated some Chinese words into my speech.

I said, "When you speak to me, you have no right to mention my private affairs, especially not those concerning my husband."

"Your husband was in prison for a long time. You've been influenced by him. We only want to protect you, Rebiya. Think about your future." His reply was nonchalant, as though he were talking about the weather. I knew that his underlying motivation was to try to nudge me toward divorcing Sidik and thus freeing myself from my husband's influence.

I asked him, "Did I take bribes? Have I killed anyone? Have I distributed pamphlets against you in the streets? What mistakes did I make? I've rightfully informed the president about the true conditions in our land. If we want to maintain stability in the region, we should first improve the standard of living for the population. I don't have any big expectations for this government. I only want it to act in favor of and not against the people."

At least I succeeded in wiping that grin off of his face. But unfortunately, it was replaced by an expression of blatant displeasure.

Unperturbed, I reflected it right back at him. "If you continue to exercise your power so bureaucratically and unjustly, if you continue to throw innocent people into jail every day, if you continue to ignore the anger of the population, then you've yet to see what's building up before your own eyes. You can't have the entire population arrested. In my opinion, my conversation with the president was good support for us because it's only when we identify the injustices that we'll then be able to bring peace to our land. Yes, it's true that you gave me a lot of power. I also know that I've been awarded a number of distinctions, but only because you hope by these awards to gain something from me."

When the translator relayed my last statements to him, his body stiffened as though it were carved of wood. He gave no verbal response for awhile. Then slowly in a cool voice, said, "I now see that you're a traitor. Now you'll feel the consequences."

I replied, "You've lost our duel of words. There is a Chinese proverb that applies to you well: 'If one cannot find the words, one shows the fist.' So now you've shown me your fist. But I have to warn you as well. If you continue to treat us Uyghurs so unjustly, you'll be punished for it."

He inhaled sharply. "Your future is now over."

"My future is determined by God alone," I said as I grabbed my handbag. "I'll go now."

"No you will not! Ablat Abdurexit still wants to talk to you."

Then his secretary and an escort took me to Uyghur Governor of the Xinjiang Uyghur Autonomous Region, Ablat Abdurexit. He and I knew each other well. I had even met with him and his wife socially outside of work.

"Ah, come in, come in . . . how nice to see you. How are you? How are your children and your husband?"

He liked to laugh and, as a sign of respect for the person he was addressing, continuously put his hand to his breast. His nickname, due to his sunny disposition, was "Sweet Ablait." We continued to chat about our personal lives. "Have you paid off the debts on your department store? How is business?"

Finally, he broached the unpleasant topic that he actually wanted to speak with me about: "You and I, we can't solve all of the problems in our land. But you should also not let yourself get into trouble over a few trifles. It was right that you addressed certain problems in Beijing. The people in charge there are always worried about our population. But we also have to admit that the standard of living for our population has improved compared to the past."

I looked deeply into his eyes. He then asked me nervously, "Why do you look at me that way?"

"I just thought that you must have forgotten your past, your childhood. You came from the north, as I did, from the Ili area. Do you still remember what the villages that you grew up in looked like? Do you remember the times when we were happy? When we celebrated together?

"In those days it was rare to find anyone who lied to others. Can you explain to me why the same population has now become belligerent and fraudulent? Don't constantly repeat, 'Good. Everything has become good.' Speak for once about the downturn in our lives. If one always speaks untruths, they'll eventually make one sick."

He looked troubled as he worked over the knot in his tie; perhaps it was too tight and was cutting off his breathing. "Please stop. Please, let's speak about something else. What deals are you currently making?"

There was no point in discussing matters much further with him. We talked a little bit more about general affairs, then I tried to go, but he held me back and invited me to his house. He said his wife would be delighted to see me, and I could not say no.

The secretary and escort who had brought me to the governor remained waiting in the entranceway. Probably they had expected that I would get into an argument with him just as I had with Wang Lequan. The governor turned to the two and told them to accompany me out. He joined us and walked me all the way to the door.

Ablat Abdurexit was known as a "soft" politician. Many of the issues he heard about he would not take a position on. It was also hard for him to witness how brutally Wang Lequan treated our people. But still, he never complained. It was only privately, when he was at home, that he showed how deeply subordinate he felt to Wang Lequan.

At work, his strategy was to simply hold down his position as governor. He and his wife had gotten used to prosperity. The government had even allowed his wife to take a trip to Germany. Ever since then, she had gushed about the freedom in that democratic country. She was so euphoric that she could hardly be quieted.

My new fifteen-storey building was to be named Akida, after my daughter. When I arrived home in the evening, Honzohre sat down with me. She really missed her brother Tayir, so we had the sixteen-year-old brought back from the orphanage.

Not long after that, Turjan—who I had lost to the Dungan gangs—telephoned me. It was his first communication since he had visited his sister a year before. At that time, he had bought her a new dress and given her a bit of money. The two of them arranged to meet again—as did he and I.

Turjan had become a tall, handsome man. When he saw me, he took me in his arms and hugged me. While we were dining at a restaurant I offered him a position in my holding company. But he could not accept the offer. He said, "In order for Honzohre to be safe, I have to stay. Nobody is bad to me Rebiya. I do a good job at whatever they ask of me."

"What is it that you do?"

"I earn my money."

"How do you earn your money?"

"That I can't tell you."

"How many are with you? Are you alone?"

"No, there are five of us, sometimes ten."

"Will you come back?"

"It's going to be hard for me to visit you. I have to go back to the Chinese interior."

With these words, he left us again. I suspected that he had something to do with drug running.

Ironically, shortly thereafter more and more parents turned to me to help them with their own children who had become heroin addicts. During drug busts, the police would arrest everybody but would eventually release any dealers who shared a percentage of their profits with them. In this way, the officials involved would pull in money twice: they would be rewarded by the state for making drug arrests, and then paid again by the drug dealers for being released. Among the people, drug dealers and drug users were simply referred to as "children of the police."

Drug arrests also took on a distorted and competitive nature. Any officer who arrested thirty dealers in one month received a larger apartment, or even a promotion. Every policeman had at least four or five homes in the city. And every family wished that their son would take up law enforcement as a profession.

At the Congressional assemblies, I petitioned several times for something to be done about the spread of drugs. I suggested that we finance an anti-drug campaign. But the cadres were of the opinion that education through media outlets was sufficient.

Instead of taking no for an answer, I promptly created my own security forces. They were instructed to immediately report to the authorities anyone who was selling drugs in my department store. At the same time, a second force provided education about drug abuse. It did not take long before the assigned Communist official came to visit me. In his words, I was prohibited from continuing my program because these policy enforcements were solely within the jurisdiction of the government, not private citizens, and certainly not Rebiya Kadeer.

I then suggested to the state-run television stations that they broadcast a program exclusively on this topic. But even this request was denied. I was not left with many options, but there was one more to try. There was a monthly assembly in my building to discuss general topics such as safety in case of fire. Within this framework I immediately began educational activities about drug abuse.

The further I progressed, the more obvious it became that the illegal economy was more and more indistinguishable from the legal one. Officials and some politicians too were on the drug lords' salary lists.

I CAME HOME TO URUMQI only on short visits at that time. I was constantly on the road for business, especially in Central Asia. My husband worried when the door bolted shut behind me as I left for as long as several months. When I came home again, we talked to each other incessantly. There was so much to tell. My absences were tough on our marriage. Somehow we managed to sustain our love with very little actual time together during those years. Sidik's outlook and sensitivity were a great source of support and inspiration. My successes in turn inspired his thinking and helped him develop deeper insights, not just about our Uyghur nation, but about humanity as well. Admittedly, it was sad when I felt he looked at me as though I were a mirage that would soon disappear again, the way I always did, only to then reappear at some other unexpected time.

As his occupation, my husband had only wanted to teach his subject at the university, to write, and to keep educating himself. For him, all of the money I was earning, all of those millions, had little value in comparison to the intellectual gratification he gained from his work. He considered his most important responsibility on this earth to be the education of Uyghurs.

Ever since the student protests in Tiananmen Square in Beijing, teachers at universities and other educational institutions had been muzzled even more tightly by the government. The topics for all lectures and for all instructors were censored. Lectures related to history and democracy were not allowed. Among Sidik's forty-five students, he was certain that at least five worked in *An Chuan Ting* secret operations. Every single one of his words was parsed by the cadres. Speaking about Uyghur nationality during class would have been the end for him. His earlier successful efforts to outsmart the censors had reached their limits under the tightened restrictions. He had run out of countermeasures for avoiding the censors' wrath while educating his students.

Once, even before Sidik had returned to the university after a semester break, someone had filed a complaint about him. Two Communist Party members at the higher learning institute within the university

where he worked accused him of having said that the time of Marx was over. But he had not said any such thing or anything remotely close to that in class. To be safe, after that experience, my husband began submitting in writing to university authorities all questions that his students had asked him.

Even when Sidik's lectures included a statement favorable to the Uyghurs, a general statement about culture or crafts, he was reprimanded. Once his supervisors reprimanded him because he included in a lecture a critique of a book by an Iranian author. The book was about women's rights, or, more accurately, about how women should not have any rights. Sidik expressed an opinion in the lecture rebuking such fanatics and arguing that they should not interfere with cultural traditions of equality by using their false logic. When he indicated to his supervisors that the Communist Party also rebuked this book, they immediately dropped the conversation and sent him back to his students. It was not only Sidik, but the entire faculty was troubled.

Sidik was ordered to constantly interject into his lectures slogans like "Mao Zedong was a great man." "The Communist regime is the best." And, "Our brothers are free." At night he was restless; tossing and talking in his sleep. Unable to rest, he would get up for awhile, then come back and try to sleep again. Each night became a test of his will to fall asleep. His eyes were the scorekeeper in this test and he was losing badly. His eyes were sunk deeply into their sockets, and getting deeper.

My husband was a thinker who was not allowed to think.

He said to me, "I can't live with it anymore—constantly lying to my students. I carry many things in my heart that I would like to share with my students. But I'm not allowed. They even prohibit my lectures on world-famous philosophers. Rebiya, I have come to the decision to leave the university."

I understood how hard this must have been for him. But I too did not see any other options in that environment. In time, the officials would have destroyed his soul. With his decision made, there was almost an immediate change in him. He became very sensitive and chose quiet solitude and contemplation over interaction. He simply did not want to talk much anymore. The only exception was the occasional get-together with one of his best friends, such as the writer Abdurayim Ötkür.

My husband spent most of his time in his home office. But if I needed help, he was at my side immediately. This change led to him accompanying me more often to help protect me when I traveled. It actually brought us closer.

The government later spread a rumor that my husband had not quit, but rather had been fired from the university.

OF THE 1.3 BILLION CHINESE, by the year 1993 up until the time of my arrest in 1999 I was the wealthiest woman, and the seventh wealthiest person behind six men, in all of China and its controlled regions. My department store was now only one part of my economic empire. One of my subsidiary companies was in real estate. Another produced food products. In Kazakhstan I owned, among other businesses, a leather factory and a two-storey department store. In Kirghizstan and Uzbekistan, my subsidiaries dealt with imports and exports. It was my practice to hire young talented Uyghurs as directors of operations for these subsidiaries.

It is true that I had developed this large holding company on my own and that I had made all of the important decisions by myself. But I also had several important advisors within my circle of trust: my oldest son Kahar, my brother Mehmet, and my driver and confidante Rehmutulla. And of course, I had my husband. There was a vice director below me who also provided excellent service. Two trusted colleagues from the finance department were quite helpful as well in analyzing the global economy. In total, there were ten of us overseeing the management of my seven primary companies. I worked a minimum of ten hours a day.

On business trips throughout our homeland, I continued my habit of broadening my knowledge of the lives of the Uyghur population. I visited all of the cultural monuments and was interested in all subjects related to our people.

I even visited the Muzart Pass through which once upon a time my grandparents had fled to find safety. The road was so steep that it felt like our driver was taking us on a vertical climb. Sidik clutched his seat tightly and told me over and over to calm down.

On another occasion I visited pipelines and petroleum towers in the Tarim Basin. "The Sea of Hope" is what the Chinese called it. From a swimming pool to their own health clinic, the Chinese oil workers lacked nothing. Meanwhile, our Uyghurs lived nearby in slums: hungry,

dirty, unhealthy, and empty-handed. The Chinese were literally stealing our resources right before our eyes.

At one point I was receiving an increasing number of reports about the catastrophic conditions surrounding the Uyghur area known as Lop Nur. It was a favorite atomic test site for the Chinese. To their way of thinking, it was better to detonate atomic bombs in the occupied Uyghur land than in their own motherland.

There was unconfirmed talk of two-hundred-thousand radiation victims as a result of the more than thirty above-ground atomic bomb tests in Lop Nur. What I witnessed there was an unspeakable horror. About eighty percent of the people I saw were physically handicapped. Some of them had bloody sores around their mouths. Other relatively young people had disfigurements such as mutilated limbs. Newborns were missing eyes and ears. Many people had lost their hair. Adding to their suffering was their complete unawareness as to why they had become so sick. I can only imagine the psychological damage they suffered just from not knowing why these things had happened, let alone from the actual visible results of the atomic tests.

Back in Beijing at the National People's Congress, I demanded compensation for these radiation victims. The response itself was an atrocity. The information about these atomic tests was totally foreign to the other representatives, as was the concept of government compensation. They knew nothing. In China there was an enormous void in knowledge about human rights, both for the rulers and for those they ruled.

I WAS TIRED OF GETTING PLUNDERED in our own land in ever more brazen ways by those in power. I therefore escaped my homeland for months at a time by visiting Central Asia. Even there though the Chinese were cashing in handsomely. At least from me they received only what was permissible by Central Asian laws. As corrupt as some conditions in Central Asia were, they were luxurious compared to the inhuman blight caused by Chinese laws against Uyghurs.

The absences may have helped me, but they began to take a devastating toll on my husband. Any time my husband was not traveling with me and my business trips involved a change of plans, even in the smallest way, my husband suffered from visions that I would be hurt and that he would never see me again. When I came back, he stood before me in visible pain. I was clearly unharmed, yet he was not.

"Have you come back healthy? Is that really you?"

Because of this constant worry, I became fearful too that something bad could happen to me.

In February 1994, my driver Rehmutulla and I were transporting goods to Korgas in Kazakhstan. We had hardly crossed the border when I started to brood about Sidik and about how he was doing without me there. As soon as I had finished my business, I urged Rehmutulla to get home as quickly as possible. Sidik was fine, thank God.

On our next trip, returning from Kazakhstan, Rehmutulla and I were leading a convoy of forty trucks that were fully loaded with scrap iron. At the border, the Kazak officials informed us that crossing was closed for the next six months. They explained that the Kazak government, in an agreement with China, wanted to seed the zone between their borders with bombs and to construct other obstacles to make it more difficult for smugglers to cross.

I was worried about Sidik and felt like I had just been struck by a hammer. How would I not be able to see my husband for six months? I sank down, lost in thoughts of my husband lying unconscious on the ground. I pulled myself up and rushed from one official to the next. I would pay them any sum they asked if they would only let me cross the border. But they would have none of it. In straightforward language, a language beyond the reach of bribes or exceptions, they emphatically said that the border would remain closed.

I constantly tried to reach Sidik by telephone. I had deliberately gotten him a mobile phone just for times like this so that he would not worry, but he never carried it with him.

After ten days, I finally reached one of his friends and asked him if he had seen my husband. The friend said, "How much more money do you want to earn? You can't imagine how worried your husband has been about you. You'll drive him to insanity."

"Please, please tell him I'm fine."

"I think you're a woman who has married the most kind-hearted man in the world. And I believe that you're taking him away from his true path for the sake of money."

One after another, I telephoned various Kazak members of parliament and ministers. I even tried to reach the president of Kazakhstan

himself, but did not succeed. Thanks to my stubbornness, and a little money on the side, the Kazaks finally agreed to contact the Chinese.

In the end, both sides agreed to open their borders for one hour. The Chinese did not want to break their agreement, but as it turned out, among the seventy people unexpectedly stopped at the border along with us were many high-ranking Chinese officials.

One of the Kazak guards at the border gate called my name: "Rebiya, there is a soldier coming from the Chinese side now to pick you up first. After that, the others will cross."

I arrived home two weeks later than I had promised Sidik. When I saw my husband, I felt touched to the core of my being. His face was covered in dust. Later I found out that for days he had stood along the China–Kazakhstan border from early morning until late at night looking for me. By the light of a torch, he had written for me:

> *I will make my eyelashes into a bridge for you.*
> *I will make my tears into a river for you*
> *to come swimming over on them.*

He said, "Your love opened that barrier." As we embraced, I breathed in deeply, but it seemed like I took in hardly any air. I could hear how he too was also having trouble breathing.

I HAD LOST ALL HOPE with regard to my work in the National People's Congress. It was a complete waste of time. Nobody in the world wanted to hear about Uyghurs being exterminated in a program of ethnic cleansing. In our own nation, there were no laws to protect us.

In 1994 my husband began trying to spur our countrymen to action by writing newspaper articles. If the state-controlled media unabashedly claimed that Uyghur songs and poems were of Chinese origin, Sidik provided the evening newspaper with a scholarly, fact-based response to such audacious lies that concluded, "Your theories are an insult to the ancient high culture of the Uyghurs."

In one of his next articles, my husband addressed the government's opinion that Uyghurs, from a historical perspective, were a part of China: "In the years 745 to 840, the old Turkic Uyghurs dominated large parts of Central Asia. In the following centuries, it was mostly Turkic and

Mongolian khans who controlled the trading centers along the Silk Road. In actuality, China never had a lot of influence in this region."

Another respected Uyghur scholar thanked the editor-in-chief of the evening newspaper by telephone. He praised the editor for having the courage to publish such texts. Even if the editors worked for the Chinese, all of them were Uyghurs. They also felt strongly about Uyghur topics. But as expected, the editor-in-chief was punished for printing Sidik's articles. He was fined three-thousand yuan. The normal fine for that type of infringement was typically one-hundred yuan.

Sidik wanted to pay the fine but the editor-in-chief kindly refused, explaining that he wanted to pay it himself. After all, the article represented not only Sidik's opinion but the opinion of most Uyghurs. In 1996, the editor-in-chief was suspended.

While Sidik advocated for the common people through his articles, I tried to help the population through my own means. Because of my wealth, many Uyghurs began to call me "The Savior." I clearly was no savior, but I also knew how much the population suffered and how much hope they had placed in me to help them.

I looked out my office window and noticed ragged children who should have been in elementary school. So I set up an elementary school for these street kids on the fifth floor of my department store. Of course, it was not like a proper school and had no yard, but at least the children would learn to read and write.

I had planned the school for fifty street children, but after only a short period of time, there were approximately five-hundred of them. We arranged the program so that advancement through grade levels could be established for each student who successfully completed the sequenced curriculum. Eventually, one grade level was taught in the morning, another at noontime, and so on. The pupils brought friends with them and they in turn passed the news to more friends. The enrollment numbers continued to grow through this process of word of mouth. Parents were profoundly grateful that their children were being given a chance to learn.

If the Chinese had opened such a school, state-controlled television would have broadcast reports about it on all of the channels. Our school was given no mention. Furthermore, efforts were made to dismiss the school altogether as completely meaningless.

The government targeted our school from the very beginning. They claimed that because of the busy streets and dangerous automobiles, it was too risky for the children to walk to the school. Besides, they were concerned that such a model made a bad impression overseas because it underscored the illiteracy and ignorance of our people, which the government had largely brought about itself through neglect.

For a year-and-a-half I fought against the school being closed. Six times officials sealed the doors to our classrooms. But I kept fighting. Meanwhile, we had managed to teach many of our students to read and write. Then orders came from the government that the school in my department store was not a good influence and that the children should be sent to receive lessons in their own neighborhoods. With that order, the school was permanently closed. I was heartbroken.

Through my travels in Central Asia I had learned how important it was to be proficient in foreign languages. Until 1987 it was forbidden in China to learn other languages besides Russian. That is why I offered rent-free and tuition-free a language school where Uyghurs who spoke English or other foreign languages could teach. Soon English, German, Japanese, and Arabic were being taught in my department store. This time, nobody from the government sealed our doors. Two-hundred young people were enrolled in several classes. On later occasions when I was abroad, I sometimes met one of my many countrymen who told me that he or she had attended my language school. I was overjoyed every time I met one of these alumni.

More foreign language schools soon opened in Kashgar, Khotan, and Aksu. But almost immediately this growth was too fast for the government. The school in Kashgar had to close, but the others remained open. My institute existed until I was sent to prison. The Uyghur director of our language school was also arrested.

The government lived by the motto "Ignorance secures obedience." Chinese children were allowed to go to school free of charge in our Uyghur nation, yet Uyghurs were allowed to go only if they had the money to pay for it. But money was exactly what Uyghur children lacked. The majority of our population at that time was thus illiterate.

Since then, literacy rates have improved. Our urban populations are more literate, and the remaining literacy problems occur mostly within outlying areas. Elementary education has become mandatory and school fees have been abolished for all elementary schools—for Uyghurs, Chinese, and others.

Uyghur teenagers were urged almost daily by radio and television programs to come to work in the Chinese interior. The Chinese however were told to move from their overpopulated provinces to the Uyghur nation to make a living. Uyghur girls in particular were recruited to work at Chinese hotels and restaurants. The ads said to them, "You should be slim, tall, and good-looking."

Many people believed the government's claim that following this measure would fight high unemployment among Uyghurs. Several thousand girls, especially from the countryside, were taken in busloads to the inland provinces under the slogan "Gaining Work Experience."

Back in Beijing, Uyghur businesspeople and students began approaching me with the repulsive information that rather suddenly, many of those recruited young Uyghur women were working in whorehouses right there in the capital city. Some of them had been sent to Hong Kong, Taiwan, or Japan to work in the sex trade there. I immediately made contact with some of the victims.

These young women had been promised salaries of one-hundred yuan a month if they worked in the interior eastern provinces. It was also reported that Chinese who went to work in our Uyghur nation earned two-thousand yuan a month. Uyghur girls were not overtly forced to prostitute themselves; it was more a case of being in a compromising situation where they needed to sell themselves to survive. For many of these proud young women, it was impossible to accept their fate. Some tried to flee. Some committed suicide. Some died from beatings by their pimps.

Shaken, I told Sidik at home in Urumqi about what I had learned from the girls and asked him to write about it. His resulting article, "A Plea to Our Daughters and Mothers" created quite a stir. Sidik called upon mothers to protect their daughters. He explained how these young women were being used as sexual fodder. He also explained how the employment bureau and their coordinators responsible for the recruitment of these young Uyghur girls were nothing more than human traffickers.

The article said, "Regardless of how bad conditions are in our land, do not sell the pride of our people—our daughters—because they are our future." He went on to write that courageous people who went to the authorities as witnesses of such misdeeds were themselves accused of intentionally spreading rumors against the Chinese government and then taken into custody.

Sidik's article had an immediate effect. In the Ili prefecture, two buses were parked and ready to leave with seventy Uyghur girls on board, but their parents rushed over and demanded that their daughters be returned to them. In Kashgar, the human traffickers had already placed twenty-three girls in a hotel. The mothers retrieved their daughters and angrily ripped up the contracts that they had previously signed.

To appease our incensed population, the Chinese government attempted to return the girls who were already working in the interior provinces. Even the television and radio programs that were announcing the recruitment drives were discontinued. But more quietly, the employees and publisher of the newspaper that had published Sidik's article were also punished.

The disruption of this human trafficking proved only temporary. In the year 2006, Chinese overlords in Kashgar proudly proclaimed on their web site that forty-two-thousand Uyghur girls in Yarkand had been recruited to work in the Chinese interior.

IN THE 1990S, THE HAN CHINESE population increased by thirty-one percent in the Uyghur nation. The cityscape had also changed as a result of this influx. Uniform prefabricated buildings were built on the fringes of the largest cities in our land and huge industrial zones were created, just as in most Chinese provinces. Traditional Uyghur neighborhoods with tearooms, shady courtyards, and low-slung mud-brick houses were flattened by bulldozers and replaced with modern office complexes.

In neighboring Kazakhstan, change was under way as well. Even though there had been some differences of opinion with Uyghur merchants, the young state wanted to create its own new currency: the tenge. At the same time, the Kazaks wanted to devalue the Russian ruble, which had been in circulation until then. Because the currency conversion was meant to take place within only five days, Kazak banks would no longer accept large amounts of rubles.

Many of my Uyghur colleagues pressured me to help them with the currency exchanges, so I sought a resolution on their behalf. They gave me their remaining rubles—twenty-three sacks full, which then had to be transported by truck. My approach was to use the money to open future purchase orders on goods. For example, I paid in advance with rubles for scrap iron that would then be delivered a year or even two years later. But strangely, a rumor was spread that I had become insolvent. Suddenly all of the merchants who I had helped wanted to cash in their promissory notes right away. They insisted on having their rubles returned to them in yuan immediately.

Anger is not the right word for what I felt. Disbelief, betrayal, and disillusionment are better words. For the first time in my life, I doubted my own people. As soon as a transaction of mine had been completed, people stood in line at my desk demanding their money back. It took me a year-and-a-half to pay back the debts.

Meanwhile, in the National People's Congress, my Uyghur colleagues and I were increasingly disagreeing. Some religious leaders who were on advisory councils to Congress and received state support preached that it was most important to follow the government's laws. They preached that the Communist Party's ideology dovetailed excellently with religious values.

I was aghast at this analysis. Among other matters, a religious leader wrote that in order to prevent radical movements, youth should be prohibited from performing all types of religious functions. Such functions should be left only to adults. Furthermore, this person argued that the abortions ordered by the government were taking place in the name of God. Still more heartlessly, these leaders asked why people were even complaining if they had enough to eat and drink and they lived in homes.

In regard to the dire straits of the Uyghur population, the cheerful response from Congress was that under the government's watchful eye, these problems would take care of themselves. In our Uyghur nation, there were no real strains between the different ethnic groups because all of us were equally discriminated against and all had no rights.

One imam named Harunhan reminded me of a mad dog. I felt he would attack anyone for the sake of a bone that was for him and him alone. The Chinese officials were delighted with him. As soon as a delegation arrived from abroad, he was introduced to them as the religious representative of the Uyghurs. In appearance, the tall, strong imam with the white turban, the long white beard, and the long coat was quite impressive.

To delegations from other countries he would always complain about the radicalism and ignorance of Uyghurs who did not know how to handle their religious freedom. The delegations were persuaded by him and the Chinese wooed him all the more ardently.

When I encountered Harunhan at the next session of Congress, I saw that he had lost an ear, as I had already heard was the case. It was common knowledge by that time that a Uyghur man, along with a few of his friends, had sought out the imam. The man was deeply distressed because birth control officers wanted to remove his unborn child from his wife.

But the imam defended the government's abortion mandate. At that, the outraged men cut off his ear and threatened to cut out his tongue. One of the perpetrators later was sentenced to death and another received a life sentence. All of the others received long prison terms.

IN 1995, THE APPARATCHIKS sent me as a member of the official Chinese delegation to the United Nations Fourth World Conference on Women in Beijing. For the first time, I met with representatives from the West, including then United States First Lady Hillary Rodham Clinton.

The government had placed three Chinese women at my side for this conference—not for companionship, but for confinement. They watched my every move and their presence alone prevented me from speaking freely. The high officials justified my entourage by saying that I could not speak any foreign languages and that these women would translate for me. But they did not translate what I said. In fact, my relationship with them reminded me more of one between a hostage and her kidnappers. Their presence did give me some insight though into just how much the officials feared me.

Three Tibetan women bound themselves hand and foot in front of the conference building to protest their Chinese oppressors. I listened with fascination to the Tibetan women as they fearlessly described the problems in their land. All of the foreign journalists followed their story with great interest. But no one from abroad reported on virtually the same Chinese oppression of the Uyghur population. *Why*, I thought, *are we Uyghurs not allowed to speak about the difficulties in our own homeland? Why am I not allowed to talk about the suffering of our people?*

Politicians and human rights organizations from all over the world were active on behalf of Tibet. The conditions in the Uyghur nation were much the same. But interest from abroad in the two, though literally we were next-door neighbors sharing a common border and both under Chinese occupation, could not have been more dissimilar. The Tibetans were successfully represented by His Holiness The Dalai Lama, a beautiful spiritual leader whose voice has been heard by the world. There was no well-known voice speaking on behalf of Uyghurs. In fact, hardly anyone in the world knew about our suffering.

I wanted to continue listening to the three Tibetan women talk, but my escorts forced me to leave with them. At that moment, a thought sparked inside of me. *I would have to go abroad to be allowed to talk freely. Only then would I be able to represent Uyghur interests.*

How proudly and eloquently the Tibetan women had expressed themselves that day. We Uyghur women at the conference remained silent, though we had so much to share as well.

Why Don't You Just Shoot Us

Sidik had been wondering for quite some time why the government had not shown any reaction toward his newspaper articles. In December 1995, about a year after his writings were published, members of the government called together an assembly to discuss history and literature.

This conference, however, was not held to grapple with classical literature, but rather to discuss my husband's articles. Those present found fault with their content but did not criticize Sidik personally. There were also Uyghur participants at the conference; among them was a person, who through our own means, we had already become well informed about. He worked in the bureau for external affairs, which was linked to the *An Chuan Ting*, and had been given the assignment of gaining our confidence. For this reason he vehemently defended Sidik's articles to the Chinese leaders at the conference. The government's intention was to keep focused surveillance on our family. In short, my husband was in danger.

As a Congressional representative, in extreme secrecy, I had also been advised of newly forthcoming restrictive laws summarized in Party Document Number Seven. This large-scale re-education and propaganda campaign that went by the name "Strike Hard" was implemented by the government in 1996 making the severity of our situation all the more clear to me. The campaign was not directed at criminals but at "thinking people"—intellectuals and dissidents. Anyone who publicly stood up for human rights was immediately denounced as a "nationalist" and promptly prosecuted. They were subjected to ridiculous sham trials which contradicted all constitutional principles and rules of law.

Wang Lequan, Chinese Communist Party Secretary of the Xinjiang Uyghur Autonomous Region, was attributed with the following quote in support of "Strike Hard": "If we have condemned one-hundred people to death and there is only one among them who is guilty, then ninety-nine were forced to die for him."

The government called for a "rigorous fight against any form of separatism and all religious intrigue." As a precaution, religious lessons were prohibited, even at home. All religious books and audio recordings had to be officially approved as well.

Even general literature about Uyghur history and culture was subject to censorship. In the wake of this campaign, many books on our history by famous German and Swedish scholars were no longer allowed. Foreign literature about democracy or human rights had been banned long before. The government was so fastidious about enforcement that it formed a new department exclusively devoted to reviewing each line of every book. Every paragraph and every footnote, no matter how small, was under the scrutiny of this new bureau.

The writer Turghun Almas, a good friend of ours, had written three books: one about Uyghur traditions, a second about the Huns, and a third about the Uyghur people. All three works were banned. But they did not arrest our friend because he had cleverly referenced Chinese sources for virtually every citation in each of his books.

All Uyghurs also had to take part in training sessions for a number of weeks, including business people, government employees, farmers, and even homeless people who lived in the streets. In these training presentations, the population was specifically warned that those who brought Uyghur history books back from abroad would be severely punished. The prison sentence would depend on the significance of the content and would vary from between three years to life.

Over the course of time, Sidik had amassed a huge library. We therefore made arrangements to ensure that the books openly appearing on our shelves were allowed by the government, and that those that had been banned remained hidden.

The government's imagination seemed almost limitless to the point of absurdity when it came to restricting Uyghurs' private lives: "It is not permitted to have discussions about the government and politics at weddings or funerals" was just one example.

Around that time the government also established control points between city districts where all Uyghurs were stopped and searched, while Chinese were simply waved through. In government bureaus, business offices, and everywhere else where Uyghurs were employed, *An Chuan Ting* officials searched through their desks and workspaces. Ladies' handbags were checked when they came to work and then again when they went home. The discrimination became ever more blatant.

Many Chinese students preferred to study abroad, and their requests were largely granted. However, Uyghur students essentially would have to accept their status as fugitives as many of them fled on foot across borders and over mountain passes to further their education. It was hard enough for a Uyghur to gain admission to a university in our own homeland. Those who did successfully graduate from universities—including Kazaks, Mongolians, and other ethnicities—could not find commensurate work afterward. Instead, they had to work as waiters and waitresses or as farm workers.

At the next session of the Xinjiang Uyghur Autonomous Region advisory commission, I asked some uncomfortable questions of Chinese Communist Party Secretary Wang Lequan:

"Why do you enact such laws?"

"Do the people who make these laws have any pride or honor?"

"Why don't you just shoot us all right now?"

"Are you eager to see our blood flow?"

"This one isn't a question. Don't force the common people to rise up."

ELABORATE SHAM TRIALS were a daily occurrence in Urumqi. We constantly saw fully loaded trucks rolling slowly through the city, each transporting four or five prisoners in blue inmate uniforms. Their hands were tied behind their backs and white signs identifying them as separatists hung around their necks. Some heads drooped forward lifelessly.

The government liked to conduct their sham trials in large halls or public squares. Staging them in front of one of the government buildings was certain to frighten the common people. Uniformed officers dragged an accused man up to a podium to plead his case. After the trial, the officers brutally threw him back onto the flatbed of the truck like he was nothing more than a sack of garbage.

The executions themselves took place in two Urumqi suburbs near the prisons Baijiahu and Liudaowan. There, the condemned were shot in a hollow located between two hills. The rules were that corpses of political prisoners would be kept by the authorities. Corpses associated with other crimes were permitted to be returned to the relatives, but with conditions. The first condition was that they had to pay a fee to gain possession of the corpse. The second condition was that they had to pay a fee for the transportation costs incurred in bringing the condemned to his execution site. The third condition was that they had to pay for the services of the executioners. And the fourth condition was that they had to pay for the ammunition used to execute the condemned.

IN APRIL 1996, THE NATIONS of China, Russia, Kazakhstan, Tajikistan, and Kirghizstan signed a treaty in Shanghai to "strengthen military measures" governing zones in all of the common border areas. In the treaty, each nation pledged to take action against separatists, fundamentalists, drug dealers, and weapons smugglers. Networks of armed units were assembled and other controls were implemented to enforce the new border treaty. In essence, the treaty marked an end to Uyghurs openly organizing regular protests in Kazakhstan and Kirghizstan against Beijing.

Uyghur trade with Central Asia, which had previously been good and had shown long-term potential, now ceased. For me personally, the transport of goods to and from Central Asia was already over before the Shanghai treaty. I ceased this business when Chinese Communist Party Secretary Wang Lequan retracted my import/export license. Motivated by these conditions, I had already secretly started to dismantle my firms in order to divert my assets elsewhere.

In Urumqi, the *An Chuan Ting* officials seized all of the goods that local merchants had imported from the treaty nations. Sometimes the merchants even had to pay fines for possession of these goods in addition to the losses incurred from the actual seizures of their property. If the tax for an import had previously been ten percent, under certain conditions that import might still be allowed but with an astounding increased tax of fifty percent. Just as was the case within our nation with its checkpoints between main Uyghur cities, at the treaty nations' border crossings Uyghurs were always stopped and searched, while merchants of other nationalities were simply waved through like tourists.

As tensions mounted and life became more difficult for us, many Uyghurs fled to Kazakhstan to escape the Chinese government's oppression. But even there it was not safe, and their lives were tormented by instability.

At the Turkish embassy, other Chinese citizens would receive a visa

immediately, but Uyghurs had to file paperwork and wait for two or three months for a decision on their visa request. Even though Turkey had not signed the Shanghai treaty, there was an unwritten diplomatic understanding in place. China promised not to get involved in Turkey's Kurdish problems, and in return, Turkey promised not to get involved in China's Uyghur problems.

In 1996, the Chinese government also started a new resettlement program in our Uyghur nation. It was an insidious one where all Chinese nationals who had become infected with AIDS were sent to our land. Our people were particularly vulnerable to the AIDS virus because of the Chinese government's intentional act of quarantining within our population those infected. Coupled with the government's intentional stifling of AIDS reporting and education, the result was an alarmingly high and disproportionate rate of AIDS patients living in our Uyghur nation, which is still true to this day.

I MET WITH THREE CHINESE OFFICIALS in 1996 in a Urumqi hotel suite as requested by the *An Chuan Ting* central ministry. I was told, "What you've accomplished in your life so far is the dream of millions of people. Because you play such a vital role in the stability of the Uyghur population, the Chinese central government would like to improve your position even more. But you must cease to give public talks. You must become more obedient.

"If you accept our offer, we'll send you to Beijing. There we'll educate you further for three to six months. But with our offer, we would like to emphasize once more and strongly that your attitude is quite nationalistic and therefore will require your transformation to greater obedience to the Party. All too often, you don't publicly agree with our politics. But we believe that privately, perhaps you don't really think this way—that it's really others who have made you form those opinions. Please don't listen to them. We are your true friends."

The three looked at me waiting for my reply. When none came, the second man broke the silence. "What do you think of our plans?"

After a few moments, the first man rescued them again from my silence. "Do you want to go to the Communist Party School? Even though you're not a Party member, we'll allow it. We have great hopes for you and would like to announce your advancement today to all

Uyghurs. You realize, of course, that this is a privilege reserved for only a small number of people. You should consider yourself quite honored to be invited."

I sat back in my chair, wrinkling my forehead in contemplation. "You're from the central ministry? So I would like to hear from you how you can honestly speak about our shared homeland when the most influential positions are always occupied by Han Chinese—not Uyghurs. So why then do the Chinese want to have all of the power for themselves?"

The first man choked on his tea. I offered, "Here, let me get you a napkin."

"No. No. Just now we spoke about how you shouldn't talk so much. I think you're a . . . stubborn woman. By getting involved constantly and everywhere, you'll never accomplish much. It seems rather that you aren't capable of learning from your own behavior. That's incredibly sad for you. You're a very likable woman; we've already noticed that. But only if you improve your conversational skills will you achieve a position of leadership. The central government believes in you. Think about this. You're only a woman and you can't solve the problems of an entire people. But if you carry on like this, you'll soon be standing all alone."

"Would you get just as angry as I did now if someone were to speak to you about the poor economic conditions of the Chinese population?" I responded.

That prompted the third man to speak. "We've laid out everything clearly before you. We'll give you a chance. With the power we want to transfer to you you'll be able to benefit your people. You receive the offer we are making to you only this once. Now. This one time only. You should be aware that people who don't want to work with us have encountered many problems, entirely of their own making. Finally, we want to emphasize one thing: The Xinjiang Uyghur Autonomous Region belongs to China. They are inseparable."

I stood up to leave, but at the door I turned around once more. "I invite you to come to Khotan with me."

"Why would we go to Khotan with you?"

"There we will see a dried-out lake, a lake that became desiccated because the Chinese settlers diverted its waters." I started to turn again to leave.

"If you were better informed about the Uyghur leaders in history, you would already know that they all failed."

"Goodbye," I said, and left the room.

THE GOVERNMENT BEGAN TO ARREST a series of scholars whose primary area of study was Uyghur history. I could sense that Sidik would be arrested soon too because he had collected many important documents surrounding the period of Chinese occupation. He had also methodically archived them for further scholarly research.

Recently too, the Chinese government began to mention his name in public. That was a clear warning—clear even for Sidik.

I felt that regardless of what happened to me, Sidik should go abroad and report through his writings about our homeland. I had begged him several times to go into exile. But Sidik had weighed this move in his mind and was still unconvinced that he would be any better off doing so than if he stayed. He looked at it from several different perspectives. For one thing, it was clear to him that to start over in a foreign country and to learn a new language would be quite difficult at the age of fifty-two. Even in Turkey, in Uzbekistan, or in another neighboring Turkic republic, he would still be quite challenged—perhaps too much so to survive let alone to be of any service to his people. But one invigorating idea did stay with him: "I'm excited about democracy in the West. If I had to leave the country, I would go to America."

In complete secrecy, with my older sons Kahar and Ablikim, we made preparations for a "vacation." Only later did I tell Sidik about our scheduled flight to the United States.

But he immediately liked my suggestion of taking a brief vacation together. Yes, I tricked my husband into boarding an airplane to go into exile under the pretense of going on vacation together. Otherwise he would have never left behind his family, friends, or his library.

Ablikim and Kahar traveled with us to Beijing and said goodbye there. We had hardly left the airplane after our touchdown in the United States when I presented my husband with the *fait accompli*: "Sidik, you have to stay here. I don't want you going to prison again."

He was quite angry with me. "Are you the government? What right do you have to do such a thing?"

I rented a vacation home in Virginia for us. The scenery and climate was beautiful, but inside our home the atmosphere was icy. I explained to Sidik in great detail what service he could be to our people if he stayed and worked in a free, democratic country like the United States.

I added, "I don't like the idea of you being so far away from me. But if you don't stay here, they will throw you in jail. If you go to jail, we'll never see each other again. But here we'll see each other again, alive."

We spent an entire month together in America. We had a lovely time, but the last week before my departure Sidik became extremely reclusive. He started reminiscing about his family; how he would like to visit Kashgar, Gulja, and Khotan; how he wished he could have said his farewells before his departure.

With every concern a new wrinkle forged itself into his furrowed brow or around his eyes. I said, "If you love me, Sidik, then keep fighting from within the United States. Keep fighting with me for the freedom of our people."

"Then you are really coming here too?"

I caressed his cheek and in that moment realized that he had agreed to stay.

"Yes. I still have many important documents and papers at home that we'll need here. I have to bring them. I have to prepare. Then I'll come."

He held me in his arms for a long time.

I rented a small apartment for him in Virginia where one of his first tasks was to learn English. But he could not seem to put his mind to it. Then he wanted to write something. But where could he have it published? I called him frequently from Urumqi and tried to ease his mind during those first months of his exile.

He told me, "I'm in a prison, a prison that has a different form. I don't know the language. I have no friends. No one comes to visit. I stand at the window and look outside. But my beloved wife isn't here."

We had no idea that we would not see each other again for nine years.

IN THE WINTER OF 1997, an earthquake in Payziwat near Kashgar changed the course of my work. It was one of the worst natural disasters that had occurred in the Uyghur nation in recent memory. More than one-hundred villages and one-thousand homes were leveled to the ground. As usual, nobody but the highest Party officials had information on the number of casualties buried beneath the rubble.

The whole region was sealed off by soldiers—not for reasons of safety, but for public relations purposes. The government did not want international aides to bear witness to the general state of affairs in the Uyghur region. They knew by experience to hide from outsiders any unattended dead bodies and the prospect of even more casualties concealed amidst debris.

Because the government had been unsuccessful in organizing enough donations for the reconstruction, a few high-ranking Chinese officials looked to me for help. First, within my own circle of friends I spread news about the sum of money I intended to donate to this cause. Soon after, virtually all other businesspeople proved themselves to be extremely generous. In some cases, I was told to take freely all of the goods from their stockpiles that could be helpful. There was no time to go to their businesses individually, so I asked them to deliver to me money, clothing, and other items they wanted to donate.

The donors made one stipulation: that I was not to give their donations to the government, but instead deliver them personally to the devastated Payziwats. Like me, they knew all too well about valuables disappearing down government dark holes.

We had to wait sixteen days before the government let us enter Payziwat. While we waited, they were busy burying corpses and clearing the worst damage in the earthquake-stricken region. We drove into the area with a convoy of twenty trucks. Our plan was to distribute the donations at government locations. When town leaders led local residents to us, as soon as the people were offered this aid they looked with great doubt toward their leaders. They had to be reassured before they would help themselves.

We succeeded in distributing all of the donations. For our farewell, the village leaders invited all of the residents to assemble together at a large square to thank us. One leader shouted a blessing and the crowd repeated it in chorus. Again and again we listened to this joyous gratitude. It was lovely to see happiness in their faces as I stepped forward to say a few words: "When I see that there's laughter in your hearts today then I too am happy."

"Long live Chairman Mao!" they shouted. "Long live Chairman Mao!"

"Mao died a long time ago!" I shouted back. A hushed murmur spread through the crowd.

"These supplies come from generous businesspeople in Urumqi. All of the people who gave donations to you wish you happiness, security, and good health. Just one more comment in conclusion: You should occasionally read the newspaper and stay informed about current events in our country."

A young man stepped up to me hesitantly, "We aren't allowed to read the newspaper here."

The cadres then escorted our convoy out. They had even prohibited us from taking photographs.

WELL OVER TEN-THOUSAND PEOPLE had arrived to honor me with a celebration at Kashgar's huge square. By this time, it had been prohibited for Uyghurs to assemble in one place. Chinese snipers with machine guns lay on the surrounding rooftops, ready to quell any uprising. A row of army trucks fully loaded with armed units blockaded both sides of the street. Every other soldier had an attack dog at his side. An explosive tension hung in the air and I sensed that a riot could erupt at any moment.

Though our population did not seem intent on taking any action against the armed soldiers, the soldiers were definitely upset about something. I would soon find out what that something was. At the very moment when I stepped onto the square, drums and flutes began to play and people began to dance. Two minarets decorated with blue and white glazed tiles flanked the entrance to the square. Normally, our people danced wordlessly. But these dancers repeated a dangerous sounding "Ho!" in quick succession and put their arms in the air every time. That gesture cut me to the bone.

As I made my way through the crowd to address the people from one of the towers, the people yelled "Ho!" three times and then abruptly came to a stop. Somebody brought me a microphone as I looked around at the rooftops surrounding us.

I said to the crowd, "I congratulate you! I congratulate every family in Kashgar on this occasion! I see that people are afraid. But people can still enjoy themselves, despite their fears. Please, I would not like this square to be wet with blood today. Look around at the rooftops. The barrels of their machine guns are sighted on your heads: just a squeeze of the trigger for them. Just a squeeze.

"I would like you to please go home peacefully after the dance today. I promise all of you that I will take on the honorable assignment to work on your behalf to solve our problems without violence."

When I went back down the stairs, I found myself suddenly being carried over the heads of the crowd. I asked them to please put me down, but in their excitement they would not.

Just as I had hoped, the people went home without an uprising. But before we had even left the square that day, I received an urgent phone call telling me that only one day before, February 5, 1997, a rebellion had been brutally suppressed in the city of Gulja. I understood then why there had been so many armed officers posted here at the Kashgar gathering. It was a pre-emptive stance to avoid another Gulja problem. My assistant Ramila and I flew directly there.

AT THE GULJA AIRPORT, I held my red Congressional badge before me like a shield against the security patrol, forcing them to step aside. It was one of my responsibilities as a representative, after all, to know the current conditions in our homeland.

From our taxi window on the drive to the city, I saw no Uyghurs on the streets—only policemen, heavy artillery, and armed soldiers, some even in full combat gear. All of the evidence had already been swept up and cleaned away. There were no traces of a street battle or even of a life lost. The stores operated by Uyghurs and Dungans were closed. The unaffected Chinese merchants though hawked their wares as usual.

Our first stop was to see Ramila's brother. He looked around to the left, then carefully to the right before quickly pulling us by our arms into his apartment, saying, "You'll be shot if you move around outside."

In his opinion, we should wait in his apartment for two or three days until the situation had further defused. We agreed to this, but also suggested that we should telephone neighbors to check on their well-being. "No, you had better not do that. Our calls are being monitored."

House searches were being conducted. A curfew had been imposed. Death sentences were being handed out based on just a whisper of suspicion. The Chinese vowed that anyone who had been involved in the rebellion would be flushed out.

After three days in the apartment, we went out looking for Dungan and Uyghur witnesses who could speak about some part of the tragedy in their own words. In some cases, we met these people in hiding. Ramila's brother and his friends also gathered many statements from witnesses.

Around eight-thousand people from Gulja had been reported as missing following the demonstrations. Those who came back often reported being subjected to gruesome physical abuse. Some of them had their teeth pulled out, one by one. Many were executed. Many were imprisoned immediately and remain so to this day—locked up by some mysterious court system operating without any legal basis. These people received harsh prison sentences based on whims, hunches, and impatience.

There had been several reasons for the demonstrations. One was that numerous women and teenagers met in private homes to celebrate a traditional Uyghur gathering. But security officers armed with clubs forced their way into these homes and arrested all of the residents. The government had decided to forbid our *meshrep*—according to our traditions, we met each other at least once a month to play, sing, laugh, and spend the day together at these gatherings. But the government considered all assemblages of Uyghurs to be a threat to state security. Even our *meshrep*. Another precipitator was that their new controls prohibited even a soccer tournament that the youth in Gulja had planned. Not only was their soccer prohibited, but they destroyed their soccer field with bulldozers.

Over time, those in power took away the Uyghurs' personal freedoms, forcing the inhabitants of Gulja into rebellion. That is why the youth were coming together for protest marches and why they were not offering to negotiate a settlement with the Chinese government, but rather were demanding that the Chinese acknowledge our independence and unequivocally leave our Uyghur nation. According to these young minds, the Chinese government had no right to even take a breath of Uyghur air. "Just leave!" they argued.

Slowly, our research began to unfold the rest of the story of the Gulja demonstration. In anticipation of an eruption from the growing tensions, the government had ordered an estimated five-hundred-thousand troops from across several provinces to gather by the city.

With the soldiers in position, the first line of demonstrators were mowed down by machine guns. In a break from these methodical killings, the soldiers were then ordered to shoot blindly into the throngs of people standing on the sidewalks. Old people, women, and children were splattered with bullets from rapid-fire weapons.

After these shootings against civilians, the soldiers tore through the crowd, shattering kneecaps and cracking skulls with their billy-clubs which sliced like swinging scythes through fields of wheat.

One witness could not forget the wounded screaming for help. Another eyewitness had found safety by sliding underneath a car. The demonstrators were unarmed, she explained to us. The youth had been marching peacefully.

Clean-up duty was left to the dogs which gnawed at legs and arms and faces. When people laid motionless on the ground—although some might have actually still been alive—the soldiers threw them onto the flatbeds of waiting trucks. Most of the young people who were still alive in the flatbeds were unable to move, suffocating miserably under the weight of others. They soon learned though that this immobility was a better option, as the soldiers slammed their clubs down on anyone who moved.

At some point, the dead were sorted out. The wounded were transported to prisons while some were thrown on the ground in a courtyard where they were hosed down with water.

These people, with their broken bones and wounded bodies, were helpless in that courtyard. Desperately, they huddled toward each other thinking there was "safety in numbers." They also sought out each other's bodily warmth, as the temperature that day was about four degrees below zero Fahrenheit. Tragically, beyond human imagination, over four-hundred of these people froze to death, melded together in chunks of ice.

Later, I personally saw these events in police videos. I also heard in the accompanying audio the screams of the victims. It was not only from civilian testimonials that we gathered this information, but also from Uyghur prison guards who spoke to us under conditions of anonymity.

From another anonymous *An Chuan Ting* informant, I was told that agents had staged an event featuring Uyghur drug addicts setting fire to taxis. This fabrication was perpetrated to create propaganda which might counter any world sympathy for the demonstrators. The informant had been personally involved in this setup. I believed him in particular because

I had met the man years before through business transactions in Kazakhstan, and knew him to be trustworthy.

The next day the Chinese security forces continued their raids. Five children, the oldest fifteen and the youngest two, lived on a farm and had locked themselves in during the period of the rebellion. They were still waiting for their missing parents to return when the Chinese soldiers knocked on the farm door. Apparently the children hesitated, then opened the door. All of the children were shot down in cold blood right there in the doorway.

A woman who watched these murders was herself hiding in a large bread oven. In utter dismay, she told people about the murder of these children. Tragically, her statements seemed to bring about her own disappearance a few days later. Another woman and her five-year-old child, who were holding hands while standing on a bridge, were reported by witnesses to have been executed in cold blood by Chinese soldiers.

The respected Uyghur politician Hamudan Niyaz was sent by the government to investigate the Gulja massacres. Until that point, he and I had maintained a friendly relationship and had visited each other often. He viewed the same videos that I did—images that the troops themselves had photographed and that the Chinese officials had assembled as evidence.

A bizarre twist of events followed. Soon after he viewed those genocidal pictures he suffered a heart attack and was immediately flown to Urumqi for emergency medical treatment. After his recovery, at least to the point where he could be released from the hospital, the government directed him to give a report on his findings. Such a report would normally be written and would reflect the evidence he had witnessed, the same evidence I had witnessed. One would also expect that after a heart attack, he would not be subjected to a high-pressured presentation.

Instead, this report was orchestrated as a live program on national television. In it, he emphatically condemned the protesters, holding them entirely responsible for the violent response of the government. Specifically, he asserted that none of the state forces had mistreated the demonstrators. He went on to refer to the demonstrators as traitors, separatists, and then, suddenly, in the middle of his report, the television screen went blank. Minutes later, the program was restored, but with an announcement that Hamudan Niyaz had suffered a second heart attack at that very moment, live in the television studio. After his recovery, he was promoted to First General Secretary of the Communist Party in the Xinjiang Uyghur Autonomous Region. He gave no further reports on Gulja.

Toward the end of our third week in Gulja, my assistant Ramila and I gained possession of videos and still photographs taken on the day of the rebellion. The arrangements to obtain these were made through anonymous sources. As gruesome as the images were, we felt grateful that they were in our custody.

I had sixty-thousand yuan with me, and I distributed this money amongst the families who had lost their husbands, wives, parents, and children. Some of the widows had been at the rebellion themselves. Many of them told me that they had been raped.

My travel bag was filled with film, photographs, and witness statements. Among the materials was a list with the names of those who had been murdered or still were missing. In my mind, I began assembling an irrefutable presentation of it all to the National People's Congress in Beijing—including such evidence as video of a child clutching her mother's hand as she is torn away by two officers. They could see for themselves next how four dogs bit into the tender stomach of this child. Their biting quickly turning into a mauling. I would show them the look on this mother's face. I would show them!

But officers there had already received orders to detain me on the way to the airport and all of this damning material was taken away from me. They searched my belongings and the clothes I was wearing, and they dumped open every suitcase.

"I'm a representative of the people." I knew that according to the law, a representative had immunity from such searches and seizures.

Their only response was, "By order from the central government, we can't even allow our own Governor Ablat Abdurexit to take any papers with him from Gulja."

Ramila and I may have left Gulja with empty pockets, but they could not empty our minds. The pictures, the testimonials, and the lists of names had burned themselves into my brain as well as into hers, in all of their details, as sharp as photographs.

Later, it was reported in state-controlled media that the rebellion had been initiated by Uyghur criminals and all of them had since been killed or imprisoned. The government released some estimates too of how many people had been shot: there was mention of about ten dead.

Until that point, Gulja had been known for its scholars, poets, and writers. Many veterans of the Three Province Rebellion also lived there—just lovely people who liked to sing, dance, and tell jokes. But after this rebellion, Gulja became as silent as a churchyard, not just in grief or in homage, but by decree. Under threat of severe punishment, the population was commanded to maintain absolute silence about the events of February 5, 1997.

While in Gulja, I was able to arrange a secure phone call to Sidik. His response, just days later, was to organize a demonstration in Washington, D.C., which was a first for us. Sidik's demonstration, which took place on February 15, 1997, drew some notice locally but gained even more immediate attention back in Beijing.

One month after the Gulja rebellion, three bombs exploded on buses in Urumqi. That day had been designated by the government as one of mourning for the recently deceased leader of the Communist Party of China, Deng Xiaoping.

FROM OUT OF NOWHERE, Turjan telephoned us from Liudaowan Prison. His sister Honzohre and I immediately left to see him. When she saw her brother in the visitor's room, she put the palms of her hands up to his, their touch separated by a partition of glass. After a few moments of loud, heated conversation, she became enraged, causing the guards to pull her back. Exhausted from reaching for the glass and from screaming for so long, she finally collapsed on the ground.

We found out that five Dungan gang members had beaten him up. I did not know why—maybe because he had not completed what they had told him to do. In any case, he retaliated by stabbing their leader to death. Turjan was captured and given the death sentence for the murder.

I tried to appeal the sentence wherever I could. I hired three attorneys to work on the case. Turjan told one of his attorneys that a Dungan gang had murdered his mother, leaving him and his siblings as orphans; that the gang had taken him in from an early age and that he had agreed to their life of crime only in exchange for a promise to leave his siblings alone. "I killed the Dungan gang leader so that other orphaned children wouldn't become like me."

No one could get Turjan even a second hearing. The police, the black-marketers, and even the judges had profited from his gang-related crimes but despite all of our efforts, the government would not repeal Turjan's death sentence. Shortly before his execution, the warden asked the young man for his last wish. It was to hug his sister Honzohre one more time. Turjan looked overjoyed when we stepped into the visitor's room. There was no separating glass wall this time.

He said, "Don't cry, my sister. I'm only going to another world, a better world. Finally, I'll be free from these difficulties here. I'm very sorry for what I've done to you and that I lived in a world full of lies. But I love you. That's the truth."

We made arrangements to take possession of Turjan's body after the execution. Though clearly the executioner's gunshot was the actual cause of death, when Turjan's corpse was returned to us we could see by his skin that the twenty-two-year-old had been tied up in a way to cause a painful death. The rope burns were reminiscent of another popular technique used by Chinese authorities for executing prisoners. That gruesome approach was to wrap the condemned's naked body with wet rope so that their blood could not circulate. The prisoner was then clothed again. He might look normal, but as the ropes dried, they torturously constricted blood circulation to the point of death. Eventually, water was gone from the rope and life was gone from the condemned.

In Urumqi, Uyghur executions were announced publicly but were carried out privately. This is noteworthy, because in other areas of our homeland, the Chinese made public spectacles of our executions. Furthermore, if the deceased Uyghur was in relatively good health, it was possible that the family would not receive the corpse back. Instead, his organs might be sold on the black market.

WHEN OUR PEOPLE STUDIED RELIGION or in any other way occupied themselves with God, they were considered by the authorities to be rebellious elements. This was especially true for students of esteemed Uyghur scholars. These scholars gave lessons not only in religion, but also in basic subjects such as history, geography, and mathematics. Each had taught thousands of students over their long lives.

About that time, the cadres were forcing many of these scholars to relocate to Beijing, literally moving them from Khotan, Artush, Urumqi, and wherever else they resided in the Uyghur nation. There they were allowed to continue teaching and even to open schools, but only using teaching materials that the government had provided. In addition, they were allowed to teach only government approved students.

One of these scholars was a rather large man, graced with an equally large amount of charisma. I knew him to be an open-minded, mature person. He accepted all religions, and in the era we lived in, made a point of openly, publicly, and undeniably rejecting any form of fanaticism. He would say to me, "God made the world for all people. He also made women to be strong here in this world. He didn't say they had to walk around with downcast eyes. No. The whole population of the world, regardless of what nationality they are, or what religion they belong to if they belong to one at all, was created by God.

"Rebiya, I constantly hear that people around me are being arrested. If I'm not mistaken, they are all my students. If they don't like my students, then they most certainly don't like their teacher either. So I ask myself, why do they just arrest my students? Why don't they arrest me too?"

I answered, "What makes you different from other teachers?"

"No one's ever asked me that. I don't know."

"Why do you think the government is afraid of you?"

"Because the people I teach also become teachers themselves."

Later I had taken part in the meeting at which it was decreed that all of this scholar's students must be arrested. After that decree, the young men associated with him went into hiding or fled abroad. But it was not just a problem with religion. In China, virtually anyone who thought differently was considered a threat. They particularly applied their intolerance to Uyghurs.

Going abroad was a Uyghur's only chance. But if one of our people applied for a passport, he was detained by the authorities. He essentially risked imprisonment in an attempt to gain freedom. Many Uyghurs had fled over the mountains after the earlier "Strike Hard" campaign. They emigrated to Turkey or to Europe.

Or they looked for hiding places in Central Asia. But after the border treaty with China, our formerly friendly neighboring countries started to detain Uyghur refugees and deport them back to China. In response, Uyghurs wandered even farther, to Afghanistan, Pakistan, and Kashmir. Since China's invasion of our nation in 1949, educated estimates are that about one-million Uyghurs have been forced to flee for their lives.

According to Amnesty International, today only Uyghur political prisoners receive the death sentence in China. Even though Han Chinese comprise more than half of the population in the Uyghur nation, eighty percent of the prison inmates are Uyghurs.

OUR CHILDREN CONSTANTLY BADGERED ME about when their father would finally come back home from America. At the time, I thought I was doing the right thing by consoling them with words of assurance that he would be home soon. But one day, after my fourteen-year-old son Mustafa came home from school, I realized I had been making a mistake.

On the school playground, the principal told my son that his father was one of those people who caused nothing but problems for everyone else. My son was one of the most diligent students in the middle school, so the principal's rebuke greatly undermined his confidence to keep working hard. I wanted to confront the principal promptly, but my son asked me not to do it. I could not agree though because I knew that the matter would not just disappear on its own: "You have a right to understand why the principal said that to you." At that point, I revealed the truth to him about his father's absence.

When I entered the middle school office, everyone immediately stood up as a sign of respect in greeting me. They knew me quite well and honored me because I fully supported the poor children at the school. I could see one exception though; the principal looked rather uncomfortable with himself.

Once we were inside his office, his hands were shaking. However, he still managed to pour a cup of tea for me.

"I don't want any tea."

"All right," he said as he moved behind his desk to sit down.

"What mistake did my husband make? You're a scholar. You must be able to tell me."

"I myself was a student of his. We are proud of Sidik. It's my opinion that every Uyghur should make it their responsibility to protect you and your family. I've thought about it a lot. What I said to your son—what I said was wrong.

"We received an order from the government to watch Mustafa closely because his father, we were told, was abroad working with the separatist movement. I didn't show this order to any other teacher but regardless they sent agents to us who made the directive public at our staff meetings.

"Among the teachers here there are several who work for the *An Chuan Ting*. I feel like they're trying to take control of me. One of the teachers reported to me that your son was talking to many other students in the playground. I was directed to monitor what he was talking about. So I did that and overheard him explaining their lesson material to his classmates. Actually, I was planning on praising him at that moment. But to my deep regret I said something completely different. I'm so sorry."

I thought it was likely that our other children's schools had also received similar directives. I thanked the principal for his service and his honesty with me.

After that conversation, I began planning for the exile of my youngest children. I raised no suspicions as I acquired their passports. In fact, Akida, Honzohre, Mustafa, and Kekenos stayed in school until shortly before their departures.

BEIJING HELD MANY MEMORIES FOR ME. But at the airport that day, I felt suspended in time. No memories, no future plans, just the moment. Although it was hard to separate myself from our four youngest children, I was sure that I would follow them to the United States soon.

"Each of you should study hard for your people because you'll come back. Your land needs you." I stood on my tiptoes to see them for as long as possible. With one last wave before boarding, I called after them, "My children, the time will come soon and we'll win!"

"You have always talked about victory, even when I was young," my older son Kahar said as he put his arm around my shoulders.

My two older children Kahar and Ablikim and I stayed at a hotel near the Beijing airport. From the room, I telephoned my husband.

Sidik cried aloud. At first I did not know if it was from joy or from shock. But then he said, "What kind of a woman are you? You always strike like a bomb. You've torn the whole family apart."

"Sidik, listen to me. You'll not be alone anymore and our children will no longer live under constant threat. They are now above the clouds and safe in an airplane. Soon I'll be with you too."

I handed the receiver back to my sons. Both of them assured him that they would be following soon. Sidik did not consider that to be a good idea: "No, no. Please don't leave our country. Stay and work there."

After that, he wanted to speak with me again about where he should pick up the little ones. I told him we had sent him all the information by email. Suddenly, he was completely beside himself with joy: "But why didn't you let me know beforehand?"

"If I had risked sending you even a small message, you might never have gotten to see your children at all."

My two sons and I spoke little that evening. Back at home in Urumqi, I felt lonely in the big apartment without my little children. Of course, I still had my older children with me. Kahar, his wife, and their child were going to move from Aksu and live in the apartment. Ablikim had already moved in with me. My daughter Rushengül came to visit occasionally, as did Alim, my twenty-two-year old who was studying medicine in Beijing.

A few weeks later, a group of *An Chuan Ting* men came to my office with a message that someone wanted to kill me. I cooperated as they dressed me in a bulletproof vest and escorted me home. Eight others stood guard in and around my home. They would not allow me to take even one step outside.

After three days they left, with the explanation that the people who had wanted to kill me had disappeared for now. Later, I learned that during those three days, representatives from an international human rights organization had been in Urumqi.

It Was a Time When Those in Power Dropped Their Masks

$\mathcal{A}$t the next meeting of the advisory commission in Beijing, about sixty to eighty representatives were present. My Uyghur colleagues remained grimly silent as I assailed the central government.

"The blood of our people is wet on your hands and wet on those of Chinese Communist Party Secretary Wang Lequan. The events in Gulja were not a rebellion as has been claimed. There were no terrorists active there. Rather, it was a peaceful movement during which ordinary civilians took to the streets because they wanted more freedom for themselves and their families. I have a list of sixteen different crimes that were perpetrated by government units."

Shortly thereafter several officials from the central government were waiting for me—high officials whose job it was to bring the politics of the government "down to the level of the people," or so they said. Among them was Uyghur Ismail Tilivaldi who tried to calm me and "bring me to my senses." He explained to me that it was important "how" I represented our people, meaning that sometimes it was good to leave some matters alone and to take up other matters in a more appropriate fashion. After all, I could not win every fight, so it was best to pick the winnable ones. He spoke of how I should concentrate on building alliances for the sake of those winnable fights and said that squandering other opportunities on unwinnable matters was a disservice to our people. He said, "Rebiya, every human being has to sleep. Even you can't be awake continuously."

I told him, "I want to stay awake as often as possible to accomplish as much as possible."

Whether I was speaking to Uyghur scientists, doctors, or scholars, to mothers, bakers, or merchants, to poor farmers, taxi drivers, or laborers—all of them told me how much they wished those in power would please listen to their concerns. I thought Ismail Tilivaldi was concerned only with himself and his family. He had no vision for others anymore. He lived in great wealth. He had become cynical, as had so many others in power—once they rose in station above their people, they also left behind their morals with those who they had once seen as equals. Ismail Tilivaldi naively thought that all Uyghurs, if they just worked a little harder, could follow in his footsteps.

While the situation in our homeland was being whitewashed in the National People's Congress, on March 8, 1997, several more bombs exploded on buses in Beijing. News of previous such bombings had been suppressed, but the government made this news known immediately. I felt sad that the bombings had occurred. They defied our own peaceful non-violent resistance and were tragically misguided expressions of deep distress and rage as a result of Chinese government-sanctioned brutality, violence, and heartless oppression. The government wanted to exterminate us. It was bigotry, prejudice, and discrimination—familiar words to describe unabashed hatred against a particular group of people simply because they were that particular group of people. Just the existence of these people justified their oppression in the minds of the perpetrators. The perpetrators were so glib, so sure of themselves, so easily willing and able to punish our people with death sentences. I had to believe for the sake of my own faith in God that this policy left the people in the government utterly barren. I had to believe that their heartlessness was punishment enough for them.

WHEN A DELEGATE WANTED to formally present a speech at a primary session of the National People's Congress in Beijing, he or she was required to submit the speech in advance. The cadres would then review the text carefully and select the passages that they determined to be the most suitable.

So I submitted the manuscript for my speech, but it was a different version of the speech that I knew I would present publicly. I kept this version to myself because I knew the censors would not have approved a single sentence of it. Even though the apparatchiks were my opponents, I felt ashamed of my intentions to flagrantly violate protocol. Yet, I needed to confront these Chinese delegates about their blissful ignorance of Uyghur suffering. In the end, I could think of no other way to gain their attention.

The censors allowed five or six other speakers and me permission to address the entire audience in the enormous Great Hall of the People. The decoy speech I had turned in was peppered with praise and veneration. I had mentioned in it, citing the government's own statistics, how wealthy the Uyghur population had grown in places like Kashgar and Khotan and how much the Uyghurs had benefited from the support of the Party to achieve such wealth. I had said how together the government and the people had tapped new oilfields and built railroads. "We used to be so ignorant. But thanks to the Chinese, now all our people can read and write." These were the glorifications that my false version presented.

I was quite nervous. One day before delivering the speech I secretly met with the interpreter who would translate my Uyghur into Chinese. I gingerly pushed across the table the real speech I would deliver, saying, "You'll not have any problems. After all, you're only translating my words, not yours." I slept badly that night.

It was the first time I would have the opportunity to speak in front of the National People's Congress. On the way to the podium, I accidentally tipped over a pitcher of tea sitting on one of the tables. My heart was beating fast.

It is not good to lie. I already knew that as the members of the State Council sat behind me on the stage. About three-thousand congressional representatives sat in front of me in the Great Hall's first and second tiers; journalists sat in the tiers above them.

Protocol dictated that no one had the right to interrupt a speaker, much less to remove them from the podium. That rule gave me the courage to carry out my intentions. I removed a copy of the real speech from my briefcase and without hesitation handed it to my translator standing next to me. He began with a strong voice, faltered for a moment, then continued reading aloud: "Who are we? Who were we? Is it our fault that the Chinese have occupied our land? That we live under such horrible conditions?"

The translator was in such a hurry to get through the words that each syllable practically tripped over the previous one. He dabbed sweat from his brow. At that point, I decided to present the most important elements of the speech myself—I was agitated but I also felt sympathy for the translator. He remained next to me and I found some comfort in that.

I could not read Chinese, but if I remained calm, I was quite able to speak freely in proper, respectful, colloquial Chinese. So I thought I would concentrate on three areas: the impoverished farmers, the educational situation, and the government's treatment of political prisoners.

I took over, saying, "Our farmers aren't allowed to take up a different line of work, such as manufacturing. And when they extract natural resources from a farmer's land, the government doesn't compensate him even five-hundred yuan or even so much as employ him as a worker. Instead, they send in their own people."

One after the other, I enumerated the many tax burdens that were suffocating our business owners: "We pay so much to Chinese middlemen and so much for imports and exports. Why aren't we allowed to conduct business with other Uyghurs?"

I did not have to think hard to know what I wanted to say. The ideas came to me quickly and spontaneously. I simply wanted to characterize as many problems in a short amount of time as I could.

"Why does the government bring AIDS-infected people from inland China all the way to Khotan, Kashgar, and Ili? The Uyghurs don't know how to protect themselves from infection and the government offers no AIDS education. What's the government's motivation for these actions?"

I moved on to the topic of political prisoners. "To murder one of our people has become almost as commonplace as shooting a bird." At this point, I noticed that several delegates were wiping their eyes. That gave me more courage. It's likely no one present had ever heard such an inflammatory speech in the Great Hall of the People.

I continued, "I'm quite sure that the president and the delegates in this hall aren't accurately informed about the true conditions I've spoken of. The right to self-determination in our Autonomous Region should be put into action. If that happens, we will experience the stability that the government and the Uyghur people wish for. We all need peace."

My inner tension subsided only when I had spoken my last word. In total, I had presented sixteen different points within twenty-seven minutes. The delegates applauded loudly for a long time.

Afterward, the censors cornered the translator and began questioning him, asking why he did not stop right in the beginning. He responded, "That's against the law. No one is allowed to interrupt. If I had stopped reading, she would've probably ripped the paper from my hands and read it herself."

I had not been afraid that I would be arrested during the speech itself, but I was certain some form of punishment was likely to follow.

AFTER ALL OF THE STRESS of the previous few weeks, I felt like a weight of several tons had been lifted from my shoulders. I felt so light and happy. Normally after the session the president and the members of the State Council would leave through the hall's back door. But this time, the session ended in a different way. Some of the Communist Party officials came up to me directly.

One of them grabbed my hands and said, "You've spoken extremely beautifully. You should always speak like that." He added that he would research what I had described and find suitable solutions. "We'll pay special attention to everything you've spoken about today."

Premier of China Li Peng also congratulated me: "A very good speech, but you must discuss such problems with us first privately."

After that, these high officials left through the hall's back door as usual. When the other representatives saw, from a safe distance, how these important men had approached me they also dared to approach. Many of them clustered around me, wanting to have a picture taken of us together. They said things like, "What Wang Lequan did was wrong." Some of them demanded his dismissal. "Day in and day out, he talks about separatism, and then he does nothing about it." These good people, from all corners of China, showed themselves to be genuinely moved as they heard for the first time about the conditions under which Uyghurs lived.

Other high officials pushed forward around me. I soon realized that they were feigning interest as a way to escort me out. They managed to shield me from the others and keep journalists away too.

Later that afternoon, I had a luncheon appointment in one of the Congressional meeting rooms. Afterward, a Chinese vice chairman of the advisory board escorted me personally to my hotel in his chauffeured limousine. He was among the nine most powerful people in all of China. He and a select few others were the ones making decisions for a population of 1.3 billion people. Even though our region encompassed one-sixth of China's entire landmass, he had visited the area only once before.

He said, "What you've told us today is very impressive. That helps our work. We'll have people sent to your region and look into the heart of the matter."

Underneath my warm smile of gratitude, I actually no longer trusted any promise the government made. I replied, "I think this may be our last meeting together. As soon as I get back, there will be great difficulties waiting for me."

He said, "No, no, no; why should that be? It's the political advisory commission that is supposed to grapple with such topics. You did the right thing. If I were a Uyghur, I too would like to have spoken like that. Don't worry. If someone gives you a difficult time, I'll get involved. None of us are such bad people as you might think."

"Thank you."

I knew very well that these were nice but usually empty words. They always sounded so hopeful, but the deeds that followed were very different from the promises. Maybe he really was a decent person. Maybe he just did not have the necessary power to stand his ground. Maybe none of the ministers were in positions to assert themselves against the interests of powerful provincial bosses or state enterprises. Maybe.

Back in my hotel room, the first thing I did was call Sidik: "I've had a great victory today, my love. You must celebrate with me."

But he did not feel like celebrating. Instead, he said, "No, you shouldn't have done that. You shouldn't speak out like that until you're safe here with me. Rebiya, you're someone who just can't be controlled. I have to stop hoping that I'll ever see you again."

"No, I did the right thing. I have only one wish right now: celebrate with me!"

"Rebiya, you're just venting your anger. Of course you gave a good speech. I have no doubt about your abilities. But things aren't going to change as you would like. Nothing will change. You're a member of the advisory committee of the central government, so they will not attack you immediately. But later, they will show you just how much they disapprove of your behavior."

"It doesn't matter what they do to me, as long as they find solutions for our people. But today, for once I've reached my goal. Please celebrate with me."

"Okay," he replied. "It's hard for me to express how much I miss you."

If among those three-thousand representatives, only a handful of people gained an understanding of the true conditions that we face, that would have been a victory. At the time, I thought it was a victory.

In the news articles that appeared the next day, only two points from my speech were discussed: relief for farmers and development of the educational system. Everything else had been censored. The members of the press were like birds in a cage—allowed to flap their wings a bit, but not to fly.

I HAD BEEN EXPECTING IT, so I was not surprised. Three months after my return from Beijing, I was stripped of all titles, offices, and responsibilities. They had made my demotion public in May. In July they put it into effect.

The unity committee of the Xinjiang Uyghur Autonomous Region summoned me. The committee members were the first to know when a new law had been passed, and it was their responsibility to inform the people about these new laws. Virtually all of the respected, and not-so-respected but authoritative, people in our nation served on this committee. The president, who was Chinese, flashed a triumphant smile as he said to me, "On the basis of the laws of the Communist Party, your status as a representative in the Xinjiang Uyghur Autonomous Region People's Congress, as well as in the National People's Congress of the People's Republic of China, and also your responsibilities as vice president of the Xinjiang Uyghur Autonomous Region Chamber of Commerce,"—he droned on, listing all the offices I held, some of which I had not even been aware of—"are now removed. Starting today, you're an ordinary citizen."

I asked, "Why have you left me this simple right of citizenship? You can also strip me of that and send me to America."

"If you don't agree with the removal of your responsibilities, you may submit your complaints to the superior court at any time."

It was not hard for me to accept these losses. Quite the contrary: I was greatly relieved. At times, my official positions had been a burden. For example, I had wanted to be helpful to the people, but I also felt that I shared responsibility for the government's behavior. It kept me boxed in an uncomfortable and often unethical position simply by my association with the government. By shedding these status symbols, I felt I had regained my status as a human being with some common sense.

I was fully aware, however, that Chinese Communist Party Secretary Wang Lequan would relentlessly exploit my new vulnerability. In fact, as I later found out, he had almost instantaneously shut down all of my business enterprises.

One of those enterprises involved a contract I had signed with a Chinese woman from the interior. My partners in Tajikistan were going to deliver cotton to her. I had already made a deposit of fifteen percent of the sale price and was going to take possession of the first two-hundred-tons personally. I thought that my personal involvement was necessary because I did not trust my partners in Tajikistan beyond their garden gates.

I was scheduled to fly from Urumqi to Almaty and from there on to Tajikistan. But at the Urumqi airport security checkpoint, the officers confiscated my passport. Their argument was that my husband had violated Communist Party laws once too often. They recommended that he curtail his public criticism of the government's treatment of Uyghurs in his new position as a commentator for *Radio Free Asia*. In addition, the central government had announced effective immediately, that I was no longer permitted to travel abroad in part because my activities were also under surveillance. Even my lawyer, who was accompanying me, could not find any flexibility with these officers.

I had not anticipated that they would take my passport. Wang Lequan brought great hardship onto me with this measure, destroying my hopes of a speedy reunion with my husband and children. Back in our apartment, I immediately called the United States.

"Sidik—they took my passport away."

"Oh no. Now we're finished. I've told you so often that they don't follow any laws. They don't have any morals."

"But that's no reason for despair. I hope that I'll find another way to get to you."

After we hung up, I had to turn my attention back to business. If I did not get the cotton to the Chinese woman on time, our contract stipulated that I would then have to pay the sizable costs to the middlemen. I immediately sent my lawyer to Tajikistan on my behalf, but my business partners would not release to him the cotton I had purchased. Twenty-four trucks loaded with cotton disappeared into Central Asia along with my significant down payment. The Chinese woman sued me and I was ordered to compensate her 2.7 million yuan. Overall my losses on the project totaled thirteen-million yuan.

I began to see the government's new rules of the game. First, they confiscated my passport. Then they determined the penalty I had to pay for the confiscation of my passport. Subsequently, they also confiscated my children's and brother's passports.

I persevered with my business deals as well as I could and continued to offer financial aid to people in need. My friends stood by me as they always had. The wife of Governor Ablat Abdurexit also continued to shop at my stores.

As another obstacle, I was no longer allowed to travel between city districts without permission from the *An Chuan Ting*. Their men in dark suits followed me like shadows. It was irrelevant where I was going. If I looked behind me while shopping in a boutique, they too would turn and look back. If I was invited for dinner, they would be sitting at one of the tables.

DESPITE MY OWN PROBLEMS, it was still important to me to keep helping the Uyghur population. I felt that I had not done enough just with the creation of schools and the support of poor children. We Uyghur women really had no part in the government. It seemed to me that women's only option for making progress would be based on our own individual strengths.

It was traditional in our society that men supported the family. In my opinion, whoever had the most talent for it should feed the family. I thought that it was possible to create change through mothers. In fact, I was sure of it. Though most of these women were impoverished and had no formal education, they controlled the future through their influence on their children. But Uyghur women needed more self-confidence. Just a few days before, I had spoken with three young women in my office who had been abandoned by their husbands. They were convinced that their lives were over. So I asked them, "Do you mean to say that your happiness is tied to your husband by a rope?"

There were also educated Uyghur women, many of whom would criticize the conditions in our society, but did not yet know how to bring about change. The time had come to redefine the roles of girls and women in our society. That is why I decided to strengthen women economically by creating a holding company just for them. The women would be able to mobilize their strengths in new ways. But to join required that the women to be personally independent. I called upon women who wanted a good education for their children, who wanted to do business with me, and who wanted to change society. The event was set. I was expecting about one-hundred guests for a lunchtime meeting. But closer to one-thousand women arrived that day at the restaurant in my department store.

Many of the women had collected banknotes in their headscarves to give to me to invest. At first, I did not know what they were thinking. Maybe they thought that I wanted to immediately set up an enterprise with their money. But in actuality, I had planned only to discuss with these women an organization for the holding company. I had not even prepared a speech. But three hours passed as we spoke heart to heart.

I said, "We thousand mothers can help another ten-thousand. No—a hundred-thousand other women and mothers! I'm a woman who only went as far as the seventh grade in school. I've seen so many highly educated women among you who should really be my teachers. I've also noticed among you some who have the potential to become top politicians. I assume that my wish is the same as yours. That's what brought us here together today.

"Your eyes have been covered until now with a blindfold. You've looked for each other in the darkness and now found each other here. Please take off your blindfolds now. Look around you."

We became a sisterhood. It was something that I had not expected. Together in that short time, these women blossomed. It was beautiful to share with them our collective tears, laughs and smiles.

I went on: "So who among you wants to participate?"

First ten, then twenty women raised their hands. Then, in one burst, all one-thousand had their hands raised. The women who had brought their money in their headscarves lined up behind each other. They seriously believed that I would be collecting their money. I explained that it was not enough to simply hand over money like that. Then I selected a commission of twenty women. Only when this group had planned everything carefully, I explained, could the members consider depositing their money.

"You're meant to work at this enterprise yourselves, with your heart, your passion, and your enthusiasm. It is for the future of your children! With your contribution, you may be able to earn ten or a hundred times that amount and to change our society with the profits!"

Among those in attendance was a woman considered to have a bad reputation because her ten children had all become criminals. Her husband had a little shop. I had heard that she was a difficult person. She had brought with her a large box of money and seemed to be following me around at my heels. Finally, I had nowhere else to go and found myself face to face with her.

She held the box out to me and said, "Please take it right away. None of my children had the opportunity to receive an education. That's why they went wrong. We were farmers; we were poor and couldn't send them to school. Yes, I know people say that I'm bad. Because of my children, I also constantly get into arguments with others. It's so easy for them to criticize me. I would like to do something for the children of other poor families now. My husband and I have made a lot of money recently—please take this."

"All right. You can go home for today; but I will call you back in two weeks."

Later, when I was incarcerated, I saw this same woman shucking corn in the courtyard of the prison. She had received a life sentence for drug dealing. It made me sad to think that when we had met previously, she'd had a chance to change her life, but wasn't able to.

Our commission planned to train all of the women in business. Each of them was then to invest a fixed amount, according to her own particular situation, into the holding company. If a woman was unable to invest her allotted amount, then I would provide the balance on her behalf. The commission advised that ten or twenty women should form a group and do business with each other. After they had gained experience, we would send them to Central Asia and the Chinese interior.

With the earnings, among other things, we planned to open a school in every district and a supermarket in every city. We also planned on supporting artists who would spread our beautiful Uyghur culture across the whole country. Furthermore, we would bring to market local specialties such as pomegranates from Kashgar or melons from Hami. We even had hopes of building a security force that would combat the trafficking of women and children.

WE FORMED THE "Thousand Mothers Movement" with the approval of the authorities. At the formal opening celebration, our membership increased again. Word was spreading across the entire Uyghur nation, and we began receiving requests from women in many areas about establishing auxiliary groups in their districts too. Supportive letters kept pouring in by the crate-load.

Among the guests of honor at our opening ceremony was the wife of Governor Ablat Abdurexit; the wife of the mayor of Urumqi; and Maynur Kasim, vice president of the Chinese Women's Union. All of the important figures from the province were also there—politicians, bankers, and officers. Even the Chinese apparatchiks apparently were aware that we were advocating a good cause.

Journalists interviewed many people and videotaped segments to air on television. It was a delightful event with great community support. So I was rather surprised that evening when the radio and television news did not report on our opening celebration. I telephoned one of the journalists I knew and asked him why there were no news stories about the Thousand Mothers Movement.

He told me, "This afternoon the editorial staff received a written command not to report anything about your organization."

"Why?"

"I'm reading to you what they wrote here: 'A report about the Thousand Mothers Movement would be a report on a separatist movement.'"

News spread like wildfire that the government wanted to silence our Thousand Mothers Movement into nonexistence. High-ranking male officials in government bureaus, even at the top-secret *An Chuan Ting*, and banks, were all ashamed. How could they explain this suppression to their wives who were unanimously enthusiastic members of our organization? In the end, the government's miscalculated intervention benefited our cause even more by increasing the public attention on it.

We started with Uyghur women. But then Uzbek, Tatar, Kazak, Dungan, Kirghiz, and Mongolian women began joining us. Of course, the government did not like to see such cooperation among ethnic minorities. But perhaps they had learned their lesson about intervening—in any case, they kept only their own Han Chinese women away from the movement.

We wanted to be a shining example for society. We wanted to start opening branches in the largest Uyghur cities. Aside from our economic growth agenda, we also put forth plans to establish health and social services departments, including some with outreach programs for women who could not come to us. Serving homeless women was an important part of our agenda; we planned for twenty to thirty percent of our holding company's profits to be given to orphans and poor families.

Older women worked as volunteers. There had never been anything like this in Uyghur or in Chinese history. We had accomplished a lot. But in such a short amount of time we were not able to accomplish many of the things we had set out to do.

As part of a business training program, in one room of my department store we displayed an "audience" of dolls. In front of the figurines women practiced stating their opinions out loud as a way to improve their self-confidence.

I continuously affirmed that we wanted only stability in the land and not to engage in politics. I knew that politically sensitive problems could not be fixed by us. In hindsight though I should have realized that in China, all topics are politically sensitive.

At our next meeting, I made an error by using the word "international."

I said, "If all mothers unite when we cry together about an injustice, that injustice will be washed away by the might of our tears. When we laugh together, the dark clouds in the sky will drift away. When we manage to help the orphans and socially disadvantaged, the international community will also support us." The Communists voiced concerns that instead of "international" I should have said "Chinese."

Three days after this speech and only three months after our successful start, *An Chuan Ting* officers sealed the door to our offices. The beautiful dreams of one-thousand mothers were destroyed with one stroke of a pen by government command. I was afraid they would confiscate the money that had been collected, but they did not. I urgently called together one last assembly.

The central government had published the command in red lettering, which indicated Security Level One—this meant something that "endangers the stability of our country." This color was normally used in times of war or for the promulgation of important laws. The women whose husbands worked for the *An Chuan Ting* secret service told me about this red command. Apparently, the government feared that we could gain international influence.

During this assembly, the women called me the "mother of mothers" and crafted a crown for me to wear during my farewell speech. I said to them, "We had a very good wish. Unfortunately, we can't realize our dreams despite our good intentions."

All of the money that had been collected was placed in a large trunk and brought to the center of the room. I said, regretfully, to each woman as she stepped up to retrieve her share, "Please excuse me. I took some of your precious time."

Then a teacher stood up from amidst the crowd and said, "Today is an unforgettable day for all Uyghur women. We can no longer permit actions that hurt our pride. The organization of the Thousand Mothers hasn't been dissolved—no. This society will exist forever!"

But with those words, we went our separate ways.

IT WAS AS IF THE WALLS TO OUR CELLS were closing in on us a bit more every day. We Uyghurs already felt like we had been locked up, but the confinement was getting even tighter. If a Uyghur boy wanted to learn boxing out of a simple interest in the sport, he was detained as a separatist. If a countryman with a mustache applied for employment, he was forced to shave it off. If someone recited a Uyghur poem, he was considered a fundamentalist.

This was a time during which those in power dropped their masks. The high functionaries decided that our Uyghur nation was a part of China and should therefore be settled by even more Chinese. There were scenes in the streets where Chinese would beat Uyghurs, forcing them off sidewalks or buses with the words, "Get out of here! This is our land!" Women working in civil service were prohibited from wearing long skirts because that garment was considered a symbol of religious values. In the job market there were positions offered exclusively to Chinese—it said so on the signs.

I had reached my breaking point. I decided to write down all of these human rights violations and send them to the United States. It was only with this all-consuming assignment that I was able to temporarily soothe my heart, which ached for my husband and children.

Everywhere I was invited, people still asked me to speak at least a few sentences. Once at a wedding with around one-thousand guests, I said "Though I'm still standing on the soil of my country, I can no longer feel it beneath me. You're standing right before me, my dear countrymen, but there is a huge distance between us all. I miss you here. I don't know how to advise you to become happy. Maybe the Uyghurs don't have the right to enjoy a bit of freedom on this earth. I've seen beautiful dances here and heard beautiful music, but I covered my ears. If we listen to our songs closely, then we know that we really should be weeping. Our songs are full of suffering, full of mourning, and full of pain. Should we wait until we are destroyed?"

As I handed back the microphone, the wedding guests began to clap their hands. A boy got up and yelled, "You're our only hope. If you say to come, I'll join you immediately."

But I replied, "Let's start the music and dancing." I did not want the police to come and disperse this gathering. More talk from me would have turned that lovely wedding into a meeting. As it was, after the celebration, the boy who had spoken out was taken into custody and locked up.

I HAD ALREADY DUG DEEP into my pockets for the bribe money to receive the final rubber stamp needed to start construction on the Akida department store. But after the divestment of my government and civic titles, the Party began nullifying some of the previous permits granted.

I had contracted with a Chinese construction company and felt that I had no choice but to give the foreman the order to begin excavation. The authorities left me alone through the completion of the second floor of the building. Then they demanded to see the permit for the construction firm. Not coincidentally, the government had confiscated that permit from me shortly before. For that, they fined me two-hundred-and-twenty-thousand-yuan, dismissed the contractors, and then shut down the entire construction site.

In response, the construction firm went to court against the Urumqi city planning office. Maybe bribe money helped, but in any case, the government gave them permission to resume the contract again. The construction foreman came to me. He offered to pay me back the two-hundred-and-twenty-thousand yuan fine if his crew could continue working. I agreed, and construction of the fifteen-storey building progressed smoothly. Finally, it seemed to no longer be of any government concern.

At around the same time, my father began to sense that something bad was going to happen: "My daughter, I'm having bad dreams. It looks to me like the government is going to cause you great pain sometime soon."

I was mentally, emotionally, and physically exhausted from among other reasons the recent battles with the government over construction of the Akida department store. My siblings suffered along with me regarding our living arrangements and circumstances under Chinese rule. They tried to cheer me up. Friends tried to lift my spirits. I talked to Sidik every day on the telephone. But I had no time or energy to think about our relationship, or any relationship, as I grew increasingly despondent.

Every time Sidik passed the receiver to our little daughter Kekenos, she started to cry. I cried along with her. Our other young daughter, Akida, asked, "Why did you take us here? Why don't you come here yourself?" Our daughter Honzohre cried, "I just want to go home to you." Our son Mustafa begged, "Come mother, come to us."

Those conversations took away whatever remaining strength I had. During the next few calls, I had to avoid speaking to the children. Inside of me was a burning wish to leave my homeland. I had even considered leaving by illegal means—perhaps over the Khunjerab Pass to Pakistan. But Sidik vehemently rejected this idea, saying, "You have to find a legal way. They're watching every step you make."

I do not know how the construction of my Akida department store was completed in 1999. I was already in prison at that time.

In Hell One Day the Fire Will Go Out
Part One

Sidik was called to appear as a witness before The United States Congress on July 15, 1999 concerning the human rights violations in our land. Subsequently he would become a Congressional witness several more times over the years. I was busy in Urumqi collecting supporting documentation in the midst of his first Congressional testimony. During the years from 1996 to 1999, the newspapers had published many stories about the changes that had occurred due to the influence of the Chinese government. I collected these articles from, among others, the Gulja evening newspaper and the Kashgar morning newspaper. I had attempted to send copies to Sidik in the mail but the packages were intercepted.

One night as I was talking with Sidik on the telephone, he told me that a delegation from The United States Congress would soon be spending time in Urumqi. Immediately, my assistant Ramila and I reconstructed a list of the murdered and missing from the Gulja massacre.

Shortly thereafter, on August 6, 1999, a representative from the United States Congress telephoned me. She and some others on a fact-finding mission on behalf of the United States wanted to visit with me as soon as possible. I was delighted. I immediately packed copies of the newspaper articles I had assembled and placed them in my handbag. With Ramila and my translator, Alim, I went downstairs. The original plan was for a driver to take us in my Audi to the hotel for our 5:00 P.M. appointment with the delegation. But my son Kahar stopped us: "Mother, we've seen government people watching your car."

He was right, so we took a taxi instead. Just half-a-block before the hotel entrance, a large vehicle suddenly sped toward us head-on. My instantaneous thought was that it was coming to assassinate me in a car "accident." But the taxi driver reacted with lightning speed and quickly turned the steering wheel to the right. The oncoming vehicle careened full force into the car directly behind us.

With a quick look back, I realized that the compact car was completely destroyed. A hand was dangling lifelessly from the open window. In the next moment, someone yelled to us to get out of the taxi, while black cars from all directions raced toward us. Nobody showed any concern for the dead or dying victims in the car behind us. Plainclothes *An Chuan Ting* men flashed their automatic weapons as they cordoned off the area. They shouted, "Nobody comes in this direction!"

They will kill me I thought. It all happened so quickly. I turned and tried to scurry across the car hood to get away, but they were already waiting for me on the other side. I screamed: "I'm Rebiya Kadeer! Are there Uyghurs here? Are there Uyghurs here? I'm Rebiya Kadeer!"

Two or three countrymen who had been stopped because of the roadblock lunged out of their cars. But they immediately were surrounded by armed men. They were arrested, and just as quickly all other witnesses were rounded up and apprehended as well.

Out of the corner of my eye I saw a boy running away. I shouted to him, "I'm Rebiya Kadeer! Tell everyone that I've been taken into custody!" Officers chased after him, but they were too slow. I was afraid of simply disappearing so I continued to scream at the top of my lungs, "They want to arrest me! They want to arrest me!"

Another group of uniformed men ran toward me. One forced his hand over my mouth while others shoved me into a vehicle. My assistant Ramila protested too as men restrained her on the ground. My translator Alim stood there motionless with guns pointing at his head.

After a short drive, they brought the three of us to the *An Chuan Ting* bureau in Urumqi. The whole building was eerily deserted. Once we were inside one of the offices, an official accused me of having caused the automobile accident. Then another official held up a little paper bag with white contents. It looked like laundry powder. He dangled it in front of my nose and said, "We also found this in your possession. So you're involved in the drug trade too?"

Ramila scoffed. "Not a single person out there will believe you."

"Be quiet."

Then Ramila and Alim were led into an adjoining room. Thankfully, the two of them were eventually set free—although they were held for three days.

By releasing them, the authorities hoped to find out more about me. They followed Ramila. Later, they arrested her one more time. She knew many people in our human rights movement and the movement to liberate our Uyghur homeland. I worried whether she would be able to keep those affiliations to herself during the harsh interrogations.

But my worrying was for naught. I admired Ramila. If she had betrayed any of those people to the authorities, they would have been arrested, and along with them most likely about three-hundred more of their colleagues. A few months later I found out that Ramila and her husband were moved abroad. Of course they wanted to bring their nine-year-old son and twelve-year-old daughter. But to assure their silence, the government held their children as collateral.

For awhile I was left to sit alone in the room at the *An Chuan Ting* bureau. Then suddenly someone came in and pressed a cloth to my mouth and nose. I tried to resist, but it all happened so quickly. I must have lost consciousness immediately.

WHILE I WAS STILL UNCONSCIOUS, with my mouth open, my head tilted to one side, all four limbs stretched out and tied down, they unbuttoned my blouse, rolled up the envelope with the newspaper articles I had collected, and placed it inside my undershirt. Their intention was to make it look like I had hidden the documents underneath my garments. I later saw for myself a videotape of this staging. In order to damage my reputation further, they showed parts of these images on television.

I do not know how long I was in this unconscious state. While I was still groggy, other men in plainclothes quietly drove me to a hotel, then helped me to a room. One said, "You have to sign these documents now."

My head slowly began to clear as I massaged my temples with both hands.

"And what about these state secrets that you had on you?" A finger pointed to the newspaper articles.

I said, "That isn't against the law. Those are normal documents and newspaper articles."

"No, no. You've broken the law. You must sign now."

"No, on my life before God I will not sign."

"Fine. If you don't sign it makes no difference."

It was dark as they led me back out of the hotel. I was pushed into a car and driven away, but we were not alone. We were in a convoy with many other cars. In front of and behind our car were trucks loaded with heavily armed soldiers. At the lead and at the tail end were more government cars with red lights flashing and sirens wailing. I was convinced that they were going to finish me off at that point. Then I changed my mind. *Maybe they are taking me to prison.* Sidik had told me about his time in prison. I thought I might have to go through worse. But I was prepared for it. I just had to survive this battle.

A tall black iron gate loomed before me. There were guards standing at attention on both sides. I recognized this place from the outside. It was the Liudaowan Prison, only about four miles north of Urumqi and well-known for mercilessly torturing its prisoners. Legend was that you either died or went insane there.

I was told to get out of the car and then to step forward. I began moving forward until one of the Chinese guards yelled something incomprehensible to me. Spooked, I pulled myself back, but they pushed me out again.

"Go on!" When I put myself in motion once more, the Chinese guard raged like a madman. So I stopped.

From behind me I heard someone yell, "You have to shout '*Baodao!*'"

I still had to learn the language of prison. "*Baodao!*" was said before someone wanted to speak or before someone wanted to enter a place. Only when the counterpart replied, "Speak!" or "Come in!" was the person then allowed to do so. But I refused to do this. The Chinese guard cursed at me, his voice cracking under the strain. Up on the tower, two other guards manning a machine gun were also screaming at me.

Finally, a Uyghur security chief made his way forward. The prison guards greeted him with a click of their heels and a salute. They discussed something together. Afterward, this chief instructed me politely, "You must say '*Baodao*' loudly."

"I will not do it."

At that, the chief commanded the guards, "Open that gate right now!"

The large gate opened with a hellish squeak. The walls immediately in front of me were black concrete. Then I went through another door. Behind me, I could still hear the cursing voices of the guards. A uniformed woman behind glass in a small chamber reached out her hand to me. Like all of the officers in the prison, she wore a dark blue uniform. After walking a few more feet into a neighboring room, I was searched by this woman, but was allowed to keep my own clothes.

Right after my arrest, some officers had gone to my apartment and gotten a blanket and some food for me. This is how my children found out that I had been arrested. I saw my things lying there on the ground.

"Pick that up!" another female officer ordered.

"No, I will not."

"Then we'll beat you."

"You can go ahead and hit me."

I thought to myself, *I don't care about anything anymore. But I'm not going to let them destroy my pride.*

Then a different female officer charged up to me. I found out later that her name was Ye.

"Carry your things," she ordered.

"No, I will not do that."

"Carry them!" My eardrums reverberated but I continued to stand still.

Again she yelled, "I'll only tell you once more. Carry them!"

I did not answer. When she tried to slap me, the security chief pulled her away for a private conversation. After the two of them had spoken, she left and returned with a female prisoner.

The woman they brought in was a Uyghur. She bent down to pick up my belongings and then looked up. She recognized me at first glance and began to cry from seeing me in such a sorry place. I bent down and took my belongings from her. She whispered to me, "No, Mrs. Kadeer, please leave it. I'll carry these by myself."

When I went to step through the next door, another uniformed woman descended on me like a vulture, "Say 'Baodao!'"

"No, I will not say that."

Immediately, Ye and the chief showed up. He said, "It's okay. Let her pass."

NEWS OF MY ARREST SPREAD across the prison floor as the iron door to my cell slammed shut behind me. The room was a bit bigger than fifty-square-feet. They had emptied the cell for my arrival. Otherwise, there would have normally been up to twenty prisoners already in there.

The toilet was nothing more than a hole with a little hose next to it to flush away the waste. The light bulb in the ceiling fixture had been removed. The walls were damp, green, and crumbly. On one side of the room was a concrete ledge meant as a place for sleeping. I heard voices

in front of the door and keys turning in the lock. Two female prisoners—
a Chinese and a Uyghur—stepped inside.

I spread my blanket on the concrete ledge and lay down on it. The
Uyghur woman chatted on about so much random detail from her life
that I got a headache from it. Meanwhile the Chinese woman made
notes on a pad. She seemed to be jotting down everything I did, including I found out ridiculous details such as I had turned my head to the
side. I nodded off. When I woke up, the Uyghur woman next to me was
still talking.

I sank back into a deep and dreamless sleep. In the morning, a scream
awakened me. "What was that?"

The Uyghur woman yawned. "They're beating someone." The
Chinese prisoner pulled out her notepad and started writing.

"Why are they being beaten?"

"When someone isn't obedient, they get into trouble."

The Chinese woman spoke for the first time, saying, "There are fifty-
eight rules here. You have to memorize them." She handed me a little
notebook with the rules translated into Uyghur:

Some of these were: "I am a prisoner. I will admit my mistakes. My
behavior is disgusting. I belong to the lowest class. I have no right to look
up from the ground. I will never mention God's name. I will not pray.
When I sleep, I will not cover my head with my blanket. When I see other
prisoners making mistakes, I will report them immediately . . . I will repeat
these fifty-eight rules from memory once every day in front of the guards."

If I accepted these fifty-eight rules, my dignity and self-respect would
be destroyed. But I was told that if I failed to learn them within a week,
I would not receive my meals.

I heard footsteps coming closer down the hallway. Then Ye entered
the cell with another officer. My two cellmates jumped up immediately
and yelled as if from the same mouth, "*Baodao*!" I remained seated.

Ye said to me, "Stand up!"

"No. Why do you tell me I should get up? It's my personal decision
whether I get up or sit down."

Ye's face deformed itself into an ugly grimace. "I'll silence your rude
mouth!"

I told her, "I will not get up, but if you like you can try to force me."

"Just you wait!" She turned on her heels and the two officers left,
slamming the cell door behind them.

A short while later, an older female officer entered the cell accompanied by two male guards.

"Rebiya Kadeer, you have to work with us. You aren't allowed to cause problems for us. As of today, you're just a guilty prisoner."

Then I did stand up and locked my eyes onto hers.

"It's irrelevant to me whether you see me as guilty or as a prisoner. I'll never see myself in that way. It's of no consequence to me whether you beat me up or kill me. I will not accept your command. I will not."

She breathed in deeply and let her breath out very slowly. "Have you already heard how we've beaten other people here? Have you heard their screams?"

"Now I no longer want to speak with you."

"We aren't going to let you get away with anything here!"

But I pretended as though I could no longer hear her.

"I'm speaking to you."

Still I remained detached.

"Answer me!"

In part I found an answer to one of my own questions. It was clear that this officer and the others had been prohibited from beating me. I said, "You must know that this place is just where you belong. You'll stay here forever. But not me. I'll leave this prison again."

She clenched her fingers tightly into the fabric of her pants, gasping as though choking on something stuck just a little too far down her throat.

My CHINESE CELLMATE STEPPED onto the open threshold and said, "Baodao!"

When I tried to follow her out, someone shouted at me, "Stop!"

It was Ye standing outside. She asked me, "What did the prisoner just say when she exited the cell? Do you have a piece of cotton in your ear? Should I translate for you?"

She crossed her arms in front of her chest.

I did the same.

Then she said, "Even if you had the power before, you're still in my hands now. You're in my cage!"

At that she uncrossed her arms and screamed, "Out!"

I took one jump over the threshold and stepped into the corridor. My

Chinese cellmate marched before me, goose-stepping like a soldier, her arms swinging back and forth in cadence. I followed her down the long, gray corridor. I could hear the sounds of doors being unlocked and locked again. Ye followed behind us. Words rattled out of her mouth like buckshot: "Soon you'll see what else is waiting for you."

I could barely understand her. She continued, "Don't forget that we've also brought many rebellious men under control here. We know how to do this."

When we arrived in front of an office, Ye ordered the Chinese prisoner, "Go back to your cell."

"As you wish." She turned around sharply and walked away in goose-step.

Some men and women from the *An Chuan Ting* secret service were waiting inside the office. Some of them were Uyghurs. I had barely taken a step forward when the obligatory "Stop!" resounded. It seemed that they were all united in this one wish: that I would finally say their special word. "Step back!"

I made a step backward and remained standing with my arms crossed.

"Keep your hands down!" These shrill commands hurt my ears. I let my hands fall, not out of fear but out of respect—out of simple politeness when speaking to another person. When they saw this gesture, they looked at each other triumphantly. With a paternal tone, as though he were taming a wild animal, one of the men encouraged me, "Now you have to say '*Baodao!*'" They were already overjoyed that they had gotten me to put my hands down.

I told them, "Even if you had transported me here on a stretcher, I would not say that word. Why do you incessantly demand that I say that word?"

A Chinese man in uniform who appeared to have the most authority in the group spoke to me in a friendly tone, "Please come in." His hands rested on both thighs.

Ye swore at me, "Damn it. Stand up straight!"

I replied, "Why do you scream all day long? I'm still a human being!"

"Okay, okay, okay," the Chinese man in uniform intervened with a soothing voice. "Ye, please bring her a chair." That was a blow to her, because normally a prisoner had to stand. He upset her further by saying, "You can go now—and it's true, you shouldn't scream so much."

Next, he turned to me.

"Rebiya, how are you? Did you sleep well? Of course the two of us, you and I, will work well together. You know us. We didn't arrest you and bring you here. We only carry out the orders. You know how that is. But if you continue on as you've been, we'll not be able to control the other inmates. You're setting an unfortunate example here.

"We have murderers, drug dealers—every kind of scum. We're convinced that you're a good woman. We hope that during these investigations your innocence will come out too.

"If someone curses you or beats you, abuses your honor or your human rights, you can tell us about that. If you get sick, they should bring you to a hospital. Otherwise, you should file reports against these guards. We have shown you a lot of respect. We've given you a large cell for only three people. But one day and one night have not even passed yet since your arrival and you've already provoked arguments. You have to understand that even someone whose been given a death sentence has to call out the word 'Baodao' to the guards. Please cooperate with us."

He talked and talked; his sentences did not know periods. But because he used such a friendly tone, I showed myself to be equally agreeable. "Okay, I'll cooperate. But please understand that I don't want to play along with that 'word' game. Since yesterday, I've hated this word "Baodao." I can't accept it because I don't think that I should be a prisoner. You have to tell your guards that they'll never bring me under control with whips.

"Those who are responsible for me should behave like decent human beings. Yesterday, I heard screams coming from the abused all night long. They should stop with these beatings."

"Beatings? Really? Of course there shouldn't be beatings."

After that, nobody in the prison required that I say their word 'Baodao.'

On the second day, they even placed a light bulb in the ceiling fixture. I received the same food that the officers did, not what the other prisoners were given. Once a week they let me out into a courtyard, which was just a small paved square. The other prisoners were not allowed to look at me or come near me. I was in detention for forty-five days, and on every single one of them I was cross-examined.

IN THE INTERROGATION ROOM, there was a small window on the right side and a plain table in the middle. A matching wooden chair was nearby. For three days in a row I sat in that chair and was not permitted to sleep. Two Chinese and two Uyghurs stood before me. Every six hours the watch would change. If I dozed off, they would shake me awake. Again and again they asked their questions.

When someone is kept from sleeping for that long, he or she starts talking gibberish and falls into a state of mind where reality and dreams become so strangely intertwined that it is nearly impossible to separate the two from each other. It is a state where the brain has long ago fallen asleep, when the person's body slumps over, folding itself up into a numb, senseless cocoon, where semiconscious words may be spoken or may be hallucinated. Prisoners who are not permitted reasonable sleep for fifteen to twenty days in the end admit to anything about themselves or another.

The hypnotic voice of the interrogator rose and fell with the waves in his ocean of words. If he gently said to me, "Rebiya, you killed someone, is that right?" then maybe I would have replied "Yes" because I no longer knew what was happening around me. Like pebbles of hail, the questions showered down on my head. Pounding, pounding, pounding, pounding . . . If a "yes" slipped off my tongue in the wrong place at the wrong time, this admission was immediately noted as proof.

Later they confronted me with my own statements: "You admitted that, and you also admitted this." After thirty or forty hours, what I had said twenty hours before was a fuzzy memory at best. When my own words were played back for me, I was surprised at myself. I felt as though I were on drugs.

As soon as I felt a resurgence of energy, I rescinded everything. "No, no, no. That isn't what I said. Heh! Heh!" Saying "Heh!" was an attempt to wake myself up. I was so exhausted. "What did you say? Will you say that again?"

Then I heard my voice played back to me again. I would think to myself, *I thought I had just dreamed that.*

At first the officers tried to hold against me all kinds of transgressions:

"You tried to pass secret materials abroad. Your husband is a separatist."

At the end of their long cascade of words I was asked, "Is that right?"

I had long since drifted off again and mumbled "yes" or "no," half-asleep. If this officer succeeded in getting the right "yes" or the right "no," he would celebrate with his colleagues: "Oh, she admitted everything!"

He would get a reward for that. And some people might lose their lives for admissions gained by such methods.

EVERY MORNING AT NINE O'CLOCK they picked me up, and every evening around eight they led me back to my cell. In one of the interrogation rooms stood a high chair with armrest. My hands and feet were fastened with iron clamps to the arms and legs of the chair. I could see that there was still dried blood nearby on the walls.

Before me stood a row of chairs. Sometimes there were three, sometimes five; it varied all the way up to eight, depending on how many men would be joining in the interrogation. Torture instruments previously unknown to me lay neatly arranged on a side table. Next to the table were electrical instruments for "giving a shock," I was told.

At the beginning of each day, my interrogators dove right in. "Who brought you here, Rebiya? You did. Why do you interfere with government laws? Why don't you think of your children instead? We're expecting a good decision from you."

I said, "I made that decision a long time ago. Why do all of you waste your time? It isn't about me—it's about millions of people."

He said, "You're a romantic. You must know that many crazy people like you have found their ruin here in this prison. We sweep their bones out this door. This one! This door!"

I tried to prepare for these interrogations by telling myself, *Okay, for hours they're going to work on me to wear me down.*

And they did. "What tasks do you take on for the various foreign resistance movements? What position do you hold among those in exile? What role does your husband have abroad? What groups in Xinjiang work together with all of you? How many are there? By what means and where did you collate the documents that were with you when you were arrested? What goal are you pursuing? How much money did you give to the foreign Uyghur resistance organizations? Which organizations did you build?"

Next, the officers dragged in every paper, letter, and photograph from my apartment. They spread out the pictures in front of me one by one: "Who is this man? Who is that in the back?"

The next interrogator intervened, "Why were you so desperate to send these newspapers to your husband in the mail?"

"Well, they're just newspapers, and I wanted my husband to know what's happening in our land. Every person can buy these newspapers on the street and take them home. That's hardly a state secret."

As though he had not heard anything I had said, another man began anew: "Why did you want to send these state secrets abroad? What's your relationship to the United States? By what means did they teach you to start such organizations here?"

Because I always treated the Chinese interrogators dismissively, they tried sending in Uyghurs as interrogators instead. Sometimes the interrogations would take eight hours, sometimes up to fourteen.

If they tried to teach me something, I tried the same in return with them. Once a Uyghur lost his self-control and came straight toward me. He was about to grab me by the throat when the others pulled him back by both arms.

At night, when I came back to my cell, I could hear how the female guards mistreated other prisoners. If they were bored or in a bad mood, the guards would kick the defenseless women in the face or humiliate them with the ugliest language.

The little flap in the cell door to see outside was almost always open. I stood on my tiptoes and watched how they chased women from the *Falun Gong* religious sect, naked, up and down the corridors with electric batons.

My Uyghur cellmate told me that the male officers, when they were drunk on brandy, liked to take the pretty young girls from their cells and rape them. The ways in which the prisoners were tormented were incredibly diverse. Some were allowed to sleep only sitting up. As soon as they moved, the female guards would strike them. I heard another woman's cries for help as loudly as though she were standing right next to me: "I'm a journalist! I'll sue all of you!" After every new beating, the guards would make fun of her: "Fine, go ahead and sue us!" Fortunately, the woman had been arrested on false suspicions and after twenty days was set free.

Officer Ye had a Chinese officer friend named Qing. The two of them had it in for a particular Dungan woman. With a broken voice, the victim begged for mercy. But these officers had no intention of letting up on her. In her despair, the Dungan woman ripped a piece of metal from the sole of her shoe and swallowed it. It was not fatal.

Though I am sure she wished it had been because afterward all of the inmates had to stand on both sides of the corridors to witness the officers' punitive actions against this woman. Qing squeezed a white laxative paste into the woman's mouth until she gagged it back up. Then Ye shoved it back down with a baton. The louder the woman wailed, the more Ye beat her with her fists. Some of the prisoners turned their eyes away in disgust. But right away Qing ordered, "Look here! You have to watch this." The Dungan woman then teetered from cell to cell. Her hands and feet were bound and she had red welts on her throat from being choked. At each cell door she was forced to repeat, "I've made a mistake. I regret it."

ONE OF THE INTERROGATORS would play the role of the good guy and the other the role of the bad guy. If one of them was abusive, the other tried to sweet-talk me with his understanding manner. More and more often though, they both bared their teeth.

Finally, one of them pointed his finger so close to me it was as though he wanted to poke my eye out: "Until now, we've offered you the most pleasant form of interrogation. This is the first time that we've ever introduced ourselves to a prisoner so nicely. But now, this special treatment is over."

The next day they led me down one of the long corridors. The room we entered was about sixty-square-feet in size. I was instructed to take a seat on one of the concrete blocks. Five minutes had not gone by when strange noises could be heard through the walls. I paused, but could not distinguish whether the sound came from a human being or an animal.

Suddenly there was a shrill shriek from the left, followed by a deep moaning from the right. This pattern alternated a few times until silence finally fell. After four or five minutes, the sounds of pain started again. Then came a piercing scream.

My God, I prayed silently.

Moaning from the right started again. It sent a shiver through my body. Then I had a feeling that the concrete block I was sitting on was vibrating. I did not know whether this came from my own shaking in fear, or if the whole ground was really shaking. It went on like this for two hours.

The officers, who remained in the room with me, shifted a bit but still made a show of coolness. They said, "Well, did you hear those voices? That's the music we listen to every day. See Rebiya, every person will fall apart at some point. Look at that—your face is as white as a sheet."

All of my energy had been drained from me. I felt as though I were someone else, somewhere else—as though the old Rebiya had left me behind alone. My own heartbeat felt like it had become too loud to bear. The sound of it almost made me vomit.

The interrogators motioned for me to stand up. Slowly, I followed them.

As we stood in the corridor and looked into another room, they introduced me to the origins of those tortuous sounds. They were two Uyghur boys, young men in their early twenties. Their heads were shaved bald.

One of these boys was bleeding from his genitals. His pants were stained red in a blotchy circle at that spot. Blood was dripping out of the bottom of his pant legs. His head hung down and he no longer showed any reactions.

The other boy had a thickly swollen face that looked like one giant contusion. Threads of blood and saliva hung from the corners of his mouth. Two male guards held him upright. One of the other guards teased me, saying, "Rebiya Kadeer, do you see this? Look here, your heroes."

When the guard said my name the boy slowly lifted his head. He pulled his hands away from the two prison guards holding him upright and said, "Why did you come here my mother? We're already here for you. For all of you."

A guard barreled his fist into the back of the young man's head knocking him unconscious. The guard said, "You've been enough trouble for us today. We'll see about tomorrow." Then they carried him away.

They briefly pulled up the head of the other boy and showed me his face. Then they dragged him like a piece of wet laundry up the corridor; his dripping blood left a smeared path.

THAT AWFUL DAY WAS THE FIRST of my imprisonment in which I could feel my own powerlessness. It was clear that I could not save those two boys. I felt guilty for their punishment because I had not shared their beatings. Visions of the boys seemed to wait for the darkness to visit me. When I closed my eyes at night, the wailing sounds in my ears of the two would wake me. I prayed for them.

There seemed to be nothing left of me but the pain in my chest. I no longer consumed food or drink. I had started a hunger strike. On the first, second, and third days, they continued as before to take me into the interrogations. When my lips were white and chapped on the fourth day, they left me in the cell. Every morning and evening they put different dishes in front of me, but I did not touch any of it.

As a Congressional representative, I had heard a lot about the mistreatment of prisoners. I knew of a boy who had bitten off his own tongue to avoid betraying his friends. I heard about another prisoner whose stomach had been opened and his intestines removed. A silent sorrow trickled through me like a poisonous liquid.

My physical condition did not suit the female guards well. They had to push and pull my body into position every time to get me to be able to sit up. My chin hung to my chest during the interrogations. For three or four days, I did not speak a word.

In the next interrogation, I looked directly into the eyes of the Uyghur who was leading the session. I did not even close my eyes to blink anymore. The man came up close to me, waved his hand before my eyes, and checked to see whether I still had reflexes. After that, he took a seat in front of me again. "Please don't look at me like that." But I kept looking at him.

ON THE SEVENTH DAY OF MY HUNGER STRIKE, a group of Uyghur and Chinese *An Chuan Ting* agents came into my cell and directed my two cellmates to pull me up.

One of the Uyghurs looked at me for a moment, then lowered his head to avoid seeing me. He said, "You haven't eaten anything for seven days, but you look very good. I think you can take a lot. You're the mother of eleven children. You've survived so many difficulties. Maybe you still have wishes you want to fulfill for yourself. Does ruining yourself fit with your morality? There are two doctors among us. We're going to inject you with some dextrose now. We'll not allow you to die because there are still many duties waiting for you."

I looked at him mutely.

"We want to correct our mistakes. Please tell us your conditions to resume eating."

A glimmer of hope stirred inside of me. Maybe I did have the power to change something. I wet my lips. My voice was hoarse as I finally spoke.

"First, my Chinese cellmate should be removed.

"Second, every day I hear the voices of girls, maybe fifteen or twenty-years-old, who are being tortured. This torture should stop immediately.

"Third, I want to speak to the two young men who were punished so brutally. But they should first be brought to a hospital. I also want to know what instruments you tortured them with.

"Fourth, you should stop interrogating me.

"Fifth, I don't know if my children are aware that I'm in this prison. I wish for them to write me one or two lines. They should say: 'We know that you're in Liudaowan.'"

I thought briefly before continuing. "In a cell on this corridor there is a woman who begs day and night for a bowl of soup. I wish for her to be transferred to my cell. Please bring me also butter, hot water, and a few packages of cellophane noodles. I also want an investigation committee to be organized for me. And I want to speak with my attorney."

The officer responded, "Okay. We'll think about your conditions."

The next day, they brought me into one of the interrogation rooms. The same men who had been in my cell the day before were also present. They consented to replace the Chinese prisoner with the cellmate I had requested and to provide me with several packages of cellophane noodles.

"Regarding one of your other conditions, we don't actually beat anyone in the corridors. The people scream of their own accord. We're honorable Communist Party members." I spit at his feet. The faces of the other Chinese turned bright red with anger.

Another officer stepped forward and said, "It's also beyond our influence to stop your interrogations. We have to notify the central government of every little detail of your time here—even in regards to your meals."

The man standing next to him held out to me a letter from my children:

> Dear Mother,
>
> We looked for you everywhere, but we couldn't find you. We were so sad, so hopeless. It was only when we were told to send money for you that we knew where you were. Our father Sidik is almost crazy with worry about you.
>
> You're our mother. But you're also the mother of our people who love you and who are proud of you. We believe that you'll continue to show yourself to be strong. Our wish for you is that you take care of yourself and stay healthy.

My daughter Rushengül had written the letter. The other children all signed it. After I read it, one of the Chinese said, "You can see how just we are. We brought you the letter without censoring it. Oh, there is one other matter. Your children and grandchildren have come to the prison gate today."

I was led to a window from which I had a view of the large black entrance gate. It was opened and I saw my children standing there. But they were so far away from me that I could not see their faces. Carefully I raised my hand and waved to them—they were so excited that they each waved to me with both arms. This was permitted for about twenty seconds. Then I was led back to the interrogation room.

In the evening, two male guards brought my requested cellmate, Amina, in on a stretcher. One of the men commented with a smirk, "She has stomach cancer and will not live much longer." Before he had locked the door behind him, he affirmed, "We've stopped the beatings here and we'll not beat anyone in the future either."

They had not met all of my conditions. But at least I had achieved something. I had also not wanted porridge pumped into my stomach with a tube, so I began to eat again.

AMINA WAS A PEASANT WOMAN of about fifty, a mother of five from Gulja. She was so poor that she hadn't been able to marry her children off. But many gangs in her village had grown wealthy dealing in drugs.

Soon there were two or three addicts in every family. Three of Amina's sons were among them and all three were in prison for dealing. Every night, the police caroused with the gang members. And every night Amina climbed on her roof and yelled at the top of her lungs, "My God, if you're just, please give me back my sons!"

The gangs increasingly considered this woman to be a threat to their business and so they offered her money to be quiet. Instead of accepting it though, she denounced them for drug dealing. On that very same evening, the police took Amina into custody. Normally, someone would spend only two or three months in detention while awaiting trial, but Amina had not been brought to trial in two-and-a-half years.

For days I heard her shouts echoing through the halls, "I've eaten *laghman* noodles my whole life! Why am I not allowed to eat them now?" She looked like a skeleton. She gasped for breath as she made her way toward the toilet on all fours. Sometimes she could not even manage that and I had to help her.

The guards had also followed through and brought the cellophane noodles with hot water. Greedily, Amina stuffed the noodles into her mouth and said, "Now that I must finally die, God has fulfilled my dream."

After one week, Amina could go to the toilet without help. Her once-beautiful face soon regained a bit of color. But she still cried every day when she spoke of her husband, her daughters, and her three sons.

At the interrogation the next day, I brought up the subject of my new cellmate. "I'll go before the court because I know exactly what it says in your laws. If a prisoner is suffering from a terminal illness, she is permitted to spend the remaining days of her life at home. In those cases, the prisoner is allowed to buy their freedom. I'll make out a check for Amina's release."

Days later, they escorted Amina out of the cell. She clung to my skirt in a panic. It was with great difficulty that the guards separated her from me. One of the Uyghur female guards explained to her, "You can go home now. The money for your release has been paid for by a company," and she winked at me.

Delirious with joy, Amina folded her blanket and asked if she could take two boxes of the cellophane noodles with her. I said, "This is all for you. Please take it."

Without Amina, I felt alone again. I closed my eyes and drew pictures in my mind. I saw my girlfriend and her children sitting down at a banquet feast. I saw the joy in all of the faces, and smiled.

I do not know whether Amina was ever truly released.

ONCE WHEN I WAS BEING LED BACK to my cell after an interrogation, I saw two prisoners in the corridor ripping up playing cards and handing the shreds to a Uyghur woman who was wearing nothing but her underwear. A female guard was squatting on a chair nearby, forcing the half-naked woman to eat the pieces. The prisoner had told people that she could read her future and theirs from the cards. As punishment, the guard made her eat the cards until the very last one was gone.

On the forty-fifth day, the interrogators had fun with me: "Since today is our last day together, we're going to elevate your position." At this point, they laughed loudly. "We think that you're a happy woman because you've been allowed to receive a warm-hearted interrogation. We didn't beat you, we didn't force you to do anything, and we didn't threaten you. So will you please sign off on that now?"

I took the pen and wrote, "They haven't beaten me, but they've tortured me emotionally. In order to intimidate me, they tortured and killed two boys."

An interrogator said, "No, the two of them are still alive. They aren't dead yet."

Another shrugged his shoulders and said, "It doesn't matter what you write. In any case, you'll miss our style of communication."

I soon found out the interrogators' "elevated position" meant solitary confinement in the high-security area. A female guard took away my soiled white outfit, the same one that I was arrested in and had been living in for the last two months. In its place I was handed a worn-out pair of underpants, a dark blue pair of pants, a white T-shirt, and a jacket. I was allowed to keep my ankle-high leather boots.

There were no words to describe the smell in my new cell—it was unspeakable. My confinement was about thirty-square-feet in size. There was an iron bed on one side, with a dilapidated blanket lying on top of it. There was a hole in the floor at the front that was to be used as a toilet. The waste remained there for up to four days until an automatic flushing system briefly sprayed water through it. I spent my days sitting on a tiny stool. I was not allowed to move from that spot. I decided to obey that order, but I told myself that it did not mean I had given up my resistance. I just wanted to avoid unnecessary arguments. Besides, there was nothing else I could have occupied myself with. So I sat on the stool.

Up in one corner of the cell ceiling, a video camera was trained on me. A loudspeaker hung next to it. The door had a look-out flap, but it was usually closed. I was allowed to see out the flap only when a man put my meal through it. I saw just his hand. I never saw the face connected with it.

For breakfast, I received mushy dumplings in hot water. For lunch, mushy dumplings in hot water, but with rotting vegetables that undoubtedly belonged in the garbage.

In the evening, mushy dumplings in hot water. When I was eating, I always managed to devour my dinner in the five minutes that were allotted. Then I pushed the tin plate, tin cup, and cutlery back through the flap opening. Often I had to vomit afterward.

To my right and high up on the wall was a crevice the size of a brick in which a milky piece of glass allowed slivers of light to pass through. The walls were so high that my hand could not reach even half-way up. Not even insects crawled through the cell. I wished they had. There was nothing to relieve the monotony.

The first few nights, I could not sleep. Then I slowly got used to my new surroundings. We inmates were allowed a few minutes to wash our faces and brush our teeth every morning over a little washing bowl. During these tasks, the guards did not watch the clock as carefully as they did for everything else.

If Uyghur female guards were responsible for me, they would let me into the courtyard every fifteen days to see the sky. Sometimes they allowed me to spend up to an hour-and-a-half outdoors. I never found out why they allowed it, but the time passed quickly—half-an-hour felt like two minutes. Their Chinese counterparts were much more predictable. They let me outside only once in forty-five days, for five or ten minutes at the most. For me, that was like breathing in and out once. Then it was back to the cell.

The interior courtyard was small: approximately fifty-feet-long and twenty-feet-wide. Sometimes I got to see other inmates there, but we were not allowed to get near each other. When I stepped outside, the other inmates were immediately ordered to move over to the opposite side of the courtyard. "This woman is Rebiya Kadeer," I sometimes heard the prisoners whisper. As a political prisoner, I was not allowed to make eye contact with them and was in fact commanded to look in the opposite direction.

On a few occasions I was sent outside at the same time as was a beautiful young woman of about eighteen. Chains bound her hands to her ankles, so she was all hunched over, unable to really look up at the sky. I guessed that she was probably a political prisoner too.

After I saw this young woman all chained up, a song emerged out of the mystery of life within me and would not leave my head. It was a song about a mother who had to watch as her daughter was being tortured. It had lyrics about a world in which nobody was allowed to touch anything. I sang it to myself:

> If I had the ability to fly like a bird,
> there would still be no place for me to land.

The guards were constantly commanding me, "Come in here!" or "Come out here!" Once I had been a respected woman but now I had descended into humiliation. At some point—I do not know when—I even gave in sometimes to their commands to say their special word: "*Baodao!*" I would call out for permission to speak. "*Baodao!*" I would call out for permission to leave my cell. "*Baodao!*" for this; "*Baodao!*" for that.

This change seemed sudden to me but in reality it was a long, drawn-out, drip-by-drip deterioration. I found myself giving up. When I sat in that solitary confinement for hour after hour, every single wish and every single hope that I ever had in my whole life appeared before my eyes. The entirety of my time on earth passed by like a film: my hometown, my children, my husband, and my friends. They were all in my head twenty-four hours a day.

I started to hallucinate, which worried me. The mouths of the guards looked as if they were ripped wide open; I could see inside the black tunnels that led down their throats. It hurt my eyes to look at them because their eyes shot out piercing laser beams. Their faces seemed to be distorted into grotesqueries that were unlike any real human face. During this period I thought *I'm scared of myself.*

Though I could not get a pencil with which to mark a line on the wall for each of the days that passed, each of them so unremarkable, I did muster the spirit to find an alternative. I went back to the toilet or to the bed during mealtime and secretly took with me a chopstick with which to quickly scratch a line on the wall. When I was caught doing it a voice squawked over the loudspeaker, "Sit down, you." They watched me all night too. Once I accidentally covered my face with the blanket and immediately a voice thundered, "Take the blanket away!"

In those first months in prison, I missed my family and my friends with every fiber of my being. After months of solitary confinement, I yearned for just the proximity of another human. I even hoped that someone might come to interrogate me.

As it turned out, that was exactly the situation they waited for. I knew it and they knew it, as the interrogators did indeed come for me. They said, "Did you miss us a lot Rebiya?"

How pleasant it was to hear their voices. "You can stay wealthy, but don't get involved any more in political affairs."

"I—" I started to talk just like in the old days, but the interrogator immediately interrupted me.

"Normally, we would be re-educating you at this stage. But we realize that you're constantly trying to do the same to us. So the same interrogators will never interrogate you twice in a row, or you might have an unexpected influence on them."

Then he ordered me immediately back into solitary confinement.

I STARTED TO TALK TO MYSELF QUIETLY while sitting on my stool. "I have to get out of this prison alive. I have to learn to accept my situation. I'm not alone. God is with me. The two of us will remain friends. Just us two."

I began having conversations with God. I shared my wishes and dreams with Him and asked Him questions. It seemed to me as though a real figure would appear before me—a pale shimmering light full of sensibilities that could discern what was best for me. Surely this was just a figment of my imagination, but it helped me.

I regularly felt my face. I wanted to know if I was still there or if this was just a dream. Was I slowly drifting into a world from which there was no return?

With the stern voice of a teacher I would ask myself questions and answer myself.

How much is ten times ten? One-hundred.
How many children do I have? Eleven.
Who is my husband? Sidik Rouzi.

After each answer I would breathe a sigh of relief. With the passage of time I brought new life into myself with additional exercises: opening and closing my right hand into a fist. Opening and closing; opening and closing. At the same time, I bounced up and down on my heels. Up and down; up and down. I did each exercise one-thousand-five-hundred times, every single day. I crossed one leg over the other knee and flexed and relaxed my toes. Flex and relax; flex and relax. Then I changed legs. Flex and relax; flex and relax.

Sitting there on the stool, with only my upper body moving, I swung my arms back and forth. Then I rotated my head and my shoulders around and around. I massaged my legs. When I exercised, a voice over the loudspeaker crackled, "Why do you do that?"

After lunch, I very quietly started to recite the Koran. Then I switched to a Uyghur prayer of Shamanic origins and used a deep, monotone singsong voice: "God help me, God will help me. God help me, God will help me. God help me, God will help me." I repeated this prayer three-thousand times. I continued, "God is leading me on the right path. God is leading me on the right path," and repeated this three-thousand times as well. And finally, "I will get out of here alive. I will get out of here alive," three-thousand times.

I divided each day up systematically in this way. Instead of sitting on the stool motionless, I massaged the backs of my knees to keep my circulation going. I dampened my hands with saliva and tried to smooth out the wrinkles under my eyes. Occasionally, I slowly raised myself from the stool and carefully made two or three steps forward. "Okay, fine, but that's enough now," the voice from the loudspeaker would instruct me. With the help of all these different tactics I was able to successfully kill thirteen hours a day.

When a meal was passed through the door's flap, another dim light from above went on for five minutes. Before bedtime it went on for fifteen minutes. Otherwise, there was only the steady tiny beam of light that passed through that murky pane of glass at the top of the wall. My eyes adapted to the poor lighting. It was only when I came back from the courtyard that it took a few minutes in what seemed like pitch-black darkness for me to be able to see again.

For a while longer I tried to keep track of time by my tally on the wall, but then the guards completely stopped it. From that point on, I lost track of the days and weeks, then months, and eventually years.

The wall behind my bed was full of graffiti in Uyghur, Chinese, Russian, and Manchu:

> *This room robbed me of my life.*
> *They have condemned me to death.*
> *No human being should enter into this hell.*
> *They are fascists!*
> *God, are you still there?*

Mixed in with the graffiti were bloody handprints. One day I started to scratch my own thoughts into the wall with a chopstick.

Of course this act did not escape the camera. Over the loudspeaker I heard, "Don't dare write something."

"I'm writing something about love."

"What do you still need love for, old lady?"

I scratched my inscription into the wall anyway and nobody ever came to bother me about it:

> *When I cry and lament*
> *And say the name of my love,*
> *My land, again and again,*
> *Who can have sympathy for me?*
>
> ~
>
> *If you are ice,*
> *I will be like a hot drop,*
> *And melt you.*
>
> ~
>
> *You should not underestimate yourself*
> *In hell*
> *One day the fire will go out,*
> *Do not think that you will be here forever.*

My senses began to sharpen again. Soon I knew who was coming from the sound of their footsteps. I was also capable of differentiating the voices coming from over the loudspeaker. A squeaky voice belonged to a particular guard and meant a bad day ahead. On that day, I would have to spend my twenty-four hours motionless.

I also recognized the voice of a Uyghur female guard, who once commanded me through the loudspeaker, "Tell me something about you." I knew that she was the same guard who sometimes took me into the courtyard to see the sunshine.

So I made up a poem for her. It was called "Don't Go Away." I integrated into it a lot of compliments for her about how interesting, how intelligent, and how beautiful she was.

The response from over the loudspeaker was, "Thank you. On that Sunday when you sang in the courtyard, I was the one supervising you."

WITHIN A FEW HOURS, the court was going to sentence me to death. The execution was to take place immediately afterward. The whole prison and many of the citizens were already aware of this situation. After months in pretrial detention, my day in court had at last arrived. May 7th of 2000.

I knew the verdict had long ago been decided and that mine, like those of so many others before me, would merely be a sham trial. I wanted to scream out "I will not die!" defiantly and proudly. But my brazen thoughts about a savior angel slowly became melancholy as I turned my mind more deeply inward. I thought, *I'm prepared to die in order to become a symbol of hope for our people. I must be fearless— if not for myself, then for my family and the people.*

They asked me which clothes I wanted to wear. For them, it was just a simple errand of sending someone over to the apartment to gather my things. I heard myself speaking my final requests out loud to the guards: "I want to wear my white long skirt and my white leather coat with the fur trimming. I want my *tomak*, my beautiful white fur hat. I also want to wash my hair and wear it out long. I want to put on makeup."

"Yes."

"May I see my children one more time?"

"No, That's not allowed."

"May I look at myself in a large mirror?"

This wish was granted. I saw a beautiful woman. When I looked at my reflection, my mind was at peace for the first time in a long time. I took in a deep breath and let the stillness envelop me. But then it all came undone. Everything around me became blurry and jumbled: the guards, the cell, the light, the floor. At first it seemed like I was the only one there who continued to exist. But in a moment the scenario was reversed—*maybe I was the only one there who didn't exist.*

The Chinese guards standing behind me put their heads together and whispered to each other. I could see that they felt sorry for me. I immersed myself in a kind of inner contentment. I was alone with still-ness, with death, and with an image in a mirror. Many of the women inmates locked in their cells cried loudly over my fate. Even some of the Uyghur female officers and guards dabbed tears from their eyes as one of the other officers shackled me into hand and ankle cuffs. "All of the wishes that you still have . . . we want to fill them for you."

"As you don't want to let me see my children, I ask only to see myself once more in the mirror with the hand and ankle cuffs on."

A Uyghur officer came into the room and told her Chinese colleague, "You're being asked for by someone. You'd better go." The Chinese woman had hardly left when the Uyghur woman pulled a camera from her pocket. Sobbing, she took a few photographs of me. She asked me what last words I had for her. But I was in a different state of mind— one that no longer had anything to do with her world.

I said aloud, "How beautiful I've become. Someone who belongs to the people doesn't look good in gold chains, but looks beautiful in hand and ankle cuffs. The only human who is truly free is the one who is able to burst through these confines. God will do that for me."

I cannot explain why I spoke like that. Perhaps it was due to my long solitary confinement or that I was facing execution. I do not know. In my mind's eye, I called upon my husband and our eleven children. I asked each of the children, especially Kekenos because she was the youngest: *How can your father live without me now?*

"Time is up, Mrs. Kadeer . . ."

. . . After the trial, as they drove me back to Liudaowan Prison, images of that courtroom kept passing before my eyes. I wrote a poem in my mind to soothe myself:

> *Innocent before the court she was placed today,*
> *Jingling, her voice filled the room,*
> *"So come out with it!" she said, "What am I guilty of?*
> *Who holds the balance of the people in their hands?"*

Though earlier I had been in a state of mind far removed in time and space from the present moment, my senses began to return—to nestle back into the real world, the world in which I could feel myself breathing, the world in which I could feel myself participating . . . the world of the living.

Gradually, I began to recover from the trauma caused by the way in which the Chinese officials had orchestrated the staged trial and my presumed execution afterward. My feelings in the face of my anticipated execution, my inner tension, my despair, and my shredded inner peace took me over so suddenly. It was an experience that had brought me to the edge of the bearable. But from it I also drew energy for everything that was yet to come.

The prison director was the next person I saw. He was as dumbfounded as I was—we both could not believe that I had not been sentenced to death. The other officers also seemed to be highly confused. It was all so surreal, so contrary to expectations. One of the Uyghur female guards even let out a cry of jubilation, "Mrs. Kadeer has come back healthy!" As news spread throughout the prison, we could hear the inmates banging their tin bowls together in celebration.

At first they placed me back in my old cell from the days before solitary confinement. I received paper and a pen so that I could write my claim against the eight-year sentence by the Superior People's Court of the Xinjiang Uyghur Autonomous Region. According to the law, I would receive a reply within one-and-a-half to two months. I was also receiving money. I was fairly sure that it was being sent by my children, but when I asked the guards who had been sending it they did not answer me. The guards only let me know how much I had in my account and then had me sign a receipt for the statement.

Several times, I tried to gain information about my children from the guards. Only once did I get a response, which was more of an admonishment than information: "You could've spent your money in peace and continued living like a queen. Do you know what all of your children have to go through now because of you?"

"Do you know something specific about my children?" I asked. But the guard just went away.

After that, I agonized over whether one or maybe even several of my children had been arrested. One day as we made our way in a group to the washroom, another prisoner whispered to me, "Your son is here."

We were standing at the wall that was connected to the men's side of the prison. I was completely bewildered after I managed to finally get someone to tell me that my son Ablikim had been sentenced to two years and my secretary Kahriman to three years. Their imprisonments were termed "re-education through work" and were imposed without arraignments or trials.

Before long, they locked me up in solitary confinement again. Months had passed since my claim for more justice and ultimately for my immediate release from prison, but I had not received an answer from the Superior Court.

Perhaps they had not given me the death penalty only so they could maintain appearances for the outside world. I was afraid that at some point they would inject me with poison and then tell the outside world I had suffered from heart problems and died. This kind of hoax was frequently perpetrated. Much later I found out that I would surely have stayed in solitary confinement for many more years had my loving husband not engaged several international human rights organizations to work for my release. Tirelessly he wrote to the president of the United States, United States Congress, European Union, Amnesty International, and many other human rights organizations. The United States government probably became involved on my behalf because I had been arrested while on my way to a meeting with their representatives. In the year 2000, for my work in China, I was honored by Human Rights Watch with their highest award. But I had no idea about any of that at the time.

I WAS GETTING WHAT FELT LIKE stomach ulcers from a lack of nutrition, and my legs had swollen because I was forced to remain motionless. When I requested medication be bought for me with my money, I was told by a cool voice, "If you should happen to die of this, then die."

My situation was dire and growing more so. I decided to present demands to the prison officials and go on a hunger strike until my demands were met. I told them, "First, I want to meet with my children.

"Second, I want to see one of my secretaries about all of the unfinished work I left behind.

"Third, I want to meet with my attorney.

"Fourth, you have to take me to the hospital.

"Fifth, you have to improve the quality of my food.

"Sixth, my appeal to the Superior Court was filed six months ago. I want an answer.

"Seventh, you'll allow me to walk up and down in my cell for two hours a day—six steps up and six steps back.

"When you meet these demands, I'll eat again."

Nine days into my second hunger strike, the cadres had fulfilled almost all of my demands. They even allowed me to walk up and down for two hours—six steps up and six steps back. Because my conviction was deemed completed and lawful, I was allowed to see my children once every three months from then on, effective immediately.

I was so excited to see my children that I was hardly aware of my feet touching the ground as they escorted me into a visitor's room. It was stark and completely separated down the middle by a glass partition and other barriers that went all the way up from the floor to the ceiling. A telephone and tape recorder sat on a table on each side of the partition. There were countless prison guards and other uniformed officers on both sides too.

The rules of conduct had been clearly explained beforehand. Only general questions such as how I was feeling overall or the quality of the food were allowed. If I did not strictly follow the rules, there would be no further visits. I was also informed that on the days when I met with my children, none of the other inmates would be allowed to receive visitors due to heightened security.

My son Kahar, my daughter Rushengül, and my secretary were led in. My legs almost gave way from excitement. When my secretary and the two children saw me, they began to cry uncontrollably. *Probably my face has changed a lot* I thought to myself. I picked up the receiver.

Kahar picked up the other receiver and I heard him say, "Did you admit your guilt? Please work well together with the authorities. Admit your mistakes, mother. Please abide by the government's directives with gratitude and follow them with your full heart. You have to take a stand against separatism. This land is a part of China. It's an inseparable part of it."

We were standing across from each other, each of us holding a receiver in our hands. I was so confused by what he had said that I could hardly contain myself. I said, "Where are your siblings?"

"Ablikim is in jail. Alim was in jail, but they released him after fifteen days. Each of us working in your business was in jail for at least ten days. If you agree, we would like you to please write a letter for us. The letter should state that your decision is for your son Alim to take over the leading role in your company. Otherwise, your businesses will be in danger."

I was not expecting this conversation. And my mind had slowed so that I could no longer concentrate on such details. Looking at my son through the glass, I thought to myself, *The government scripted this well for him. Alim was my youngest son. He had studied medicine, not business, and had just graduated. The Chinese authorities are compelling my children and Alim to take over the management of my businesses. What else are they doing to my children?*

"Please Kahar, how are Sidik and your younger siblings doing in the United States?"

"They are all doing well. They are healthy."

A guard set a plate of meat and fresh vegetables on my side of the partition. Clearly, it was put there only to give the impression that I was being well taken care of. After ten minutes, someone said, "Time is up."

I watched as my son spoke intensely to one of the officers but the man just stood there unflinching and unresponsive. Then one of the Chinese guards on my side of the room wrapped a slice of apple, a little piece of meat, and grapes in a napkin for me. While he was doing this, he grinned broadly and said, "Have you noticed how just the Party's policies are? Look, we even brought along meat for you."

I could see that my children were watching whether the guard would hand me the food. So that they would not worry, I took the napkin and said, "Thank you." I kept my true thoughts to myself as I walked in the opposite direction without turning around again. I did not want my children to see my face.

WHEN THE CENTRAL GOVERNMENT in Beijing realized just how intensely my case was being scrutinized abroad, the high officials seemed to have lost their composure. They decided to end my solitary confinement and transferred me a month later to the higher-security neighboring prison facility at Baijiahu.

After about a twenty-minute drive, we reached the multilevel women's penitentiary. It was well known that the prisoners there were forced to do heavy labor. Even without official reports, citizens knew that many prisoners died there.

As I was marched down the corridors, I was shocked to see so many young men. It was only when I looked closely that I saw these "men" were women with shaven heads or very short haircuts. At home, it was customary for Uyghur women to move gracefully with careful, small steps. But here they shuffled along with wide movements as though they had lead weights on their feet. I was also surprised to see such a large number of young female prisoners, aged eighteen to twenty.

In the office of the vice director for the prison, the female guards loosened my hand and ankle cuffs. The director looked at me thoroughly from head to toe.

"So this is the famous lady . . . Take her."

A female guard turned to me: "Pick up your blanket, your tin bowls, and all of your other things on the floor. Carry them to your cell."

"I'll make two trips. I've been in solitary confinement for a long time. I don't have enough strength to carry this all at once."

"Do what I tell you!"

"But I tell you that I can't make it." I sank down on top of my things.

"Stand up!"

I did not want to argue and so got up again.

"Take them now!"

When I staggered away, loaded down, she grabbed my shoulder and pulled me back. I lost my balance and only a nearby wall kept me from falling all the way to the ground. That made me so angry—and I really do not know where I got the strength—that I grabbed the woman and pushed her. She just barely steadied herself with a hand to the wall. White with anger, she grabbed an electric baton from the table. She immediately spun me around and wrenched my arm behind my back.

The director said, "Be careful. Stop it. We have orders from above." Then she turned to me. "You've been rude to a guard. For that you'll receive an additional three years on top of your eight-year sentence."

"This guard assaulted a prisoner, and for this you should lock her up also for three years. The regulations you must follow are ones that I helped sign into law as a representative in the National People's Congress."

The next moment more uniformed guards came into the room. The others moved aside as a large, Chinese female officer came directly toward me. She stopped a breath away, her face to mine.

She said, "I am Lei and I'm responsible for you. You have to practice obedience because you belong to the dirtiest of all rungs of society. You're nothing but garbage."

I had never been able to tolerate someone placing themselves above others. "I see then that you haul the garbage."

"Shut up! Who allowed you to speak? Unless I allow you to speak, you're to remain quiet."

"If you're a human being, then I also have the right to speak to you as a human being."

Her eyes twitched.

"Take that away!" She meant me.

ON THE SECOND FLOOR more than twenty cells were lined along the hallway, each with its heavy wooden door held open. An iron door blocked the line of sight at one end of the hallway. At the opposite end was a large meeting room. To the side were four rooms serving as the base for the guards on duty.

Officer Lei summoned a Chinese prisoner named Qiao-Qiao. "Qiao-Qiao, take off what she's wearing. Burn it and put her in prisoner clothing." Then she added something that I did not understand at first. "And get rid of the hair!"

Qiao-Qiao was a murderess. She had stabbed her boyfriend to death out of jealousy. She had already spent fourteen years in that prison. The prison administrators had decided that she was the right one to be my mentor. As I would soon find out, she was the most awful of them all.

At the clothing distribution booth, she leaned far over the counter and whispered something to the woman on duty there. The woman pulled out a dark gray jacket and pair of pants that were full of holes and three sizes too big for me. The waistband hung down almost to my knees. She gave me a string for a belt.

I could barely walk in that pair of pants. Even with the string belt, they were too wide and long. Qiao-Qiao and another Chinese prisoner led me through the corridor to the next room. There they pushed me down on a bench as Qiao-Qiao waved a Uyghur inmate over to us. She instructed the inmate, "Cut off her hair!"

I jumped up and grabbed my braids protectively. "No!"

So they called in more women inmates to help. Two held down my left arm and two others my right. Somebody pushed me down from behind. Then they cut off my braids just below my ears.

Qiao-Qiao worked on me some more with the scissors. In my eyes she resembled an evil spirit more than a human being. She snipped at me from all angles and all sides. After that the prisoners pulled me in front of a mirror and had a good laugh. "Look at yourself," they said.

I turned around and looked at myself from all sides. Inside, my heart was bleeding, but I would never let them know that. Then I was once again taken back to Officer Lei.

In addition to her, a Uyghur female officer named Mihri was also made responsible for me. She had long black braids, bright blue eyes, and a long thin body. Over the next several years, Officer Mihri would never have a nice word to say about me. She would treat me like a lower life form. But sometimes she would also silently hold a protective hand over me.

Officer Lei told me, "You'll learn the fifty-eight rules by heart within the next fifteen days. I know you didn't do this in the first prison. But you will here. There are many people out there watching for you, but they're only dreamers. I'll keep you here with me until I'm old. Even your spirit will not leave this prison. So why don't you speak up now? Just a short while ago you were singing like a bird."

"I can sing like a bird. I've learned to do that. But I can't bray like a donkey as you do or bark like a dog as you do. In contrast, I've never learned such inhumanity."

She slammed her fist on the table. "I must show you who I am. I am Lei! Don't forget it!"

"You're just an employee who works for a few yuan to pay your rent and buy your food. If you fight with me like this every day, sooner or later it'll make you sick."

Officer Mihri stepped in, "Today she shouldn't be put to work. I'll take her to her cell."

I was led me down the long corridors without a word. Once we arrived at my cell, Officer Mihri reprimanded Qiao-Qiao for getting me such a ragged blanket and ill-fitting clothes. "What kind of strange things did you get? We have enough clothing here that will fit her!"

Qiao-Qiao babbled something to herself.

"Qiao-Qiao!"

"*Baodao*!"

"Closer!"

"I'm very sorry that I've done something wrong."

After that, I was given a new blanket and clothing in my size. I was deeply grateful to Officer Mihri for these actions. But I could not show her this because she never looked at my face. I also found it strange that she spoke to me only in the third person. "Her." "She." "This woman." But never "You."

"She is under my authority. And I hope that nothing happens to her in this cell."

Officer Mihri had hardly left when Qiao-Qiao threw my clothes from the bed to the floor with one sweep of her hand. "I'm not the sort who will carry the clothes for a prisoner like you. You'll have to take that over yourself."

Silently I picked up my clothes and put them back in their place.

As BEFORE, THE INTRUSIVE, glaring eye of a video camera mounted into the ceiling was always watching me. There were iron bars at the window. On one side of the cell were four bunk beds; on the other side there were three. There were fourteen inmates in this cell—one Kazak, four Uyghurs, and the remaining eight Chinese. My cell was unusual; in no other cell were there as many Chinese women incarcerated together. It was impossible not to notice this, as the total population inside the prison was eighty percent Uyghur.

There was a little stool for each inmate. We stowed them under the beds when we were not sitting on them. We were ordered to keep one pair of underpants and one T-shirt inside our pillowcase and one jacket and one pair of pants tucked into our beds. There were no personal belongings allowed aside from these.

There were between one-hundred-and-eighty to two-hundred female prisoners on every floor of this prison, and one bathroom on each floor. Two women guards would always accompany us there and watch us while we were on the toilet. If a prisoner was not granted permission to visit the toilet, she had no other choice but to soil herself. Only late at night, after work, would she then be able to remove her wet and stinking clothes.

Each prisoner also had her own tin pail stowed under the beds. We kept our bowl, spoon, piece of soap, toothpaste, shoes, and socks in the pail. Fourteen pairs of worn out shoes and socks took on a noxious odor after a while.

THE INMATES SEWED from early in the morning until midnight. They made suits for women and men, shoes, children's clothing—absolutely everything that someone might want in the marketplace. About three-hundred sewing machines for this assignment had been set up in a large room. The room itself had dark green mold growing along the floor-boards, up the walls and ceiling, and especially in the corners.

I was ordered to sit on a stool in the back of the room. I was to remain inactive and just watch the seamstresses work. And that is all they did. They looked neither left nor right—they just worked nonstop. Qiao-Qiao stayed nearby as my watchdog. She worked just as quickly and silently as the others. She would snap at me, "Sit up straight!" If I tried to offer a nearby seamstress help, Qiao-Qiao went wild, "Don't touch anything!"

It was only my second day at Baijiahu. Since I had gotten there, I had been thinking *This is like paradise. This is much better than my old prison.* After work, when we had returned to our cell, I found out that Qiao-Qiao had dumped water on my blanket. Without saying anything, I put my jacket over it and easily fell asleep.

But after only two hours the guards started making noise: "Wake up!" Everyone jerked themselves upright and hurried away. I ran after them, not knowing where we were going. It turned out to be the washroom.

It was small and windowless. Wash basins were suspended from the walls, with about a hundred women crowding around them. Someone jammed their elbow into my side, but there was nowhere for me to move to. The women cursed and ranted. Within five minutes, we were sup-posed to have brushed our teeth, washed our faces, and used the toilet. Under certain conditions that might have been possible, but when there was such a long line it was impossible.

In the middle of the washroom was a somewhat larger basin. I found out that once a month in the winter and every two weeks in the sum-mer, we were allowed to wash our clothes, dishes, and bodies. We were given a total of forty-five minutes for that.

After the five-minute washing we hurried back to our workplaces. On the way there, several of the women fell down, scrambled to get back up, and kept running. Just as briskly as we had jumped out of our beds only minutes before, my fellow inmates jumped into their chairs and started sewing. I took my place on the stool and watched as I had been commanded.

Two or three hours later, we were told, "Grab your meals!" All of the inmates dashed toward a large iron kettle that had been dragged in. Each prisoner held out her tin bowl and scurried back to her sewing machine chair right away. The food was black. I had trouble just getting it into my mouth, so I set it aside at first. Within the viscous mass was supposedly a dumpling.

Since mold on the ceiling would sporadically detach itself and sprinkle down, I was afraid that some of it might fall into my food. So I took a piece of paper from the floor and covered my bowl with it. Then tentatively put the spoon in my mouth but gagged immediately. "I can't eat this today. Excuse me."

Qiao-Qiao yelled, "Eat!"

I had no intention of doing what Qiao-Qiao told me to do. "You're not a warden. Do you really have to bother me all the time?"

Immediately she jumped up, shouting "*Baodao*! *Baodao*!" and ran out in the direction of the guards' station.

A moment later she came back, accompanied by Officers Lei and Mihri. Officer Lei wanted to know what I had done to Qiao-Qiao. "Why do you hurt her so much?"

Qiao-Qiao sobbed melodramatically. Apparently she had reported to them that since yesterday I had been scolding her incessantly, even in the middle of the night. She also said that because I did not like the food, I had thrown my bowl at her.

"Everyone stand!" About three-hundred women jumped up at Officer Lei's command. "Look in this direction!"

Suddenly the room hummed with whispers. A lone voice called out, "That's our mother Rebiya Kadeer." Then a second voice. Then a third and on.

"Who said the name Rebiya Kadeer?" Several Uyghur women came forward. Officer Lei admonished them, "You'll stand."

That meant the women would stand still in one spot for twenty-four hours without sleeping or eating. That would be difficult enough, but there were also likely beatings and other punishments that would make it even harder. I felt miserable because I had already brought hardship to these women on the first full day after my arrival.

Officer Lei added, "If any of you in this room even speak to Rebiya Kadeer you'll lose points."

I later learned if a prisoner lost three points for bad conduct, she would forfeit receiving visitors one time. She might also receive one little piece of meat instead of three at the next meal. And if she lost even more points, she would be incarcerated in darkness.

Officer Lei continued, "Nobody is allowed to even look at Rebiya Kadeer. This person is an enemy of the people! She once earned a lot of money and achieved for herself, for herself only, great fame. You shouldn't talk about what a great lady this person was in the past. Maybe you didn't understand her correctly in those days. Back to work!" Immediately the sewing machines began to clatter again.

She turned to Officer Mihri, "I'm going to a meeting. See you."

"See you." Then she summoned back the Uyghur women ordered to stand. In her usual third person communication with prisoners she asked, "Why did they say the name of Rebiya Kadeer out loud?"

They just shook their heads not knowing what to say.

"Will they do that again?"

"No," each woman answered.

"Then sign here." Officer Mihri held a piece of paper out to them and the women signed their names to it.

"Now keep working."

A warm feeling spread inside of me. I thought, *I believe this woman is a caring person.* Although she was in this place and in this position, she still had feelings for her people.

"Rebiya Kadeer!" she called.

"I'm here!"

"Come with me to my office."

When I moved to step into her office, she gently held me back. "She first has to say '*Baodao*!'"

Because she was a Uyghur and because she had protected those women, I did her the favor. "*Baodao*!" I even had some sympathy for her, as I suspected it was probably not easy to work in the prison. I resolved not to cause her any more problems.

Officer Mihri asked, "Why did she clash with this person? She should explain."

I answered, "I would never get into an argument with a woman like her. That doesn't reflect my character. I'm a prisoner like she is. Maybe I'll get along well with Qiao-Qiao in the future."

"Fine, then. I'll not get involved in it."

Over the next two-and-a-half years, Qiao-Qiao still continued to concoct the most evil stories about me. She would put her belongings underneath my blanket and then accuse me of having stolen them. Other times, she complained that I had thrown dirt into her meal bowl. I never defended myself much against these absurd accusations.

In Hell One Day the Fire Will Go Out
Part Two

Officer Lei denigrated me in front of the director and vice director of the prison. She complained that she was not allowed to use corporal punishment on me and because of that I was a threat to the entire internal structure of the prison population. As a result, the administrators contacted the security bureau for the Xinjiang Uyghur Autonomous Region, which forwarded the query to Beijing. In order to punish me more severely, they needed permission from the very top.

Shortly thereafter, seven Chinese officials from Beijing arrived at the prison and ordered me to their office. One of them commanded me to sit down and said, "It hasn't even been a year since you were transferred here, but we've already received twenty complaints against you from Baijiahu prison officials. I think you don't want to accept your new situation. However, if you don't change your behavior now, we'll have you sent to Peylo Prison in the Tarim Basin."

Peylo was the largest of twenty-nine labor camps in the Xinjiang Uyghur Autonomous Region. Of one-thousand inmates, perhaps thirty would survive over the course of their sentence. More specifically, the survival rate was commonly estimated to be less than five percent. If a weakened prisoner fell onto the sand at Peylo, several thousand ants immediately swarmed over the body. In a short amount of time, the ants would bite off piece after piece of the body, leaving only the skeleton as evidence of their appetite.

Another of the seven Chinese officials waved Officer Mihri over and asked her, "Have you neglected your supervisory duties for this prisoner?"

"No I have not. I request to speak to the gentlemen alone please."

I waited outside the door for two-and-a-half hours. After the door reopened, the group appeared to be in good spirits. Mihri most likely told the men that Lei had purposely brought trouble upon me and that in fact I had done nothing wrong.

One of the men summoned me back into the office. He told me,

"You aren't a prisoner like the rest of them. The central government has determined that you aren't allowed to speak to anyone for eight years. You're permitted to speak only with Officers Lei and Mihri. Every two weeks all of the prisoners are allowed to watch television in a large hall. That doesn't apply to you. You may not write or read. You may not grow your hair longer than your ears. You will not request that your children bring you more to eat. You will obey the commands of Officers Lei and Mihri."

I nodded. Another Chinese man spoke up: "We've assigned a total of ten people here to you." He listed their names: Mihri, Lei, the prison vice director, and Qiao-Qiao were among them. "You may leave now."

Qiao-Qiao gave me a confused look when I came back to the cell. Then she immediately began to scream. Frightened, I jumped aside. The other women in the cell shook their heads. But Qiao-Qiao was already in the hallway with the prison officers, accusing me of having grimaced at her in such a threatening way that she was scared from the moment I had returned.

Lei came into the cell with Mihri and said, "The government officials from Beijing haven't even left yet and already there's more trouble. Poor Qiao-Qiao is suffering from constant intimidation by this person. We should send her to the prison at Peylo."

At that instant, I spoke directly to Mihri for the first time: "You can ask my cellmates. I didn't do anything."

Though the others knew exactly how Qiao-Qiao was tyrannizing me, they were afraid to help. A young Kazak woman finally forced herself to describe to Mihri in great detail all that Qiao-Qiao had done to me.

THAT THE YOUNG KAZAK WOMAN had stood up for me was a thorn in the side of the prison administrators. She also helped me clean my meal bowls in the washroom. For these reasons, she was moved to another cell and replaced by an insane Chinese woman.

This new cellmate deluged us all with an arsenal of curses throughout the night and then, while we slept, kept herself busy by stealing our blankets. Sometimes she laughed for no reason. The next moment she paced from wall to wall in utter madness, wailing and pulling out her hair.

After her arrival, major upsets occurred in our cell every day. Amazingly, I was the only one this crazy woman left alone. To the other prisoners, she described me as a "holy woman." Those prisoners then reported her to the officers for being nice to me.

So that no alliances would form, the administration exchanged the women prisoners in my cell every two weeks. Each day, three of the cellmates would file a report on me and would denounce each other as well. If a prisoner had not written anything bad about me for a week, she was replaced.

Every two weeks, the uniformed officers gathered in their office and came back to me with their assessments: "You aren't developing as you should. You aren't accusing your fellow inmates of anything, yet they constantly report you for the smallest matters."

I thought about this situation for a long time. *Why were my cellmates denouncing me?* I recognized that at some point, due to the conditions in the prison, each had lost their humanity, their empathy, and their sympathy. The worst part is that they each probably believed these things had been taken from them forever.

If I had to use the toilet, two prisoners followed me. If I sat on a stool, two others sat down next to me. If I wanted to sit at the table, three others sat there with me. This constant togetherness made us all aggressive.

After I was released from solitary confinement, my courtyard exercise privileges had been withdrawn. Only if I was expecting guests or when I went to the sewing room did I pass through the courtyard. I enjoyed it very much each time. Even for just those few moments a sense of freedom wafted around me.

TWO WEEKS AFTER A VISIT had actually been authorized, the prison director finally contacted my relatives. I was told, "Your children are coming tomorrow."

I sat up that whole night and silently counted every second. The next morning I waited impatiently for someone to come get me. But it was not until noon that I finally heard Mihri call my name. I was at the door immediately, saying, "I'm here!"

"Her children have come." I moved forward but Mihri restrained me. "She should walk slower. She shouldn't walk ahead of me."

I tried, really, but I could feel that my children were near and I couldn't walk any slower. Mihri put her hand tightly on my shoulder. "She should walk slower . . . slower."

This time they led me into a visitation room that was without a partition to separate us. There was a little table between two sofas. Microphones for listening in stood on the table. I was instructed to sit on the sofa at all times and was not allowed to stand up when my children entered the room. A male warden with a video camera was positioned a few feet away to record the meeting too. Countless officers were in the room and I could see that many soldiers stood guard outside as well.

"Just so you could meet with your children, hundreds of us were ordered to be here," one of the officers chastised me.

Another broke in, "If you tell your children anything about your daily life in prison, you'll never see them again. You'll tell them that your life is good here and that the food is good. You'll not mention other topics."

Even more officers were talking to me from all sides, but I did not actually notice any of them. I thought only about my loved ones. I wanted to know what they looked like and how they had changed.

"Mother." My son Kahar's familiar voice brought my head around instinctively, but the officers stopped me roughly. Behind me I heard, "My dear mother, my dear mother."

Alim, Rushengül, and Kahar cautiously stepped forward and stopped in front of me. In unison, they said, "Mother." They must have been in shock, never before having seen me in such a condition: emaciated, weak, with closely shaved hair and gray prison clothing.

One of the officers grew annoyed upon seeing my children stand there speechless. Their tears were the only communication they could muster. He said, "When they don't see their mother, they cry. And now that they see her, they still cry. Sit down now, all of you."

But my children could not stop crying, so the officer ordered them to stand in front of me. One after the other, they greeted me. Their whole bodies were shaking.

I said, "I ask for your forgiveness for looking so poorly."

"Dear mother, we see how beautiful you are regardless."

I consoled my children as they sobbed, "It doesn't bother me that they cut my hair and took my clothes. What has changed around me is completely meaningless. I'm bearing it all with my head held high and I ask that you not feel sorry for me."

After that, my children—who were growing into fine young adults—recovered a little bit.

"I'm doing well and I'm healthy. I live here just the way all of the other prisoners live. This time in prison now is just a part of my life, the way wealth was a part of my life."

Rushengül looked into my eyes. "Dear mother, your words haven't changed. You speak just as beautifully as you did before. Our hearts have found their places again."

I asked, "Kahar, how are Sidik and the children?"

"They are doing well, they are healthy."

"And my father?"

I had forbidden my children from the beginning, even when I first entered Liudaowan, from telling my father that I was in prison. They were to tell him that I was in the United States on business. But my father could not understand why I did not call him even once in all of the years of my absence.

Minutes later, without allowance for even a proper good-bye to my children, I was pushed from the room and marched back down the corridor to my other life. For a moment, I was not sure which world I was in.

AROUND FOUR OR FIVE O'CLOCK every morning, the guards led us from our cells to the sewing hall. More than twenty hours later, around one or two o'clock in the morning, they herded us back. After one month of my required sitting quietly in the corner, I requested to be allowed to work like the other inmates. Sitting on a stool for twenty-one hours doing nothing was strenuous. I would rather work. Later, when I was in the West, I saw many articles of clothing that had been made in Chinese prisons being sold in stores.

When we showed up in the morning, the guards patted me down first and allowed me to enter the sewing hall first. If I stood farther back in the line, the other women formed rows on both sides, creating a runway that I could pass through toward the door of the sewing hall.

"The dangerous prisoner has come," they used to say.

"The queen has come. Please clear the path for her," the Uyghur women would joke.

From that day onward, I was assigned to sew on buttons. Though I did not just meet my quota but surpassed it, I was unable to stay awake for eighteen to twenty-two hours a day. One side of my face would begin to ache. Then other pains I could not even identify arose. I hurt everywhere. Other prisoners had similar reactions. Every day, up to twenty women collapsed unconscious on the ground.

The female guards would shove the unconscious women aside with their feet as if they were shifting sacks of laundry. After about fifteen minutes, the women would come to, pull themselves back up onto their chairs, pale as ghosts, and continue sewing. These conditions were intolerable, which is why I decided to speak to the prison's deputy director.

I said, "If a prisoner doesn't sleep enough, she will fall to pieces. I request that you allow us at least eight hours for recuperation. You say that the laws in this country are just. But I've met many innocent women in prison, along with those who the courts have had good reason to send here. You should strive to keep all of us prisoners alive. If the conditions don't change, then every one of us will die before our time."

In response I was told, "This is a prison. Don't forget where you are."

I said, "You call it a prison, but actually it is a workplace for slaves. You don't even allow us one hour of free time during the week."

"Are you trying to ignite a rebellion?" Her question hung in the room for a while. "Yes, you're a very dangerous woman. You're always trying to start a rebellion. Get out of here!"

The next day I was thrown into an abyss.

"WE'LL SEE EACH OTHER AGAIN in fifteen days." The prison's vice director walked away. For minor infractions, the term was ten days, but for serious infractions, such as mine, she added to my "days of guilt."

The cell door slammed shut and I was immediately surrounded by absolute darkness. They had taken me into the basement. Not even a glimmer of light entered my cell from the corridor. I held my hand in front of my face but could not see it. There was no cot in the room, no blanket—nothing. It was completely empty. I sat down on the bare concrete floor. The cell was barely big enough for me to stretch out my small frame when I laid down. If I stretched my arms, I hit the walls on both sides. The air in the cell was stuffy and humid. Sweat dripped seemingly from every one of my pores. I worried that if they did not come quickly enough I would die of dehydration. As I soon learned, food and drink were brought twice a day. I was instructed to perform bathroom functions into a cup.

I lay there not knowing whether minutes or hours had passed. After a few days, I lost the energy to sit up. I collapsed like a rag doll. I started talking to myself so that I would not have a panic attack. "Breathe, Rebiya, breathe. Stay calm, Rebiya, stay calm."

I strained to see something, anything, in the pitch black. But there was nothing to see. I shut my eyes very tightly so that I could at least see the dots of light under my eyelids. Despite my physical weakness, I started to stretch my hands and toes. Open and close. Open and close. Open and close. Open and close. I massaged my ears and rubbed my legs.

Many prisoners went insane or became ill when incarcerated in such darkness and had to be taken to the hospital afterward. For most, the hospital was their last stop. I sang in the darkness, talked to my children, and discussed matters with my husband. And I asked questions of God.

"Fifteen days are over." An eternity seemed to have passed by when that voice from outside penetrated my imaginary world. The light blinded me so completely that I could not see at all. I went from one blindness to another. I kept shutting my eyes to ease the pain. For five or six days afterward I still had to shield my eyes with my hands. At first, I was allowed to stay in my cell. Qiao-Qiao and another girl watched me. "Well, was it nice in the guesthouse?" they mocked me.

I have had some difficulty organizing these torturous sessions in the dark chronologically. These events pile on top of one another in my mind. I was held in darkness about six times, but I can no longer say for sure exactly when each particular time was.

FOUR WEEKS LATER THE PRISON DIRECTOR came to see me. He said, "We've heard that you have to work hard for up to twenty-two hours a day. Now there will be reforms. Effective immediately, every prisoner will be allowed eight hours of sleep. We'll also serve meat once a week. Furthermore, we'll allow you all to take half-a-day's rest once a week."

We continued to stumble into our cells after work and to get back up at five o'clock in the morning. But at least there were some improvements. We congratulated each other.

Not once during the entire time of my imprisonment did I hear a nice word from the female officers or guards. Instead they yelled constantly until their voices were hoarse. They said things like, "Lift your head higher!"

One time, a female guard could no longer keep her thoughts about me to herself. She told me, "Normally, they would've carried your corpse out of here long ago, or at least beaten you half to death. The only reason this hasn't happened yet is because your husband is China's Public Enemy Number One. I just can't understand why the prison department thinks that you're so special. They always say that you're a bad person, but at the same time, they're concerned about you."

I could sense that there must be some kind of support for me abroad. But I told her, "I don't know what my husband is doing. We haven't seen each other for a long time."

She took notes on what I had said. I believed as well that the extensive international attention apparently directed toward me had played a role in the latest reforms at the prison. Perhaps the central government was frightened that something would happen to me and that the abuses at Chinese prisons would then come to light.

I was not always successful at appearing calm and composed on the outside. On one occasion, a photograph I received in the mail from the United States overwhelmed me. My children Akida, Honzohre, Mustafa, and Kekenos were sitting on a carpet in the street, all looking in the same direction. Akida had written on the back of the photo, "Every day we wait for you. We miss you."

On the half-days that we had off, the guards sometimes permitted us for a short while to hold onto our photos. I pressed the picture of my children to my body as though I could feel their hearts beating.

My children's visits were the high points in my life during my incarceration. Our conversations usually unfolded in the same pattern within the usual allotted half-hour.

I would say, "How is your father doing in America? And the children?

How are your businesses going? I'm doing well here, you don't need to worry." An officer once said to them, "Your mother lives like a queen here. Look at how her face glows."

Once my son Kahar winked at me. The guards took note of this on the video recording later and then prohibited him from meeting with me for six months.

It was forbidden to hold hands. It was also forbidden to smile. We were meant to exchange our news while remaining as unmoved as possible. If the children shed tears, the officer would interrupt, "If you cry, you'll not be allowed to see your mother next time."

Despite my best efforts, I could not find out how my son Ablikim was doing. The children would only say that he was "good", nothing more.

Only one of my children could speak at a time, generally in turn according to where they stood or sat. Sometimes one of them would repeat phrases that one of their siblings had already said before: "Did you admit your guilt? Please cooperate with them. Admit your mistakes."

We lost a lot of precious time that way. My daughter once whispered, "Mother, you know we have to say that." As punishment, she was not permitted to visit me the next three times.

The officers made me recite the fifty-eight rules from memory after every visit: "I am a prisoner. I will admit my mistakes. My behavior is disgusting. I belong to the lowest class. I have no right to look up from the ground. I will never mention God's name. I will not pray. When I sleep, I will not cover my head with my blanket. When I see other prisoners making mistakes, I will report them immediately . . ."

On a cold spring day when prison administrators called a meeting under the open sky, every prisoner had her chair with her, but I had been barred from taking mine. There was a damp meadow adjacent to the prison courtyard which only shortly before had been flooded with rainwater. The administrators wanted to introduce a new law, the so-called One Hundred Days Struggle. The law stated, "If a prisoner is not re-educated properly in prison, her sentence will automatically be extended by one-hundred days."

I wanted to sit on the dry concrete surface next to the grass, but I was ordered back to the grassy field. To protect myself from the damp-ness, I positioned myself in a squat, at least until another order came: "Sit down on your backside." So I sat in the grass in wet pants for an hour. The cold slowly crept into my abdomen and nested there. Soon I felt as though it had taken over my whole body. To the right and left of me, two Chinese guards sat on their chairs, like they were on their thrones. "*Baodao*!" I said, as I tried to let them know that I was feel-ing ill. "*Baodao*!" But the two of them pushed me back down by my shoulders.

When the meeting was over, I stumbled back into my cell. It felt to me as though my inner organs were failing. The next morning, I could no longer urinate. I painfully excreted just one drop, which burned like fire. Every five minutes, I felt the urge to urinate but my body would not respond.

The first time I needed to, the female guards gave me their permis-sion to go to the toilet, but not the second time. I no longer had control over my body and urinated while I was sitting at my workplace. Then I collapsed to the floor and simply remained there. The guards hardly took notice of me or of the other seamstresses lying on the floor, each of us in our own physical and emotional misery. I curled up into a fetal position and spread my jacket over my abdomen to keep myself warm. Flies swarmed around me. At midnight, the end of the workday, I was no longer able to stand. Two women pulled me up and helped me back to my cell.

Once they had put me on my bed, they pulled off my wet pants. That is when they noticed that I was covered in blood. Qiao-Qiao then reported this to Lei. Not long after, the officer was standing at my bed-side.

She said, "So it's really true that you've become sick. I'll bring you to the doctor's office tomorrow. But for now, just lie down. It's not going to kill you."

I was frequently urinating blood and screamed in pain the whole night, begging my cellmates for help: "I'm losing so much blood. I'm afraid that I'll bleed to death."

But Qiao-Qiao would not permit them to help me—or even to speak to me.

The next morning Lei ordered, "Come along." But I could not obey. I remained lying down with my hands pressed to my abdomen.

Following Lei's orders, some women prisoners dragged me to the medical ward.

A Chinese woman and a Uyghur woman were sitting at two tables next to the entrance. The Chinese woman said, "What's wrong with you? Stand up straight."

But I was unable to comply. Once the women realized this they dragged me to a bed and laid me down. A female doctor came in and examined my urine, then gave me a blood transfusion. Under Lei's supervision, some prisoners then dragged me back down the corridor. Again I felt a sharp pain in my abdomen. I pressed my hands against it and pulled them away bloodied. As I lifted my head, I saw Mihri standing over me. I said to her, "I beg of you. If you're a Uyghur's daughter, then please save me."

Mihri said, "Where are you taking her Lei?"

"Back to her cell."

"No. Carry her back to the sick ward."

A strong Uyghur prisoner flung me over her shoulder and brought me there. In the medical ward, it was hard to miss Mihri's loud admonition to the staff on duty. "If she dies, the vice director and I will lose our jobs. We are to keep this person a prisoner here. Nothing else. I'm responsible for her. You're to keep her in the ward here for three or four days. As soon as she is well, I will personally come get her."

I had the feeling that the Tatar female doctor was relieved by this directive. She had wanted to keep me there from the very beginning, but Lei had not listened to her objections. I received an additional transfusion. The Tatar doctor watched over me for a while, nursing and comforting me. She said, "Would you like to see yourself in a mirror?"

"Yes." I gasped. I saw that the area around my mouth was white. My face resembled that of a dead person.

The next morning, Mihri came to visit me briefly. She asked me, "Why didn't she inform me in a timely manner?"

I was at a loss for an answer. While I was lying on the ground all day long, no officer or guard had spared even a minute to assist me. I did not know what had made me sick and the doctor had not yet given me a diagnosis. Some nurses brought me a hot water bottle to soothe my abdomen. They also boiled water for me to drink. I drank gulps in an attempt to satisfy what seemed to be an unquenchable thirst.

Four days later I was taken back to my cell. But just two more days after my body swelled up like a balloon. All of this occurred shortly before a scheduled visitation with my children. Because the prison administrators did not want them to see me in this condition, they cancelled the visit.

As fate would have it, the strong Uyghur prisoner who had carried me on her shoulder to the medical ward was released one week later. She went from the prison directly to my department store. She then stood at the entrance and called out to all passers-by that I had become ill. Our security people took the woman to my sons, to whom she then gave a full report.

NEWS OF THE STATE OF MY HEALTH spread with lighting speed. In Washington, D.C., my youngest daughter Kekenos hung a poster with my photo on it from her neck and stood in a high-traffic area. My husband wanted to take her back home each day for lunch, but she refused and instead stood there in a solemn vigil for five days.

In another act of protest, a group of fifty of my relatives marched at Baijiahu Prison, but only four of these visitors were allowed in to see me. The prison administrators had ordered Qiao-Qiao to wash me and rub my skin with oil. I managed to walk slowly to the visitation room and waited for a while there. Kahar, Alim, and Rushengül stepped inside. Ablikim followed behind. I rejoiced within, *Praise be to God— Ablikim is free again!* I found out later that he had been released without any stated reasons nine months earlier.

My brother, my sister-in-law, two of my grandchildren, and a few other relatives were waiting in the hallway—if I tilted my head toward the door a bit, I could see each of them. The officers tried to appeal to my incensed relatives, saying, "It's normal for a person to get sick at some point. But now she's well again and you can speak with her."

My son Kahar brushed by him and stood in front of me. "Mother, you gave us life. We wish there was more we could do for you."

Rushengül said, "Mother, your granddaughter won recognition in school for her essay. Her topic was 'My Grandmother.'" She was not permitted to give me any more information than that. I fondly recall seeing my grandchildren during these visits over the years. Later, after my release, I read her essay:

I notice that all of the people who look into my eyes feel sorry for me. They look at me and believe that they can find my grandmother in my eyes. But they are afraid to say her name . . . My grandmother once said to me from prison, 'You shouldn't believe that I'm guilty.' At that moment I thought, 'My grandmother assumes that I'm still a child.' Each time I left the prison after visiting her, I was very proud that she is my grandmother . . . I will become like my grandmother. There are beautiful birds with spectacular feathers in our country. One of them—the Bül-bül bird—is particularly splendid. And my grandmother, when she is free, is like this bird.

Ablikim sobbed before managing to collect himself. He said, "We are prepared to let our blood flow. We are prepared to die. We aren't afraid that they will throw us in jail." He was promptly punished for his words, as the officers immediately led him out and prohibited him from visiting again for a long time.

But their tactics did not scare my son Alim either. He said, "Your blood flows in our veins. Don't worry about us. We'll remain strong." After that, the officers led him out as well. They stopped the visitation entirely after only ten minutes. Normally we had half-an-hour.

THE VICE DIRECTOR OF THE PRISON summoned me to her office on September 11, 2001 and informed me that violent attacks had been committed against the United States.

She continued, "You've always admired America. That's why you sent your husband and children there. But now you see that country too is destined for downfall. The Americans, unfortunately for you, will not have time to worry about you because they have their own problems now. In addition, Uyghur terrorists participated in this crime. We will arrest them and then you can face off with them, terrorist to terrorist."

She did not tell me any details about the September 11th attacks, but visibly enjoyed talking about them. I was scared and angered at the same time. If the United States was being attacked, how then could the rest of the world stand up for itself?

I did not believe the vice director about Uyghurs having been involved in this international crime. But how September 11th would alter life in our Uyghur nation was beyond my imagination. It was only after my release that I found out just how imaginative the Chinese government had become in manipulating the horrific American tragedy for their own political purposes.

The government called upon the cooperation of all foreign powers in combating Uyghurs. They falsely accused Uyghur fighters of having been and continuing to be trained in Afghan terrorist camps. The government's massive propaganda campaign resulted in even more arrests of anyone who spoke up in favor of Uyghur independence. In short, the worldwide war on terrorism gave Beijing a flimsy excuse for additional inhuman, brutal actions against us.

Before September 11th, bilingual signs in both Uyghur and Chinese for traveling or shopping were prevalent throughout the Xinjiang Uyghur Autonomous Region. After September 11th, Uyghur signage was removed. The implication was clear: Chinese was the official language of the Uyghur nation, not our native Uyghur language. Furthermore, the government laid bare its real plans for our land.

A Uyghur scholar was sentenced to twenty years in prison because he translated the United Nations' Universal Declaration of Human Rights into Uyghur. Judges used absurd logic in defending death sentences handed down to our countrymen. One such excuse was that these people were actually terrorists attacking China's ideology, but disguising themselves as peaceful activists. The Communists turned every person against every other person. Everywhere people gathered, spies swarmed. Even inside families, children were instructed to spy on their parents and parents on their children. Then they were to file reports with the relevant authorities.

September 11th changed the whole world. But we Uyghurs, approximately twenty-million of us worldwide, were also among the casualties.

THERE WERE SIXTY-FOUR political prisoners incarcerated with us, including me. Shortly after September 11th, thirty more political prisoners joined us. Once a week, we were taken into a room one by one. There we were forced to strip naked and kneel down on all fours while female guards inspected our body cavities from the front and from behind. I was completely humiliated by this process.

Later, I told myself that it was not I, but the female guards who should be ashamed. Each time I set foot in that room I was filled with repugnance. In the beginning, I refused to take my clothes off. But later, as the punishments increased, I just wordlessly let my clothes drop to the ground and kneeled down.

Once a month, political prisoners also had to take part in re-education classes. The first rule was, "There is no God." The instructor taught that all religions were a lie. Only the high moral standing of the Communist Party and the Chinese government could serve as guidelines for people. The second rule was that the Xinjiang Uyghur Autonomous Region was a permanent part of China. That had always been the case and that would always remain the case. During class, we had to chant aloud fifty times, "We never want to separate from China!"

The teacher then spoke about the United States and how capitalists scorned human rights. Afterward, she turned to the European nations and emphasized the moral and political corrosion caused by capitalism there. At the end of her lesson, she always repeated that the system of capitalism would fail. And finally, she stated that the Chinese president would eventually rule the world because China was strong, rich, and just.

Sometimes these indoctrinations would last two or three hours, sometimes half-a-day. Occasionally the instructor compelled one of the students to stand up, curse God, and swear eternal loyalty to Communism. Of course she eventually demanded this of me as well, but it did not work out the way she had in mind. I stood up from my chair with the words, "There is only one God."

Once I requested of the instructor to be allowed to say something. Without waiting for her to agree, I stood and explained: "Not only have religions provided us with the first laws of human history, but they've helped form the basis for a good and moral way for human beings to live side by side. Religions should bind people together, not separate us from one another."

With that, the instructor leapt toward me and held her hand over my mouth. There were always female guards in the room to watch our lessons. They had the instructor fired because she had let me talk for so long. Although we political prisoners were not allowed to talk with each other, we were still able to find out the crimes some of us had been accused of. These revelations were a part of our mandatory self-criticism practice during the lessons.

Among us was a seventy-one-year-old woman from Shaja whose husband and two children had been executed by the government. She said, "I now doubt that there is a God and believe that what the Communists say is true. Our mistake was that we secretly gave our children lessons on religion. We thought we were doing something good. But religion is what brought my husband and my two children to their deaths." This elderly woman and another ninety-year-old woman had both been condemned to life in prison.

The beautiful young woman who I had seen shackled and hunched over in the courtyard when I was at the old prison, Liudaowan, had been transferred here to Baijiahu Prison too. I hoped to arrange her marriage to my son Ablikim as soon as she was set free. She would surely be pleased with him. He was a handsome man with the heart of a lion. When a woman like her was released from prison, no one else would dare take her as a wife. But destiny had other plans. When she was released several years later, Ablikim had planned to pick her up at Baijiahu Prison, but authorities arrested and jailed him beforehand.

Political prisoners were generally not allowed to be released. After they had completed their terms, they were usually provoked into some kind of punishable behavior by the authorities as a way of being imprisoned again further.

This process is illustrated by the story of another political prisoner in her late twenties who said the following in her self-criticism session, "I founded an organization to free my land. We read many books. We studied our history. We made copies of the material and distributed it to the population. Many of us were killed. Because I was still young, they labeled me as a co-conspirator and sentenced me to four years in prison. But I wasn't very good at being re-educated because I always insisted that what I'd done was right. That's why they lengthened my sentence by four more years. These eight years were over last year. But other prisoners observed how I prayed secretly under the bed covers. That's why an additional three years were added to my prison term."

"Well then, you can tell us once more whether there is a God." The instructor's face grew red when the young woman did not give her an answer.

The instructor demanded, "Does the Xinjiang Uyghur Autonomous Region belong to China or not?"

The woman still remained silent.

❧ ❧

I WAS TRANSFERRED to a three-bed cell with Qiao-Qiao and another murderess whose execution had been delayed for three to four years.

To my surprise, the authorities also improved my work assignment. I embroidered flowers onto sweaters along with a group of other women. We were seated single-file in two long rows in our workroom. The threads and yarns for each workstation were kept between the rows. One woman was responsible exclusively for threading needles and another was assigned to distributing them. As was the case in the larger sewing hall, seamstresses in this smaller workroom also frequently collapsed unconscious onto the floor. When they came to, they just got back in their chairs and resumed working.

Before our lunch break we were required to recite the fifty-eight rules and repeat them again at midnight: "I am a prisoner. I will admit my mistakes. I belong to the lowest class . . ."

I was ordered to eat my lunch apart from the other prisoners. Many of my fellow inmates had already been in prison for twenty years, so not a single one of them took the risk of looking at me, much less talking with me. While I was embroidering green leaves onto a rose, other inmates took notes about me. I did not understand what they had to write about, but every prisoner in our workgroup had one of these little notebooks.

Every two hours the female officers ordered us to line up. I was usually last in line. The constant repetition of false accusations was tiring.

"Why did you smile at the woman in front of you?"

"Why did you elbow your neighbor while receiving your meal?"

"Why did you make obscene gestures with your hands?"

"I haven't done anything. I haven't seen anything. I just did my work. Every day I embroider five sweaters. If I were constantly disturbing someone as you say, I could hardly get my work done."

"Admit it already. The others have witnessed it."

When they called me out the next time, I just let my head hang down. They asked their questions, but got no answers. There were always at least four of them questioning me—presumably so that they could spy on each other as well. Officer Mihri was usually present too.

Sometimes the officers and guards kept me with them over the lunch break as punishment. Sometimes they brought me in for an interrogation long after midnight.

They said to me, "We're making a lot of effort to re-educate you—even working with you into the night. If there were no Communist Party, then we wouldn't be able to invest so much time in you. Maybe you would no longer even exist. What do you think about that?"

I thought to myself *If there were no Communist Party, I wouldn't have to sit here in the middle of the night and put up with listening to these silly questions.*

The Chinese guards had a real talent for saying awful things with a smile on their faces. "We treat you so well. Why do you torture yourself? Answer and you'll be allowed to go. You're not only boring yourself, but us as well. Just answer and let us go to sleep."

If I had said anything, their next move would have been to accuse me of arguing with them, and everything would have started over again from the beginning.

One of their favorite tactics was provocation. "You were a separatist. You were a nationalist. You endangered the stability of our country. The authorities have assigned two cellmates just to observe you and an additional ten people for a broader surveillance of you. With this additional financial burden, you've caused great damage to the Party."

"Yes it's true. I've caused you great damage." I wrongly assumed that this response would bring the questioning to an end sooner, but after that they delved deeper into the subject.

They did not allow me to rest for even one second. If I wanted to go to the toilet, I had to wait for up to half-an-hour for approval. I would stand there sweating and shifting from one leg to the next until sometimes I could no longer wait. When the resulting unpleasant smell caught their attention, they hovered around me like flies and ordered me to wash myself.

I would barely have finished changing my clothes when the officers would then take me from my cell again for another four hours of interrogation. They lamented that my guilt had put them in such an impossible situation. They looked with pity at Qiao-Qiao and the other cellmate, who in turn feigned servitude as my minders. The cellmates told the guards, "We'll continue to suffer with her behavior for the government. There are so many worse things that she does to us, but we'll not tell you about them. We'll bear it alone."

At that, one of the officers immediately interrupted Qiao-Qiao, "No, you must take note of everything. We have to know exactly what kind of horrible life you lead with this person."

Only the prospect of seeing my children again kept me thinking straight. I could concentrate on nothing else anymore. Even if we were not allowed to talk about anything, at least we were allowed to see each other.

"Our father is trying to help you." For that remark, my son Kahar was permanently denied visitation rights.

For five-and-a-half years, I did not really know that people abroad were lobbying for my release. But I understood from Kahar's remark that some action was being taken on my behalf. It seemed that the Chinese were doing some of their own strategizing in regards to Sidik's activities. The prison administrators became increasingly more accommodating toward me. Another Chinese woman succeeded Officer Lei. Although the replacement was not much better, Lei's transfer was a clue for me that discussions of some sort were being held.

MY FATHER COULD NO LONGER remain quiet in the face of my unexplained absence. He asked for Sidik's telephone number in Virginia. Then he went to the post office and called Sidik. He wanted to know where I was. Sidik explained that I was on a business trip. My father did not believe a word of what his son-in-law told him and angrily slammed the receiver down.

After that, my father asked all acquaintances he saw about my whereabouts. At a mourning ceremony for a neighbor, he explained to the guests that he had not received a word from me in several years. He appealed to them, saying that he did not believe what he was being told, that I was doing business somewhere: "Please tell me the truth."

A friend answered that we all had to accept the fate that God had decided for us. But my father interrupted him—he was absolutely sure that his daughter had not died. He was certain I was still alive. He could feel it. After that, the friend grew silent. Then my father collapsed to the ground.

Because he was doing so poorly, my oldest sister Zohre telephoned him twice and tried to impersonate my voice. Her voice and mine were quite similar. My father simultaneously believed that he had spoken with me and also seriously doubted it was me. Finally, he grew very ill and said that he had only one wish left: to see me.

During my children's next visitation, they briefly alluded to how sick my father was and how much he missed me. I was aware that the Chinese New Year festivities were approaching and thought that perhaps the prison administrators would be merciful on such an important holiday. So I requested a paper and pen in order to draft a letter to the officials:

> *During the New Year's festivities, the entire population everywhere in the land is permitted to be happy. Please bring me to my father's door. Then take off my wrist and ankle chains and give me thirty minutes' time with him. Just once, I want to encourage my father, to give him joy. If he had to come to the prison himself, he would not be able to bear it. Please, you can send ten officers to accompany me and I will pay for each and every one of them.*

Their written reply was brief, " In order to put this plan into action, we would need two battalions of soldiers."

In May 2004, my son Alim tried to help. "I'll talk to them. They should at least allow you to speak to your father on the telephone." But it was too late. One month later, the prison director informed me that my father had passed on.

No one had told him that I was in prison. None of us wanted him to go over to the other world with pain in his heart. I did not want to cry. I still do not. But I get tears in my eyes every time I think about him.

BECAUSE MY EARLIER ABDOMINAL PAINS had been so serious, the prison administrators ordered that I be taken to the prison hospital for any and every health concern I experienced. The hospital was much cleaner than the medical ward where I had been treated for my earlier abdominal pain. The next doctor's visit was due to my skin swelling from malnourishment.

A Chinese doctor came to me and said, "Please sit down. Could you please roll up your sleeve?"

He had said "please," used the polite form of address, and looked at me in a friendly way. I had not experienced such courtesy in five years. The doctor had treated me as if I were a human being. My eyes welled up with tears of gratitude. I wanted to control myself, but simply could not. He was taken aback: "Did I do something wrong?"

The female officer taunted me, "Oh, look at that, she's just a human after all and can actually cry."

"That's enough, officer."

"Doctor, you should just examine her without looking her in the eyes."

After that, he interrupted the examination and the two of them left the room. When they came back, the doctor was much more reserved with me.

I had no problem with my heart, but the doctor insisted that I had heart trouble. He prescribed what he said was the appropriate medication and said that the female officers were to watch and confirm that I took it. I had no idea what they were dispensing when they put a pill in my hand, along with a glass of water. I drank the water but kept the pill tucked inside my cheek. Later I pulled it out as inconspicuously as possible. Then pulverized it between my fingers so that they would not find any residue.

But they were constantly watching me and asking why I was always rubbing my fingers together. Sometimes I tried to crush the pill between my toes by pretending to be scratching myself there. Unfortunately, Qiao-Qiao was also watching me closely, and she discovered what I had been doing.

From that point on, officers and guards were assigned to scrutinize me constantly if I scratched myself, combed my hand through my hair, or touched behind my ear. I was under close surveillance twenty-four hours a day.

IT WAS THE WINTER OF 2004 when the prison director, the vice director, and several other high officials guided me into the large assembly hall. All of the political prisoners were present and I was ordered to stand before them. One of the officials gave a speech, "Rebiya Kadeer has been successfully re-educated. She has internalized the doctrines of the Communist Party very well."

My knees turned to rubber. I thought *What was that supposed to mean?* The entire time, I had remained true to myself. I had not been re-educated. Some of the women prisoners looked at me angrily as the officials continued their compliments toward me. Because I had assimilated so well, they said, my sentence had been reduced by one year. I felt like a traitor and was ashamed of myself. Previously, all of the political prisoners greeted me with their eyes. After that meeting, not one of them greeted me anymore.

In January of the following year, Qiao-Qiao packed up her belongings. She admitted, with complete candor, "It was my job to spy on you and to mistreat you so that I could get my sentence shortened. I don't care whether you live or die." Her sentence had been reduced by three years.

The other Chinese woman cellmate remained the same, but Qiao-Qiao was replaced by a different woman, a swindler who had received a life sentence. If I coughed, she documented it in her notebook. If I brushed my teeth, she stood very close and stared at me. This woman had two protruding yellow teeth and wretchedly bad breath. While I ate, she perched in a squat, breathing heavily, not an inch from my food bowl. I felt every breath she let out. "Go somewhere else. What do you want from me?" But she never reacted to my words.

I was amazed by the authorities' ability to keep finding such unusual creatures for me. These two women worked very hard to mistreat me in order to get their own sentences reduced—even while I slept. Each night, when the ceiling light had dimmed, one of them would scream in my ear or throw things at the wall.

If I turned to one side, the swindler jumped up next to me on the bed like a troll and yelled, "What are you doing there?" On one occasion, the two of them even jumped on my bed together. One of them pulled at my shirt, the other at my foot. In retrospect I do not understand how they themselves could have taken this stress. But they always appeared satisfied as soon as they got me to rail against them.

Eventually, I stopped reacting to them entirely, at which point they immediately started attacking each other until female officers pulled them apart. The two of them swore that I was to blame for their disputes. One of the officers admonished me, "Why don't you leave your cellmates alone?"

At some point, I also stopped reacting so much to the officers. And for this they scorned me, "How could you've been one of the most well-known women in China? You aren't right in the head."

No comment passed my lips in response. But their tirades did not end: "Why do you constantly look out the window of your cell?" In reality, my cellmates hardly ever allowed me to get to the window. "When we read what the other prisoners write about you, we are nauseated." The female officers definitely knew that all of those accusations were not true, but they had been ordered to behave this way toward me.

Once as I was holding out my bowl during food servings, a prisoner knocked it from my hand. She had it refilled and gave it back to me. In the process she dipped her fingers into the porridge. Although I had seen only her fingers, I did not know what had been hidden underneath them. I ate around that spot. Right away, a few prisoners surrounded me, saying, "Why didn't you eat it all?"

The female officer who had witnessed the whole incident reprimanded me for my behavior. "Why couldn't you take the meal with your own two hands? Why do you have others do it for you?" One of the other officers then pinched me on my cheek. I pushed her hand away. Not long afterward, more female officers came into the cell and wanted to know why I had lifted a hand against them.

"Well, you just hit my colleague. For striking an officer, a prisoner gets an additional three years. That applies to you too, of course."

My cellmates confirmed everything the officers wanted to hear. "She always beats us up too," the swindler reported.

One of the officers apologized to her. "She will pay for the tears that the two of you have shed."

Once, during a visit by Ablikim in January 2005, I told him about the conditions inside the prison. "Ablikim, they've put two prisoners in my cell to torture me."

Somehow I was not reprimanded for doing so. Or, more likely the prison administrators took note of what I had said and passed the information higher up.

It was becoming apparent that some public pressure was growing more effective because right after that visitation my two cellmates suddenly restrained themselves from tormenting me.

During the last several visits, I could see that Ablikim wanted to give me an important message. But the guards, especially the Chinese ones, hovered over every word. One day, when there were mostly Uyghur officers present, after a brief inner conflict with himself, Ablikim said, "Mother you've been awarded the Norwegian Thorolf Rafto Memorial Prize. We are proud of you."

The Rafto Prize is a highly esteemed honor presented each year to a persecuted human rights activist. I had no idea at the time that I had actually been awarded the prize the year before, in 2004.

"Silence!" The Uyghur officers had to react like this or they themselves would have been punished. At least they had let him finish speaking. Ablikim was immediately led out and prevented from visiting for a long time. I cried, forgetting that I was in prison. I told myself, *I will get out of here.*

In March I gathered a few bits of wool that had been discarded in our workroom and asked a Uyghur officer if I could please be allowed to use scissors and glue in order to craft something. From these scraps I sculpted a small flying blackbird and put something into his beak. I reveled in delight, thinking to myself *I'm like this blackbird. I'll fly too and one day help our people reclaim our land.*

I glued my little blackbird to the ceiling above my bed. Looking at it gave me inspiration. I thought, *Rebiya some things seem to flow through us and they don't happen by coincidence. It's God sending a sign. I only have to know how to interpret it.*

On March 8, 2005, I received clean inmate clothing for a meeting with officials from the *An Chuan Ting*. They had summoned me to the prison administration office.

After a long silence, one of the men began by expressing pity for me. He said, "You're doing very poorly. You're suffering from heart problems. Because of the medical treatment you require, we'll release you. So how do things look? Will you commit wrongful acts out there again?"

At first I could not believe what I had heard, so I took a moment to process his words again. Maybe the supposed heart problems were just a pretext for my release.

I told the men, "I'll never commit a wrongdoing."

"What do you mean by that?"

I did not reply.

"If we send you abroad, will you work against us from over there?"

"I will work for the people—for nobody else."

"Will you stand up for separatists?"

"I've never been a separatist. In my eyes, all humans are equal."

"We are now thinking about your medical treatment."

I did not know what he meant by that. Was I to get medical treatment outside? Then he gave me a hint:

"If we let you out in your homeland you'll create even bigger problems for us. That's all for now."

I was led back to my cell. After that visit, I was given better food, and one of my cellmates was swapped out and replaced by a Dungan. This Chinese Muslim woman flattered me and talked with me, but constantly took notes on everything I said and did. She wanted to know what I was going to do when I was released from prison and what hopes I had for my future. I told her, "I'll do what every normal human being would do. I'll hug my children."

"Rebiya!" An officer was calling me into the corridor. After a short pause, she added, "Kadeer!" They led me outside for some courtyard exercise. After all those years, I was finally allowed to see the sky again. Three days later, the prison administrators called me back into their offices. This time, they took a picture with a paper tablet hanging around my neck. Something was written on it in Chinese but I did not see what it said.

After that, some officers took me to the prison hospital. One said, "You're seriously ill so you must get some rest." I spent three days there without anything being wrong with me. They gave me those "heart pills" again, which as before, I took into my mouth and secretly spit out later.

A doctor asked me, "Where do you feel pain?"

"I don't have any pain."

The doctor shrugged his shoulders. "Then why are you here?"

At that, one of the officers cut him off. "Don't ask so many questions."

The officer herself did not know why I was in the hospital. As soon as the doctor left the room, she whispered to me, "What did you talk about with the *An Chuan Ting*?"

This time the other guards cut her off, "Don't ask so many questions."

A week after meeting with the secret service officials, the prison administrators asked what my clothing size was. A thousand voices rejoiced inside of me. I thought, *They are looking for new clothes for me. I'm really going to be released.*

On March 11, 2005, my children received permission to visit me.

Many guards stood outside the door, but we were escorted into the same room where we had always visited—the room that always had guards all around and where video cameras and microphones were always in place. This time though only one Politburo high official sat there alone. My children and I sat across from each other on the sofa and visited as usual. I found out later that the visitation had been kept a close secret, even from the prison director himself.

A Fable About a Little Ant

"Rebiya Kadeer!" On March 16, 2005 a prison officer shouted out my name as she entered my cell at three o'clock in the morning.

I jumped up. She spoke no other words. None were really necessary. I hastily dressed in anticipation of my release from prison. Just as I was about to leave my cell, I stopped, remembering my handmade blackbird. I looked at the officer as I tentatively reached for it. She said, "Oh that's not so important. You can take it with you."

Men in dark suits were waiting for me at the end of the corridor. They escorted me to the clothing dispensary where I received a pair of pants, shoes, a blouse, and a coat.

After I had changed into these clothes, they escorted me in the direction of the main gate. On the way there I saw only Chinese soldiers in olive-green uniforms, no prison officials. I could not help but notice that at the gate no one demanded I say "*Baodao!*"

In front of the gate stood a vehicle with its engine running. Beside it was the empty truck that had carried the Chinese soldiers, and beyond were more cars for the *An Chuan Ting* who were escorting me. Farther away, sirens wailed.

The prison gate was located on Beijing Street, which I knew also led to the airport. As we drove, I sensed that we were indeed to embark on a flight to . . . somewhere.

It was odd at the airport. The halls were completely empty, as though they had been swept out. Usually that airport teemed with people twenty-four hours a day. My next thought was that perhaps there was a war, as they hurried me across the tarmac toward a military airplane.

Once I boarded, I saw Officer Mihri and one of her female officers waiting for me, along with a group of additional Chinese prison guards. Not a single word was exchanged. Four hours later, I recognized from above the approaching Beijing landscape. After we landed, Officer Mihri and her companion prison officer were replaced by two other women. There was no opportunity for me to say anything to Mihri though I would have liked to.

Even now, to this day, I think that if I ever had the opportunity to be face to face with Officer Mihri I would hug her tightly. With tears in my eyes, I would thank her for being kind to me. Tell her how in that Communist and brutal country, there is at least one officer who is humane at heart. I would tell her that without the kindness she had shown me, the time I spent at that horrid prison would have passed with greater despair and suffering. I would tell her that her kindness is what gave me the ability to cope with the harsh environment. That during those dark times, and in those dark places, her kindness showed me some good still existed. That is what I would like to say to Officer Mihri.

Then I was taken to a suite in a nice hotel nearby. Diplomats from the Chinese foreign ministry arrived just minutes afterward. They explained to me that I would be flown abroad due to the critically necessary medical treatment I was to undergo.

"When you leave here Mrs. Kadeer, you'll still have the opportunity to work for us abroad. If you choose to do that, you'll also be allowed to continue conducting your business here and to continue to be a multimillionaire. However, if you should choose to reveal to the worldwide community what you've experienced here or continue to be involved in human rights causes, then that would be quite unfortunate. If you choose the latter, you'll experience actions against your children and your businesses to a degree that you haven't yet imagined possible. They'll be finished."

Another added, "You can decide for yourself whether you want to live in prosperity or in constant difficulty. You have the choice."

Until that point, the high-level cadres had not said where they intended to send me. Instead, they emphasized that regardless of my new destination, I would always remain classified in China as a convict. And then I learned their plan. "We will turn you over to the Americans."

My blood felt hot, then cold. *Was this possible?* I had always trusted in God's voice. God had not forgotten me.

The diplomat continued, "You have to remember one thing Mrs. Kadeer. Twenty years from now, there will not be any more people known as Uyghurs. You're an intelligent woman and you should learn to work with us.

"You have permission to stay in the United States only for eighteen months to undergo your medical treatment. If you feel well after your care, we'll bring you back. Then you can return to your businesses and be an example for your people. All of your five children here in China will also be well off. We know how much you love them. You must know too that we have made mistakes and that you have made mistakes."

I promised, "I will never do harm to the Chinese people."

Later, the Chinese government denounced me in an article, claiming, "Mrs. Rebiya Kadeer did not keep her promise." But that was not true of my promise, as I intended it. I am not fighting against the Chinese people, but rather—just like many Chinese people themselves—I am fighting for a democratically based government and for the unequivocal observance of human rights.

Soon after this conversation, officials from the American Embassy arrived at the hotel to complete more diplomatic formalities. One asked me, "Do you want to travel to the United States?"

"Yes, I do."

About an hour later, they anxiously looked at their watches as they led me across a runway. The minutes passed as slowly as if each were a whole day. A mobile phone rang.

"Stop," someone commanded. "There could still be changes." This happened twice more as we were about to board the plane. Year after year, I had given myself the courage to believe that I would leave prison alive. Standing on the runway, I looked up the staircase to the airplane. It was so close.

Just before the handover to the United States embassy diplomats, one of the Chinese diplomats emphasized, "You aren't allowed to receive political support in the United States."

One of the men from the United States embassy hugged me. He told the Chinese diplomat, "Sir, as long as this woman doesn't break the laws of our country, she can do what she wants there." This man's hug made me feel like I had already arrived in The United States of America.

At last, we boarded the airplane. Only a few hours before I had been sleeping in my cell. I pinched myself. This was not a dream. In my pocket I could feel my little blackbird. Some day, with nourishment in my beak, I would fly back to my homeland—just like this bird did in my imagination.

During the flight I realized that I could not tell whether I was looking forward to what was ahead, as I had no idea what awaited me. The attaché from the United States politely tried to carry on a conversation about my life, including my life in prison. I tried to answer but couldn't concentrate and gave confused answers to his questions.

He said, "I understand. It's an overwhelming moment right now." He also handed me some American money from his briefcase. I didn't know how much it was. I didn't count it, I just thanked him. He told me, "If you need any other kind of help, please get in touch with me directly."

During a one-hour stopover in Chicago, a reporter for Radio Free Asia was waiting for me. He asked whether I planned to be careful with my public statements since my children were still in the hands of the Chinese, or if I planned to speak freely. I responded, "As of right now, I can speak. I'm allowed to scream. I'm allowed to laugh. I'm allowed to cry. I'm allowed to go wherever I want. Today is like a birthday for me. I feel reborn."

Even today, people speculate about the real reasons for my release. It was well known that United States Secretary of State Condoleezza Rice had traveled to China shortly thereafter. There was also discussion of "horse-trading" in regards to my internationally announced release and the resulting lack of condemnation of China by the United Nations Human Rights Commission, which was meeting at that time in Geneva.

Today, the Chinese government deeply regrets that they set me free.

As I set foot on American soil, I had not even thought about the possibilities I would have in this country. My whole life I had wanted to help the Uyghur people. Now fate seemed to have brought me to the doorstep of a new opportunity for that.

Hundreds of journalists and Uyghurs had come to the airport in Washington, D.C. to greet me. In the middle of this cheering crowd, I heard the calls of my children.

In the next instant, Akida threw her arms around my neck. When we had said goodbye seven years ago, she had still been a teenager. Standing in front of me now was a young woman of twenty-four. Many hands reached out to me—my son Mustafa, my daughters Kekenos and Honzohre. I did not recognize my own children. I felt like a distant relative.

How very much I had missed my husband. Every minute of our separation, I had yearned for him. There he stood, in the middle of all the bustle. Next to him was a woman from the State Department. She held him firmly by the hand. He had been to her office countless times to lobby on my behalf. Sidik had been such a strong, handsome man. He was still strong and handsome, though now an older, white-haired man. Certainly at that moment he saw me through those lenses of the past and the present as well. Because of malnourishment in prison, my body had swollen and my face was pale. My hair was cut quite short, just above the ears.

Nine years apart is a long time in a human life. Recovery was no different for him than it was for me, as we would eventually find out. He knew what prison could do to a person. Sidik made a pathway for himself. When we finally were face to face, he first kissed me on the forehead and then hugged me. The crowd was jostling around us but he just held on to me. "We've won," he whispered.

At home I hung my blackbird near the front of our bed. I was a different woman—a stranger to myself. It almost broke Akida's heart. She took her father's hand and together they went into the other room. She said to him, "Papa, mother doesn't hug me. She doesn't even look at me."

"Your mother is still living in another world. Please be patient. You can't imagine what Chinese prisons are like. And do you know what, Akida? She doesn't yet recognize me either."

That night, we slept together—all six of us in a row. I woke up and looked at the peaceful faces beside me. *Where are my little children?* I asked myself, still searching for the time that had been lost.

We had missed each other so painfully over the years. Our dreams of reunion had sustained us. But in real life, with our fragile human hearts, we now stood before each other in fear.

Whenever I did speak with my family, my words revolved around the Uyghur fight for freedom. I was so obsessive, so repetitive. I always started every conversation with the same remarks about how miserable the people were in our homeland. I did not speak about my children's or my husband's feelings, or even my own.

Sidik said to me, "Rebiya, my wife . . . patience. You need to find yourself again. You don't have to accomplish everything at once. We'll make our plans. Patience."

"Forgive me please. This time I didn't come back as a wife or a mother. I think I was brought back to life because I'm to speak about human rights in our homeland."

Akida calmed me down, saying, "It's okay. It's okay. Mother, you're here with us now."

"*Dao!*" I answered as if still in the prison. "*Dao!*" I said, still lowering my gaze to the ground. They looked at me as though I had lost my mind.

I felt less worthy, completely intimidated, and so small. But Sidik returned my soul to me. He knew from his own personal experience in a Chinese prison that I would remain disoriented for awhile. "*Baodao!*" I called out if I wanted to speak. That word! The same one that I had once despised and refused to say now just came out automatically.

In the streets, I thought that all the passersby were shouting at me. If someone wanted something from me, I always said yes. I could not say no to anyone.

At home, sitting at the kitchen table, I would talk to myself out loud, reliving past conversations. "It's irrelevant to me whether you see me as guilty or as a prisoner. I'll never see myself in that way. It's of no consequence to me whether you beat me up or you kill me. I will not accept your command. I will not!"

Other times, out of feelings of guilt, I would say to my family, "You brought me here, but there are thousands of children who are still waiting for their parents. Except they'll never arrive. Never."

Externally, I began to appear functional again, but it was only much later when I actually began to find myself. At first I was afraid to visit other people, but I accepted every invitation anyway. I would not allow myself even one day of rest. I met with politicians and gave a speech to the United States Congress.

I often said to my children, "When our people are free again, then we'll lead a better life." My daughter Akida always smiled at that. Once she answered, "Yes, I'm happy to have a mother like you and a father like my father. You aren't only concerned for us but you're concerned for everyone."

"If someone wants to work for the freedom of their people, their family has to make a lot of sacrifices. And if we aren't prepared to do this, we will not be successful." They understood me a little bit more each day. Slowly I could feel again that these were my children, and that this was my family.

Later Akida asked, "Your grandparents fled, you fled, we fled—how long will this go on, mother?"

ON MAY 10, 2005, I WAS INVITED to a conference at the United States Capitol Building. On that same day I also gave interviews to the television, radio and newspaper reporters who had gathered in front of the White House to cover the conference.

The next morning in Urumqi, hundreds of Chinese security forces sealed off my two department stores, which my sons were running at the time. They searched my offices and my apartment. My vice director was pulled by her hair from the office to a waiting vehicle. They took my secretary away as well. Other co-workers at the company were beaten and threatened with further punishment.

They confiscated fifteen sacks full of documents from my home. I had taken out a loan of nine-million yuan for my Akida Holding Company. After the seizure of all of my business documents, our debts were announced publicly as being far in excess of the actual amount. On that same day, my five children still in China were detained and interrogated for two days.

The Communists also started bringing my children in twice a month for questioning. The *An Chuan Ting* created a special unit named "Office 307." Its only task was to keep my family under surveillance. My five children were followed wherever they went. Their telephones were wiretapped. They lived each hour in fear of what measures would be carried out against them.

Ablikim went underground for a while until authorities interrogated and beat up a friend of his. Two hours later, my son resurfaced. In exchange for his freedom, he signed a declaration that he would never again seek contact with any members of the Kadeer family.

TODAY MANY PEOPLE FEAR for my safety. But I no longer feel fear, no doubt because of all that I have experienced emotionally and physically. I have touched the hand of the angel of death so many times before. Yes, my telephones are tapped by Chinese emissaries here in America too. Yes, I am always watched by them here too. Yes, I am threatened by them here too.

In January of 2006, my assistant Sureyya was driving me home from our office in Washington, D.C. when all of the sudden a white Ford van accelerated, moving against the one-way flow of traffic and into our lane directly toward us. My assistant shouted, "What's going on?"

Before I had time to respond to Sureyya, much less to think, it was already too late. Everything was a blur as the van slammed into our compact car. My assistant clutched the steering wheel and looked across at me. I had been tossed forward and was holding my forehead. Later she recalled that at that moment she had a glimpse of the face of the man driving the van. She described it as being filled with hatred.

Sureyya sat upright and tried to get out of the car as the van reversed. "He's coming at us again! Rebiya, quick! Get out!" Immediately I released my seatbelt. But in the next instant the van was ramming us again.

I still remember hearing her screaming for a third time, "We have to get out! He's coming again!"

The compact car was so completely damaged that I do not know how we managed to force the crumpled doors open. I only know that we ran from somebody who was trying to kill us. It was instinctual—it was survival—I have no idea how we made it. After that, everything went black.

I woke up in the hospital. My children and husband were standing around me, crying. I had a large wound on my head. One of my vertebrae had been cracked. The doctor told me how lucky I had been, as I escaped becoming a quadriplegic by just inches. Sureyya was badly battered as well, but stabilized. The driver had abandoned the stolen van and run away on foot after we escaped the wreckage. The FBI to this day has not found him.

Apparently the Chinese government was paying serious attention to our work. Not even a year after that first assassination attempt, on May 19, 2006, we were all away from the house. Our daughter Reyila and her son Elyar, who had been able to escape from China on their own and relocate near us, came to the house. As they were walking toward the front door, Reyila noticed a white delivery van. As she approached, she saw three Chinese men taking photographs and videotaping the outside of our apartment. "What are you doing?" she shouted. They sped away, but not before my daughter had memorized their license plate number. The federal authorities traced it to the Chinese Embassy in Washington, D.C.

In an attempt to ruin my good reputation with the Uyghur people, the Chinese government financed and produced a dramatized twenty-eight-part television series based on my life, which was broadcast throughout the Xinjiang Uyghur Autonomous Region. They portrayed me as a woman who reached the top in business and influence only because of the support of the Chinese government, but who later lost her life in a bitter death as a terrorist. In the last segment of the series, they showed her putting a gun to her temple and shooting herself.

The name "Rebiya Kadeer" is not mentioned in the program, but the woman's life story is virtually identical to mine. They even cast a former friend of mine from Urumqi in the lead role. The actress wore a near perfect imitation of my clothing style.

I AM SURE THAT THE CHINESE GOVERNMENT sends secret agents from the *An Chuan Ting* to the United States and elsewhere to strategically disrupt our human rights activities. It was a great effort for my colleagues and me to unite all of the Uyghur associations from around the world under one umbrella organization. We accomplished this in order to speak with one voice and work mutually on one plan for our Uyghur nation.

The formation of this united body was greatly impeded by a major Chinese propaganda campaign. The Communist government's new campaign in the Xinjiang Uyghur Autonomous Region centered on me. They said that I embodied the three most evil traits of all the state's enemies: terrorism, radical Islamism, and separatism. Whenever there is mention of me in the government-controlled media—still to this day—the catchphrase "We have to fight the Three Evils" is employed.

IT IS DIFFICULT, IF NOT IMPOSSIBLE, for a Uyghur to obtain a passport in China. A family or a family member wishing to travel abroad must first be qualified as "clean." "Clean" refers to the Chinese perspective that there have been no political involvements by the family. Sometimes officials check as far back as four generations.

Those who are allowed to go abroad as merchants, scholars, or university students all are "clean" and have a satisfactory record with the *An Chuan Ting* secret service. There are many Uyghurs in the United

States who support me and our cause, but who would never stand up in public. They live in fear in America, just as they did in China. Understandably, they want to stay "clean." Otherwise, they will be sent back to China or else live in exile from then on.

The Chinese do not allow Uyghurs to leave China because they fear the alternative to Communism. They are afraid that life under their system of government does not measure up to a life lived in peace. They fear their own darkness even more among people in the light of free will.

On May 28, 2006, Uyghurs living in exile in the United States selected me to join the Uyghur American Association.

The very next day, officers in Urumqi again arrested my three sons and daughter. In reaction to the imprisonment of our children, a human rights delegation from the United States, which happened to be in China at the same time, filed a protest against the Chinese government. Immediately afterward, the authorities released my children. They were allowed back home, but each of them was kept under round-the-clock surveillance.

The first of June is World Children's Day. It is widely celebrated throughout China—children everywhere have a vacation day from school. The authorities encouraged our four children remaining in the country—Kahar, Rushengül, Ablikim, and Alim—to drive into the mountains to celebrate as other people would and enjoy the holiday. Paradoxically, only a short while earlier, the head of *An Chuan Ting* Commission Number Three had expressed himself to my daughter Rushengül in a completely different manner: "You're all criminals. You're all guilty. Even your two-month-old daughter is guilty."

Just before leaving for the mountains, Rushengül telephoned me once more and said, "I have my doubts about going." I was suspicious of anything that the government urged them to do. But my son Alim was of a different opinion: "They're only human. They have families just as we do. When they see our seven- and nine-year-olds, they'll have compassion for them just as we would for their children."

A few hours later the telephone rang again. I heard Rushengül, who was out of breath, scream, "Mother, there are officers here! They're beating Ablikim now! He's lying on the ground! I think he's unconscious!"

In the background I heard shouts from my family. I heard my grandchildren crying. A loud moaning sound passed over the telephone connection. *That was Alim* I thought with a shudder. The officers were screaming that my children had tried to flee. The last sounds I heard were hurried words from Rushengül, "Mother, they set a trap for us." Then the line went dead.

I understood that the *An Chuan Ting* had let me listen in on purpose. Otherwise, they would have never let Rushengül use her cell phone in a situation like that. They wanted me to know that my children were in their hands and under their control. Since that day in June 2006, two of my sons have been in prison. My daughter Rushengül remains under house arrest.

One day later—June 2, 2006—my twelve-year-old granddaughter called me from a telephone booth. "Grandma, nobody saw me," she whispered and described how she had fled from the security station. "I'm staying with a school friend. Those policemen were kicking and beating Uncle Ablikim. Uncle Alim tried to help but they beat him down also. Grandma, I'm afraid. If I go home, the Chinese will take me into custody. Then I'll not be able to call you anymore."

I said to her, "Please, please go home. If they discover that you're in hiding, it will be very bad." But that day she did not go home. The next day, she telephoned again. This time I took a more severe tone, "Go to the home of your paternal grandparents."

Soon, thank God, she was back with her mother, Rushengül. She also received permission to go back to school. On her first day back in class, the school administrators called an assembly. In front of the entire student body, the principal accused her of being the child of separatists. He instructed all other students to keep a safe distance from her. Since then, my granddaughter has continued to suffer emotionally from this isolation at her school.

On June 14, 2006, the Communists accused my sons Kahar and Ablikim of tax evasion. Ablikim was also accused of wanting to topple the Chinese government. We had not received any other information about Ablikim since his beating and imprisonment earlier on World Children's Day. In response to the accusations, seventy-two United States Congressmen wrote a letter to Chinese President Hu Jintao calling for Ablikim's release.

My other relatives also remain under pressure. My brother in Altai has been interrogated several times. Even my late father's elderly widow has been brought into the station several times for questioning.

In November 2006, shortly before my departure to Germany for a World Uyghur Congress meeting, my brother Mehmet telephoned. "Rebiya, I'm supposed to give you a message. Your sons could expect some mercy if you don't accept a position with Uyghur activists."

One day after my election to the position of President of the World Uyghur Congress in Munich, my son Alim was sentenced to seven years in prison. My son Ablikim soon after received a nine-year prison sentence. My son Kahar was heavily fined.

I BELIEVE THAT I WILL RETURN to my homeland one day. Throughout my life, I have always been led by my feelings. That is why I trust my feelings now as well. When I felt like I would make it, I always did make it. I have had the feeling for a long time that one day our Uyghur nation will be an independent, free, democratically based, nonsecretarian, multicultural country. And every day this feeling strengthens in me.

For my countrymen, I wish for basic human rights. That is our goal. The rest will develop outwardly from respect for human rights. We are fighting a difficult battle against a large adversary. We want the Chinese government brought in front of an international human rights tribunal for its criminal suppression of the Uyghur population.

Do I feel tired sometimes? That would be the worst thing for me—a day on which I was too tired to work for our people. Prison made me strong. And every day, I gain even more strength. When sometimes I do not know where to turn, I think of that fable my father told me about the little ant: "We each have the power to unlock the secrets of the world, as long as we have courage and self-confidence."

ACKNOWLEDGMENTS

Numerous people and organizations actively worked on behalf of my release from prison and have since supported with great dedication our fight for human rights in the Uyghur nation. I thank all of you from the bottom of my heart for your efforts.

My special thanks go to Amnesty International, especially T. Kumar; to Human Rights Watch, especially M. Spiegel; and to the Norwegian Rafto Foundation for Human Rights. I would also like to make special mention of the Dui Hua Foundation, a human rights organization that specializes in China, as well as the United Nations Human Rights Council: The Unrepresented Nations and Peoples Organization (UNPO), which has been tracking and responding to our concerns for years. And of course I must thank the World Uyghur Congress.

I wish to thank also the United States Congress, especially the late Congressman Tom Lantos; Hans Hogrefe, Director of the Congressional Human Rights Caucus of the House International Relations Committee; as well as Susan O'Sullivan of the U.S. State Department. The Norwegian Parliament, the Canadian Parliament, and the Foreign Office of Canada have also openly listened to our concerns, as have the Foreign Ministry of Germany and the European Parliament. I also wish to make special mention of Margarita Bause, Head of the Green Party in Germany, and of Annelie Enochson, member of the Swedish Parliament Christian Democratic Party.

Beyond this, my thanks extend to the international press, which has contributed to a wider global awareness of our cause. I wish to make special mention of the British Broadcasting Corporation (BBC); the *Washington Post*; the Norwegian news agencies and media, especially *Bergens Tidene*; the news magazine *Der Spiegel*; *Voice of America*; and *Radio Free Asia*.

Rebiya Kadeer
April 2009

On the Evolution of This Book
—An Epilogue by Alexandra Cavelius

It was through a short newspaper article that I became aware of Rebiya Kadeer: "Once the richest woman in China, mother of eleven children; today, China's public enemy number one." It was obvious from just these few words that this was an extremely unusual woman and that, in addition to Tibetans, another large ethnic minority in China existed. Unlike the Tibetans though, the Uyghurs were almost unknown in the West. This ethnic minority was Muslim and was being oppressed by the Chinese occupiers in ways no less brutal than those used on the Tibetans.

This woman's courage immediately fascinated me as she bravely faced discrimination and state terror with her head held high, leaving behind her wealth, and surviving five-and-a-half years in one of the most brutal prisons in the world. I introduced myself to her at an Amnesty International event in Munich, Germany and asked whether I might be permitted to collaborate with her on her life story.

Months passed before we could finally begin the interviews. Since her release in 2005, this Nobel Peace Prize–nominated human rights activist has been living in exile in Washington, D.C. and traveling around the world tirelessly to increase awareness about the difficulties of her people. Uyghurs up until this time have remained largely isolated from the public limelight. But in February 2006, our first working meeting was finally going to take place.

Just a few days before her departure for Germany however, Rebiya was the victim of an assassination attempt that almost took her life.

When we were finally able to begin our conversations together in April 2006, the "mother of all Uyghurs" was still noticeably affected by the physical consequences of that attack. She was wearing a neck brace, her eyes were heavily shadowed, and she had a laceration on her forehead. Still, her husband Sidik had to step in to settle her down because despite her doctor's orders, she was prone to doing things like tearing off her neck brace in order to demonstrate, with her braids flying, how Uyghur women dance. During our series of interviews, she flew back to the United States for a few days to give a talk on the subject of birth control in the Xinjiang Uyghur Autonomous Region. It is unbelievable what tremendous energy this slight, delicate person harbors. And what a gripping story she has to tell.

It became clear very quickly that we would need more time than was originally arranged. We planned for the remaining conversations to take place at Rebiya's house in the United States. But all of a sudden, our Uyghur translator began to behave very strangely. He canceled flights that he knew were nonrefundable and refused to release cassette recordings and other materials. In short, he tried to ruin our book project.

After others had taken over his responsibilities he admitted that he had been pressured by Chinese authorities to sabotage our book project. Consequently, his sister had been thrown out of her university in the Xinjiang Uyghur Autonomous Region. His telephone had been tapped. In China, Rebiya Kadeer—similarly to the Dalai Lama in Tibet—is considered a terrorist.

The episode with the translator is just one example of how far the reach of the Chinese government extends. Threats of this nature are a daily bitter reality for Uyghurs living in exile who advocate for their people by peaceful means. Every step Rebiya takes today is scrutinized by the Chinese government. For her children remaining in the Xinjiang Uyghur Autonomous Region, whom the government retains as a sort of collateral, repercussions are a constant threat.

Rebiya Kadeer's descriptions show another face of China—the dark side of a superpower whose influence is growing constantly across the globe. Thus, it has become even more important to promote discussions on the topic of human rights in China.

Alexandra Cavelius
April 2009

Appendix

CQ Congressional Quarterly
The Nation's Leader in Political Journalism Since 1945

October 6, 2006

The Long Arm of China's Secret Police Reaches Into the U.S.

by Jeff Stein, CQ National Security Editor

The white van gunned into a busy Fairfax County, Va., intersection last January, turned right and sped at the line of cars across the yellow line, seeming to aim at the Hyundai Elantra waiting for the light to change.

In the car was Rebiya Kadeer, a prominent political refugee from China who has been nominated for the Nobel Peace Prize, and her assistant. The truck careened off her door, then backed up. Its engine revved and then the van rammed hard into the Hyundai again, throwing the women back in their seats, shaking them like rag dolls.

To Kadeer, 60, a former businesswoman who spent five years in a political prison for advocating civil rights in her native Uyghar Province, a mostly Muslim enclave in the far western part of the country, the January incident was just one example of a brazen Chinese campaign of harassment and intimidation against her and many other exiled human rights advocates in the United States.

Previously her daughter had confronted "Chinese-looking men" videotaping her ground-floor Fairfax apartment from the parking lot, she said. Before they sped off, she wrote down a license number, which was traced to a local car rental agency, and from there to China's embassy, according to aides to Rep. Frank R. Wolf, R-Va., who discussed her case with the FBI. (An FBI source confirmed the incident on the basis of anonymity.)

Activists who visit her get anonymous phone calls from Chinese men who threaten to harm their relatives back home—or try to entice them into spying against her and other activists, she and others said. What appear to be Chinese agents park ominously near their homes and trail them around.

"They seem to watch me closely," Kadeer said. "They follow me wherever I go."

Including to a restaurant recently in suburban Virginia, she said. A couple of Chinese men who had been sitting at a nearby table followed her when she went to the rest room and pressed their ears to the door. She surprised them when she walked out.

Chinese authorities keep the pressure on her back home, too. Authorities have imprisoned three of her sons, and put a daughter under house arrest, in a failed effort to get her to give up her campaign for Uyghar (pronounced "wee-gar") autonomy.

Alim Seytoff, general secretary of the Uyghar American Association, says he and other rights advocates get constant telephone calls from China threatening them and smearing Kadeer.

Uyghars traveling to the United States are offered inducements such as houses and cars to spy on activists in the U.S., he and others say.

And then there are the automated phone calls from China, which ping their phones at night like unsolicited pre-recorded sales pitches Americans have come to detest.

Erping Zhang, a former employee of a Chinese government travel agency, says he has "personally received numerous, numerous recorded messages" denouncing human rights leaders, as well as "two death threats from people who speak Chinese." Radio Free Asia recently broadcast one that he recorded.

Zhang, a human rights activist who just graduated from Harvard at age 45, was warned not to testify to a congressional committee last week. But he went ahead anyway.

Not that he didn't take the threats seriously.

Zhang thinks Rebiya Kadeer's life could be in danger, especially now, with the heightened credibility conferred by her nomination for the Nobel Peace Prize, which will be awarded Oct. 13.

"It could be," he said, "It could be, because she has the courage to step forward. "They could create an accident."

Pressure

The Beijing regime's main concern here, however, appears to be Falun Gong, the quasi-religious spiritual movement with a high profile in the United States that advocates freedom of religion and speech.

"Hundreds, perhaps thousands" of its practitioners have been jailed and tortured to death in China, which regards the Buddhist-like movement as a serious political threat, said Rep. Christopher H. Smith, R-N.J., chairman of a House International Relations Subcommittee, at a July 2005 hearing.

Citing a 2004 State Department report, Smith said "tens of thousands are jailed without trial, held in labor camps, prisons and mental hospitals where they are forced to endure torture and brainwashing sessions."

But the long arms of China's secret police have reached into the United States, according to witnesses at the hearing, who recounted physical intimidation, beatings and even death threats against Falun Gong practitioners in Atlanta, New York and Chicago, where assault charges were filed against a Chinese consulate official.

In upstate New York, according to a congressional staffer, Chinese agents took pictures of license plates at a Falun Gong event, and then apparently traced them through their owners back to relatives in China, who started getting threats.

In Providence, R.I., activists took pictures of a Chinese man who regularly emptied newspaper boxes selling periodicals critical of the regime.

Anywhere in the U.S. that Falun Gong activists apply for protest permits or sponsor human rights-oriented events, Chinese diplomats or their agents can be counted on to pressure local officials, according to news reports and independent sources.

In a heretofore unreported incident in Austin, Texas, last year, a senior manager at a major Internet technology company with extensive business in China was pressured into resigning after getting involved in a pro-human rights art exhibit, according to two sources. With legal action pending, the persons involved were reluctant to discuss the issue further.

Sole Task

China may have sent more than a thousand secret agents to the U.S. to neutralize human rights activity here, a former official in China's

Department of External Security Affairs suggested at last year's hearing. That number would be in addition to thousands of Chinese spies working to steal secrets in U.S. government defense agencies and industries.

The FBI is "keeping tabs on more than 3,000 companies in the U.S. suspected of collecting information for China," BNN reported on Feb. 14, 2005.

Yonglin Chen, whose official title was first secretary and consul for political affairs in China's consulate in Sydney, Australia, from April 2001 to May 2005, said his real job was running a special unit whose "sole task is to monitor and persecute" Falun Gong.

"To my knowledge, similar groups have been established in the Chinese missions in the United States and other countries where the Falun Gong is active," Chen testified.

"Besides the diplomatic system, there is an intelligence collection system working against the Falun Gong as well," he said. "I am aware there are over 1,000 Chinese secret agents and informants in Australia, and the number in the United States should not be less."

A spokesman at China's embassy in Washington did not return a call asking for comment.

"It never ceases to amaze me how paranoid they are," says Rudy Guerin, who ran FBI counterintelligence operations against Chinese agents for three decades until his recent retirement. "They see Falun Gong as a real threat."

"It's amazing to me how much time and effort they put into it," he added. The heavy-handed skullduggery is "like driving a nail with a power drill."

Guerin says the FBI urges the activists to report harassment to local law enforcement agencies, but most have an ingrained distrust of police.

The FBI has also asked the U.S. State Department, which is in charge of diplomatic relations, "to rein [China] in on a number of occasions," Guerin says. And from time to time, State "has called in the [Chinese] ambassador or DCM [deputy chief of mission, the number two official] and told them to knock it off."

The State Department did not respond to an inquiry on the subject.

The last time a Chinese official was declared persona non grata for inappropriate activity and sent packing was 1987, Guerin said. It was an espionage case.

Guerin, who began tracking Chinese agents here in 1979, said he could not recall any official booted out of the U.S. for harassing or threatening human rights activists.

But the law is clear, Guerin said: "You cannot use your intelligence apparatus to infiltrate a group or stop [activists] from exercising their Constitutional rights."

Privately, senior FBI officials say they don't want the U.S. to take any steps that would provoke a tit-for-tat reaction from Beijing: the expulsion of CIA or FBI agents from China.

"Outing" the secret agents in China's embassy and five consulates here—providing the media with their true names, pictures and assignments—would have the same effect, they say.

9/11 Victim

Over the past 10 years, China's portion of the U.S. global trade deficit has grown to 26 percent, or $19.1 billion. Economic experts say that if China, which holds $262.6 billion worth of the U.S. national debt, were to stop buying U.S. treasury bonds, Washington would face a deep financial crisis.

Such a predicament checks the hands of U.S. officials, experts say, but some officials responsible for Chinese affairs say their behind-the-scenes efforts have paid off, too.

Kadeer agrees, crediting State Department officials by name for successfully exerting pressure on Beijing to gain her release from prison in 2005.

On the other hand, she says, "Yes, it would help in many ways" if U.S. officials met openly with human rights activists in China. "Not just meet, but pressure China to abandon the death penalty for Uyghar activists."

China has also effectively insinuated itself into the Bush administration's "global war on terror," she says. By branding the Uyghar autonomy movement Islamic extremists connected to al Qaeda, she says China creates doubt about their legitimacy.

"We are a victim of 9/11 also," Kadeer said quietly, but firmly, during an interview in her tiny Washington office. Dressed in black and looking frail, she said Uyghar's Muslims—ethnically Turkmen, far more Central Asian than Chinese—have little in common with their Arab co-religionists.

"We have nothing to do with al Qaeda," she said. "We are only interested in human rights."

The Bush administration's soft-peddling of human rights concerns enrages some members of Congress.

Last summer Rep. Wolf complained to Bush administration officials that "while we engage China on trade issues the plight of Chinese dissidents [is] often ignored." He implored officials to meet publicly with dissidents, and practicing Christians, when they visit China.

"Members of the Reagan administration often met with dissidents when visiting Russia and other communist countries," he said in his July 12 letter to every cabinet secretary and their deputies. "Few, if any, in this administration do this when they visit China."

Wolf and other members of Congress have pressed the FBI about Chinese activities here, with little effect.

"I called FBI a couple weeks ago to follow up, and they never got back to me," a congressional aide said, reflecting a common experience.

The first Bush administration, in the late 1980s, "de-coupled" trade from human rights issues, a tilt that continued through the Clinton years, experts agree.

Rep. Dana Rohrabacher, R-Calif., calls the practice "shameful."

Expectations that China's behavior could be moderated through trade and quiet diplomacy have created "a Frankenstein's monster," Rohrabacher maintains. "There has been not one inch of reform . . . We've lost ground in the last 10 years."

Rarely moderate himself on the subject, Rohrabacher says he "wouldn't be surprised" to learn that Chinese secret agents have even "killed people here, but we just can't know for sure because they covered it up."

"We're dealing with guys here who have zero respect for human rights. I was theorizing, but I would not be surprised at all," he said.

Even human rights activists haven't gone that far, and if one of their leaders disappeared here under mysterious circumstances, it's certain the world would quickly know about it.

There's a grisly precedent.

Years ago, in the depths of the Cold War, few U.S. officials thought that Chile's military dictatorship, a close anti-communist ally of the Nixon and Ford administrations, would dare send secret agents into the U.S. to kill one of its leading dissidents abroad.

But it did. On Sept. 21, 1976, a Chilean agent set off a massive car bomb less than a mile from the White House, killing a dissident former official, Orlando Letelier.

The assassination was preceded by death threats.

Rebiya Kadeer sounds fatalistic about the death threats she gets.

"I gave myself to the care of God," she says.

Reprinted with permission.
Source: CQ Homeland Security

MEMORANDUM

To: Chairman Henry J. Hyde and Ranking Member Tom Lantos

From: Dennis P. Halpin and Hans Hogrefe

Date: October 30, 2006

Findings of Staff Delegation Visit to Urumqi, PRC, May 30-June 2, 2006

RE: Incidents Involving the Family of Rebiya Kadeer, advocate for Uyghur minority rights

---

This report has been drafted in response to a number of inquiries that the Committee on International Relations has received, both from other Congressional offices and the NGO community, regarding the circumstances surrounding the cancellation of a portion of an International Relations Committee staff delegation visit to Xinjiang Uyghur Autonomous Region of the People's Republic of China in May and June 2006.

Dennis P. Halpin, professional staff of the House International Relations Committee (HIRC–Majority), and Hans Hogrefe, Staff Director, Congressional Human Rights Caucus (HIRC–Minority) traveled on official business to Beijing and Urumqi from May 26 to June 5, 2006. The purpose of this trip was to discuss certain trade issues, diplomatic issues, UN issues, regional relations, human rights questions and American citizen emergency cases with staff at the American Embassy and with the Chinese Foreign Ministry in Beijing and to examine the current human rights situation, education, health and cultural issues, media/internet issues, state of minority rights, energy issues, and counterterrorism concerns in the Xinjiang Uyghur Autonomous Region of the People's Republic of China.

Staff met with area experts for briefings prior to the commencement of the trip. One of those meetings was with Ms. Rebiya Kadeer, Nobel Peace Prize nominee and leading advocate for Uyghur minority rights. Ms. Kadeer presented her frank assessment of some of the difficulties encountered by the Uyghur minority in western China. Halpin specifically stated to Ms. Kadeer during this meeting that, due to the sensitivity of the situation, there was no intention to attempt to make direct contact with her remaining children in Urumqi during the visit there.

The visit to Xinjiang, Uyghur Autonomous Prefecture (May 30-June 2), was undertaken at the invitation of the National People's Congress (NPC), and representatives of the NPC accompanied the staff delegation during the visit. In addition, two officers from the American Embassy in Beijing, Mr. Eric Richardson, the Political Section's human rights officer, and Ms. Caroline Katzin, Special Assistant to the Ambassador, accompanied the delegation. The original staff delegation schedule included a proposed visit to the city of Kashgar, a center of traditional Uyghur culture located near the Pakistani border. Official meetings with local officials in Kashgar had been scheduled.

The trip to Kashgar, however, was suddenly cancelled by Congressional staff due to actions taken by local authorities against the children of Ms. Kadeer. The timing of these official actions coincided exactly with the staff delegation visit to this region, an area of particular sensitivity to the Chinese Government. Given the proximity of this region of China to volatile areas of south and central Asia, including Afghanistan and Pakistan, the religious and cultural influence of Islam, and the different ethnicity of the Uyghur minority (a people of Turkic background rather than Han Chinese), Beijing has long feared irredentist influences from adjacent Central Asian Islamic nations and neighbors with similar ethnic and religious traditions.

The designation by the United States, following the September 11, 2001 attacks, of a Uyghur organization, the East Turkestan Islamic Movement (ETIM) as a terrorist organization, was a welcomed development in Beijing and was perceived as a key determinant in soliciting Beijing's cooperation in the war on terrorism. This development, however, has heightened both Congressional concerns, and those of the human rights NGO community, that Beijing has utilized this terrorist designation to discourage comprehensive discussion of the suppression of the cultural and religious rights of the Uyghur minority in western China. Branding all

Uyghur political, religious and cultural activism with the label of "Islamic terrorism" has served as a convenient means for Beijing to dismiss discussion of Uyghur minority rights, in marked contrast to the vigorous international dialogue concerning the rights of the Tibetan minority.

The primary objective of the Congressional staff delegation visit to Xinjiang was to probe into these issues further. The harsh treatment administered by officials to the children of Rebiya Kadeer at the time of the staff delegation visit can only serve to reinforce perceptions in the Congress that there is a grave situation regarding minority rights in Xinjiang similar to what has been observed in Tibet. (Seventy-two Members of the House of Representatives expressed their grave concern over the arrests and brutal treatment of Ms. Kadeer's children in a July 26, 2006 letter to Chinese President Hu Jintao.) The successful propaganda campaign by Beijing of painting legitimate Uyghur aspirations as terrorism has left Rebiya Kadeer as the sole major voice for the Uyghur people in the international community. The treatment of her children only reinforces the perception that Beijing fears that Ms. Kadeer is emerging as a Dalai Lama figure for the Uyghur people on the international stage.

This leads to the inevitable conclusion that the detentions and beatings of her family members were directly connected to the visit of staff from the U.S. House of Representatives. This conclusion is further reinforced by the fact that Ms. Kadeer herself was detained by local authorities in August 1999 as she was entering a hotel to meet with a member of the staff of the Congressional Research Service (CRS). Ms. Kadeer was charged with "providing state secrets to foreigners"—even though the documents in her possession were newspaper articles which were publicly available. Ms. Kadeer was tried in secret and sentenced in March 2000 to eight years' imprisonment, a sentence which was later reduced by one year. In March 2005, Ms. Kadeer was released and allowed to travel to the United States.

This followed a pattern of "hostage diplomacy" as Ms. Kadeer's release immediately preceded the first visit to Beijing of the new Secretary of State Condoleezza Rice. Ms. Kadeer's release was also followed immediately by an announcement from Washington that the United States would not pursue a resolution concerning China's human rights violations at the (former) UN Human Rights Commission's annual meeting in Geneva, as the United States had done the year before. While both sides denied a *quid pro quo*, the timing of events left the impression that a deal for Ms. Kadeer's release had been struck. A number of Ms. Kadeer's family members remained in China following her release and some of them were involved in managing her remaining business interests.

The circumstances of what occurred to Ms. Kadeer's family members during the staff delegation visit are as follows:

Ms. Kadeer was warned by Chinese authorities at the time of her release from incarceration and exile to the United States in March 2005 not to become an advocate for Uyghur rights in the United States or her family in China would suffer the consequences. Despite these warnings, Ms. Kadeer appeared several times before the Congressional Human Rights Caucus and gave testimony, as well as at a hearing conducted by the International Relations Committee's Subcommittee on Africa, Global Human Rights and International Operations.

Unknown at the time, some days prior to the staff delegation visit to Urumqi, Ms. Kadeer's family members residing in Urumqi were approached by security forces and warned not to have any contact with the upcoming Congressional staff delegation during its visit. Initial discussions with Embassy Beijing underlined the sensitive circumstances of the Kadeer family, confirming the delegation's decision not to request from our Chinese hosts a meeting with any family members.

On the day before the arrival of the staff delegation in Urumqi on Tuesday evening, May 30, 2006, three of Ms. Kadeer's children, her sons Ablikim and Alim Abdiriyim and her daughter Rushangul, were taken into police custody, apparently to prevent contact with the delegation. Late on the evening of May 30, Hans Holgrefe received a call on his cell phone from the United States reliably informing him of the detention of Ms. Kadeer's children. He immediately raised the grave concerns over this action with the representatives of the National People's Congress (NPC) and indicated that this could affect the delegation's schedule. After initial denials by the Chinese hosts, who were seemingly unaware of this situation, the delegation was informed the next morning by Uyghur sources in the U.S. that Ms. Kadeer's three children had been released from detention, but were put under house arrest, with a heavy, permanent police presence on the premises. According to this information, the police forces acted in an extremely hostile manner toward Ms. Kadeer's sons and daughter, as well as her grandchildren, and had severely threatened them with what would happen to them once the U.S. delegation had left. There was still no official confirmation of the exact circumstances of the family members. A phone call placed to a number reported as being for Ablikim was answered by a person responding in broken English "Thank you, America" and "Help!" It is unclear if this person was Ablikim.

Mr. Hogrefe then informed the NPC representatives that, due to the detention, he felt it necessary to request a formal meeting with Ms. Kadeer's children, to determine the situation while the delegation was in Urumqi , unless they were verifiably released from any form of detention. The NPC representatives appeared unnerved by this request. Surveillance of the delegation was immediately heightened, with a Public Security Bureau (PSB) vehicle even following delegation members when they met in the hotel parking lot to discuss the situation with the American Embassy's human rights officer. Local authorities appeared quite agitated over the possibility that delegation members might attempt a surreptitious meeting with Kadeer family members, although this was not our intention. With this request pending, the delegation proceeded with its scheduled meetings with local officials in Urumqi.

On Thursday morning, June 1, while the delegation was visiting the Xinjiang People's Publishing House to discuss minority language publications with the staff, Mr. Hogrefe received a further cell phone call from the United States indicating that security officials had told Ms. Kadeer's family members to board a waiting minibus. Her two sons and one daughter, along with other family members, boarded the bus and were driven to an isolated location outside the regional capital of Urumqi. Seven police cars reportedly arrived. Ablikim and Alim were dragged off the bus and severely beaten by the police as four of Ms. Kadeer's grandchildren watched. Ablikim was reportedly so severely beaten that he had to be taken to a hospital. Ms. Kadeer's daughter Rushangul was told to call her mother on her cell phone, so that she could hear the screams of her children. Upon being informed of this, Mr. Hogrefe informed the National People's Congress that, given the disturbing news and unjustifiable actions taken, he would be terminating his visit to the Xinjiang Uyghur Autonomous Region. He asked arrangements be made for him to travel to Beijing as soon as possible. He asked the United States Embassy to arrange his onward travel back to Washington. Mr. Halpin informed the representatives of the National People's Congress that the staff delegation visit could only proceed if the family members of Ms. Kadeer were immediately released. He informed the NPC hosts that he would not be flying to Kashgar that evening as originally scheduled.

The NPC hosts spoke separately with Halpin on the bus outside of the Norgay mosque which the delegation was visiting that afternoon as part of its survey of religious and cultural issues in the Xinjiang Uyghur Autonomous Region. The NPC hosts suggested that the U.S. delegation included a "splittist" who was causing disharmony. They further suggested that Halpin should go forward with the schedule as planned for the sake of friendly bilateral relations. Halpin responded that his ultimate responsibility was to the International Relations Committee Chairman, Henry Hyde, and he would act accordingly—as Chairman Hyde would expect.

The NPC informed Mr. Hogrefe that he could leave for Beijing on the morning of June 2, with the American Embassy's human rights officer, Eric Richardson. Mr. Halpin and Ms. Katzin could proceed to Kasghar the next morning if the Kadeer issue were resolved. At midnight, delegation members were suddenly awakened and summoned to the hotel conference room. There the Chinese hosts read an official statement which suggested that the Congressional staff delegation had engaged in "interference in the internal affairs of China" and should desist from doing so. The Chinese hosts also stated that the Congressional staff delegation should assume full responsibility for the failure of the delegation to proceed to Kashgar as planned and for any ensuing disharmony in relations between the U.S. Congress and the National People's Congress. Mr. Hogrefe repeated Congressional concern, and those of Mr. Lantos, over the gross human rights violations represented by the beatings and detention of Ms. Kadeer's children and repeated his determination to depart China as soon as possible. Mr. Halpin stated that Chairman Hyde had sent him to China to ask the Foreign Ministry to release a number of American citizens and prisoners of conscience and now, instead of telling the Chairman he had succeeded in his mission, he must report that the visit had resulted in more people being detained rather than released. Halpin stated his own intention to return to Beijing with Mr. Hogrefe in the morning.

The staff delegation returned to Beijing by air on Friday morning, June 2, 2006, with the NPC hosts. On the way to Urumqi Airport, the NPC hosts provided the delegation with copies of a local newspaper which stated that Ms. Kadeer's sons, Ablikim and Alim Abdiriyim, had been incarcerated and formally charged with tax evasion. (Ms. Kadeer's daughter, Rushangul, remained under house arrest.) It appeared that Chinese authorities wished to ensure that the Congressional staff delegation was fully aware that they had not been swayed by objections concerning what had transpired. It also was a likely indication that the hard-line Secretary of the Communist Party in the Xinjiang Uyghur Autonomous Region, Wang Lequan, who reportedly has a personal vendetta against Ms. Kadeer and her family, wanted to present Beijing with a *fait accompli*—published formal charges against Ms. Kadeer's children. This would assure that there would be no backtracking on the actions taken due to official American pressure.

Mr. Hogrefe took a connecting flight in Beijing and immediately returned to the United States. Mr. Halpin had meetings scheduled at the American Embassy regarding the continued detention of a U.S. citizen so he remained in Beijing to attend these meetings.

Postscript: A third son of Ms. Kadeer, Kahar Abdureyim, was arrested a few days after the delegation departed Urumqi. All three of Ms. Kadeer's sons, Kahar, Ablikim Abdureyim, and Alim Abdureyim, remain in detention while her daughter, Rushangul, remains under house arrest. Judicial proceedings are being carried forward in the Chinese courts, with a credible NGO report of torture to extract a confession in the case of at least one of the sons. A verdict is expected in the near future.

How deeply concerned the Beijing Government is over the perceived threat of this one woman, Rebiya Kadeer, to Chinese absolute control of Xinjiang was confirmed by a September 22, 2006 press report in Oslo. The Oslo Daily *Aftenposten* reported that "Chinese authorities have warned Norway that relations between the two countries would suffer if Norway awarded the Nobel Peace Prize to Chinese human rights activist Rebiya Kadeer…The Chinese Deputy Foreign Minister Zhang Yesui told members of a Norwegian Foreign Ministry delegation in Beijing Thursday that the relationship of the two countries would 'be damaged' if the Chinese human rights activist was awarded the prize. State Secretary at the Foreign Ministry Raymond Johansen said Friday that the Chinese threat was 'totally unacceptable and inappropriate.'

The Norwegian Nobel Prize Committee was completely independent of the government, he said." Norwegian media compared the Chinese attitude to the prize with that of the Nazis to the decision to award the prize to Carl von Ossietzy (a German pacifist) in 1935. In that case, Nazi threats were unable to prevent Oslo from awarding the prize.

HRES 497
EH

H. Res. 497
In the House of Representatives, U. S.

September 17, 2007

Whereas the protection of the human rights of minority groups is consistent with the actions of a responsible stakeholder in the international community and with the role of a host of a major international event such as the Olympic Games;

Whereas recent actions taken against the Uyghur minority by authorities in the People's Republic of China and, specifically, by local officials in the Xinjiang Uyghur Autonomous Region, have included major violations of human rights and acts of cultural suppression;

Whereas the authorities of the People's Republic of China have manipulated the strategic objectives of the international war on terror to increase their cultural and religious oppression of the Muslim population residing in the Xinjiang Uyghur Autonomous Region;

Whereas an official campaign to encourage Han Chinese migration into the Xinjiang Uyghur Autonomous Region has resulted in the Uyghur population becoming a minority in their traditional homeland and has placed immense pressure on those who are seeking to preserve the linguistic, cultural, and religious traditions of the Uyghur people;

Whereas the House of Representatives has a particular interest in the fate of Uyghur human rights leader Rebiya Kadeer, a Nobel Peace Prize nominee, and her family as Ms. Kadeer was first arrested in August 1999 while she was en route to meet with a delegation from the

Congressional Research Service and was held in prison on spurious charges until her release and exile to the United States in the spring of 2005;

Whereas upon her release, Ms. Kadeer was warned by her Chinese jailers not to advocate for human rights in Xinjiang and throughout China while in the United States or elsewhere, and was reminded that she had several family members residing in the Xinjiang Uyghur Autonomous Region;

Whereas while residing in the United States, Ms. Kadeer founded the International Uyghur Human Rights and Democracy Foundation and was elected President of the Uyghur American Association and President of the World Uyghur Congress in Munich, Germany;

Whereas two of Ms. Kadeer's sons were detained and beaten and one of her daughters was placed under house arrest in June 2006;

Whereas President George W. Bush recognized the importance of Ms. Kadeer's human rights work in a June 5, 2007, speech in Prague, Czech Republic, when he stated: 'Another dissident I will meet here is Rebiyah Kadeer of China, whose sons have been jailed in what we believe is an act of retaliation for her human rights activities. The talent of men and women like Rebiyah is the greatest resource of their nations, far more valuable than the weapons of their army or their oil under the ground.';

Whereas Kahar Abdureyim, Ms. Kadeer's eldest son, was fined $12,500 for tax evasion and another son, Alim Abdureyim, was sentenced to seven years in prison and fined $62,500 for tax evasion in a blatant attempt by local authorities to take control of the Kadeer family's remaining business assets in the People's Republic of China;

Whereas another of Ms. Kadeer's sons, Ablikim Abdureyim, was beaten by local police to the point of requiring medical attention in June 2006 and has been subjected to continued physical abuse and torture while being held incommunicado in custody since that time;

Whereas Ablikim Abdureyim was also convicted by a kangaroo court on April 17, 2007, for 'instigating and engaging in secessionist' activities and was sentenced to nine years of imprisonment, this trial being held in secrecy and Mr. Abdureyim reportedly being denied the right to legal representation;

Whereas two days later, on April 19, 2007, another court in Urumqi, the capital of Xinjiang Uyghur Autonomous Region, sentenced Canadian citizen Huseyin Celil to life in prison for 'splittism' and also for 'being party to a terrorist organization' after having successfully sought his extradition from Uzbekistan where he was visiting relatives;

Whereas Chinese authorities have continued to refuse to recognize Mr. Celil's Canadian citizenship, although he was naturalized in 2005, denied Canadian diplomats access to the courtroom when Mr. Celil was sentenced, and have refused to grant consular access to Mr. Celil in prison;

Whereas a Chinese Foreign Ministry spokesperson publicly warned Canada 'not to interfere in China's domestic affairs' after Mr. Celil's sentencing; and

Whereas Mr. Celil's case was a major topic of conversation in a recent Beijing meeting between the Canadian and Chinese Foreign Ministers: Now, therefore, be it

Resolved, That it is the sense of the House of Representatives that the Government of the People's Republic of China—

> (1) should recognize, and seek to ensure, the linguistic, cultural, and religious rights of the Uyghur people of the Xinjiang Uyghur Autonomous Region;

> (2) should immediately release the children of Rebiya Kadeer from both incarceration and house arrest and cease harassment and intimidation of the Kadeer family members; and

(3) should immediately release Canadian citizen Huseyin Celil and allow him to rejoin his family in Canada.

Attest:
Clerk.

Sep 17, 2007: This bill passed in the House of Representatives by voice vote. A record of each representative's position was not kept.

U.S. Department of State

Country Reports on Human Rights Practices - <u>2007</u>
Released by the Bureau of Democracy, Human Rights, and Labor
March 11, 2008

Abridged version. For the full report please visit the website
http://www.state.gov/g/drl/rls/hrrpt/2007/100518.htm

The People's Republic of China (PRC) is an authoritarian state in which, as specified in its constitution, the Chinese Communist Party (CCP) is the paramount source of power. Party members hold almost all top government, police, and military positions. Ultimate authority rests with the 25-member political bureau (Politburo) of the CCP and its nine-member standing committee. Hu Jintao holds the three most powerful positions as CCP general secretary, president, and chairman of the Central Military Commission. The party's authority rested primarily on the government's ability to maintain social stability; appeals to nationalism and patriotism; party control of personnel, media, and the security apparatus; and continued improvement in the living standards of most of the country's 1.3 billion citizens.

According to 2005 official statistics, the Ministry of Justice administered more than 700 prisons with a population of more than 1.8 million inmates. In addition 30 jails for juveniles held approximately 22,000 juvenile offenders. The country also operated hundreds of administrative detention centers, which were run by security ministries and administered separately from the formal court system.

Since 2001 authorities have increased repression in the Xinjiang Uighur Autonomous Region, targeting in particular the region's ethnic Uighur population. In January Xinjiang Uighur Autonomous Region Party Secretary Wang Lequan again urged government organs to crack down on the "three forces" of religious extremism, "splittism," and terrorism, and to "firmly establish the idea that stability overrides all." It was sometimes difficult to determine whether raids, detentions, and judicial punishments directed at individuals or organizations suspected of promoting the "three forces," were instead actually used to target those peacefully seeking to express their political or religious views.

The government tightly controlled the practice of Islam, and official repression in the Xinjiang Uighur Autonomous Region targeted at Uighur Muslims tightened in some areas. Regulations restricting Muslims' religious activity, teaching, and places of worship continued to be implemented forcefully in the Xinjiang Uighur Autonomous Region, sometimes citing counterterrorism as the basis for taking action that was repressive. Xinjiang Uighur Autonomous Region authorities detained and arrested persons engaged in unauthorized religious activities. In addition the Xinjiang Uighur Autonomous Region government maintained the most severe legal restrictions in China on children's right to practice religion. In recent years authorities often charged religious believers with committing the "three evils" of terrorism, separatism, and extremism.

The government's policy to encourage Han migration into minority areas resulted in significant increases in the population of Han Chinese in the Xinjiang Uighur Autonomous Region. According to 2005 statistics published by Xinjiang Uighur Autonomous Region officials, 7.98 million of the 20 million official residents were Han. Hui, Kazakhs, Kyrgyz, Uighur, and other ethnic minorities comprised approximately 12 million Xinjiang Uighur Autonomous Region residents. Official statistics understated the Han population, because they did not count the tens of thousands of Han Chinese who were long-term "temporary workers." Nonetheless, Han officials held most of the most powerful party and government positions in minority autonomous regions, particularly the Xinjiang Uighur Autonomous Region.

The migration of ethnic Han into the Xinjiang Uighur Autonomous Region in recent decades caused the Han-Uighur ratio in the capital of Urumqi to shift from 20 to 80 to 80 to 20 and was a deep source of Uighur resentment. Discriminatory hiring practices gave preference to Han and discouraged job prospects for ethnic minorities. In June 2006 the Xinjiang Production and Construction Corps announced that it would recruit 840 employees from the Xinjiang Uighur Autonomous

Region designating nearly all of the job openings for Han Chinese. While the government promoted Han migration into the Xinjiang Uighur Autonomous Region, overseas human rights organizations alleged that government-sponsored labor programs forced Uighur girls and young women to work in factories in eastern China on false pretenses and without regular wages. Although government policies brought economic improvements to the Xinjiang Uighur Autonomous Region, Han residents received a disproportionate share of the benefits.

The Xinjiang Uighur Autonomous Region government tightened measures that diluted expressions of Uighur identity, including measures to reduce education in ethnic minority languages and to institute language requirements that disadvantage ethnic minority teachers. The government continued moving away from the two-track school systems that used either standard Chinese or the local minority language and toward a new system that required schools to teach both standard Chinese and local minority languages or to teach standard Chinese only. Prior to adopting the new policy, the vast majority of Uighur children in the Xinjiang Uighur Autonomous Region attended Uighur-language schools and generally received an hour's Chinese-language instruction per day.

During the year authorities in Urumqi, Xinjiang Uighur Autonomous Region, destroyed over 25,000 "illegal" religious books. In 2006 Xinjiang Uighur Autonomous Region authorities reported confiscating publications about Islam with "unhealthy content." Uighur writers and editors, including the editor of the Kashgar Literature Journal, Korash Huseyin, reportedly were jailed in 2005 for publishing stories that authorities maintained advocated separatism. Authorities continued to ban books containing content they deemed controversial. Most of the banned titles dealt with China's recent history, including Zhang Yihe's Past Stories of Peking Opera Actors.

Possession of publications or audiovisual materials discussing independence or other sensitive subjects was not permitted. According to reports, possession of such materials resulted in lengthy prison sentences. In 2005 writer Abdulla Jamal was detained in the Xinjiang Uighur Autonomous Region, reportedly for writings that promoted Uighur independence. Other Uighurs who remained in prison at year's end for peaceful expression included Tohti Tunyaz, Adduhelil Zunun, Abdulghani Memetemin, Nurmuhemmet Yasin, and Korash Huseyin.

In addition there continued to be frequent reports that police and other elements of the security apparatus employed widespread torture and degrading treatment when dealing with some detainees and prisoners. During the year there were reports that officials used electric shocks, beatings, shackles, and other forms of abuse. In June 2006 authorities detained and beat Alim and Ablikim, the sons of prominent Uighur human rights activist Rebiya Kadeer, and Alim reportedly confessed to the charges against him after being tortured by security officials. In June 2006 authorities charged Alim, Ablikim, and Qahar Abdureyim, three of Rebiya Kadeer's sons, with state security and economic crimes. In April Ablikim was sentenced to nine years in prison and three years deprivation of political rights, reportedly after confessing to charges of "instigating and engaging in secessionist activities." In November 2006 Alim was sentenced to seven years in prison and fined $62,500.

In March 2006 UN Special Rapporteur Nowak reaffirmed earlier findings that torture, although on a decline—particularly in urban areas—remained widespread, and that procedural and substantive measures were inadequate to prevent torture. Nowak reported that beatings with fists, sticks, and electric batons continued to be the most common forms of torture. He also found that prisoners continued to suffer cigarette burns, prolonged periods of solitary confinement, and submersion in water or sewage, and that they were made to hold extreme positions for long periods, were denied medical treatment, and were forced to do hard labor. Death row inmates were shackled or handcuffed 24 hours per day and systematically abused to break their will and force confessions. According to Nowak, officials specifically targeted for abuse house church groups, Falun Gong adherents, Tibetans, and Uighur prisoners.

Conditions in penal institutions for both political prisoners and common criminals generally were harsh and degrading. Prisoners and detainees often were kept in overcrowded conditions with poor sanitation. Inadequate prison capacity was an increasing problem in some areas. Food often was inadequate and of poor quality, and many detainees relied on supplemental food and medicines provided by relatives; some prominent dissidents were not allowed to receive such goods.

Many inmates in penal and reeducation-through-labor facilities were required to work, with minimal or no remuneration. In some cases prisoners worked in facilities directly connected with penal institutions; in other cases they were contracted to nonprison enterprises. Former prison inmates reported that workers who refused to work in some prisons were beaten. Facilities and their management profited from inmate labor.

Authorities arrested persons on charges of revealing state secrets, subversion, and common crimes to suppress political dissent and social advocacy. Citizens also were detained and prosecuted under broad and ambiguous state secrets laws for, among other actions, disclosing information on criminal trials, meetings, and government activity. Information could retroactively be classified a state secret by the government.

In January Ministry of Health spokesman Mao Qunan reportedly acknowledged that the government harvested organs from executed prisoners. On May 1, new regulations came into effect that include a ban on the trade of human organs and on live organ transplants from persons under the age of 18. The regulations also stipulate that the donation of human organs for transplant should be free and voluntary. However, the new regulations make no specific reference to the extraction of organs from death penalty prisoners.

Conditions in administrative detention facilities, such as reeducation-through-labor camps, were similar to those in prisons. Beating deaths occurred in administrative detention and reeducation-through-labor facilities.

The government continued to use house arrest as a nonjudicial punishment and control measure against dissidents, former political prisoners, family members of political prisoners, petitioners, underground religious figures, and others it deemed politically sensitive. Authorities in the Xinjiang Uighur Autonomous Region used house arrest and other forms of arbitrary detention against those accused of the "three evils" of extremism, "splittism," and terrorism. House arrest encompassed varying degrees of stringency but sometimes included complete isolation in one's own home or another location under lock and guard. In some cases house arrest involved constant monitoring, but the target of house arrest was occasionally permitted to leave the home to work or run errands. When outside the home, the subject of house arrest was usually, but not always, under surveillance. In some instances security officials assumed invasive positions within the family home, rather than monitoring from the outside.

Several underground Catholic priests and bishops were under house arrest for varying periods during the year. The longest serving among them may be Bishop Su Zhimin, who has reportedly been detained in a form of house arrest in Baoding, Hebei Province, since 1997. An unverified press report circulated in June 2006 stated that Bishop Su had died in custody. The government has not responded to inquiries about Bishop Su.

Criminal punishments included "deprivation of political rights" for a fixed period after release from prison, during which the individual is denied the already-limited rights of free speech and association granted to other citizens. Former prisoners sometimes found their status in society, ability to find employment, freedom to travel, and access to residence permits and social services severely restricted. Former political prisoners and their families frequently were subjected to police surveillance, telephone wiretaps, searches, and other forms of harassment, and some encountered difficulty in obtaining or keeping employment and housing.

Trials involving capital offenses sometimes took place under circumstances involving severe lack of due process and with no meaningful appeal. Some executions took place on the day of conviction or failed appeal. Executions of Uighurs whom authorities accused of separatism, but which some observers claimed were politically motivated, were reported. Many alleged acts of torture occurred in pretrial criminal detention centers or reeducation-through-labor centers.

Uighurs were sentenced to long prison terms, and in some cases executed, on charges of separatism. On February 8, authorities executed Ismail Semed, an ethnic Uighur from the Xinjiang Uighur Autonomous Region, following convictions in 2005 for "attempting to split the motherland" and other counts related to possession of firearms and explosives. During his trial Semed claimed that his confession was coerced. Semed was forcibly returned from Pakistan in 2003. On April 19, foreign citizen Huseyin Celil was sentenced to life in prison for allegedly plotting to split the country and 10 years in prison for belonging to a terrorist organization, reportedly after being extradited from Uzbekistan and tortured into giving a confession. Although Celil was granted Canadian citizenship, Chinese authorities refused to recognize this and consequently denied Celil access to consular officials. During the year the government reportedly sought the repatriation of Uighurs living outside the country, where they faced the risk of persecution.

The country's population control policy relied on education, propaganda, and economic incentives, as well as on more coercive measures such as the threat of job loss or demotion and social compensation fees. Psychological and economic pressures were common. Those who violated the child limit policy by having an unapproved child or helping another to do so faced disciplinary measures such as job loss or demotion, loss of promotion opportunity, expulsion from the party (membership in which was an unofficial requirement for certain jobs), and other administrative punishments, including in some cases the destruction of property. In the case of families that already had two children, one parent was often pressured to undergo sterilization. The penalties sometimes left women with little practical choice but to undergo abortion or sterilization. The government continued its coercive birth limitation policy, in some cases resulting in forced abortion and sterilization.

THE AMERICAN SOCIETY OF HUMAN GENETICS

Analysis of Genomic Admixture in Uyghur and Its Implication in Mapping Strategy

Shuhua Xu[1,2], Wei Huang[3], Ji Qian[2] and Li Jin[1,2],

[1] Chinese Academy of Sciences and Max Planck Society (CAS-MPG) Partner Institute for Computational Biology, Shanghai Institutes for Biological Sciences, Chinese Academy of Sciences, Shanghai 200031, China

[2] Ministry of Education (MOE) Key Laboratory of Contemporary Anthropology and Center for Evolutionary Biology, School of Life Sciences and Institutes of Biomedical Sciences, Fudan University, Shanghai 200433, China

[3] Chinese National Human Genome Center at Shanghai, Shanghai 201203, China

Abstract

The Uyghur (UIG) population, settled in Xinjiang, China, is a population presenting a typical admixture of Eastern and Western anthropometric traits. We dissected its genomic structure at population level, individual level, and chromosome level by using 20,177 SNPs spanning nearly the entire chromosome 21. Our results showed that UIG was formed by two-way admixture, with 60% European ancestry and 40% East Asian ancestry. Overall linkage disequilibrium (LD) in UIG was similar to that in its parental populations represented in East Asia and Europe with regard to common alleles, and UIG manifested elevation of LD only within 500 kb and at a level of $0.1 < r^2 < 0.8$ when ancestry-informative markers (AIMs) were used. The size of chromosomal segments that were derived from East Asian and European ancestries averaged 2.4 cM and 4.1 cM, respectively. Both the magnitude of LD and fragmentary ancestral chromosome segments indicated a long history of

Uyghur. Under the assumption of a hybrid isolation (HI) model, we estimated that the admixture event of UIG occurred about 126 [107146] generations ago, or 2520 [21402920] years ago assuming 20 years per generation. In spite of the long history and short LD of Uyghur compared with recent admixture populations such as the African-American population, we suggest that mapping by admixture LD (MALD) is still applicable in the Uyghur population but 10-fold AIMs are necessary for a whole-genome scan.